Helen of Troy

Helen of Troy

Beauty, Myth, Devastation

RUBY BLONDELL

OXFORD
UNIVERSITY PRESS

OXFORD
UNIVERSITY PRESS

Oxford University Press is a department of the University of Oxford.
It furthers the University's objective of excellence in research,
scholarship, and education by publishing worldwide.

Oxford   New York
Auckland   Cape Town   Dar es Salaam   Hong Kong   Karachi
Kuala Lumpur   Madrid   Melbourne   Mexico City   Nairobi
New Delhi   Shanghai   Taipei   Toronto

With offices in
Argentina   Austria   Brazil   Chile   Czech Republic   France   Greece
Guatemala   Hungary   Italy   Japan   Poland   Portugal   Singapore
South Korea   Switzerland   Thailand   Turkey   Ukraine   Vietnam

Oxford is a registered trade mark of Oxford University Press
in the UK and certain other countries.

Published in the United States of America by
Oxford University Press
198 Madison Avenue, New York, NY 10016

Library of Congress Cataloging-in-Publication Data
Blondell, Ruby, 1954–
Helen of Troy : beauty, myth, devastation / Ruby Blondell.
    pages. cm.
Includes bibliographical references and index.
ISBN 978-0-19-973160-2 (hardcover : alk. paper)
1. Helen of Troy (Greek mythology) in literature.
2. Greek literature—History and criticism. 3. Latin literature—History and criticism. I. Title.
PA3015.R5H3725   2013
880.9'351—dc23   2012036954

9 8 7 6 5 4 3 2 1

Printed in the United States of America
on acid-free paper

To Douglas

Love is like jazz.
You make it up as you go along
and you act as
if you really knew the song . . .

Contents

Preface

Helen of Troy is the mythical incarnation of an ancient Greek obsession: the control of female sexuality and of women's sexual power over men. As the most beautiful woman in the world, and the most destructive, she is both the most in need of control and the least controllable. When she escapes male oversight by absconding to Troy with her lover, Paris, she triggers the greatest war of all time: the Trojan War. Though her departure is typically referred to as an "abduction," none of our sources claims that Paris took Helen by force against her will. Her complicity is essential to her story. Yet the men who set out in hot pursuit share responsibility for the devastation that results. The war is caused not only by their inability to control the beautiful Helen but by their equal inability to dismiss or destroy her.

Helen's defining action, her elopement, raises a whole series of questions about gender, agency, and ethics. As an object of patriarchal control who yet has agency of her own, she models the position of women in Greek culture generally. As a beautiful object of desire who yet has desires of her own, she models, in particular, the figure of the bride, becoming an emblem of the instability of marriage itself, which must be secured by retrieving her. As the iconic errant woman who must be reincorporated into patriarchal social structures, she is also the foundation of Greek masculinity, insofar as this is grounded in the control of women. As a woman who ran off with a "barbarian," she is a vehicle for defining Greek identity and values vis-à-vis the larger non-Greek world. Finally, as the cause of the Trojan War, she also causes its commemoration in song and story, making her a kind of Muse, associated with poetic immortality, the seductions of discourse, and mimetic fluidity, all of which are linked, in turn, with the threat of female beauty and female desire.

Having constructed female beauty as a threat, and imagined an absolute standard of beauty fulfilled by a single woman in whom that threat culminates, Greek men spent considerable energy attempting to analyze, contain, disarm, deny, or appropriate the power accorded to their own creation. The most obvious containment strategy is blame. The ancient Greeks had a well-developed discourse of praise and blame that functioned as a means of social control. But Helen can never be *just* a scapegoat, since the behavior for which she is to blame is inseparable from her infinitely desirable beauty. Greek culture does not distinguish easily between moral and physical beauty, and is deeply uncomfortable with the potential dissonance between them. But this dissonance makes Helen who she is. Like Pandora, the first woman, she is a *kalon kakon*—a "beautiful evil." Since she embodies both aspects of this paradox—its allure as well as its threat, its glorious splendor as well as its destructiveness—it is impossible to reduce Helen to a mere object of abuse. Male desire introduces a second reason for ambivalence. The Greek warriors' willingness to pursue an adulterous woman at such enormous cost risks exacerbating the shame of losing control of her in the first place. Overt abuse of Helen forces them to confront her hold over them, and hence the embarrassing spectacle of their own emasculation. Blame of Helen brings blame of men in its train.

Consequently, ancient authors excuse or palliate Helen's behavior as often as they censure it. Some actively defend her, often in quite outlandish ways, as we shall see. Insofar as blame is an acknowledgment of power, however, such texts disempower Helen by the very refusal of blame. The ancient "defenses" all turn out to be in their own way modes of containment.

Another strategy is to appropriate Helen's power by transforming her into an emblem of the masculine heroism produced and displayed on the battle-field. The men driven to war by her beauty assert their own agency at her expense, transforming her recovery into a heroic enterprise and herself into a token of their glory. The lust for beauty that "attacks" men and destroys their manhood becomes a lust for heroic combat that proves their manhood even while taking their lives for the sake of a woman. Greek authors are far from unanimous, however, in their attitudes toward the Trojan War. While some treat it as a tragic yet noble arena for the display of manly heroism, others view the war itself as a pointless calamity and the lust for glory as a ruthless and irresponsible greed for power. As an emblem of warfare, Helen's fortunes vary accordingly.

Since the rise of gender studies in the 1970s, the transgressive heroines of Greek myth have been a source of fascination both to scholars and to the general public. Until recently, this seemed less true of Helen than of others, such as Clytemnestra or Medea. This may, perhaps, be the result of a certain embarrassment. It is easy—too easy—to perceive Helen as, at best, no more than a passive victim of Greek patriarchy and at worst, fickle, self-centered, and irresponsible. If one focuses, instead, on her power over men, that takes a form from which the influential "second-wave" feminism of the 1970s understandably distanced itself. Helen's destructive power, vested in her seductive "feminine" beauty, is less congenial from some perspectives than the "manly" physical violence of heroines like Medea or Clytemnestra, whose criminal behavior can be construed as a way of striking back defiantly against male mistreatment.

In the last fifteen years or so, however, Helen has received an increasing amount of scholarly attention. This has been paralleled, to judge by her recent prominence in popular culture, by a distinct blossoming of interest among the general public. All this suggests that she is touching some kind of contemporary nerve. For better or worse, "femininity" is back in the "postfeminist" twenty-first century, and Helen remains a lightning rod for its meaning and value. "Third-wave" feminism has prompted us to revisit the problematic power of female beauty, and the historical study of women and gender has focused increasingly not just on women's victimization but on the exercise of agency even under patriarchal constraints. The time therefore seems ripe to revisit Helen from the perspective of her beauty and its power.

While I was working on this project, interested people would often ask me if Helen "really" existed or what she "really" looked like. I should therefore make it clear from the outset that this book is not about the "real" Helen. Or rather, it *is* about the real Helen, whom I take to be in her essence unreal. If a skeleton were dug up with Helen's name on the tomb, this would have no impact on my project. Whether or not the Trojan War was started by a historical person is irrelevant for my purposes, since no such person—even if her name were Helen and she really eloped to Troy with a man named Paris— could be "Helen of Troy." As the woman who was—and is—by definition the most beautiful woman of all time, Helen of Troy could never have existed. She is in her very essence a creature of myth—a concept, not a person. It is that concept, and its meaning for ancient Greek authors, that is my subject.

No other character in ancient Greek mythology plays such a prominent role in so many disparate kinds of work: epic, lyric poetry, tragedy, historiography, rhetoric, comedy, even philosophy. This book examines the surviving texts from the archaic and classical periods in which Helen has a significant presence, focusing especially on the twin themes of beauty and female agency. It begins, however, with two preliminary chapters, which are intended to provide a broad, synchronic, cultural context. Chapter 1 lays out some of the essentials of ancient Greek gender ideology, focusing on female beauty, the conceptual position of women between objectification and agency, and the intrinsic ambiguity of the female as embodied in the first woman, Pandora. Chapter 2 introduces Helen's myth through a narrative of her basic story, elaborated with attention to the major themes that concern me, plus a discussion of the mythic significance of her beauty and her place in cult. In this chapter I employ early sources as far as possible, and present, for the most part, the most widespread and authoritative versions of Helen's story, but I also draw on later or more idiosyncratic accounts where they are pertinent to the rest of the book.

Homeric epic provides not only the first and most influential representation of Helen's character, but the most complex. Only in Homer is she simultaneously guilty and sympathetic, with the sympathy elicited in spite of the guilt, and even, in part, because of it. The *Iliad*—the most canonical version of her story—is the subject of chapter 3, which focuses primarily on the various attitudes of different characters (including Helen herself) toward her guilt and agency in causing the Trojan War. Chapter 4 turns to the Helen of the *Odyssey*, who is in some ways still more memorable, thanks to her skill with supernatural drugs and magical, mimetic powers. This epic reevaluates Helen's story from a postwar perspective, questioning both the true success of the war in regaining control of her and the advisability of recovering her at such cost.

Homer's Helen has haunted the imagination through antiquity and beyond, shaping and participating in every retelling of her tale. Those retellings begin with the lyric poets who are the subject of chapter 5. This chapter examines Helen's presence in a number of short poems and fragments from the archaic period, which are quite varied in poetic type but all conventionally grouped under the rubric of "lyric." It includes works by Semonides, Alcaeus, Sappho, and Ibycus, focusing especially on the ways in which they respond to the legacy of epic. The chapter concludes with the overt rejection of Homer enshrined in the story of Stesichorus's Palinode. This poem, now lost but famous in antiquity, denied that Helen went to Troy at all, claiming instead that she was replaced by a double created for that purpose by the gods.

Three chapters are devoted to Athenian tragedy, a genre in which Helen has a varied and extensive presence thanks to the playwrights' preoccupation with the Trojan War as a paradigm for heroism and a source of Greek identity. The subject of my first tragic chapter is Aeschylus's *Oresteia*. In *Agamemnon*, which initiates the trilogy, Helen has a significant offstage role, complementing her more conspicuously destructive sister, Clytemnestra, who dominates the stage. I pursue themes linked with Helen in this play to the end of the trilogy, where, I argue, Helen as well as Clytemnestra is suppressed in the interests of establishing Athenian democracy.

Two further chapters are devoted to another tragic playwright, Euripides. First, however, I turn to two early prose authors who may have influenced him. Chapter 7 surveys Helen's three main appearances in Herodotus's *Histories*. As a historian, Herodotus takes a rationalistic approach to the Trojan War, dismissing the transcendent power of Helen's beauty as a credible casus belli. I argue, however, that the threat of her beauty remains latent in his narrative. The subject of chapter 8 is the sophist Gorgias. Like his predecessors, though in a rather different way, Gorgias makes Helen a vehicle for exploring both Greek masculinity and the human condition. In his *Encomium of Helen* he uses her to scrutinize not the glory of war but philosophical issues surrounding agency, responsibility, and gender, albeit in the guise of a "joke" or "amusement."

Since Euripides was known even in his own day for seeking out the dangerous territory of female eroticism, it is not surprising to find him taking an extensive interest in Helen. She has a background presence in all his Trojan War plays and enters the stage as a dramatic character in three of them. I focus, in chapters 9 and 10, on the two dramas in which Helen has a substantial speaking role, namely *Trojan Women* and *Helen*. Between them, these two plays provide a distinctively Euripidean perspective on the ambiguity of the desirable female. The first shows Helen, in a fifth-century reimagining of Hesiod's "beautiful evil," as a shameless sophist; the second employs the Stesichorean device of the double to present her, I claim, as an unattainable fantasy of virtuous female beauty.

My last chapter concerns Isocrates, a contemporary and rival of Plato who responds to Gorgias with a bizarre encomium of his own. Isocrates is the last Greek author from the classical period to make Helen the focus of a substantial work. Harking back to Homer, he presents her as an emblem of Panhellenic masculine achievement, but does so, I argue, in a trivializing fashion, at least where Helen herself is concerned. Though he insists strenuously on his own seriousness, Isocrates seems in the end less serious than the overtly playful Gorgias in his attention to the ethical and conceptual challenges that surround her. Finally, a brief epilogue points forward to just a few of my personal favorites among the Helens that were yet to come.

I hope this book will have something to say to scholars and students of the ancient world, but also that it will reach a wider audience. Accordingly, although my interpretations are built on a foundation of scholarly research, this bedrock is rarely visible in the text, and footnotes have been kept to a minimum. I am grateful to Stefan Vranka of Oxford University Press for encouraging me to take this approach. I regret, however, that it leaves me unable to express specific debts to those whose work has influenced me in ways both large and small. I beg scholarly indulgence, too, for all the places where I have oversimplified complex matters or simply cut the Gordian knot. The bibliographical notes are intended, in part, to remedy these deficits, as well as providing signposts for readers who would like to pursue matters further.

This work was made possible in part by a fellowship in the Society of Scholars and an NEH 2008 Summer Stipend Incentive Award, both from the University of Washington's Simpson Center for the Humanities. It would have taken even longer without sabbatical leave granted by the university. A fellowship from the Liguria Study Center for the Arts and Humanities in Bogliasco provided a paradisiacal month of writing, at a critical stage, in the congenial and stimulating company of my fellow Fellows and the center's supportive staff. The Department of Classics at the University of Washington provided generous financial support for the illustrations.

I am most grateful to everyone who helped make this a better book by reading and commenting on parts of it at different stages of its development, including the Press's anonymous referees. I reiterate my thanks to Lucia Athanassaki, Ewen Bowie, Patricia Rosenmeyer, and the *AJP* referees for substantially improving much of what is now chapter 5. Alex Hollmann provided detailed comments on an early draft of chapter 7, saving me from my woeful ignorance of Herodotus. David Konstan kindly gave me feedback on chapter 3. Students in my two graduate seminars on Helen provided much food for thought, especially participants in the 2011 seminar who plowed through an embarrassingly inchoate early draft. Among civilians I owe a special debt of gratitude to Bucky Harris and Douglas Roach, each of whom read the entire manuscript with a fresh mind and a sharp eye.

Innumerable people have assisted me in other ways. Colleagues at the University of Washington and elsewhere generously answered questions about the many, many things of which I knew nothing when I started this project, including Larry Bliquez, Catherine Connors, Sara Goering, Stephen Hinds, Alex Hollmann, Deb Kamen, Peg Laird, Olga Levaniouk, Sarah Levin-Richardson, Toph Marshall, Kirk Ormand, Corinne Pache, and Kate Topper. I have also profited from comments made by members of the audience when presenting portions of this work in various contexts. Many scholars shared their unpublished work with me, including Carin Calabrese, Toph Marshall, Ellen Millender, Kirk Ormand, and Bella Vivante. Helene Foley, Tony Long, Bridget Murnaghan, Greg Nagy, and Jim Tatum provided much-needed encouragement and moral support. I have benefited from countless stimulating discussions—mostly about gender, women, and robots—with my former students Alex Dressler, Lindsay Morse, Ryan Platte, Zoe Selengut, and especially Yurie Hong. I am also grateful to several graduate students for research assistance, especially Rachel Carlson, who helped prepare the bibliography.

The list of friends who have sustained me over the years with cocktails and conversation more or less directly related to this project is a long one and includes many whom I have already named. Among them, however, I must reiterate my special gratitude to Deb Kamen and Kate Topper for their intellectual generosity and insight. During the writing of this book Deb has been my go-to colleague for questions about all aspects of Greek culture, and Kate a mine of information on everything to do with Greek art, from iconography to caption writing. I count myself exceptionally fortunate to work in a department so remarkably learned, supportive, and replete with goodwill. These qualities are personified in Alain Gowing, who served as chair during most of the writing of this book and did all he could to foster its progress.

Finally, I thank Douglas Roach for his love and support over the last decade. This book is dedicated to him, for making the years spent writing it the happiest of my life.

Abbreviations

Aesch.	Aeschylus	
	Ag.	*Agamemnon*
	Eum.	*Eumenides*
	LB	*Libation Bearers*
Aeschin.	Aeschines	
Alc.	Alcaeus	
Alex.	*Alexandria*	
Anacr.	*Anacreontea*	
Anth. Pal.	*Palatine Anthology*	
Ar.	Aristophanes	
	Lys.	*Lysistrata*
	Thesm.	*Women at the Thesmophoria*
Arist.	Aristotle	
	EN	*Nicomachean Ethics*
Athen.	Athenaeus	
Cat.	*Catalogue of Women*	
Cypr.	*Cypria*	
Dial. Mort.	*Dialogues of the Dead*	
Eur.	Euripides	
	Alc.	*Alcestis*
	Andr.	*Andromache*
	Ba.	*Bacchae*
	Cyc.	*Cyclops*

	El.	*Electra*
	Hec.	*Hecuba*
	Hel.	*Helen*
	IA	*Iphigenia at Aulis*
	Med.	*Medea*
	Or.	*Orestes*
	Tro.	*Trojan Women*
fr.	fragment	
frr.	fragments	
Gorg.	Gorgias	
	Hel.	*Encomium of Helen*
Hdt.	Herodotus	
Hes.	Hesiod	
	Theog.	*Theogony*
	WD	*Works and Days*
HH	*Homeric Hymns*	
Hyg.	Hyginus	
Il.	*Iliad*	
Isoc.	Isocrates	
	Panath.	*Panathenaicus*
Ov.	Ovid	
	Met.	*Metamorphoses*
Od.	*Odyssey*	
Paus.	Pausanias	
Pyth.	*Pythian Odes*	
Pl.	Plato	
	Ap.	*Apology of Socrates*
	Euthyd.	*Euthydemus*
	Phdr.	*Phaedrus*
	Phlb.	*Philebus*
	Rep.	*Republic*
	Symp.	*Symposium*
Plut.	Plutarch	
	Lyc.	*Life of Lycurgus*
	Mor.	*Moralia*
	Thes.	*Life of Theseus*
Polyaen.	Polyaenus	
	Strat.	*Strategemata*
Semon.	Semonides	
Soph.	Sophocles	
	Ant.	*Antigone*
Theoc.	Theocritus	

Thuc.	Thucydides	
Xen.	Xenophon	
	Mem.	*Memorabilia*
	Oec.	*Oeconomicus*
	Symp.	*Symposium*

I

The Problem of Female Beauty

> Certainly it would be a very boring relationship indeed in which the robot always performed in exactly the manner expected of it by its relationship partner, forever agreeing with everything that was said to it, always carrying out its human's wishes to the letter and in precisely the desired manner. A Stepford wife. Perfection. No, that would not be perfection, because, paradoxically, a "perfect" relationship requires some imperfections of each partner to create occasional surprises.
>
> —David Levy, *Love and Sex with Robots*

Ancient Greek culture is obsessed with identifying the *best*—the swiftest, the strongest, the finest of its kind. Beauty is high on this list of prized traits. As the manifestation of bodily excellence it betokens women's readiness for marriage and men's for its male equivalent—the battlefield. It is therefore sought after in men and women alike. Yet beauty has special meaning for women. A woman's most highly valued social function is to perpetuate her husband's name and line by bearing him male heirs. A girl's acquisition of erotic beauty at adolescence marks her readiness to undertake this role, signaling her desirability as a wife and her potential to bear fine children. Other female excellences are, naturally, important, chief among them a properly virtuous disposition and skill at female crafts. As a symbol of complete womanly excellence, however, beauty was the female attribute among all others for which the "best" was sought.

When young women sang and danced in choruses, one girl was usually picked out for special attention as the most beautiful. Formal beauty contests are also attested in various parts of Greece. That beauty is the definitive female excellence is shown through the most famous of all such contests, the mythical Judgment of Paris, which was set in motion by the goddess Eris ("strife") when she assigned a golden apple "to her who is most beautiful." Paris, a handsome Trojan prince, was chosen by Zeus, king of the gods, to judge the beauty of three major goddesses who desired this accolade—Aphrodite, goddess of beauty and sex, Athena, goddess of wisdom and war, and Hera, who, as Zeus's wife, was the queen of the gods. The winner was, of course, Aphrodite. The contest was rigged in her favor, since it was designed to assess the quality that she embodies in her very essence. All goddesses are physically perfect, to be sure, but only Aphrodite stands for sexual allure as such. Yet the other two goddesses foolishly chose *this* ground on which to compete. They did not quarrel over wisdom, or military or political power, but over beauty, a trait they all share and in which they all wished to be judged supreme. As one poet playfully puts it, beauty is woman's defining power, equivalent to animals' teeth or claws or man's intelligence (*Anacr.* 24).[1]

At the Judgment each goddess offered Paris a bribe symbolic of her own sphere of influence. Aphrodite's was marriage to her human counterpart, Helen, daughter of Zeus and the most beautiful woman in the world. This book is about Helen, her beauty and its impact on the men around her. In order to understand that impact, however, it is necessary to set it in context by sketching the general significance of female beauty in ancient Greek culture.

As the story of the Judgment demonstrates, even though erotic beauty can be deployed by both genders it is construed in Greek myth as a characteristically feminine mode of power. Male beauty, too, was paraded in contests among the ever-competitive Greeks, and widely celebrated in sexual (especially homoerotic) contexts. But in men, beauty is neither exclusively erotic nor confined to one's physical prime. In Xenophon's *Symposium* a beautiful young man named Critobulus claims to value his own looks in part because beauty can enhance a man at any stage of his life—as a child, youth, man, and old man; it can be an asset, for example, for a general (Xen. *Symp.* 4.16–17). Old people are regarded almost by definition as erotically unattractive, yet Critobulus tells us that beautiful old men were chosen to carry olive branches in the procession at the Panathenaea, the great festival of Athena. The beauty of perfected masculinity adorns the broad array of male roles and activities, as a supplement to or sign of the corresponding powers—such as strength and intelligence—that are required to fulfill those roles successfully, but not as their replacement. The beauty of perfected femininity is, by contrast, construed as intrinsically erotic, and inextricably tied to the domain of sex and reproduction.

The modern cliché locates beauty in the eye of the beholder. Among the ancient Greeks, however, it was typically thought of as something that can be measured objectively. Aphrodite wins the divine beauty contest because she and her protégée simply *are* the most beautiful—not because Paris just happens to prefer this goddess, or because Helen is simply his type. In early epic, beauty is presented as a substance independent of individual human features, something that the gods can apply to a person like ointment or like gilding on a work of art

---

1. For ancient sources cited parenthetically in the text, see the list of abbreviations. Authors are identified in the glossary and index.

(below, p. 9). Artistic theories conceived of it as an abstract, objectively spec-ifiable perfection of proportions, an attitude also reflected among philosophers. Visual artists aimed to produce a perfectly beautiful human figure by culling ideal limbs from a set of models, each of whom might fall short as a whole but manifested one perfect feature. Such imaginary perfection became, in turn, an ideal—if unattainable—standard for living humans, whose beauty is often praised by likening them to works of art (especially statues). The objectivity of beauty helps explain why beautiful people were typically thought of as generic in appearance rather than uniquely individuated, and personal idiosyncrasies less a source of charm than a regrettable departure from the ideal.

It is this objectivity that makes possible the quest for the "most beautiful." That quest is complicated, however, by an ambiguity built into the ancient Greek thought-world at a fundamental level. The principal word for "beautiful" (*kalos*) is a broad term of admiration, used not only for physical beauty but for moral "beauty" or fine behavior. The word for "ugly" (*aischros*) is used, similarly, for shameful deeds as well as physical deformity. These ambiguities reflect a sense that good or bad character should be manifested in and complemented by a person's visible appearance. In the *Iliad*, Achilles, the greatest warrior and "best of the Achaeans," is also the most beautiful of the Greeks at Troy (2.673–74), while the troublesome Thersites is damned with the single word *aischistos* as both "ugliest" and "most disgraceful" (2.216). In the classical period this outlook is echoed in the notion of the *kalos kagathos*, literally "both beautiful and good," a phrase that could be applied to any successful and admirable man. Though physical appearance is rarely uppermost in this expression, it grows out of the traditional aristocratic notion that the best man should also be the best-looking.

Needless to say, this heroic ideal is not regularly fulfilled in ordinary life. The potential dissonance between inner (moral) and outer (physical) beauty, with the possibility for deception that it entails, is a persistent source of anxiety. This is true even for men, but it is especially acute where women are con-cerned. If female beauty signifies the acquisition of feminine excellence, a woman's virtue should by rights be proportionate to her beauty. Every man not only wants a beautiful wife but wants her beauty to serve as an authentic indi-cator of superiority. This fantasy retained its power. Yet it was overshadowed by a pervasive fear that where character is concerned the most beautiful women will be not merely not the best, but the very worst. An admirable male physique can also portend trouble, to be sure; but unlike female beauty it is not intrinsi-cally inclined in that direction. It is no coincidence that the feminine version of the phrase *kalos kagathos* is very rarely found and never became a catchphrase for women as it did for men. The notion of the woman who is both beautiful and good appears to be, if not an oxymoron, at least something of a paradox. Woman is, instead, a "beautiful evil" or *kalon kakon* (below, p. 16). Granted, it is not quite impossible for a beautiful woman to be virtuous, but it is generally presumed that she will not be. Nor is this simply because her beauty may cloak an evil character. Such beauty is a cause of evil in itself. Countless myths attest to the part it plays in generating conflict, starting with the Judgment of Paris, instigated by Strife herself.

Beauty exercises its power by arousing the mighty and notoriously destructive forces of *erōs*—passionate sexual desire. The god Eros and his mother, Aphrodite, operating in blithe disregard for cultural and legal boundaries, strike the heart (*thumos*) with desire,[2] destroying the rational mind (*nous*) and "wits" or good sense (*phrenes*), and with them respect for social and ethical constraints. In Sophocles' tragedy *Antigone*, after a father and son quarrel violently over a woman, the chorus sing:

> Eros, unconquered in battle;
> Eros, you plunder possessions;
> you keep your night watch
> on a young girl's soft cheeks;
> you range over the sea
> and through wild rural dwellings;
> not one of the immortals can escape you,
> not one of us human beings
> whose lives are but a day;
> and he who has you has madness.
>
> You wrench the wits aside to injustice,
> even those of the just, to their ruin;
> you have stirred up this quarrel too,
> between men bound by blood;
> radiant desire is the victor,
> shining in the eyes of the bride
> who graces the marriage bed; it is this
> that sits in rule beside the mighty ordinances;
> for the game-playing goddess
> Aphrodite is invincible in battle.
>
> (781–800)

This choral song touches on many of the themes associated with *erōs* and its power. It is one of countless texts where the impact of desire for a beautiful woman is likened to assault, disease, fire, insanity, military conquest, enslavement,

---

2. *Thumos* is not, biologically speaking, the heart (for which the usual Greek word is *kardia*), but like the metaphorical English "heart" it is the seat of passionate emotion, including both *erōs* and anger.

or death. This enables such a woman to "conquer" the physically stronger male. Aphrodite herself subdues all males, divine and mortal, with the power of desire, whether it is desire for herself (as with her lover, the war god Ares), or the desire that she inspires for others (as with her father Zeus, notorious for his erotic susceptibility). For the immortal gods such subjection is rarely more than an embarrassment, but for a human male it can be devastating.

It is, to begin with, the *sight* of a beautiful woman that fills men with desire. The most frequent word for physical beauty is *eidos*, which contains the -*id*- root denoting vision (seen in words like "video") and literally means "appearance." Innumerable Greek texts present the eyes as both the source and the instrument of erotic passion. The sight of extraordinary beauty induces "wonder" (*thauma*), an awestruck amazement that can be paralyzing in its effect. But the eyes are not only the path by which *erōs* enters the viewer; they were also considered the most beautiful part of the body and hence the most erotically charged feature of the person viewed. The cheeks, too, are often praised as a site of beauty, in part because of their close association with the eyes (other facial features are very rarely mentioned). Eyes flash with fire and radiate emotion, both expressing and eliciting the fire of desire in return. Beauty itself is conceived of as a bright light, often shining from a woman's eyes. This gives her a dangerous weapon, which can set on fire, stab, or wound its victim, rendered still more dangerous by the way it draws the eye of the observer in response. For a woman to meet a desiring gaze with her own glance is therefore a calculated act of provocation. In a fable known as the *Choice of Heracles*, by the sophist Prodicus, the hero reaches a fork in the road and meets two women, named Arete and Kakia, or Virtue and Vice. Virtue's eyes are "adorned" with modesty, but Vice looks the hero directly in the face (Xen. *Mem.* 2.1.22).

The threat of women's beauty is also intimately bound up with female discourse, which is in turn closely linked both with deception and with the power of language in such diverse forms as poetry, prophecy, and magic spells. The manipulative female voice is an essential weapon in Aphrodite's arsenal. As a mighty goddess she can, if she chooses, manifest herself in her full power, threaten and control mortals openly; but her allotted sphere is deception and "the intimate conversation of adolescent girls," along with other seductive delights (Hes. *Theog.* 205–6). In the *Iliad* she possesses a special, elaborately decorated strap (her *kestos himas*), which may be a kind of ornamental breast band:

> On it were wrought all of her magic charms;
> loving affection was on it, and desire, and intimate conversation,
> persuasive, which steals the mind even from those whose wits are sound.
>
> (14.215–17)

In such passages the lines between erotic persuasion, deception, and magic are blurred, often to the point of erasure. The kind of language ascribed to beautiful women—persuasive, seductive, and potentially deceptive—is also associated from earliest times with poets, whose art is blessed by Aphrodite's companions, the Graces and Himeros (the personification of desire) (Hes. *Theog.* 64–65).

Such seductive discourse is unlikely to be directly sexual. The word translated above as "intimate conversation" (*oaristus*) denotes not erotic talk per se, but affectionate conversation between the sexes, often flirtatious, with manipulative and competitive overtones. (The equivalent verb is used at *Il.* 6.515–16, for example, for a conversation in which a loving wife tries to dissuade her husband from returning to battle.) The *Homeric Hymn to Aphrodite* describes the goddess seducing the mortal Anchises in part by means of a duplicitous speech with which she "cast sweet desire into his heart" (*HH* 5.143–44). Yet her words are not explicitly seductive. Rather, she tells a string of outright lies designed to produce an attractive self-presentation, portraying herself as a decorous mortal virgin of noble family on the verge of marriage, who was "abducted" by the god Hermes from a group of dancing girls (5.119–21). Even in the absence of such literal lies, however, the deep-seated conflict between *erōs* and reason causes seduction to be figured as intrinsically deceptive. Aphrodite "deceives" people into going against their better judgment, by "persuading," "shrouding," or otherwise incapacitating their "wits" or good sense—in other words, inducing them to think the indulgence of the desire she inspires is right or good when it is really bad, wrong, or disastrous. This is what really lies at the heart of her deception of Anchises, who suspects that she is a goddess, and knows such a liaison is likely to harm him, but sleeps with her anyway (*HH* 5.91–106, 185–90).

Despite the intimidating power ascribed to Aphrodite and her allies, the "deception," "violence," and "insanity" that they induce do not remove their victims' responsibility for the foolish or destructive behavior that so often follows. When the chorus of *Antigone* sing of the invincible power of *erōs*, they are not excusing its victims for their unjust behavior but lamenting it. Rational self-control and the successful subordination of appetites were central to classical Greek conceptions of masculinity. When a victim of *erōs* acts against his better judgment, his rational mind "wrenched aside," in the chorus's phrase, this is not an excuse but an indictment. Such acts are still *acts*, for which one is held accountable even if the driving force is overwhelming. The mighty power of *erōs* is, to be sure, invoked from time to time in an effort to gain sympathy, but this remains a shameful admission of weakness, not an effective self-defense. The erotic weakness of Zeus, in particular, is often mentioned in such cases. If the greatest of all gods could not resist, how can a mere mortal? But not even Zeus is *excused* for such lapses. He gets away with them because he can, but moralists do not approve.

Nor are Aphrodite's human victims excused by the fact of her divinity. In ordinary Greek thinking, a mortal who acts on feelings or thoughts caused by a meddlesome god remains responsible for that action, retaining the credit or the blame. Aphrodite inspires sexual transgressions without exculpating the transgressors, just as Ares or Athena inspires a warrior to fight boldly without undermining his glory. Though mortals do occasionally blame their own wrongdoing on divine interference, this is never unproblematic as a mode of self-defense, and never became acceptable in mainstream thinking, which persisted in holding human beings responsible for such actions. Sexual misbehavior did put considerable pressure on this outlook, since Aphrodite was a busy god as well as a powerful one. Nevertheless, other things being equal, one must take the blame for any misdeeds that she provokes.

A beautiful woman who inspires such misdeeds is often the first to suffer, as an innocent target of rapacious male lust, regardless of her own desires (or lack thereof). Mythology is replete with abductions of innocent victims like Persephone (below, p. 12). The plot of the *Iliad* is initiated by a quarrel over Briseis, a hapless Trojan captive who "resembles golden Aphrodite" (19.282). Another Trojan, Cassandra, who is also likened in the *Iliad* to "golden Aphrodite," and described as Priam's "most beautiful" daughter (13.365, 24.699), became the archetypal mythic victim of violent rape (cf. figure 1.3 below).

Yet a woman may also be empowered by her beauty, if she uses it to pursue her own ends and control the men who desire her. Mortal women and goddesses alike are shown in art and texts paying careful attention to their toilette, especially prior to moments of seduction (including the wedding night). These scenes make it clear that beauty is not thought of simply as a natural fact. Rather, the production of a woman's beauty lies in her own hands. Such adornment scenes often include mirrors, suggesting a self-conscious awareness in women of their own appearance as an object of display. A mirror implies not only the threat of narcissistic self-admiration—an obvious projection of men's own desire to *see* women—but the ability to enhance one's looks, for seductive purposes, through dress, cosmetics, and grooming. Like a hero's weapons, such decorations are instruments of power, the mirror a female counterpart to the manly sword (cf. Ar. *Thesm.* 140). A hero's magnificent equipment does not compensate for weakness, but rather signifies his exceptional strength; so, too, a woman's clothing and ornaments do not conceal her beauty, or compensate for its absence, so much as express its quality. The most beautiful woman is the one with the best accessories.

Aphrodite is therefore the most richly adorned of all. She is notable even among the gods for her luminous clothing and copious shining jewelry. In figure 1.1 her lavish accoutrements include a casket full of Erotes (winged figures of desire), which literalizes the equivalence between a woman's adornments and her erotic appeal. The same kind of equation is conveyed by Homer's description of her special breast band. This is the ultimate accessory, identical with seduction itself. When Hera wants to borrow it she asks her sister for "loving affection (*philotēs*) and desire (*himeros*)" (*Il.* 14.198), and receives in

FIGURE I.I Aphrodite, in an elaborate outfit and copious jewelry, nursing an Eros. She is surrounded by erotic imagery, including a swan and a casket of Erotes. The other side (not shown) portrays Helen and Paris. Apulian red-figure lekythos, 400–330 BCE. Taranto, Museo Nazionale 4530. Gianni Dagli Orti/The Art Archive at Art Resource, NY.

return the breast band decorated with these and other feminine charms. Nor is it any accident that Aphrodite is regularly described as "golden." When she emerges from the sea at birth, the nature goddesses known as Seasons dress her in an elaborate outfit including lovely garments, a beautiful golden crown, intricate golden earrings, and golden necklaces (*HH* 6.5–13). The fact that she receives this costume at birth shows that it is intrinsic to her divine function— a function demonstrated by the resulting impact on the male gods, who all want to marry her immediately (*HH* 6.15–18). In order to seduce Anchises she dons a similar outfit (*HH* 5.61–67). According to the *Homeric Hymn*, when he laid eyes on her,

> she was wearing a dress brighter than beams of fire
> and twisted bracelets and shining earrings
> and most beautiful necklaces around her tender neck,
> beautiful, golden, very elaborate.

> (*HH* 5.86–89)

FIGURE 1.2 A bride dresses for her wedding in a lovely outfit, jewelry, and veil. Eros
fastens her sandals while an attendant brings a tray with yet more decorations. Attic
red-figure acorn lekythos, 410–400 BCE. Boston, Museum of Fine Arts 95.1402. *ARV²*
1326.71; BAD 220627. Photograph © 2013 Museum of Fine Arts, Boston.

At this sight, *erōs* naturally overcame or "captured" him (91).

In these descriptions of Aphrodite's seductive attire, the radiance of her
garments and the gleam of gold and other precious metals convey the light of
beauty itself. When she first appeared to Anchises, a light "like the moon"
shone round her breasts (5.89–90), and when at last she revealed herself as a
goddess, "immortal beauty shone forth from her cheeks" (5.174–75). Precious
metals also convey beauty's divinity, since gold and brightness in general are
strongly linked with the gods. Elsewhere, beauty and sexual charm (*charis*) are
spoken of, conversely, like erotic accessories. The Homeric gods pour beauty or
charm over their favorites as if it were perfume (*Od.* 18.190–94), or gold applied to a statue by a skilled craftsman (*Od.* 6.232–35, 23.156–62). The effect is
to make them "shine with beauty and charm (*charis*)" (*Od.* 6.237). Nor is this
equation of beauty and adornment confined to mythology. Even in classical
Athens, which provided few approved opportunities for the public display of
female beauty, brides were extravagantly dressed to maximize their charm (see
figure 1.2). The morning after her wedding the bride received gifts of clothing,
perfume, toiletries, and accessories to maintain her husband's erotic interest.

Women could own very little property, but their clothing, jewelry, and other adornments were their own, and they evidently knew how to use them.

As with almost everything to do with women, however, cultural attitudes toward female adornment were deeply conflicted. In myth such items tend to be destructive, often in a way that associates female vanity and sexual license with the improper use or excessive consumption of material goods. Vanity was therefore severely frowned upon. Thanks to beauty contests, both formal and informal, young Greek women must have been well aware of their own appearance and its potential. Yet they were expected not to glory in their beauty but to present themselves, rather, as unaware of its power. The Judgment of Paris offers a stern warning as to the dangers of competitive vanity, and the purposeful use of such power is a mark of licentiousness. In Prodicus's *Choice of Heracles*, Vice—in contrast to the modest Virtue—shows an acute awareness of her body as an object to be viewed. She scrutinizes her appearance, looking around to see if anyone (male) is watching her, and checks on how she looks (in the absence of a mirror) by glancing at her shadow (Xen. *Mem.* 2.1.22).

The anxiety surrounding female adornment is a transparent expression of the male fear—and expectation—that beautiful women will take advantage of their power over men in order to pursue their own desires. When this happens, the results are usually disastrous, since women as such were perceived as inclined to bad choices by a greed, irrationality, and lack of self-control inherent in their very nature. The choices in question are typically sexual, since women's intrinsic irrationality was linked to their gender by means of their physical makeup, their soft, porous flesh making them even more subject than men to the incursions of mind-destroying Aphrodite. A beautiful virgin—who risks abduction by predatory men—is trouble enough, but once a woman has actually experienced sex, her own desires threaten to become insatiable. In Euripides' *Trojan Women*, Andromache, a model of the ideal woman, observes that "they say" a single night of sex with a man will win over any woman—even, apparently, a virtuous wife who has been enslaved by an enemy who then rapes her (665–66). Sexually transgressive women were viewed as damaged goods, since they could not be trusted not to repeat the behavior, and in classical Athens a man was legally obliged to divorce his wife if she had sex with another man, even if she had been raped.

Since women find it so hard to control themselves, they must obviously be controlled by men. A woman in ancient Greece was a perpetual minor, always under the authority of a male guardian (normally her father or husband but in some cases an adult son). This gives men a certain responsibility for women's behavior. According to Socrates, as portrayed by Xenophon, a husband is culpable if he does not "teach" his wife how to behave (*Oec.* 3.11). The attribution of such childlike irresponsibility to women did not mean, however, that they were not held accountable for their actions. Like a child, a woman can and should learn through training and, if necessary, punishment. If her husband's teaching fails to stick, Xenophon's Socrates opines, the wife is to blame for her own dereliction. To say that women are unable to withstand the power of *erōs* is not to excuse them, but to define the deficiency that renders them prone to such culpable behavior in the first place. Because of this deficiency, the most requisite female virtue was self-control (*sōphrosunē*).[3] Failure to exercise this virtue was among the most reprehensible behaviors in Greek culture for both sexes. But it is especially insisted upon for women, because they need it most.

If all this is true of women as such, it is even more true of beautiful women. It is true, above all, of Aphrodite. The divine embodiment of female beauty is unique among goddesses for her promiscuity, erotic self-assertion, and plea-sure in sex. The symbiosis between beauty and promiscuity is reflected in her gifts to mortals, which comprise both beauty and erotic passion. The more fully one is favored by this goddess, the more of both these attributes one may expect to possess. The point is not simply that the more beautiful a woman is, the more likely she is to have opportunities for transgression (though this is presumably a factor). Rather, the woman's greater desirability to men, and the resulting increase in male attention, is configured as a more lustful nature in the woman herself. The *erōs* she inspires is projected back onto her, in propor-tion to the beauty that arouses it, as susceptibility to erotic beauty in men. The more beautiful she is, the greater the threat that is posed not just by the male interest she attracts, but by her own desires.

This comports with a fundamental and pervasive principle of Greek thought, that like is attracted to like. In other words, a beautiful person will be drawn to beauty in others, and hence to erotic transgression. The effect is fur-ther exacerbated by the inflammatory power of reciprocal vision. A beautiful woman draws the eyes of lovers, whose gaze is itself a source of provocation, inspiring desire in the woman herself. Her responsive glance fuels their desire still further, setting up a cycle of reciprocal *erōs* whose intensity is proportionate to the beauty of both participants. To make matters even worse, the most beau-tiful are most likely to embark on this cycle of vision and desire in the first place, since great beauty attracts equally great beauty to itself, affording more opportunities for misbehavior and feeding the erotic excess to which such people are already by nature inclined.

Beautiful women are, in a word, trouble. Yet a man needs a wife to provide him with children, especially sons to carry on his name, and it is beauty that makes him desire a young woman as his wife and holds out the promise of fertility. Misogynistic Greek males sometimes express a wish that they could reproduce without women (e.g., Eur. *Hipp.* 616–24). In the absence of this option, however, a man was obliged to import a bride from an alien household

---

3. *Sōphrosunē* (literally "sound-mindedness") also encompasses self-knowledge, deference, and moderation. Ideally, it means not merely that one can resist inappropriate desires, but that one does not experience them in the first place.

and install her at the very heart of his own. Wives, whose first loyalty is to their natal family, are viewed with the suspicion due to any outsider. The birth of children helps incorporate a woman into her husband's household and guarantee her status. It also cements a marriage by providing an indirect blood-tie between husband and wife and giving the latter a stake in her new family. Yet a powerful mistrust remains. As the surly Hesiod puts it, to trust a woman is to trust a swindler (*WD* 375). Even Telemachus, son of the archetypal faithful wife, Penelope, asserts that although Penelope *says* his father is Odysseus, he does not know this for a fact, since no man knows for sure who his own father is (*Od.* 1.215–16). Such mistrust is exacerbated by the very beauty that elicits men's desire for women in the first place.

Anxiety about female beauty is therefore focused on the figure of the bride. A woman is thought to be most beautiful, and hence the greatest threat to herself and others, when she is a *parthenos*, that is, an adolescent girl who is still virginal but ripe for marriage. The *parthenos* is a liminal figure, poised at a dangerous moment of exposure as she makes the transition from child to adult, from her father's house to her husband's. She embodies a feminine wildness that must be "tamed" by sex and marriage. Horse taming is therefore a frequent image in erotic contexts, with the *parthenos* portrayed as an unbroken filly running free. A *parthenos* is also thought of as a precious object, or *agalma*. An *agalma*—the word often refers to sacred statues—is a treasure whose value transcends mere economic exchange. This means it must be carefully protected against theft. Yet an *agalma* may also manifest a mysterious ability to move itself. In certain cults of Aphrodite the goddess's statue was veiled and had its feet chained, a ritual conflating the goddess with her image in a way that was presumably designed to constrain the untoward eroticism and transgressive movement that she provokes in mortal women (cf. Paus. 3.15.10–11). Like an *agalma*, the *parthenos* too is a beautiful object whose movement, whether through abduction or her own agency, is likely to leave trouble in its wake. After the culturally sanctioned transition of marriage, she is supposed to settle down, to become stable in behavior and location. But there is always a lingering danger that she will refuse to stay put and move again.

Given these anxieties, it is not surprising to find the ideal bride presented more as an object than as a subject of desire. A man "leads" (*agein*) a woman in marriage, a verb that can be used, among other things, for dragging a resistant animal (e.g., *Il.* 13.572) and for the outright abduction of women and children as plunder in war (e.g., *Il.* 6.426). In myth and ritual, marriage itself is often presented as equivalent to abduction. The standard term for this is *harpagē*, an abstract noun formed from the verb *harpazein* ("seize"). The most famous such myth is the tale of Persephone, daughter of the fertility goddess Demeter, whose kidnapping by Hades makes her an archetypal bride. Persephone's terror, as described in the *Homeric Hymn to Demeter*, conveys the fear experienced by girls at marriage, when they had to leave their childhood home for a stranger's house, while Demeter's extravagant grief underlines a daughter's preciousness to her natal family. But even though Persephone is taken against both her own and her mother's will, the final outcome is a sanctioned marriage to Hades. This model for marriage, which renders the woman a passively stolen object, reassures men both of the bride's chastity and of their own control.

Nevertheless, the bride is not constituted as a *mere* object. The wedding was a fearful journey into the unknown, but it was also a joyful day for her, and the fact that she was "led" or even "abducted" does not exclude consent or active enthusiasm on her part. (Similarly, a modern bride may be "given away" by her father and lifted over the threshold by her new husband without arousing any skepticism about her say in the matter.) Persephone herself eats a pomegranate seed in the house of Hades, symbolizing consent, and the Athenian wedding involved similar rituals (including the bride's consumption of a fruit). Nor does the language of *harpagē* by itself imply unwillingness in an abductee. In order to make it clear that the woman is not complicit it is necessary to add "by force" or "against her will." Poets and artists are well able to indicate the coerced "taking" of a woman, as opposed to one in which she acquiesces. This is clear in paintings like figure 1.3, which shows the rape of Cassandra at the sack of Troy. There is a clear contrast with wedding scenes, where the groom typically leads the bride by the hand or wrist but they often make eye contact and may be surrounded by symbols of mutual desire (see figure 1.4). In wedding preparation scenes Eros himself sometimes ties the bride's sandals, suggesting the charm of her movement but also, perhaps, hinting at her own desire to make the journey to her husband's bed (see figure 1.2).

FIGURE 1.3 At the sack of Troy, Ajax son of Oileus drags Priam's daughter Cassandra away from the statue of Athena to which she clings for protection. Detail of an Attic red-figure hydria, early fifth century BCE. Naples, Museo Archeologico Nazionale 81669; *ARV²* 189.74; BAD 201724. Scala/Art Resource, NY.

FIGURE 1.4 A bridegroom leads his bride to his house, looking back into her eyes. Erotes flutter around her head and an attendant adjusts her veil. Attic red-figure loutrophoros, 450–425 BCE. Boston, Museum of Fine Arts 03.802; BAD 15815. Photograph © 2013 Museum of Fine Arts, Boston.

The figure of the bride is thus poised between objectification and agency, desirability and desire of her own. She must be sufficiently reluctant to suggest that she will not stray once she is married, but she must also actively desire her new husband. To be sure, it was not decorous to speak of such desire directly. The notion of marriage as abduction gives a woman an ideological veil, preserving decorum and with it her reputation. When Aphrodite seduces Anchises, for example, we know perfectly well that she is driven by her own desire, but she constructs a scenario that avoids its direct expression, presenting herself as a *parthenos* abducted by Hermes and carried off to Anchises' rustic home against her will. A wife must engage in sex willingly, however, in order to gratify her husband, and—at least according to some ancient theories—must enjoy it in order to conceive a child. A desirable woman is also a woman who desires. Yet this very fact raises the specter of adultery. The same erotic subjectivity that adds to a bride's allure threatens to unleash the disastrous consequences of unbridled female sexuality.

These anxieties surrounding female beauty, agency, and sexuality are crystallized in the myth of Pandora as recounted to us by Hesiod. Pandora is both the first woman and the prototype of all women, who collectively inherit her essential characteristics. As Hesiod puts it, she is the progenitor of the female "race" or "kind" (genos) (Theog. 590). This odd expression, which seems to suggest that women are somehow an independent species, hints at a male fear—complementing men's resentment at their own reproductive dependence—that women can perpetuate themselves without any contribution from the other sex. This fear is expressed through such mythic figures as Gaea, the primordial earth mother who produced her first offspring without a mate, and the Amazons, an independent "race" of women who had no need of men except as occasional sperm donors. Pandora does not enjoy such literal independence. She is, as we shall see, the first human wife. As such, however, she embodies the threat of female agency within the patriarchal household in a way that is inseparable from the allure of her beauty.

In Hesiod's cosmology there is no creation of man. Men apparently just were. They lived together in some kind of homosocial paradise until the kindly Prometheus tried to trick the gods with an inferior offering and then stole fire from them, provoking Zeus to create the dubious "gift" of Pandora in revenge.[4] At the command of Zeus, Hephaestus, the craftsman god, molded out of clay "the likeness of a modest virgin (parthenos)" (Theog. 572, WD 71). She was a figure of awe-inspiring beauty, as lovely to look on as an immortal goddess, a parthenos whose beauty inspires erotic desire (WD 62–63). In other words, she embodies female beauty at its most dangerous and destructive. This is made clear by the gifts she receives from Aphrodite, who personally "pours" upon Pandora's head not only erotic charm (charis) but the painful desire and "limb-devouring cares" that this provokes in men (WD 65–66). Other gods helped dress and decorate her, with special attention to her head, which is veiled, garlanded, and crowned:

> Bright-eyed Athena tied her sash and adorned her
> with silver clothing; on her head she placed
> with her own hands an elaborate veil, a wonder to behold;
> Pallas Athena put delightful wreaths of freshly picked flowers around
>   her head;
> and the famous limping god [Hephaestus]
> placed on her head a golden crown that he himself had made.
>
> (Theog. 573–79)

---

4. "Pandora" means "all gifts." Hesiod's explanation is ambiguous: she either received "all gifts" from the gods or was given to men as a "gift" by "all" the gods (WD 80–82). But the name may originally have signified "giver of all gifts," with reference to Pandora's prehistoric function as an earth goddess.

> The divine Graces and lady Persuasion
> fastened golden necklaces around her throat,
> the lovely-haired Seasons wreathed her with spring flowers,
> and Pallas Athena arranged all the adornments on her body.
>
> (WD 73–76)

When gods and mortal men first laid eyes on her they were overcome with wonder (*thauma*) (*Theog.* 588–89).

Pandora is, in Hesiod's words, a "fabricated woman" (*Theog.* 513). This might make her seem like some kind of mythological Barbie doll, a fully accessorized toy, created and dressed by the gods for their amusement. But the erotic charm with which she is endowed signifies the vitality of life itself. She is also granted several key capacities that constitute her as a human agent, as distinct from a lifeless clay statue. Hephaestus gives her "strength," that is, the ability to move her own body, and "voice" (*audē*), a word that implies articulate human language; the beauty of her face implies, in addition, a glancing eye (*WD* 60–63). In order to use these capacities Pandora needs a mind, and the gods supply this as well, along with "character"; but these faculties are provided by Hermes, god of liars, thieves, and tricksters, so her mind is "doglike" and her character that of a thief (*WD* 67–68).

Hesiod calls Pandora "an evil in exchange for fire" (*Theog.* 570), and indeed, she turns out to be not only as brilliantly beautiful as fire, but equally destructive. Her beautiful appearance is, in its essence, a trick, one that is replicated internally in her sneaky, devious character. Zeus ordered Hermes to take her as a gift to Epimetheus ("afterthought"), who accepted her against the advice of his brother Prometheus ("forethought"). After Epimetheus took her in, Pandora "devised lamentable woes for mortals," opening "with her own hands" a sealed jar full of evils and releasing them into the world (*WD* 94–104). She thus fulfilled her function as a "great disaster" (*Theog.* 592; cf. *WD* 56, 82), designed by Zeus to ruin men's previously carefree lives. The success of this divine plan hinged on her godlike beauty, which made Epimetheus ignore his wiser brother's warning. Pandora is, as Hesiod puts it, an evil that will delight men's hearts in the very moment of embracing it (*WD* 57–58), or, more succinctly, a "beautiful evil" (*kalon kakon*) (*Theog.* 585). She, and with her women as such, challenges by her very existence the aristocratic ideal of the *kalos kagathos*, the harmony between physical beauty and the inner "beauty" of character.

The ambiguous gift of Pandora inaugurates the ambiguity of the human condition, by contaminating the carefree world of men not only with the evils she releases into that world but with women themselves. Pandora's jar evokes a memorable passage of the *Iliad* in which Achilles observes to Priam that no human life is unequivocally good:

Two jars stand in the storeroom of Zeus, full of gifts;
one of them holds the evils he gives us, the other one blessings.
If Zeus, the lord of the thunderbolt, gives a mixture of both
to a man, he sometimes meets with evil, sometimes with good.
But if he gives only woeful gifts to a man, he degrades him;
evil starvation drives him over the splendid earth,
and he wanders deprived of honor by gods and mortals alike.

(24.527–33)

Zeus's other gift, the "beautiful evil" that is women, equally embodies the fundamental duality of the world we live in. As Hesiod declares, in a strikingly close parallel, a bad wife brings a man utter misery, but even a good one is a mixture of good and evil (*Theog.* 607–12).

Zeus fulfills his crafty, malevolent intentions through a creation whose own mind is a malicious one. When Pandora opens the jar and "devises" woes for mortals, the gesture implicates her will and agency in the divine destruction of men. The word translated as "devise" refers to a mode of intelligence called *mētis* by the Greeks, which is, in essence, the ability to conceal one's intentions and control people through deceit. Despite its damaging impact on the rational mind, *erōs* leaves *mētis* intact. And despite the supposed rational superiority of the male, women in general, and beautiful women in particular, are often endowed with this particular form of intelligence, which they tend to employ for the seduction and betrayal of men (cf. Eur. *Hipp.* 641–43). *Mētis* is thus linked with Aphrodite. But it is also associated with Zeus himself. In Hesiod it is Metis, the female personification of cunning, who advises Zeus on good and evil (*Theog.* 899–900). And when Hesiod says Pandora "devised lamentable woes for mortals" (*WD* 95), he is repeating, word for word, a description of Zeus's own plan for revenge against Prometheus (*WD* 49). Pandora is not merely the god's instrument, but his accomplice.

When Epimetheus takes in the beautiful Pandora, he initiates the failure of rational self-control that makes men complicit in the destructive consequences of female beauty—the susceptibility to *erōs* that gives women power over men. He also inaugurates the institution of marriage, by welcoming the beautiful stranger into the very heart of his household. Pandora's virginal beauty and magnificent outfit both mark her as an archetypal bride, dressed and adorned by the gods for her wedding like the bride in figure 1.2 (above). As a fabricated object who is yet an agent, she also embodies the tension in the figure of the bride as a desirable object with desire and agency of her own. Hesiod describes Pandora, in a paradoxical phrase, as both woman (*gunē*) and *parthenos* simultaneously (*Theog.* 513–14). *Parthenos* though she is, she represents, at the same time, the threat of a mature woman, whose sexual appetite, once awakened, makes her still harder to trust or to control.

FIGURE 1.5 Pandora emerging from the earth; she looks up at Epimetheus, who returns her gaze. An Eros flies overhead, signaling her desirability, while Hermes comes from the left to escort her (he is looking back toward Zeus, not visible here). Attic red-figure volute krater, c. 450 BCE. University of Oxford, Ashmolean Museum G 275; ARV2 1562.4; BAD 275165.

There are traces of such desire in Hesiod's wording. As a "modest *parthenos*" Pandora presumably has a downcast eye, yet when he says she resembles the immortal goddesses "to look at in the face" (*WD* 62), the Greek phrase implies reciprocal eye contact, suggesting that her glance responds to the admiring gaze of gods and mortals. The rendition of her birth in figure 1.5 is more explicit, showing a Pandora who looks boldly up at Epimetheus, their eye contact emphasized by the angle of her head. Hesiod is more discreet in conveying Pandora's glancing eye, but he signals her lack of sexual self-control quite clearly when he describes her mind as "doglike." "Dog" and "dog-eyed" (implying a shameless gaze) are frequent insults in Greek, for both sexes but especially for women. Unlike the English "bitch," such language does not connote mean-spiritedness but rather uncontrolled appetite, especially for sex. This doglike quality is closely linked with Pandora's "thief's character," and the "lies and wheedling words" that crown her erotic repertoire (*WD* 77–78). Duplicity as well as lust is intrinsic

FIGURE 1.6 Ewer with breasts, eyes, necklaces, and a bird's beak. Thera, c. 1550 BCE. National Archaeological Museum, Athens, inv. no. 877. © Hellenic Ministry of Culture and Tourism/Archaeological Receipts Fund.

to her very being, and hence to that of all women, who are naturally disposed to deceive men for their own erotic purposes.

Opening the jar is, in addition, a symbolic deed with sexual overtones. Like Pandora herself, a jar is an object made out of clay by males for their own purposes—one that should be kept safely shut up at home. The jar in question is a gift to men from Zeus, as Pandora is, and like her it has a mysterious and ominous interior. The shape of an ancient storage jar is like that of a woman's body, especially her womb (at least in the view of ancient Greek medical writers). The great antiquity of this idea is strikingly conveyed by the Bronze Age jar with female breasts shown in figure 1.6, which literalizes the notion of women as containers. By opening the jar Pandora unseals herself, symbolically taking control of her own sexuality and giving birth, as a consequence, to the evils that lie within.

When the goddesses of youth, charm, and seduction adorn Pandora with jewelry and flowers, they are giving her the tools with which to accomplish such purposes. As it happens, these accessories elicit the only emotion that Hesiod attributes to the first woman. When she is first "led" into the company of mortal men, for them to gaze upon, we are told that Pandora "delighted in her adornments (kosmos)" (Theog. 587). The phrase suggests a self-conscious, narcissistic pleasure in her own beauty and, perhaps, an awareness of its power.

Athena's contribution is a further acknowledgment of feminine power. The goddess of weaving not only dresses Pandora in beautiful clothes but teaches her to do this kind of work herself (WD 63–64). Wool-working was an essential skill for ancient Greek women, whose production of textiles made a vital economic contribution to their husbands' households. In consequence, weaving became both paradigmatic of female "work" and a symbol of desirable womanhood. (Seated wool-working women are often portrayed, for example, in courtship scenes.) Like beauty itself, however, such skill was viewed by men with ambivalence. Weaving symbolizes not only valuable household labor but women's power to trap and beguile men, both erotically and otherwise. It is, in particular, a metaphor for the crafty snares of manipulative language. And, of course, it enables a woman to enhance her own beauty through clothing. Weaving was thus emblematic of Greek ambivalence about female skill and craftiness. Its positive value can be seen in the most famous of all mythological weavers, Penelope, who uses her skill to maintain her virtue; but even she uses it to control men who desire her (below, p. 90).

This capacity to act as a desiring subject is itself part of Pandora's allure. An art collector, no matter how passionate, is content to possess a beautiful object, but an erotic lover longs for a reciprocal response of a kind no mere object can supply. This point is conveyed by numerous tales where humans pine with fruitless love for a statue. The boundary between statues and persons was a source of endless fascination to the Greeks—a fascination conveyed through the many myths in which that boundary is transgressed or blurred. The most influential of these—the tale of Pygmalion—is found only later, in the Latin author Ovid. But many older stories underline the inadequacy of statues as objects of desire. In Euripides' Alcestis, for example, an amorous husband on the point of bereavement exclaims:

> An image of your body, shaped by craftsmen's
> skilled hands, will lie stretched out in my bed.
> I shall fall on it and enfold it my arms,
> and, calling out your name, I'll think I have—though I
> will not—my own dear wife in my embrace;
> the pleasure will be a cold one, yet it may help me
> to lighten the burden weighing down my soul.
>
> (348–54)

Despite the erotic overtones of this disquieting suggestion, its main rhetorical purpose is to emphasize the inadequacy of an inanimate figure in place of a living woman. Statues are, as such moments attest, erotically unavailable and intrinsically unsatisfying love objects, owing to their inability to look, move, speak, and respond to the lover's desire with desire of their own. A desirable woman must be more than an object—she must herself be a desiring subject.

The distinction between Pandora, the "fabricated woman" who is, yet, a woman, and a *mere* object, emerges still more clearly if we compare her with a set of golden robot women constructed by Hephaestus, the same god who "molded" her:

> In support of their master moved his attendants;
> they were made of gold, but looked like living young women.
> They have mind in their wits, and speech and strength,
> and from the immortal gods they know how to do women's work.
> These bustled about in service to their master.
>
> (*Il.* 18.417–21)

Like Pandora, these golden robots have mind, "voice," and "strength," and have learned from the gods to do "women's work" (an expression that typically denotes weaving). Yet their use of these capacities poses no threat to their master. They simply bustle about, tending to him as good handmaidens should. They are ideal servants, mechanical women like Stepford wives who fulfill male fantasies of subservient female perfection.[5]

These robots have the mind and physical agency required to perform their domestic tasks, but they lack the dangerous erotic subjectivity embodied in Pandora. They seem to be devoid of any feelings, including the experience of desire. Nor, significantly, are they portrayed as erotically attractive. Unlike the Stepford wives, who are designed in part as hassle-free sexbots for their husbands, the golden robots are not marked as sexually desirable. Hephaestus is married, after all, to the goddess Grace herself (a substitute, in this story, for his usual wife, Aphrodite) (18.382–83). In this respect the robot women are no different from the self-moving golden cooking pots that Hephaestus also has under construction (18.373–79). A woman must be more than a statue or even a robot if she is to fulfill the functions of a wife, which include not only important household tasks like weaving (and opening jars), but arousing and experiencing erotic passion. The same attributes that make Pandora, or any wife, potentially dangerous—her beauty, together with her capacity for independent feeling and action—are also what make her both desirable and necessary.

---

5. In Bryan Forbes's 1975 movie *The Stepford Wives*, a group of husbands "perfect" their wives by replacing them with look-alike robots. (I ignore the disastrous 2004 remake.)

The more desirable she is, however, the greater the danger that she will exercise those capacities to the detriment of men. It is no coincidence that Hephaestus's robots also lack another essential characteristic distinguishing a human being from a mere object. That is moral character—the aspect of humanity in virtue of which we can be held responsible for our actions. The golden robots, like the Stepford wives, always automatically do the "right" thing. If they fail it is a mechanical failure, not a moral one. Pandora, by contrast, can be held accountable, because she does, explicitly, have moral character. As we saw, that character is a bad one: it is "the character of a thief" (*WD* 67). This pejorative coloring extends to the quality of her voice and mind, highlighting her difference from the robots who share so many of her faculties. The robots are merely given a voice, but Pandora also receives "lies and wheedling words" (*WD* 77–80); the robots simply have a mind, but Pandora's mind is "doglike" (*WD* 67–68).

These qualities define Pandora as untrustworthy in her very essence. But this itself lies at the heart of what makes her—and all women—different from a statue. As we saw, humanity requires not just vision, voice, and strength or even mind, but the capacity to be held responsible for one's actions. But a responsible agent is one who has the power to deceive and betray. For this reason, all adult human relationships are necessarily based to some degree on trust. Trust, however, implies the possibility of mistrust. You cannot trust a golden robot or a Stepford wife, precisely because you cannot *mis*trust her. Despite the pervasive belittling of women's intellectual and moral capacities in Greek ideology, that Pandora and her "race" are human selves in this sense is all too clear. Women's ability to transgress becomes, among the misogynistic Greeks, the will to transgress, in a transparent expression of anxiety regarding female eroticism and its power. Yet it is also a mark of their autonomous humanity. A woman is more than a statue. And there's the rub.

Hence the conundrum of female beauty. As the signifier of nubile womanhood it is intrinsically desirable; yet the greater it is, the more destruction it brings, through unbridled desire not just in lustful men but in the beautiful woman herself. How, then, is this essentially uncontainable force to be kept within bounds?

Ancient Greek societies imposed many social controls on women, physically restricting their visibility, movement, and voice. Though the specifics vary by period and place, the basic agenda remains more or less constant. It appears at its most extreme, however, in Athens (the source of most of our texts from the classical period). In the course of her life an Athenian woman should relocate just once, under male auspices, when she is "led" by her bridegroom from her father's house to his. Apart from this sanctioned and ritualized transition, a good woman knows her place and stays inside as much as possible. When she does go out she should wear modest clothing, including an enveloping veil.

The female voice is especially loaded as a site of power and control. A woman's basic work (reproductive and economic), which requires movement, "strength," vision, and intelligence or "mind," can, albeit with difficulty, be accomplished without a voice (while minding one's own business or in solitude). Speech is thus the least necessary, from a functional perspective, of the faculties that constitute a person as an agent. It is, moreover, intrinsically involved with the exercise of power. Any speech aimed at an audience—that is to say, nearly all speech—is an attempt to exert power of some kind over another person. Women's voices were therefore strictly policed, and silence deemed central to the female virtue of *sōphrosunē*, or self-restraint. The ability to influence men with sweet speech does have a place, when properly controlled, in marriage. But women's opportunities for public speech were very few, and even private speech was viewed with suspicion. Ideally they should not even talk to each other, since they are liable to talk about sex and spur each other to misbehavior. A woman's mouth is an analogue for her sexual organs—a dangerous aperture that should preferably be kept closed.

Such norms are enforced ideologically as well as physically. The discourse of praise and blame was pervasive in ancient Greece, serving to cement group solidarity through affirmation and approval while mocking or reproaching outsiders and deviants. Women often serve as targets for praise or, more often, blame. The tale of Pandora exemplifies such blame, and at the same time justifies it by suggesting that women are blameworthy in their very nature. The same kind of hostility is displayed vividly in a poem by the seventh-century BCE poet Semonides, which develops in baroque fashion Hesiod's suggestion that women constitute a distinct "race." Semonides categorizes different types of women who, he says, derive from different species of animal and other natural phenomena: the sow, vixen, dog, earth, sea, donkey, weasel, mare, monkey, and bee. Despite individual variations, these women are collectively chastised for lust, deception, and greed, and even potentially good qualities, such as beauty and intelligence, are presented in a negative light. The only exception is the blameless bee woman, who grows old faithful to her husband, bears him splendid children, and eschews the company of other women with their talk about sex (7.86–91).

Such blame is an acknowledgment of agency and, in its way, of power. It is at least in part because the ugly Thersites, in the *Iliad*, voices complaints too close to those of the great Achilles that he must be humiliated verbally as well as physically chastised. Like Achilles, Thersites carps at Agamemnon's greed and failure to appreciate the labor of other warriors (2.225–42). In response, Odysseus not only scolds him roundly but beats him until he weeps, while the onlookers laugh and applaud the lesson he is learning (2.246–77). Semonides' poem exemplifies, similarly, the "appropriate" use of blame to reinforce existing hierarchies. In the course of his diatribe he complains, among other things, about the improper use of blame by women themselves, who "arm for battle" and reproach their men (7.103–5). Every woman is, it seems, a potential Thersites, who may turn on her betters, and the poet plays the part of Odysseus in countering their challenge.

"Good" women, by contrast, are typically portrayed by our male authors as misogynistic, self-policing, and male-identified. They are sensitive to public opinion and embrace their subordinate status, along with the accompanying restrictions on their freedom of speech and movement. Euripides' Iphigenia, for example, the virtuous self-sacrificing *parthenos* par excellence, accepts her own death in the cause of male glory on the ground that one man's life is worth the lives of ten thousand women (*IA* 1394). His Andromache—a model wife, as always—understands that independence of mind can only lead to trouble. In her eponymous drama she opines that a woman should put up with even a bad husband and not argue with him (*Andr.* 213–14). She goes on to play the "good woman" card against her rival, Hermione, by disparaging women in general as worse than snakes and fire (*Andr.* 269–73). In a different drama she explains that she voluntarily gave up any desire to leave the house or talk to other women (*Tro.* 645–55; see further below, p. 191).

Andromache's disparagement of her sex as a whole is an indicator of good womanhood, since it shows a proper understanding of her own inferior status. Women's personal self-deprecation is also appealing to men, particularly when voiced in remorse for transgression of their subordinate role. This affirms not only the behavioral norms prescribed for women but the judgment of female moral weakness that is used to underpin such norms. It allows men, moreover, to claim women's collusion in their own subordination. It is for this reason that the pattern of (minor) transgression followed by repentance forms part of the portrait of an ideal marriage in Xenophon's treatise on household management. When his young wife is angry with herself for having misplaced something, the speaker, a nobleman named Ischomachus, graciously explains to her how things should be organized and blames himself for not having done this sooner (*Oec.* 8.1–2). The wife (who remains nameless) is delighted to be set straight and eager to do better (9.1). Similarly, after her husband rebukes her for wearing makeup she never does such a thing again (10.9).

Praise and blame are mutually implicated: if there is a best of the Achaeans, that implies the existence of a worst. Achilles and Thersites are two sides of the same coin. Not surprisingly, then, the discourses of praise and blame are often mutually constitutive, with praise of the honoree articulated at the expense of his or her opposite. This creates a natural impulse to polarize the *kalon kakon* of the female—the irreducible complex of beauty and evil—into opposed models of "good" and "bad" womanhood. In Prodicus's *Choice of Heracles*, for example, Virtue and Vice polarize many of the qualities that coexist in Pandora. Hesiod himself declares that a man gets nothing better than a good wife, but nothing "more chilling" than a bad one (*WD* 702–3; cf. also *Theog.* 603–12). Where women are concerned, however, such polarities are rarely evenly balanced.

Many myths present a good woman as the exception, not the rule, and Semonides pits nine negative types against his single virtuous bee woman. Good women are not only far outnumbered by wicked ones but frequently complain that their reputation and that of all women is soiled as a result.

There was no shortage, then, of representations of good and bad women, which supplemented the physical controls on female independence, educating women in properly gendered behavior and, perhaps more important, educating men—the audience for most of these works—in enforcing such behavior. Yet such measures can never be entirely successful. Many myths suggest that female speech is ultimately uncontrollable. (In the story of Philomela, for example, a woman whose tongue is cut out manages to communicate through figurative weaving.) No matter how heavily she is veiled, a woman's eyes must remain visible if she is to function as a wife. It is therefore up to her to keep her own glance under control. The feet must likewise be free if a woman is to do her work. But moving feet betray a woman's capacity for self-directed locomotion, which may take her outside her prescribed boundaries (especially if she falls under Aphrodite's sway).

Nor does even the most meticulous adherence to decorum protect a woman from advances by unscrupulous men. On the contrary, modesty is itself a provocation. When chiding his wife for the use of makeup, Xenophon's Ischomachus declares simplicity and modesty to be more sexually arousing (*Oec.* 10.12). When a woman leaves the house, the drapery that conceals her body invites attention to what lies beneath, while the veil emphasizes her eyes by framing them. The veil is, to be sure, the very symbol of modesty, yet it is also a standard element in descriptions of seductive feminine adornment like Pandora's (above, p. 15). The same applies to the visual arts, where the veil is often a focus of attention (see figures 1.2 and 1.4 above). Brides, in particular, tend to hold their veil with one hand, in a distinctive gesture that signifies appropriate modesty while highlighting the beauty of the face. Decorous women are no less likely, then, than their more disreputable sisters to draw the kind of attention that may lead them astray.

Worse still, the appearance of modesty can never be trusted. A lustful woman may use decorum itself as a means of seduction. If Aphrodite can seduce Anchises by taking on the appearance and persona of a marriageable *parthenos*, abducted against her will, then the most modest-seeming *parthenos* might be a scheming Aphrodite in disguise. Even Semonides' bee woman is undercut, just a few lines after being so highly praised:

> The one who seems to be most self-controlled,
> it is she who behaves most outrageously;
> while her husband stands gaping, the neighbors
> enjoy seeing how he too is mistaken.

> (7.108–11)

The sole good woman in the poet's menagerie turns out to be, in essence, either a fraud or the fantasy of a delusional husband.

All women, even the bee woman, are thus daughters of Pandora, that likeness of a "modest virgin." Her legacy reaches its apogee, however, in the ultimate "beautiful evil," Helen of Troy. Beauty is a quality of all Greek heroines, a fundamental excellence of their gender, but only Helen is defined specifically by her supremacy in this regard. It is her beauty, along with the divine paternity that causes it, that gives Helen her heroic identity and drives her exceptional status and notoriety, making her the preeminent female subject of song and story. Through her beauty, and the transgressive desire that accompanies it, Helen causes the greatest war of all time. Other mythic women may be more violent, but none wreaks more havoc than the most beautiful of all. This is Helen's mythic essence, as it is Pandora's: the beauty is inalienable, the destruction inevitable. Unlike Pandora, however, of whom we hear no more after she opens the fatal jar, Helen is a woman with parents, husbands, offspring, a loom, and a voice—in short, a woman with a story. It is to that story that I now turn.

2

Helen, Daughter of Zeus

> A pretty woman makes her husband look small,
> And very often causes his downfall.
> As soon as he marries her then she starts
> To do the things that will break his heart.
> But if you make an ugly woman your wife,
> You'll be happy for the rest of your life.
> —Jimmy Soul

When Zeus wanted to reduce the human population, which had grown bloated and impious, a character called Momos ("blame") advised him to achieve this not by thunderbolts and flooding, but by "the birth of a beautiful daughter" and by marrying the sea nymph Thetis to a mortal man, "from which two causes, war arose between Greeks and non-Greeks" (*Cypr.* fr. 1). The daughter was, of course, Helen. As for Thetis's marriage to the mortal Peleus, that resulted in the birth of Achilles, the greatest hero of the Trojan War. Achilles and Helen are often coupled like this as complementary causes of the war. She is its principal reason, he the principal agent of the slaughter, and the Trojan battlefield the arena that proves the supremacy of both. As a pair, they represent the gendered body at its most glorious: seductive female beauty and destructive male strength. The manifestation of supreme masculinity is predicated on the manifestation of supreme femininity, each exercising its intrinsic mode of power: her beauty is as deadly as his physical strength, her body as deadly as his body. Both therefore embody the combined splendor and horror of warfare itself, symbolized in the raging fire that will engulf Troy—the fire of Achilles' strength and Helen's beauty.

Momos's advice was reported in a lost epic known as the *Cypria*. Its purpose is apparently to implicate mortals in their own destruction as a punishment for impiety. Like Pandora, then, Helen is a purposeful product of a vengeful Zeus (albeit through paternity rather than craftsmanship). As with Pandora, too, the erotic lure of her beauty is intrinsic to the god's hostile purpose. What makes the Trojan War story distinctive, despite its countless permutations over time, is the fact that it is always caused, somehow, by Helen as the embodiment of female beauty. Regardless of her presence or absence at Troy, her personal enthusiasm or reluctance, some kind of a Helen is always involved, and her beauty is always pivotal. She is conceptually essential to the Trojan War, and thus to ancient Greek constructions of Greek masculine identity, which is, in consequence, founded on the containment of the threat of female beauty.

In the *Cypria*, Helen's function as an instrument of vengeance is reflected in the identity of her mother, Nemesis ("retribution"). Zeus pursued Nemesis in the form of a goose. She tried to escape by changing into a series of wild animals, but Zeus caught her and mated with her, both of them in goose form. As a result of their union, Nemesis laid an egg from which Helen hatched (see figure 2.1). According to a more obscure tradition Helen's mother was a sea nymph, one of the daughters of Ocean (Hes. fr. 24). This underlines her eroticism, since water has

FIGURE 2.1 Helen emerging from the egg. Leda and Tyndareus stand watching on either side. Campanian red-figure bell krater, c. 340 BCE. Naples, Museo Archeologico Nazionale 147950. Scala/Art Resource, NY.

sexual connotations, and aligns her with Aphrodite—her patron goddess—who was born from the sea. In the story that became canonical, however, Zeus took the form of a swan to have sex with a mortal woman named Leda, and it was she who laid Helen's egg. (Some sources reconcile this with the Nemesis story by having Nemesis lay the egg and Leda find and adopt it.) This makes Helen unique among heroines, since Zeus has no other female offspring via mortal women. Leda's husband Tyndareus is, however, her adoptive father, and often simply referred to as her father. Leda and Tyndareus reside at Sparta, which is a fitting home for Helen's birth. Despite its dour reputation, this city was famous in ancient times for its beautiful women—a fame that was matched, unsurprisingly, by a suspicion among Sparta's enemies that their men could not control them. Though Helen was a Spartan, most texts from the classical period present her from an Athenian perspective, often reflecting negative stereotypes about Spartans of both sexes.

As a daughter of Zeus, Helen is half sister to many major divinities—including Aphrodite and the Muses—and some important mortals. She has a half–twin sister, Clytemnestra, whose mother is also Leda but whose father is the mortal Tyndareus. Clytemnestra was married to Agamemnon, son of Atreus, whose home is variously located at Mycenae, Sparta, or Argos, but who retains Spartan associations. She became notorious for taking a lover, Aegisthus, while her husband was away at Troy, and murdering Agamemnon upon his return. The sisters also have a pair of brothers, Castor and Pollux, who were likewise both born from Leda but had different fathers (Pollux was a son of Zeus and Castor of Tyndareus). Despite this divergent paternity, the boys are known as the Dioscuri, or "sons of Zeus"; in contrast to their destructive sisters, they became emblems of aristocratic brotherhood and male loyalty. Helen is also a half sister to Heracles, the mightiest of Zeus's sons by a mortal woman. Unlike Clytemnestra and the Dioscuri, however, he plays no direct part in her story.

The daughter of Zeus was destined to be repeatedly abducted and/or married (not always clearly distinguishable concepts in myth, as we have seen). These multiple marriages provide the requisite evidence of her beauty's supremacy. In view of the close causal link between beauty and *erōs*, a woman who did *not* arouse such passions could scarcely qualify as the most beautiful in the world. At the same time, the number—and inadequacy—of Helen's various male partners suggests that the forces of female beauty and desire are in their essence uncontrollable. The byways of mythology assign her many mates, but a handful stand out. The first is the Athenian hero Theseus, who abducted the young Helen with the help of his friend Pirithous while she was dancing in a group of adolescent girls (a frequent context for such occurrences) (see figure 2.2). This incident follows the standard pattern for mythic abductions, which typically lead to marriage or at least sex (two more concepts that are not always distinguishable). In some accounts, however, Theseus abducts her prior to puberty, and she remains a virgin. Either way, the Dioscuri respond by invading Attica to rescue their sister; after pillaging Athens they bring her safely home.

FIGURE 2.2 Abduction of Helen by Theseus. She reaches back toward her friends for
help, while Pirithous waits on the left with a chariot to whisk them away. Detail of an
Attic black-figure hydria, c. 510–500 BCE. London, British Museum B 310; *ABV* 361.12,
355, 695; BAD 302007. © The Trustees of the British Museum.

When Helen reached marriageable age, noble suitors came to woo her
from all over Greece. Our earliest account of their courtship comes from the
Catalogue of Women, an epic poem of uncertain authorship (though it is attributed to Hesiod), which recounts the pairings of numerous mythic heroines
with various gods and heroes. The *Catalogue* tells us that Helen's suitors wanted
to marry her sight unseen: all but one of them was drawn by her "renown"
(*kleos*)—in other words, by the very idea of such beauty (cf. 199.2–3, 199.9,
204.56–63). This begins Helen's special association with *kleos*, "renown" or
"reputation," a word that is most often used for the glory sought by warriors in
battle but which means, fundamentally, "what people say." The *Catalogue* also
subtly indicates the emasculating effect of Helen's beauty on her suitors. Typically a man desires to "lead" a woman in marriage "as his wife" (e.g., 43a.20).
This pattern is even used for Aphrodite in the *Homeric Hymns*: when the male
gods first see her, each of them wants "to lead the goddess home to be his wife"
(*HH* 6.16–17). Yet in the *Catalogue* hero after hero desires "to be the husband
of lovely-haired Helen," reversing the normal structure of marital desire and
control.

In some later accounts Helen is actually allowed to choose her own husband, a rare practice that gives a woman more prestige and power but also
makes her responsible for the consequences. One source explains that this
unusual arrangement was intended to prevent strife among the suitors and
thus curtail the threat to other men's marriages, specifically Agamemnon's to

Clytemnestra (Hyg. 78). In the *Catalogue*, Odysseus is also a suitor, though canny enough to know he cannot win (198.2–6). He is not yet married to his famous wife Penelope, of course, but his interest in Helen creates a certain tension with his more familiar status as the well-matched and loyal—if not faithful—husband of the *Odyssey*. In more traditional versions Helen's husband was chosen by her male relatives, but Tyndareus tried first to preempt strife by making the suitors swear that they would come to her husband's defense and help him seek revenge if any man should "take her from him by force" (204.78–84). In the view of one hostile source, this oath is evidence of collective mental impairment caused by desire for Helen, which blinded each man with irrational hope (Eur. *IA* 391–94). In any case it only exacerbated the problem, by transforming the conflict from a dispute among individual men into a clash of massed armies.

However the selection was made, the not-so-lucky winner was Menelaus, Agamemnon's younger brother. This might seem like a strange choice of mate for the world's most desirable woman, since Menelaus is a second-ranked hero in more ways than one. He is not only a younger son but a mediocre warrior, presented throughout the tradition as less than supremely heroic at best. In the *Catalogue*, Menelaus does not even woo Helen himself; Agamemnon does so on his behalf (197.4–5). Nevertheless, he is chosen because he provides the most courtship gifts (204.41–42). This explanation is in keeping with the impressive wealth that is a standard feature of Menelaus's legendary persona. It is this that makes him a fitting husband for the supremely precious Helen. Only he can afford her.

This seemingly odd pairing also has a certain mythic logic. Menelaus's erotic susceptibility to Helen—often strongly emphasized—parallels her own erotic weakness. Both, moreover, are a discredit to their gender. As the essence of the unfaithful wife Helen is, obviously, a failed woman, and this in turn emasculates Menelaus by rendering him the quintessential cuckold. Their marriage exemplifies, in consequence, a kind of gender reversal often found in mythological couples. The more one partner diverges from his or her gender stereotype, the more the other partner does so too. Female self-assertion emasculates men, while male weakness unleashes in women a "masculine" autonomy. This is exemplified most conspicuously in Aeschylus's portrait, in his *Agamemnon*, of the "manly" sword-wielding Clytemnestra and her feminized paramour, Aegisthus.

Helen is scarcely "masculine" in any such obvious sense. But Menelaus, like the other suitors, desires "to be Helen's husband" rather than "leading" her as his wife (*Cat.* 204.41–43). The tradition allowing her to choose her own husband develops this emasculating innuendo, assigning Helen a male prerogative that places Menelaus in the position of a bride. Nor did Helen, like most women, relocate to her husband's household upon marrying him; instead, the couple remained at her home in Sparta, an unusual practice that places the woman in a much stronger position and is associated with greater female authority. When Helen sails away to Troy with Paris she thus jeopardizes her husband's status at Sparta, which is dependent upon his wife. That departure, in pursuit of her own desire, is itself a usurping of masculine prerogative made possible by Menelaus's failure to exercise proper husbandly control. As we saw in chapter 1, a woman was expected to relocate once and once only, from her father's house to her husband's, where she is supposed to stay put. Helen inverts this arrangement. She stays put at her natal home for her first, official, marriage, and after that is constantly on the move.

Our early sources have little to say about the marriage of Helen and Menelaus. Their wedding is celebrated, however, by a chorus of unmarried girls in a poem by Theocritus composed in the third century BCE. Helen is praised as an ideal bride, not only the most beautiful of her cohort of Spartan girls (all 240 of them), but the best at running, spinning and weaving, singing, and playing the lyre (18.22–25, 32–37). The chorus anticipate that Menelaus will have Helen forever (18.14–15) and pray for the couple's *erōs* and desire to be equal and reciprocal (18.50–55). Their wedding song thus affirms the fantasy that the most beautiful woman is, indeed, the supreme embodiment of female excellence (cf. above, p. 3). Given the well-known identities of the bride and groom, however, Theocritus's poem drips with irony. When the girls praise Helen's running (18.22), then compare her to a chariot horse (18.30), the audience knows full well that this horse will not remain yoked for long. In case there were any doubt on this score, Menelaus is mocked as a sleepy-headed drunk unworthy of such a wife (18.9–11).

Theocritus's chorus also pray that Helen may bear Menelaus a child that resembles herself (18.21), and this prayer, at least, was to be granted. According to the *Odyssey*, the marriage resulted in a single child, a girl named Hermione, with "the beauty of golden Aphrodite" (4.12–14). There is something a little strange, however, about the chorus's prayer. All children should resemble their parents, of course (cf., e.g., Hes. *WD* 235), but since there is no doubt about a woman's identity as mother, the crucial point, for a husband, is that his wife's offspring should resemble *him*. It seems strange too, at a wedding, to pray in effect for a daughter, as opposed to a son and heir. The prayer thus draws attention to Helen's lack of fecundity. In some other more obscure tales she does bear additional offspring, including sons to both Menelaus and Paris; but Hermione as her only child dominates the tradition. According to this canonical account, Helen puts an end to her husband's legitimate line, denying him a vital form of patriarchal self-perpetuation. A further prayer by Theocritus's chorus, for the marriage to result in a fine line of noble descendants (18.52–53), was not to be fulfilled.

In normal circumstances such failure to bear a son would jeopardize a Greek wife's position, since it denies her a woman's primary avenue to status within her husband's household. Since she did not relocate upon marriage, however, Helen needs no sons to establish her status at Sparta. Moreover, the absence of a son helps her maintain her independence. When a son grows up, he becomes another source of male authority over his mother (cf. *Od.* 21.350–53). The production of a beautiful daughter, by contrast, perpetuates Helen herself in a way that hints at the specter of an independent "race" of females (cf. above, p. 15). Not surprisingly, Hermione was to have a troubled future. Her marriage, like her mother's, would be highly problematic, with the bride an object of violent dispute between two suitors. To make matters worse she is also, in most accounts, unable to bear children.

Meanwhile, on a hillside near Troy, Paris was busy judging the relative beauty of three great goddesses. Zeus's reasons for assigning him this exalted role are rarely addressed, but the strong association between similar things in Greek thinking suggests that his primary qualifications were his own beauty and the personality that went with it. As many myths attest, Trojan men had an extraordinary erotic appeal for both male and female admirers, generally with negative consequences for themselves and others.[1] Paris is no exception. His beauty is, however, not that of a mighty warrior like Achilles, which is an effect of perfected masculinity, a proper expression of magnificent physical power. It is, rather, a "feminine" allure of the kind associated with fine clothing and luxurious accessories. In keeping with the attraction of like to like, this feminizing type of beauty is expected to make a man attractive to women. It is also closely linked with heterosexual excess and transgressive desire on the part of the man. Paris is the archetype of this feminized variety of masculine beauty: he is the masculine "beautiful evil." The devastation he will bring his people is foreshadowed when his mother, pregnant with Paris, dreams she will bear a firebrand that will burn Troy to the ground. All this makes him a fitting judge for the fateful contest.

In the *Cypria*, Aphrodite prepares for the occasion by enhancing her beauty with perfume, clothing, and flowers, assisted by the Graces and Seasons (fr. 4). The erotic impact of her appearance may be gauged by her effect on Anchises in the *Homeric Hymn* (above, pp. 8–9). In this case, however, the desire she inspires was to be satisfied by her human surrogate, Helen, whom the goddess offers Paris as a "gift" or bribe. Like her Greek suitors, Paris desires Helen sight unseen. Excited by the prospect of marrying her, he awards Aphrodite the prize then sails off to Sparta, where he proceeds to woo Helen with courtship gifts (102–3). Many vase paintings show him appearing seductively in her boudoir, like figure 2.3, where his beauty is on full display. Menelaus simplifies matters by foolishly taking a trip to Crete, even telling Helen to take good care of their guest; Aphrodite then "leads" Helen to Paris. After consummating the relationship the couple sail away, taking with them a large number of Menelaus's possessions (103). Other sources indicate, alternatively, that they first have sex on an island called Cranae, off the coast of the Peloponnese. Either way, the marriage is subsequently ratified at Troy.

1. Other examples include Anchises (above, p. 6) and Troilus (below, pp. 107–9).

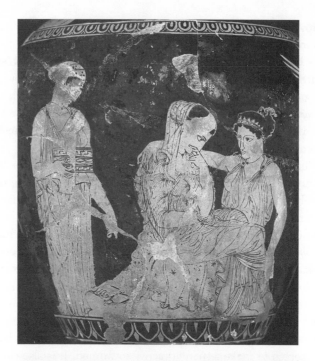

FIGURE 2.3A AND FIGURE 2.3B The meeting of Paris and Helen. In figure 2.3a an
elegantly clad Helen sits in Aphrodite's lap with her eyes cast down. The goddess

At first glance, Paris seems like a more suitable partner for Helen than Menelaus did. He is her male equivalent—the favorite of Aphrodite, marked by both erotic beauty and transgressive sexual desire. Their elopement even follows a more conventional wedding pattern than her original marriage. In contrast to Menelaus's mildly ignominious relocation to Sparta, this time the man conveys the woman from her home to his. But Paris is *too much* like Helen. He is marked throughout Greek tradition as unmanly in both appearance and behavior. His beauty, as we saw, is of a "feminine" type, his weapon of choice is the bow and arrow—typically deemed less "manly" than face-to-face combat—and he is at best a reluctant warrior. It is no accident that in Homer he is typically referred to as "Helen's husband," instead of Helen as "Paris's wife," reversing the usual naming pattern for married couples.

Paris's offense is standardly labeled an "abduction" (*harpagē*). The abduction of *parthenoi*—unmarried adolescent girls—is a frequent occurrence in myth and acceptable, in its way, as a route to marriage (cf. above, pp. 12–13). The abduction of a married woman is, however, a very different matter. Paris's crime is a heinous one, exacerbated still further by the fact that he was present in her husband's house as a guest. This makes him the archetypal violator not only of marriage but of the institution of guest-friendship (*xenia*), which mandates the hospitable treatment of strangers and creates mutual obligations between host and guest. Guest-friendship was integral to the web of reciprocities that sustained ancient society, and its norms among the most sacred in Greek culture. It was ranked alongside respect for one's parents and the gods, and lay under the protection of Zeus himself.

Paris's deed is also often described as a "theft," not only of Menelaus's possessions but of his wife, who may be regarded, with caveats, as a possession of a very special kind. This kind of objectification is also implicit in the oath of the suitors, as recounted in the *Catalogue*, which binds them to take revenge on any man who "takes" Helen "by force" (204.81–84). The verb translated as "take" is the Greek *helein*, which can also mean "capture" or "destroy," and is used here, as often, in a way that puns on Helen's name. In this case the echo underlines her status as an object for the taking. Even though Paris exercises no force against Helen herself, in her husband's eyes the abduction obviously qualifies as a "taking" in the relevant sense. Deprived against his will of both wife and goods, Menelaus may easily be seen from a masculine perspective as the victim of

Persuasion stands to their left, holding a box for cosmetics or jewelry. In 2.3b (a continuation of the same scene) Paris is pulled forward by the winged figure of Desire (Himeros). Attic red-figure amphora, 450–425 BCE. Berlin, Antikensammlung, Staatliche Museen 30036; *ARV*[2] 1173.1; BAD 215552. pbk, Berlin/Johannes Laurentius/Art Resource, NY.

another man's use of "force." From this perspective, Helen's own subjectivity and agency are irrelevant.

As we saw in chapter 1, however, the language of *harpagē* does not rule out complicity in the abductee. Though many such victims are, indeed, kidnapped against their will, including Helen herself when she was abducted by Theseus, this time she is not among them. The *Cypria's* narrative is one of seduction, not kidnapping or rape. When Aphrodite "leads" Helen to Paris, the verb indicates not external coercion but the force of Helen's own desire, which brings about a catastrophic failure in the essential womanly virtue of *sōphrosunē*, or self-control. This leads to an improper exercise of independent agency on Helen's part—one that became emblematic of the danger of female movement as such. She seems to just *go*, unimpeded by the physical and ideological constraints that govern women's lives. Our sources use three verbs in particular, over and over again, to define her transgression: "leaving," "going," and "sailing away." These active verbs make Helen, like Paris, responsible for her own erotic choices. The degree to which that responsibility is weighted varies considerably, as we shall see. Depending on the author and text, it can be minimized to the vanishing point or blown up into criminal enormity. But it is never completely elided.

The same combination of male "taking" and female complicity is reflected in the visual arts, where the abduction is normally portrayed as wedding-like. Often Paris leads Helen by the wrist, as a bridegroom would, and the couple is surrounded by symbols of desire (see figure 2.4 and compare figure 1.4, p. 14). Sometimes Eros even fastens Helen's sandals for her journey, like those of a bride (compare figure 1.2, p. 9). There is a noticeable contrast with images of her first abduction by Theseus, where she is usually shown as an unwilling victim. In figure 2.2, for example, she is bodily lifted from the ground and reaches back to her friends for help. When Theseus abducts the young Helen he uses force, and the conflict remains local. This is a mere preface to Helen's real story, however, in which she is complicit in her "abduction" and brings about the greatest war of all time. The logic of myth makes it clear that her own desire is an essential ingredient in the enormity of the destruction caused at Troy.

This is only to be expected, given the Greek tendency to project transgressive desire onto women who inspire it (above, p. 11). In Helen's case, this process appears with exceptional clarity in a famous poem by Sappho, a poet from Lesbos living around 600 BCE. Helen is identified as surpassing all others in beauty, then used to exemplify the power of *erōs* not as an object of desire but as an agent following her own desire for Paris (see further below, pp. 111–16). Similarly, Gorgias's *Encomium of Helen*, a playful rhetorical piece from fifth-century Athens, begins by extolling the power of Helen's body to arouse men's desires, but goes on to analyze the causes of *her* desire, not theirs (see further below, chapter 8). Both of these utterly different texts exemplify a tendency in

FIGURE 2.4 The abduction of Helen by Paris. Paris leads Helen away by the wrist like a bride. Aphrodite touches her head, and Eros flutters overhead. Behind Aphrodite is the goddess Persuasion. The other side (not shown) portrays the recovery of Helen by Menelaus. Attic red-figure skyphos, c. 490–480 BCE. Boston, Museum of Fine Arts 13.186; *ARV²* 458.1, 1654, 481; BAD 204681. Photograph © 2013 Museum of Fine Arts, Boston.

many of our sources to focus less on Helen's desirability to Paris than on her own susceptibility to desire for him. She is not, in modern terms, promiscuous. She is, rather, a serial monogamist—a faithful wife, if temporarily, to each man in turn. In fact, her own feelings are rarely even mentioned in connection with most of these pairings. But the elopement with Paris becomes her iconic story, a story haunted by the idea that a beautiful woman is one who cannot control her own desires.

The elopement is, of course, all part of a divine plan, initiated by Zeus and carried through with the help of Aphrodite at the Judgment and thereafter. Both Paris and Helen are subjected to divine influence, as illustrated in figure 2.3 (above). In this poignant image Helen sits on Aphrodite's lap while Paris is badgered by the god Desire (Himeros). Both mortals seem reluctant to submit to the gods that egg them on—Helen's eyes are downcast, and Paris appears to hang back. Despite such divine involvement, however, both of them remain responsible for their own actions (cf. above, pp. 6–7). Paris's instrumental function in fulfilling the plans of the gods does not excuse his erotic susceptibility, but actually depends on it. His choice at the Judgment defines his identity: it is a choice of what kind of person to be, based on the kind of person that he already is. The same applies to Helen herself. She is, to be sure, the goddess's victim, but Aphrodite's power works through her desires, not against them. When Aphrodite "gives" her to Paris this means, in essence, that if Paris seeks her out and seduces her she will succumb.

Menelaus's first reaction to Helen's departure receives little emphasis in most versions of the story. He went to Troy, accompanied by Odysseus, and tried to talk the Trojans into giving Helen back. After receiving a hostile reception (including, on one account, a murder attempt), he returned to Greece. His older brother, Agamemnon, then proceeded to assemble a vast army of allies with a total of a thousand ships. The fleet gathered at Aulis, a coastal town to the north of Athens, en route to Troy. There they were detained by contrary winds sent by the goddess Artemis (who favored the Trojans). In order to placate her, Agamemnon sacrificed his young daughter Iphigenia. This disturbing incident is mentioned nowhere in Homer, but in many other accounts of the war—especially in tragedy—it compromises the expedition by leaving the Greeks' hands stained with innocent blood.

When they finally reached Troy, the army of the Greeks (also known as the Achaeans) laid siege to the city, beginning ten years of brutal warfare against the Trojans and their many allies. The war was not only unprecedented in scale but marked the beginning of the end of the heroic world (in which gods and mortals mingled socially). Like Pandora opening the jar, Helen, by eloping, inaugurated the decline of the human race. In the classical period, starting with the Persian Wars of the early fifth century BCE, the Trojan War took on another kind of symbolic importance. When lines became drawn more sharply between east and west, or Greeks and non-Greeks, the Trojan War was used increasingly as a legendary justification for this dichotomy. As its object, Helen came to stand for Greece itself, an identity fostered by the similarity of her name to that of Hellas—the Greek word for Greece—and of its people, the Hellenes. Meanwhile the Trojans became viewed as archetypal "barbarians." In Greek, the word *barbaros* is not intrinsically negative, simply meaning "non-Greek-speaker," but it became increasingly pejorative over time. Paris, already a glamorous and less-than-manly figure in epic, became the very essence of the effeminate, luxurious barbarian, deficient in the values that made the Greeks, in their own view, superior to foreigners.

The moral case for the Trojan War rests on the violation of those values, especially the crucial institution of guest-friendship. Yet the war is never *only* about punishing Paris; it is also about reclaiming Helen. These two central motives for the war—revenge (on Paris) and retrieval (of Helen)—are variously emphasized by different authors and can be hard to disentangle from each other. Given the dim view the Greeks took of female adultery, this may seem surprising. Under the circumstances, one might not expect Menelaus to want Helen back at all. Yet her beauty makes her extraordinarily precious, just as

Zeus intended when he conceived her. It is this that enables Paris's violation of guest-friendship to bear such enormous weight. Despite the heinousness of that violation, excessive revenge is condemned, in general, from Homer onward, and the war against Troy can all too easily seem to fall into that category. It can be justified only if Helen's abduction is treated as a special case. The scale and duration of the war are not mere unfortunate side effects of her beauty. They are, rather, the evidence for its supremacy. Conversely, her exceptional value, as the beautiful daughter of Zeus, makes her worth recovering at any cost.

The suitors' oath shows the high value placed on Helen not just by Menelaus but by the Greeks collectively. Yet the oath is invoked surprisingly rarely to explain their support for him in the Trojan War. They, do, however, have other motives. The Greek warriors are concerned with plunder, status, and above all *kleos*: glory or renown deriving from heroic exploits on the battlefield. Renown is passed down to future generations through story and song—especially in epic poetry—providing great heroes with a form of immortality. A glorious death in battle also immortalizes a man by preserving his youthful beauty from the decay of age. The value of such glory, and its central role in creating heroic identity, are displayed emblematically in the choice of destinies faced by Achilles, the greatest hero of all. In the *Iliad* his divine mother, Thetis, informs her son that he can have a long and undistinguished life if he returns home, or the "imperishable *kleos*" of a youthful death upon the plains of Troy (9.413). Though he vacillates between these options, he ends up embracing death at Troy and with it his heroic identity.

The myth of Helen's origins implicitly justifies the pursuit of these goals by granting her extraordinary value as casus belli. Yet many accounts of the war display uneasiness or indignation at the enormous cost in human suffering on both sides. Was Paris's offense really such as to merit this reaction? Or put differently, was Helen really worth it? If this question is a pressing one for the Greeks it is still more urgent for the Trojans, who are risking annihilation and cannot fall back on the claims of justice. Their refusal to return Helen as the war dragged on became something of a puzzle. The only available explanation, besides the value placed on Helen herself, is loyalty to Paris. Yet such loyalty is never invoked directly. Paris is uniformly despised by the Trojans generally and seems little loved even by his relatives. Nor does his death put a stop to the war. When Paris is killed in battle, other men quarrel over who should have Helen next, and she ends up with another son of Priam, named Deiphobus. We hear little about this marriage, which seems to exist primarily to fill the vacuum created by Paris's death. Helen must always have a mate, preferably one who has had to compete for her with other men. But Deiphobus's role underscores the fact that once Helen enters Troy, the Trojans are collectively complicit in retaining her. This can be explained only by the power of her beauty.

After ten long years the Greeks finally conquered the city by means of the ruse known as the Trojan Horse. They constructed a hollow wooden image of a horse, secretly filled it with armed warriors, and tricked the Trojans into taking it into their city as a sacred object (*agalma*) to be dedicated to the gods (*Od.* 8.510). This trick, often linked with the crafty Odysseus, fittingly replicates the deed that initiated the war. As a beautiful, precious, yet dangerous object welcomed in by foolish men, the horse has a symbolic kinship with Helen—a kinship that also brings out her likeness to Pandora (above, pp. 16–17). Some say that Helen betrayed her adopted city by conspiring with Odysseus to implement the plot. Other later accounts have her signaling to the Greeks with a torch from the city walls, a motif developing a more traditional association between the torches at her wedding to the "firebrand" Paris and the conflagration that burned Troy to the ground.

The sack of the city was brutal. Old men and children were ruthlessly slaughtered and the women enslaved to the victors. Among other atrocities, Priam and Hecuba's virginal daughter, Polyxena, was sacrificed on Achilles' tomb. Neoptolemus, son of Achilles, slaughtered Priam himself at an altar and murdered his little grandchild, Hector's son Astyanax. Ajax son of Oileus dragged Priam's beautiful, prophetic daughter Cassandra from Athena's temple where she had taken refuge, forcibly separating her from the statue of the goddess (see figure 1.3 above, p. 13). This incident became a canonical case of brutal and impious rape, in contrast to the equivocal "abduction" that took Helen to Troy.

As for Helen herself, many vase paintings show Menelaus encountering her among the ruins. In some images of this famous incident—which is known as the Recovery of Helen—Menelaus's sword is raised to kill her (figure 2.5), but in others he has dropped it, overcome by her beauty (figure 2.6). Helen often retreats to the protection of Aphrodite or her statue (as in figure 2.6). In other renditions the scene is wedding-like. Menelaus sometimes grasps Helen's wrist like a bridegroom, she may hold her hand to her veil in a bridal gesture (as in figure 2.5), and Erotes often flutter overhead (as in figure 2.6; compare figure 1.4 above, p. 14). After all these years, Helen still has the allure of a nubile *parthenos*. The effect on Menelaus and his sword illustrates graphically the emasculating power of her extraordinary beauty. The husband of whom she made such a mockery not only fails to punish her but takes her home again as his wife, ignoring the fact that she should be spurned as damaged goods for her adultery.

The surviving Greeks had numerous adventures on the voyage home. The *Odyssey* recounts the wanderings of Odysseus, who took ten years to return to his faithful wife Penelope, then slaughtered the men who had been preying on his property while courting her in his absence. Agamemnon reached home only to be murdered, along with Cassandra (now his concubine), by Clytemnestra. Menelaus's own ship, with Helen on board, was blown off course and they wandered extensively around the Mediterranean. Their most important

FIGURE 2.5 Menelaus encounters Helen at the sack of Troy and raises his sword to kill her. She lifts her veil with her hand and returns his gaze. The other side (not shown) portrays a woman mourning a dead warrior. Attic black-figure amphora, sixth c. BCE. Vatican, Museo Gregoriano Etrusco 350; *ABV* 140.1, 686; BAD 310352. Scala/ Art Resource, NY.

stop was in Egypt, a place that is linked persistently with Helen. Some authors even claim that she spent the entire war there. She did not elope at all, but was replaced by an indistinguishable double or *eidōlon* fabricated by the gods. It was this that the two armies fought over at Troy, while she herself waited out the war in Egypt. On this account, Menelaus retrieved her when he landed there on his way back to Greece. One way or another, however, they eventually arrived home to renewed domestic stability at Sparta.

Unlike other erotically transgressive women in myth, Helen does not come to a bad end. In fact, she does not come to an end at all. The only surviving account of her death is a peculiar anecdote mentioned by the second-century

FIGURE 2.6 Menelaus encounters Helen at the sack of Troy and drops his sword at the sight of her. She flees to the protection of Aphrodite (on the left). A figure of Eros flies between them as they make eye contact. Attic red-figure bell krater, c. 450–440 BCE. Paris, Louvre G 424; *ARV²* 1077.5, 1682; BAD 214486. Réunion des Musées Nationaux/Art Resource, NY.

CE travel writer Pausanias. Helen was allegedly sent into exile by Megapenthes (Menelaus's illegitimate son) and Nicostratus (her own son with Menelaus); she went to the island of Rhodes, where she was killed in revenge by Polyxo, a woman whose husband had died in the Trojan War (3.19.10). Aside from this obscure local tale, we hear no reports of Helen dying. On the contrary, her myths feature a number of close brushes with death that seem to insist on her unkillability. Even the Rhodian story has a variant in which Helen escapes the vengeful Polyxo (Polyaen. *Strat.* 1.13). In another tale, the virginal Helen is chosen by lot to be sacrificed in order to avert a plague, but an eagle (the bird of Zeus) intervenes to rescue her (Plut. *Mor.* 314c). At the sack of Troy Menelaus almost kills her—but doesn't. Euripides teases us with the idea of Helen's death in his *Orestes*, which features a plot to murder her. In contrast to her well-known effect on Menelaus, this time her beauty is markedly inadequate to blunt her attacker's sword (cf. 1286–87). We even hear her voice, offstage, crying out that she is dying (1296–1301). But it turns out that she has simply disappeared (1493–98), "abducted" by Apollo under orders from Zeus (1629–37). Once again she turns out to be indestructible.

Despite this lack of a defining death story, however, Helen does pass from human life, reappearing as an immortal recipient of hero cult. Cult heroes and heroines were, typically, significant mortals who exercised supernatural powers from beyond the grave. As such they were a species of divinity, albeit with less power and status than the gods proper. If duly honored with gifts and sacrifice they provided powerful protection; if not so placated they could be very dangerous. In historical times most of the prominent figures from epic—such as Achilles, Agamemnon, and Odysseus—were worshipped in this way. Such cults were strongly local, but an individual hero might have shrines in many places, and important figures were often claimed by several localities.

Helen is the most significant of all cult heroines. As such she is unusual in several ways, starting with the strange circumstances of her birth. The egg from which she hatched had cult associations. Depictions of the event often include an altar (see figure 2.1), and Pausanias claims to have seen the shell preserved in a shrine at Sparta (3.16.1). If her birth is peculiar, so is her death, or lack thereof. Hero cult typically centers on a tomb (real or imagined), and death is usually an important feature of a hero's or heroine's myth. (Her Rhodian death story is, in fact, linked with a local cult.) Helen shared with Menelaus a shrine known as the Menelaion, at Therapne near Sparta, which did come to be thought of as their tomb, but we hear nothing about how she arrived there (see figure 2.7). As for Menelaus, not only does he lack a death story but we are explicitly told, in the *Odyssey*, that he will not die, but will live forever in Elysium because he has Helen as his wife and is thus the son-in-law of Zeus (4.561–69). This grants him special distinction even among cult heroes, most of whom were thought of as residing mysteriously underground near their tombs. Only a privileged few are given a blessed afterlife in a paradise like Elysium or the Isles of the Blessed.

Helen's cults were widespread. Most of them have some connection with her status as a supremely beautiful *parthenos* or bride and her consequent abductions. In the cult at Rhodes, her death story may represent the symbolic "death" of a *parthenos* making the transition to marriage. Another shrine, near Athens, was associated with her abduction by Theseus and retrieval by the Dioscuri. She was also linked with a shrine elsewhere in Attica, dedicated to her mother, Nemesis. This cult may have treated the Trojan War as an antecedent for Greek retribution (*nemesis*) over non-Greeks in the Persian Wars, in which Athens played a leading role. The shrine was established, however, near the beginning of the Peloponnesian War between Athens and Sparta, suggesting an Athenian desire to appropriate the Spartan Helen for themselves. Elsewhere, at Corinth and on the island of Chios, there were springs named for Helen, which may have been thought of as beautifying girls who bathed there (the Corinthian spring was known as "Helen's bath"). She was associated with a cult of Achilles in the Black Sea (see below), and both she and Menelaus may even have been worshipped in Egypt.

FIGURE 2.7 The remains of the Menelaion, the shrine of Helen and Menelaus at Therapne near Sparta, looking west toward the Taygetus Mountains. Photograph by Kirk Ormand.

Unsurprisingly, Helen's cult is best attested at Sparta. In addition to the shrine where her egg was on display, another was apparently dedicated to a sandal that she lost during her elopement. Her most prominent Spartan shrines represented the two sides of a girl's transition to marriage. At one of them, near the Platanistas ("plane trees"), Helen was worshipped by *parthenoi* in a cult that may be reflected in Theocritus's wedding poem (above, p. 32). Theocritus refers to dances and footraces, which were performed in Helen's honor, and mentions offerings of flower garlands and olive oil at a sacred plane tree. Her other major cult site was the Menelaion at Therapne. Since, as we saw, she shared this shrine with Menelaus, it presumably commemorated the marriage resumed after the Trojan War. Even there, however, Helen was associated with beautifying young women, as we shall see (below, pp. 158–60). In cult, she can be simultaneously a desirable but dangerous *parthenos*, provoking transgression in herself and others, and an errant wife brought back under male control.

The fickle Helen might seem like a strange heroine for girls to celebrate at the point of marriage, but cult figures were, in general, far from saints. Heroines, like heroes, were worshipped not for their virtue but for their awe-inspiring nature, which could be manifested in all kinds of ways, including remarkable virtue but also shocking crimes. (Medea and Clytemnestra, for example, were both cult figures.) Heroines' marriages, in particular, are typically *not* exemplary, but set them apart in one way or another from the norm for mortal women. Both heroes and heroines were, to be sure, regarded as models for human behavior, but such imitation was limited to positive qualities. The cult of Helen does not endorse her adultery. It does, however, acknowledge the bride's beauty and also, more obliquely, her desire.

Helen is an emblematic figure of the bride in art and texts as well as cult. In poetry brides are likened to Helen for their beauty, and in art her elopement with Paris is presented as a wedding scene (above, p. 36). This "wedding" far overshadows her legitimate marriage to Menelaus in our sources. The desire that drives Helen's infidelity is thus vital to her image as a bride. She is complemented, to be sure, by other legendary models for young women, such as Achilles' mother, Thetis, who was famous for rejecting sex and marriage (below, pp. 99–100). Yet Helen remains the figure of the bride par excellence, since it is she above all who embodies the anxiety surrounding female sexuality that renders marriage inherently unstable. Like Pandora, she incarnates the tension that lies at the heart of women's role as an object of male desire who yet remains an agent with desires of her own. The ambivalence attending her complicity in her own abduction echoes the problem of identifying the subjectivity of the bride, and more generally women's finely calibrated position between coercion and consent in marriage.

Helen represents, in addition, the liminality of the bride, poised between the roles of *parthenos* and wife. Her beauty makes her the emblematic virgin ripe for marriage; yet she maintains this status, paradoxically, through repeated remarriage (or reabduction); this resituates her over and over again as the desirable bride while simultaneously rendering her the promiscuous woman par excellence. Like Pandora, or Aphrodite herself—who can play the *parthenos* when it suits her—she transcends the conceptual division between *parthenos* and mature woman so as to embody both the seductive beauty of the one and the overactive sexuality of the other. She represents woman simultaneously at her most desirable and most destructive.

If Helen is an iconic bride, however, then any bride may be a Helen. With each mythic marriage she reenacts the danger to a man of incorporating such a "beautiful evil" into his household. The Trojan War narrative suggests that this threat can ultimately be contained, albeit at enormous cost, by restoring the errant wife to her rightful husband's control. Yet cult casts some doubt on this clear-cut narrative. Archaeological and literary evidence alike suggest that in the afterlife Menelaus continued to play second fiddle to his wife. In the *Odyssey* he obtains the privilege of immortality in Elysium only because of Helen, not for any special qualities of his own. Menelaus was, in general, a rather insignificant cult hero. At joint shrines like the Menelaion the female partner normally has a subordinate role (receiving, for example, less significant offerings). At the Menelaion, however, despite its name, Helen was probably the more important figure of the two. Herodotus mentions, for example, that Helen had a cult statue (*agalma*) at Therapne—a rarity for heroes, let alone heroines—but says nothing at all about Menelaus (6.61.3).

Helen's cults link her more closely with her brothers than with her husband. In Euripides' drama *Orestes*, the immortal Helen is to sit at her brothers' side and share their prerogatives, but nothing is said about immortality for Menelaus (1635–37, 1660–63). Her supernatural activities likewise associate her with the Dioscuri. She sometimes protects sailors, appearing along with them in the form of Saint Elmo's fire, a flickering luminescence on the rigging of ships known in many places as "Helen's fire."[2] She even appeared at her brothers' side to protect Sparta during a battle (Paus. 4.16.9)—an exceptionally martial role for a heroine. In other stories she acts quite independently. Like Aphrodite she can bestow the gift of beauty (below, p. 159), and in one well-known incident she blinds a poet who displeases her (below, p. 117). None of these stories mentions Menelaus. The immortal Helen seems to gad about quite independently of her husband, intervening in the human world in unusually diverse ways. Cult suggests, then, that her redomestication through the Trojan War may not have been entirely successful.

The most intriguing evidence for its failure is an anecdote in which we find Helen cohabiting in the afterlife not with Menelaus but with Achilles, at an important cult site of his in the Black Sea called White Island (Paus. 3.19.11–13). The connection is a fitting one. Achilles is, as we saw, Helen's most direct male equivalent, his supreme military prowess the masculine counterpart of her erotic power. If she is an ideal bride, he is the ideal bridegroom, and they are often intriguingly linked as (potential) marital partners. In the Hesiodic *Catalogue*, for example, the only reason Achilles is not one of Helen's suitors is that he is too young; had he been old enough, he, not Menelaus, would have won her (204.87–92). In the *Cypria*, we are told, Achilles desired to see Helen, so Aphrodite and Thetis arranged a meeting between them; having seen her, he restrained the Achaeans when they wanted to leave for home (105). And the eccentric Hellenistic poet Lycophron seems to marry them in a dream (*Alex.* 171–74). Like her cohabitation with Achilles on White Island, this takes their affinity to its logical conclusion. Achilles is clearly the "right" man for Helen. For this very reason, however, they cannot be paired in the mortal world, but only in a dream or in the afterlife. A successfully (and therefore permanently) partnered Helen would lose her raison d'être. Marriage to Achilles would eliminate her story.

Helen's exceptional features as a cult figure—her lack of a death narrative, extraordinary power, and independence—may help explain why she is often spoken of not just as a cult heroine but as a goddess. Unlike cult heroes, gods and goddesses are not, as a rule, promoted mortals. They are endowed with

2. Helen's name also probably underlies the name "Elmo" (Skutsch 1987:191–93).

immortality and supernatural powers from birth, and never die. Some scholars believe that Helen was originally a prehistoric fertility goddess, who "faded" to become the mortal heroine of epic. If this is true, however, it is not something of which our sources seem to be aware. They present Helen not as an ancient goddess but as recently elevated to divinity. Be that as it may, as a cult heroine Helen was especially prominent, powerful, and popular. Regardless of her origins, the word "goddess" serves to acknowledge this extraordinary status.

These multiple, overlapping identities—epic heroine, cult heroine, and goddess—coexist in our surviving texts in a sometimes uneasy but creative collaboration. There are some obvious fundamental differences between the mortal Helen and her divine counterpart, especially when it comes to power, beauty, and the relationship between them. In contrast to the goddess, who seems unencumbered by the constraints that men impose on mortal women, the human Helen is subjected, albeit not always successfully, to masculine control. As a result, she is inserted into men's lives in a more intimate way than her divine counterpart. Her only avenue to power is her beauty, which may exercise its spell with or without her consent. Either way it is bound up with erotic transgression, by men, women, or both, and shows its force through destruction. The divine Helen, on the other hand, can come and go, appear to men in dreams, strike them blind, or assist them in battle. She has special power to operate in the sphere of mortal female beauty, but she does not, as a goddess, control men through her personal allure.

That said, Helen's beauty remains the defining feature that unites her various personae to make her a single, though complex, mythic figure. The extraordinary nature of that beauty also helps to blur, in her case, the normally sharp line dividing humans from the gods. Beauty is a divine force, an attribute of the gods, and a manifestation of their power. Helen's paternity grants her more of this godlike charisma than any other woman. In consequence, even the human Helen never quite loses the aura of divinity, threatening boundary confusion and anxiety about the power of female beauty in the mortal world.

The line between mortal and goddess is blurred, in particular, by her beauty's timelessness. Erotic beauty is tied to youth, making it, for mortals, intrinsically evanescent. The gods, however, are not only immortal but ageless: once they reach their physical prime they remain there forever, in unchanging splendor. Helen's beauty likewise transcends the usual stages of mortal life. In art, she usually emerges from the egg looking like a nubile adolescent, as in figure 2.1 (above). In this representation her hair is nicely styled, betokening the kind of artifice associated with feminine allure. (Elsewhere she even wears jewelry.) This is typical of iconography for the births of goddesses, who are usually born fully grown, displaying their signature characteristics from the start. In the narratives of Helen's life, her abduction by Theseus prior to puberty suggests that her beauty came unseasonably early. Nor does it ever fade. Starting in Roman times, writers began to amuse themselves with the idea of an aging Helen (see, e.g., Ov. *Met.* 15.232, Lucian *Dial. Mort.* 18). But in classical Greece she remains eternally young and nubile despite her misadventures.

This freedom from the constraints of time helps explain Helen's lack of fecundity. Ancient critics explained that the gods arranged it so, because she could not have been more prolific without impairing her beauty. If nothing else, the presence of a brood of children would undermine the illusion of virginal availability and make it more difficult to avoid questions about Helen's aging. Nor is she a very good mother to Hermione, whom she abandons along with Menelaus. Her beauty outlasts its proper season and purpose, impairing her ability to fulfill the role of mother as well as wife. In this she resembles her patron goddess Aphrodite, who is a goddess of desire, not reproduction, and is distinctly unenthusiastic about maternity. (When she becomes pregnant with Anchises' son Aeneas, she swears the father to secrecy and hands the infant over to the nymphs to raise [*HH* 5.247–73].) The timelessness of Helen's beauty may also help explain her lack of a death story. Dying young gives mortals a way to remain eternally youthful, like the gods, but Helen does not need death to preserve her beauty from decay.

As the ultimate manifestation of divine beauty in the human world, Helen is not merely an extraordinarily beautiful woman but the most beautiful of all, a status that remains unsullied by the vagaries of time or taste. This may seem bizarre or even absurd to the modern reader. If beauty is in the eye of the beholder, as current thinking would have it, then the concept of "the most beautiful woman" becomes meaningless. But Helen's absolute superiority is underwritten in ancient Greek terms by a rather different conception of beauty, as something that can, in principle, be measured objectively (cf. above, pp. 2–3). It is this that makes possible the very notion of the "most beautiful," and with it the existence of Helen, as *the* most beautiful woman, without qualification. The objectivity of beauty also increases the danger posed by female beauty, by allowing for the (imaginative) existence of a woman who is perfectly beautiful. If beauty as such exercises a power akin to divinity, then its objectively determined maximum will be, in effect, irresistible. A beauty that is in the eye of the beholder may launch a ship or two, but only a beauty upon which all beholders agree can bind a generation of heroic males under oath and generate an enterprise as cataclysmic as the Trojan War.

The very concept of such beauty is enough to give it power. The story of Helen's suitors, as related in the *Catalogue of Women*, suggests that her beauty is from the outset a report, as much as a presence (cf. above, p. 30). This may seem paradoxical, given the importance of vision in Greek conceptions of *erōs*. But if beauty is an objective quality, then a universal reputation for supreme beauty will guarantee desirability. (None of the suitors seems to have changed his mind at the sight of her.) This is not simply triangulation (desiring because others desire). Rather, having the reputation of being (the most) beautiful is equated with being (the most) beautiful: it elicits an equivalent desire. Later authors would develop the idea of Helen's reputed beauty as a force in its own right, independent of her physical presence. Despite the number of men who did, in fact, attain her, she has a long history of association with the unattainable—with visions, fantasies, and dreams. This reaches its logical conclusion in the strange story of her double, which allows Helen's beauty to transcend the limitations of space as well as time.

Helen's beauty and its disastrous consequences made her a potent symbol, for philosophers, of pleasure, construed as a threat to reason and virtue. In Plato's *Republic*, Socrates likens the pleasures of food and sex, pursued by the masses, to Helen's *eidōlon* (*Rep.* 586bc). Aristotle urges us to view pleasure as the Trojan elders viewed Helen—as something to be eschewed despite its allure (*EN* 1109b7–12). These thinkers reflect the broader cultural discourse of masculinity as constructed through resistance to pleasure. A man who is "led" by pleasure puts himself in the position of a woman, who is "led" in marriage by her husband. A real man remains in control of pleasure, as of his wife. Helen's beauty makes her the mythic signifier of erotic pleasure, and thus the ultimate threat to manly excellence. Yet Plato also implies a positive use for her. If those who devote themselves to base pleasures resemble the warriors who fought over Helen's double, it follows that the "real" Helen stands for the true pleasure of philosophy.

Helen can serve such philosophical purposes because her essence is mythic and transcendent. Her meaning lies less in her beauty than in the idea of her beauty. This raises difficulties, however, for writers and especially for visual artists who wish to portray her. Absolute beauty, which transcends any particular person, would seem to be in essence unrepresentable. Artists can present *a* beautiful woman, but not *the most* beautiful. Any "realistic" portrait of Helen as a specific person, however beautiful to however many, is doomed to failure. Zeuxis, a fifth-century BCE artist renowned for his illusionistic realism, produced a famous painting of Helen. When seeking a model he allegedly held a contest of naked *parthenoi*, selected five, and used the finest body parts from each to create a composite portrait. This approach implies, on the one hand, that supreme beauty is not instantiated in any one real woman, but on the other that there is such a thing as perfect female beauty, which is in principle instantiable, whether in Helen or in her image. Zeuxis's painting does not survive. No matter what it looked like, however, if it accurately portrayed the specific charms of these five women it must still have left his Helen's beauty open to critical judgment by those who might have chosen a different five.

The vases that provide most of our visual evidence for Helen's story adopt a different approach. Because vase painting is a highly stylized medium, and thus intrinsically "unrealistic," it can use conventional signs to represent the unrepresentable. It is also well suited, as a medium, to conveying Greek ideals

of beauty, which call for simple forms and eschew particularity. Together, stylization and lack of specificity allow the viewer's imagination to roam free,
making it possible to represent not Helen but the idea of Helen by using
acknowledged signifiers of beauty. Vase painting tends to draw attention to the
eyes, for example (especially in archaic styles). This aspect of Helen's allure is
made clear in the countless scenes where her beauty disarms Menelaus at the
fall of Troy (e.g., figures 2.5, 2.6, above). Texts sometimes attribute this effect
to the sight of her naked breasts (Eur. *Andr.* 627–31; Ar. *Lys.* 155–56). In art she
is normally fully clothed, but almost always makes eye contact with her pursuer. In other images she is shown as a beautiful bride (e.g., figure 2.4, above)
or, more voyeuristically, occupied with her appearance, especially in the many
scenes where she is discovered by Paris in her boudoir. In figure 2.8, for example, she is elegantly dressed and adorned with jewelry, her hair is elaborately arranged, and she gazes into a mirror. As we saw in chapter 1, such
accoutrements betoken the conscious display of female beauty, eroticism, and
power over men.

These ornaments are the visible tokens of Helen's myth-heroic identity, like
the armaments that identify the heroic male. Most male heroes are individuated

FIGURE 2.8 Helen sits on a chest (perhaps for textiles), wearing an elaborate coiffure,
jewelry, and clothing, and looking into a mirror. Paris stands to the left and a figure of
Eros flies overhead. Attic red-figure hydria, early fourth century BCE. Berlin,
Antikensammlung, Staatliche Museen 3768; *ARV*² 1516.81, 1697; BAD 231037. pbk,
Berlin/Johannes Laurentius/Art Resource, NY.

by their special equipment. Heracles, for example, can be recognized by his lion skin and club. But Helen's accessories do not particularize her. Instead, they assimilate her to other beautiful females, especially heroines, goddesses, and nymphs. What makes her supremely beautiful is not any charming individual quirk or idiosyncrasy but the absence of such peculiarities. This can make it hard to distinguish her from other beautiful women in art, unless they are named or placed in an unambiguous narrative context. Figure 2.9, for example, shows a group of mythological women engaged in domestic tasks. All are elegantly dressed, with long, elaborately arranged hair, generic visual descriptors that identify beautiful women not by their differences, but by their similarity. We can tell who they are only because several names are inscribed on the vase. Without these labels, the heroines would be interchangeable. It can even be hard to distinguish Helen from Aphrodite (note the resemblance between them, for example, in figures 2.4 and 2.6, above). This is not merely an intellectual obstacle for scholars: rather, it speaks both to the generic character of female beauty and to the threat inherent in an aspect of women that can make them indistinguishable from a mighty goddess.

Poets and writers, like visual artists, convey Helen's appearance through the reiteration of conventional tropes. They usually avoid specific description, confining themselves to conventional epithets, such as having "lovely hair." As with the conventions of vase painting, this mode of description comports with the Greek view of beauty as both objective and generic, as opposed to subjective

FIGURE 2.9 Four women engaged in domestic tasks. On the left sits Helen working wool; Clytemnestra faces her, holding a perfume bottle; a mirror hangs on the wall between them and their names (not visible in this photograph) are inscribed above. On the right, one woman holds a basket of fruit while another lifts a fold of her garment in a veiling gesture; the name of Cassandra is inscribed above them, but it is unclear to which of the two it refers. Detail of an Attic red-figure pyxis, c. 500–470 BCE. London, British Museum E 773; ARV² 1670; BAD 209970. © The Trustees of the British Museum.

and individual. But authors can also convey beauty indirectly, without entering the dangerous ground of specificity or "realism," by describing its effect on others. Most texts wisely avoid presenting Helen directly to the eye of the audience's imagination, insisting instead on her quasi-magical impact on other characters. This power resides not just in how she looks, but how she *looks*. The impact of her glance is strongly emphasized, in texts as well as art. Euripides' Hecuba, for example, declares that Helen sacked Troy "by means of her beautiful eyes" (*Hec.* 441–43).

Not surprisingly, the association of beauty with feminine speech also comes to the fore in literature, since this is the only aspect of Helen's charm that can be conveyed directly through texts, as opposed to the visual arts. We are told that the sixth-century BCE poet Ibycus (in a work now lost to us) supplemented the story of Menelaus dropping his sword—the most famous example of Helen's visual power—by having her converse with her husband from Aphrodite's shrine (fr. 296). In our surviving texts Helen often employs the kind of intimate conversation that we saw featured as part of Aphrodite's erotic arsenal (above, pp. 5–6). She also has special ties with epic poetry, which bestows renown on the men who fight for her. As the cause and object of the Trojan War she becomes its Muse, an emblem of heroic glory and an agent of poetic immortality.

This array of associations and symbolic meanings opens Helen to an impressive number and variety of reinterpretations of her character and story. Is she divine or mortal, glorious or tawdry, powerful or powerless, agent or object, innocent or guilty, real or fictitious, absent or present (in Sparta, Troy, or Egypt)? This rich range of options and the multiple tensions among them go far to explain her perpetual allure and her special value as a vehicle for the reassessment of intellectual as well as poetic traditions. Authors in every period and genre use Helen and her story to wrestle not only with the legendary past but with questions of Greek identity, female subjectivity, human agency, and the power of discourse itself. She is, to use Hitchcock's term, the ultimate MacGuffin. She is also, as the story of her *eidōlon* betrays most starkly, a fiction or illusion in her very essence. Created by Zeus to manipulate men, men in their turn create and re-create her, striving ceaselessly to control her story and its meaning. Though Helen herself will always eludes their grasp, that does not prevent them from possessing her as an idea, a dangerous but beautiful toy that they are never quite willing to discard. In the chapters that follow we shall see one writer after another appropriating Helen for their own purposes, as they compete over her like the warriors at Troy.

3

Disarming Beauty: The *Iliad*

> She gets up and pours herself a strong one,
> And stares out at the stars up in the sky.
> Another night, it's gonna be a long one.
> She draws the shade and hangs her head to cry.
>
> My, oh my, you sure know how to arrange things.
> You set it up so well, so carefully.
> Ain't it funny how your new life didn't change things.
> You're still the same old girl you used to be.
> —The Eagles

The Greek quest for the most beautiful and best found its male fulfillment in Achilles, best and most beautiful of the warriors who went to Troy. The *Iliad*, as its opening words proclaim, is the story of his wrath and its consequences. As such it is a fundamentally masculine epic. Yet masculinity is predicated on the feminine, and Achilles' counterpart, Helen, is the most substantial, nuanced, and compelling female character in the epic.

Helen appears in three books, starting with a sequence of scenes in book 3. When we first meet her she is weaving in her room, where the goddess Iris summons her to view a duel between her two husbands; she proceeds to the walls of Troy, where she looks down on the battlefield and regales Priam with anecdotes about the Greek heroes visible below; after the duel Aphrodite appears to Helen and lures her—with threats—back home to sleep with Paris. In book 6, she and Paris are relaxing in their bedroom when Hector arrives to urge his cowardly brother into battle; Helen welcomes him and they converse affectionately. Finally, at Hector's funeral in book 24, Helen is the last of the Trojan women to mourn him with a formal lament.

The epic that opens by naming its theme as the wrath of Achilles thus ends with Helen's lamentation. In between, it betrays many traces of the long-standing kinship between them (cf. above, pp. 27, 46). In the *Iliad*, that kinship is grounded primarily in their special ties to divinity. Thanks to their divine parenthood they are both, like the war itself, a "great disaster," she because of her godlike beauty and he through his superhuman strength (3.160, 22.288; cf. 24.547). Both are not only semidivine but godlike in appearance, inspiring awe in those who see them face-to-face (3.158, 24.629–30). Both have an unusually intimate relationship to a patron goddess, whom they recognize, as most mortals cannot, by the flash of her eyes (1.199–200, 3.396–98). Both also stand up to a god or goddess, face-to-face, in a way no other mortal does. Helen famously (if temporarily) defies Aphrodite, for whom she shows bitter contempt (3.399–412), while Achilles scolds Apollo for depriving him of glory and declares that he would punish the god if only he could (22.14–20). Both go on to accept the need for submission to the divine will, but resentfully, combining defiance with an acute awareness of their place as mortals in relation to the gods.

Achilles and Helen also share a preoccupation with their reputation among future generations. While this is an obvious trait for Achilles, as for any great warrior, it is exceptional in a woman. Achilles makes the heroic choice of eternal glory over a long life (9.413), and uniquely among warriors sings like an epic bard of "men's renown" (9.189). Helen, similarly, is all too conscious of her status as a theme for future song (6.357–58)—the song that is, in fact, the *Iliad*. She also participates in the reproduction of her own reputation through a distinctively female mode of storytelling. When we first see her she is

> weaving a great fabric,
> double-width, dark red, and working into it the many struggles
> of the horse-taming Trojans and bronze-clad Achaeans,
> which they were suffering at the hands of Ares on her account.
> (3.125–28)

Iris then arrives and calls her to view the "marvelous deeds" of the men portrayed in her weaving (3.130–31). Helen's own renown depends on their willingness to continue doing so. But her role as the prize for which they are performing such deeds also makes her an emblem of the male heroic enterprise. She is thus indispensable to the glorification of Achilles, whose status as "best of the Achaeans" is revealed and confirmed through his role in the war she began.

Yet the bright blaze of Achilles' glory far outshines the discreet light of Helen's beauty. It is taken for granted, to be sure, that she is the most beautiful woman in Troy (cf. 9.139–40 = 9.281–82). Yet she is never described, like other Homeric beauties, as "most beautiful" of a group or as "resembling golden Aphrodite" (cf., e.g., 3.124, 6.252, 24.699). Nor does the poet conjure her beauty by dwelling in any detail upon her physical appearance, clothing, or adornments. Like other female characters she is simply "glorious among women," of fine appearance, with white arms, lovely hair, a long gown, and shining garments. She is, in addition, the "daughter of Zeus," and thus "of noble paternity," but her beauty is not linked with that paternity, and she has no substantive relationship with her divine father (in contrast to Achilles and his mother, Thetis). When she mentions the parents she left behind in Greece (3.140), she is presumably referring to Leda and Tyndareus—a humanizing detail that locates her securely in the mortal world.

The lavish and specific rendition of female beauty is reserved, in Homer, for goddesses. When Hera prepares to seduce her husband, she bathes and perfumes herself, carefully arranges her hair, and dresses in fine clothing, jewelry, and a beautiful veil (14.170–86). When Aphrodite appears to Helen, disguised as an old woman, Helen recognizes her nonetheless by her "most beautiful neck, desirable breasts, and sparkling eyes" (3.396–97). This ability to see through the goddess's disguise betrays the close kinship between them. Helen even views herself as a kind of proxy for the goddess, who, Helen declares, has displaced her own desire for Paris onto her mortal protégée (3.399–409). Helen's description of Aphrodite's charms thus tells us obliquely about the power of her own unseen looks. But Aphrodite renders her protégée effectively invisible—perhaps literally so, when she leads Helen away from the walls unseen by the women around her (3.419–20; cf. 3.384).

The power of Helen's beauty is, however, conveyed indirectly through her effect on other characters. When the Trojan elders see her arriving upon the walls of Troy, they declare:

> There is no cause for blame (*nemesis*) against Trojans and well-greaved
>   Achaeans
> for suffering long hardships over a woman of such a kind;
> she is terribly like the immortal goddesses to look at in the face.
> But even so, though she is the way she is, let her sail away,
> and not stay here as a disaster for us and our children.
>
> (3.156–60)

The old men's reaction to Helen's appearance recalls Hesiod's Pandora, who likewise "resembles immortal goddesses to look at in the face" (*WD* 62). But they add the word "terribly" (*ainōs*), which has the same ambiguity in Greek as in English, suggesting that Helen's beauty brings her frighteningly close to divinity. When she joins Paris in their bedroom he too conveys the impact of her beauty, this time in explicitly erotic terms, by describing not her appearance but the overwhelming desire that it arouses:

> Never before has *erōs* shrouded my wits so much,
> not even the first time, when I abducted you
> and sailed away from lovely Sparta in seafaring ships,
> and mingled with you in the bed of love on the island of Cranae,
> as much as *erōs* and sweet desire have captured me now.
>
> (3.442–46)

Like the elders on the wall, he avoids enumerating the qualities that elicit this reaction.

This reticence in detailing Helen's beauty has been much admired for the way it frees the imagination from the constraints of specificity. In the context of early Greek poetry, however, this restraint should not be seen primarily as a device to convey the exceptional nature of that beauty. As we saw in chapter 1, extraordinary beauty is typically conveyed in archaic poetry not through reticence, but through the lavish accumulation of physical detail. Decorum is maintained by keeping the focus less on the body itself than on the decorations that signify its erotic power. Helen, by contrast, is almost entirely devoid of such accoutrements. If she is, in one scholar's words, "far more than merely a sex-object or a femme fatale," she is also far less than one.[1]

The destructive power of "feminine" beauty is most ostentatiously displayed, among mortals, in the person not of Helen but of Paris. In contrast to the veiling of her looks, Paris's dangerous beauty is displayed, glorified, and also castigated. He is not only godlike in appearance (3.16) but "best" in beauty (3.39 = 13.769)—an expression normally used only of women. His appearance is unusually decorative, even in battle. His equipment is "most beautiful" (6.321), glorious, and elaborate (6.504), and his outfit includes such exotic details as a leopard skin (3.17) and "a richly decorated strap (*polukestos himas*) under his tender throat" (3.371). This last item, which nearly causes his death at Menelaus's hands, is a unique detail evocative of seductive feminine attire, most notably Aphrodite's erotically irresistible breast band (*kestos himas* 14.214; cf. above, p. 5). Aphrodite herself, who gave Paris the "gifts" of lovely hair and physical beauty (3.54–55), "seizes" him out of battle like an object of erotic abduction (3.380). She then represents him as an alluring object awaiting Helen in bed:

> Come with me! Paris is calling you to come back home.
> He is in the bedroom, on the bed with its inlaid patterns,
> shining with beauty and clothing; you would not say
> he came from fighting a man, but that he was going
> to a dance, or resting after leaving off dancing.
>
> (3.390–94)

---

1. The quotation is from Taplin 1992:97.

Like playing the lyre—another of Paris's pastimes (3.54)—skill at dancing hints at the frivolity and hedonism that accompany such glamorous looks (cf. 24.260–63).

Paris is further feminized by his behavior in battle. The mighty Greek hero Diomedes scorns his efforts with the bow and arrows as equivalent to those of a child or woman, in contrast to his own brutal course of mayhem (11.384–95). Ornate and beautiful weapons are not unusual in themselves, but such regalia should betoken the wearer's manly courage. Paris is not a weakling. He has the presence of a magnificent stallion (6.506–14) and wears the full complement of heroic armaments (3.328–38). He is also—at least part of the time—a strong and brave (if reluctant and ill-judging) warrior (6.521–22, 7.1–16, 13.765–801). But he skulks aside in battle rather than face Menelaus (3.30–57). In contrast to his martial brother, Hector, he prefers to remain indoors, in the women's domain, where he fondles his weapons instead of using them in combat (6.318–31). Even after promising to fight he continues to dally at home with Helen (6.518–19). Hector imagines the Achaeans mocking the dissonance between his beautiful appearance and his weak spirit (3.43–45), and even Helen bitterly contrasts his boasts with his actual performance (3.430–31). Paris is a male Pandora, an object of desire whose beautiful appearance belies an interior that cannot withstand scrutiny.

This decorative exterior is accompanied by an intense erotic interest in women. Like the Greek stereotype of the beautiful female, Paris allows sexual passion to overcome good judgment and a sense of shame, thanks to the instability of his *phrenes* or "wits" (3.38–51, 6.350–52). His gifts from Aphrodite comprise not only his lovely appearance (3.54–55) but "lust" (*machlosunē*) (24.30), a word associated with prostitutes that is normally used for women. Diomedes calls him an "ogler of *parthenoi*" (11.385), and Hector castigates him, in a memorable line, as "ill-omened Paris, best in beauty, woman-crazy, deceiver!" (3.39 = 13.769). The last item in this compact litany of contempt denotes the "deception" of seduction (Helen uses it at 3.399 to insult Aphrodite). And "woman-crazy" (*gunaimanēs*) suggests in Greek not only "crazy about women" but "driving women crazy." The net result is, indeed, attractive to women, both Aphrodite herself and Helen, her surrogate, who continues to be drawn to him against her better judgment.

Despite Helen's intimacy with Aphrodite, then, it is the latter's male protégé who most fully embodies her seductive power. Paris's glamorous appearance and poor performance in battle alike make him close kin to the martially challenged goddess. His power, like hers, is exercised in the bedroom, not on the battlefield. He is fully aware of the assets she has bestowed on him (3.64), and the goddess ensures that he is restored to the right arena for his—and her—prowess. After conveying him in person to the bedroom, she appears to Helen as Paris's proxy and agent, "calling" her to him on his behalf (3.383, 3.390), then "leading the way" to the bedroom (3.420); when they get there Paris in turn cajoles her with seductive speech, then "leads the way" to bed (3.437–47). Helen is used for their own ends by the man and the goddess alike, both of whom have far more freedom than she does to exploit the "feminine" power of erotic beauty.

Helen's extraordinary impact on men is thus divorced from the actively seductive appearance often associated with the threat of female desire. She is, however, endowed with a more discreet and less overtly threatening form of feminine allure: the appeal of modesty itself. She seems to spend most of her time at home weaving, and never flaunts her beauty—a discretion in which the poet collaborates, as we saw. When she appears on the walls of Troy, where the elders liken her to a goddess, she is decorously wrapped in her shining veil and chaperoned by two maids (3.141–44). Homer avoids describing her beauty, while exploiting the power of the veil (both literal and figurative) to suggest a concealed eroticism and excite the imagination of his audience.

Such modesty accords with Helen's presentation, despite the transgressive origin of her marriage, as a well-behaved wife, properly incorporated into the Trojan royal family. She addresses Priam as "respected father-in-law" (3.172), and he, in turn, calls her "dear child" (3.162, 3.192). She also enjoys an affectionate relationship with Hector, her brother-in-law, and laments him at his funeral in company with his mourning wife and mother. With this normalizing of her position at Troy comes the disempowerment of domestication. Yet it also gives her a different kind of power over Troy. Her integration into Priam's family—over a period of twenty years, as she asserts, in a rhetorical exaggeration of the usual ten (24.765)—makes it hard for them to give her up, not despite the length of the war but because of it. She is not only a "good" woman but a Trojan woman, so that the honor of Trojan men is at stake in protecting her.

This presentation of Helen as a modest woman and proper wife also helps justify the Achaean enterprise to Homer's audience, if not to the Achaeans themselves. The latter's claim to revenge on Paris would be cast into question were Helen portrayed as a shameless adulteress. Their other "official" motive, the desire to retrieve her, would be even more surely undermined. Revenge is, to be sure, treated as an intrinsically desirable goal, for which the retrieval of Helen may even be postponed (cf. 7.400–402). Nevertheless, her retrieval remains intrinsic to the undertaking. The purpose of the duel between Paris and Menelaus is to determine which man will "take the woman home" (3.72, 93), and Athena spurs Odysseus into rallying the army by urging him not to let Helen, for whom so many Achaeans have already lost their lives, remain as a "boast"—as something to glory in—for Priam and the Trojans (2.176–77; cf. 2.160–62). Agamemnon likewise underscores Helen's centrality when he declares that if Menelaus dies, the war must be abandoned. Echoing Athena, he insists that leaving Helen as a "boast" for Troy would bring Agamemnon himself unbearable disgrace (4.171–82).

The idea of sacking an entire city over a single woman was to raise eyebrows later on, but in the *Iliad* no one directly challenges Helen's worth as a casus belli. In this heroic world one woman *can* be the worthy object of a great war, just as a single warrior—an Achilles or a Hector—can win that war. But not just any warrior, and not just any woman. Achilles ruefully admits that Briseis, the woman for whom he came to blows with Agamemnon, was not worth quarreling over (19.56–64), despite her likeness to "golden Aphrodite" (19.282) and alleged equivalence to Helen (9.337–43). The extraordinary value accorded to Helen by the Achaeans is not cashed out, however, in terms of her beauty or their desire. Achilles mentions that Menelaus "loves" his wife, but his language is not that of *erōs* (9.337–43). Nor is there any mention of the suitors' oath, which would implicate the Greek kings collectively in desire for Helen. Awe at her beauty is confined to the Trojan elders, and erotic passion to the unmanly Paris.

Menelaus himself expresses desire not so much for Helen as for revenge. It is this that he "longs for in his heart" (2.589–90). The warriors on both sides (with the exception of Paris) are driven, similarly, by a lust for warfare itself. In contrast to Paris, who is excited more by women than by war, the object of their passion is combat with other men. The language of desire is transferred to the battlefield, protecting the warriors from the emasculation of fighting merely for a woman. Achilles, for example, urges on his warriors by appealing to their *erōs* for battle (16.207–8), and Menelaus attributes to the Trojans a passion for fighting that surpasses desire for any variety of sensual pleasure, including sex:

> All desires can be sated, the desire for sleep and lovemaking,
> for sweet song and innocent dancing—all objects of a desire
> that one wishes to satisfy more than the *erōs* for war;
> but the Trojans' desire for battle cannot be sated.
>
> (13.636–39)

Like Pandora, and Helen, war too is a "beautiful evil," ruining men's lives but arousing their desire by offering them the chance to reap eternal glory as they die in its embrace.

From this heroic, masculine perspective, Helen herself is less a source of erotic passion than an exceptionally precious object. She is often grouped with the property that Paris stole from Menelaus at their elopement. This objectification is most obvious in the duel scene, where Menelaus and Paris fight over Helen while she looks on from the city walls. The scene reflects a common mythic courtship pattern, in which the bride is presented as a prize on display while her suitors compete for her. When the men speak of the winner "taking" (*helōn*) Helen, along with "all the property" (3.72 = 3.93), the pun on her name underlines her objectification through reversal: she is not the taker, but the taken. "Taking" does not of itself exclude volition in the object in question, as we saw in the case of the bride (above, p. 13), but Helen has no say in the matter of the duel. A herald is sent to inform Priam of its occurrence (3.245–58), but only the divine messenger Iris notifies the woman whose personal future is at stake (3.121–38). Her intervention highlights the fact that no human being took the trouble to let Helen know her fate was hanging in the balance.

Such unabashed objectification plays to Helen's advantage in an important way. Agency entails responsibility, and responsibility entails susceptibility to blame and, most important, punishment. As long as the question at issue is whether Paris stole her, or the Trojans should return her, then she cannot be held accountable. He is to blame for starting the war and they for allowing it to continue. Helen's objectification therefore dovetails with the interesting fact that in the *Iliad* virtually no blame is directed at Helen by the men who are fighting over her. She is a "great disaster" to Troy (3.50, 160), and Achilles calls her "shudder-inducing" (19.325), but such expressions do not imply personal guilt or agency. "Shuddering" is a response to any terrifying threat, such as warfare, death, or manifestations of divine power (e.g., 16.119–21). Like the word "disaster," it allows Helen to be a cause of destruction without being its agent. She does, it is true, speak of reproaches from the Trojans (discussed further below), but these remain offstage, never voiced aloud within the epic. It is Paris who takes the blame, from Trojans as well as Achaeans. As a stolen object, Helen is not held accountable.

This skirting of Helen's responsibility serves the heroic agenda of Achaeans and Trojans alike. The attribution of blame to Helen would call her value into question and make a mockery of the heroic enterprise by undermining the rationale for fighting on both sides. Menelaus, and the Greeks generally, can afford to objectify her, since the justice of their cause depends on treating her as a stolen object that should be returned. Making Paris, not Helen, the target of blame makes the quest for revenge—for men's retribution against men—central to the complex of excuses for the war. Acknowledging Helen's agency would risk complicating that simple model of justice. It would also undermine her value as casus belli, as we saw. The legitimacy of Achaean heroism would be undercut if its object were contemptible or of illusory value, and blame would compromise Helen's value by contaminating her reputation and making her damaged goods.

It is in the Trojans' interest too, especially in the context of the duel, to present Helen as a mere object that can conveniently be reassigned to its proper owner. The theft of an object is more easily rectified than the seduction of a wife. Moreover the Trojans have an even greater stake than the Achaeans in affirming the untarnished value of that object. To begin with, they are fighting in self-defense—a situation that makes the retention of Helen ludicrous on its face. Unlike the Greeks, they cannot appeal to "justice." No Trojan ever denies that Paris is to blame, and the retention of Helen implicates them collectively in his offense (cf. 6.55–61, 13.620–27)—especially given their original refusal to return her (3.205–6, 11.123–25, 138–41). This is true above all for Priam and Hector, as the most powerful men in Troy. Priam holds titular authority as king, while Hector as his heir, and the greatest Trojan warrior, seems to exercise the most real power. They presumably have the authority, between them, to give Helen back to the Greeks, but seem reluctant or unable to exercise it. Priam leaves the matter in Paris's hands, despite the fact that the Trojans generally seem to want to return her (7.345–93).

Like the Achaeans, the Trojan warriors are driven by their passion for warfare, as Menelaus so graphically declared. In their case, however, there is nothing to justify that passion besides Helen's beauty. This is clear from the words of the Trojan elders. They view Helen, because of her godlike beauty, as a legitimate casus belli whose value trumps any ethical challenge to the war's rationale. Neither side, they say a touch defensively, should incur blame for fighting over a woman "of such a kind" (3.153–60). Exalting Helen's value and attributing the same motive for the war to the Achaeans allows the old men to avoid questions about adultery or justice. The implications of this become clear when we remember the copious censure directed at Paris for taking Helen in the first place. When Hector is at his most desperate and diminished, as he considers surrendering to Achilles, he contemplates giving up Helen along with the stolen property and even all the treasures of Troy (22.111–30). Her value crumbles with his heroic resolve and aspirations to glory. But as long as they are willing to keep fighting in solidarity with Paris the Trojans cannot afford to undermine the beautiful Helen's value by disparaging her.

Unsurprisingly, then, neither Priam nor Hector breathes a word of blame toward Helen during their conversations with her. Hector is friendly and even affectionate, but Priam goes further, explicitly denying her any responsibility:

> As far as I'm concerned you are not responsible, but the gods
> are responsible, who stirred up lamentable war with the Achaeans.
>
> (3.164–65)

Priam seems to depart here from the standard Greek view that humans are responsible for their actions even when these are caused by the gods (above, pp. 6–7). But his words serve a particular purpose in a very specific context. This is not an official or public assessment of accountability, but a face-saving maneuver. The audience are eavesdroppers, made privy to an intimate conversation between an old man and an exceptionally beautiful woman who enjoy an affectionate personal relationship. Priam is, in addition, Helen's protector, both as her father-in-law and as the king and patriarch of the royal family. He is also the father of Paris, whose transgression, like Helen's, was well known to have been motivated by Aphrodite. Priam's vague reference to "the gods" displaces divine causation away from this specific goddess and toward the larger divine plan in a way that saves face not just for Helen but for himself, his sons, and the Trojans collectively.

Like the reaction of the elders, Priam's words contribute to a poetic strategy that implies that Helen is worth fighting for to the Trojan leadership by demonstrating the disarming effect she has on them as men. Since old men are not afflicted with the unstable wits of the young (3.108–10; cf. 23.589–90, 604), the aged condition of the Trojan elders may explain their ability to recommend her removal. Yet even they affirm her beauty's transcendent value. Helen's impact on the powerful men who are exposed to her presence not only explains the war but justifies it, in masculine terms, as a dispute over an ineffably precious object. For this reason, the poet avoids showing Helen blamed to her face. That face is, after all, the cause of the trouble.

There is more to Homer's Helen than her face, however. Even in the duel scene the poet implicitly challenges the objectifying strategies of his male characters. The men may speak of the winner "taking the woman and property" and "leading her home" (3.72, 93), but Iris addresses Helen as "dear bride" (3.130) and rephrases the outcome from a woman's point of view:

> Paris and Menelaus who is dear to Ares
> will fight over you with their long spears,
> and you will be called the dear wife of the victor.
>
> (3.136–38)

She avoids both the word "take" and any mention of stolen property, and makes Helen the grammatical subject of the verb (albeit a passive verb). She focuses, moreover, on marital status, the most important of the intimate personal relationships that construct a woman's world.

In the scene on the wall that follows, Helen, too, will dwell upon that world, expressing nostalgia for the relationships that made up the fabric of her life in Greece. When she first appears, the Trojan elders' reaction constitutes her as an object of men's gaze and speech. But when Priam invites her to survey the warriors below, and questions her about the Greek leaders, she resists such objectification by introjecting traces of her own story and point of view into her responses. Agamemnon is her brother-in-law as well as a king and warrior (3.178–80); Ajax used to visit their house at Sparta (3.232–33); she wonders where her brothers are in the crowded scene below (3.234–42). She becomes not merely an object for male viewing and disposal, but a viewer of men in her turn, and one who speaks about them with authority. The scene thus offers us a hint of women's perception of themselves as subjects, if not agents, in their marriages and family relationships, in a way that is ignored entirely by the Greek men.

If Helen is more than an object, however, this complicates the question of her value as casus belli. She is innocent, of course, if Paris took her against her will. This may be suggested in an anomalous passage where the old Greek warrior Nestor urges mass rape of the Trojan women in retribution for the "struggles and laments of Helen" (2.354–56). The quoted phrase is repeated shortly afterward, where it helps explain Menelaus's motivation for revenge (2.590). Most interpreters, from ancient times on, have taken the "struggles and laments" to be Helen's own, implying that she was violently abducted by Paris. If so, the line is unique both in suggesting that she was taken against her will and in showing any concern among the Achaeans for her subjectivity. But this representation comes from Nestor's (and then Menelaus's) perspective, and thus serves the Achaean male agenda by suggesting that she resisted abduction as a good woman should. In any case, the wording is ambiguous. The Greek may indicate not Helen's own struggles, but the struggles of the men fighting for her (not "of Helen" but "for Helen").

Be that as it may, the notion that Helen was taken against her will is belied by her own attitude toward her abduction. Her opening speech to Priam is replete with regret:

> How I wish that evil death had been my pleasure
> when I followed your son here, leaving my bedroom
> and my kinsmen, my cherished daughter and charming age-mates.
> But that did not happen; so I am wasting away in lamentation.
>
> (3.173–76)

Other passages extend this litany of regrets to include her parents, her brothers, and the city as a whole (3.140, 236–42). She even misses Menelaus (3.139–40), and voices acute contempt for Paris, whom she castigates as far inferior to her first husband both as a warrior (3.428–36) and in moral character (6.350–53). Menelaus is, to be sure, less than spectacular as an epic hero. In the *Iliad* overall he falls markedly short of the greatest warriors on both sides (cf. 7.104–16, 10.114–23, 234–40, 17.587–88). Nevertheless, he is clearly a cut above Paris on the battlefield, and of course he has justice on his side. Helen's admission of his superiority amounts to a confession that eloping with Paris was wrong, not just ethically, but as a decision affecting her well-being. She endorses from her own lips the linchpin of Greek gender ideology, affirming that women's desires are excessive, unstable, and unhealthy, and leave nothing but trouble in their wake.

These sentiments go beyond regret to outright self-blame. In one particularly memorable line, Helen castigates herself as a "chilling, evil-devising dog" (6.344). As we saw in chapter 1, "dog" and "dog-eyes" are frequent insults for uncontrolled, lustful women (above, p. 18), and Helen uses such language of herself repeatedly (3.180, 6.344, 6.356). These self-reproaches serve not only to fill the vacuum left by the male characters' avoidance of blame, but to trump that avoidance. If Helen avows her guilt, then who are we—or Priam—to disagree? Yet this avowal also frees the poet to present the Achaeans and Trojans fighting heroically for an object that is uncontaminated by their disparagement.

Since she blames herself so stringently, they are freed from the necessity of doing so. It is, in fact, Helen's self-blame that allows Priam to save face for her by attributing responsibility to the gods (3.164–65). The more one is willing to accept responsibility, the more one is entitled to such face-saving gestures, and no one takes more responsibility than Helen. Priam has his own reasons, as we saw, for his paternalistic excuse, but the audience can accept it in part because Helen herself does not do so. Her self-blame assures her guilt while allowing her to retain her value in the eyes of others. She has—conveniently—put herself in her place, so that they do not have to.

Helen's self-blame does more than this, however. It not only allows the male warriors to avoid impairing her value by reproaching her, but helps restore that value by compensating for her past behavior. As we saw earlier, self-deprecation is a form of self-disempowerment characteristic of the Greek male portrayal of virtuous women, who often denigrate their sex in general and themselves in particular as inferior to men (above, p. 24). Helen's regrets thus enhance her attractiveness by characterizing her as "good" in a specifically gendered fashion. Blame by men, which would debase her value, is suppressed, or eclipsed by her beauty, but self-blame enhances her worth as a woman, and hence, indirectly, the legitimacy of the heroic struggle to (re)claim her. Ironically, she achieves this restoration of her value by casting doubt on that value—a reflection of the catch-22 in which Greek ideology traps all women, as descendants of Pandora.

The implication that a woman has learned her lesson is, in consequence, a powerful tool for manipulating men. Helen certainly knows how to use it for such purposes. Her remorse and self-blame are addressed exclusively to men whose protection is vital to her. When talking to Paris, who has other reasons for protecting her, she blames him, not herself (3.428–36, 6.349–53). Over Priam and Hector, however, she exercises not overt sexual power but the discreet charm of a demurely beautiful and well-intentioned woman, her virtue marred by an error of judgment that she now bitterly regrets. Her penchant for self-blame is integral to this use of the seductive female voice. In her conversation with Priam it contributes to a self-presentation that is clearly effective in maintaining a mutually fond relationship (3.162, 172). Later she uses "sweet" words to Hector, words that turn out to be both subtly flirtatious and full of self-flagellation (6.343–58).

Her lament for Hector at his funeral has a comparable effect. The other women mourn the consequences of losing his physical might, as their champion in battle, but Helen dwells on his gentle character, which afforded her a different kind of protection. Here again she expresses remorse, while positioning Priam as her continuing protector for the future:

> Hector, of all my husband's brothers by far the dearest
> to my heart! My husband is godlike Paris,
> who brought me to Troy. How I wish I had died first!

For it is now the twentieth year since I went
away from Greece and departed my fatherland.
But from you I never heard an evil word or an insult;
and if someone else scolded me within the halls, one of
my husband's brothers, or sisters, or his brothers' fair-robed wives,
or my mother-in-law (not my father-in-law, who was always gentle,
like a father), you restrained them by talking them out of it
with your kindheartedness and kind words.
So I weep for you and my ill-fated self together,
grieving in my heart, since no one else in wide Troy
was gentle to me or friendly. The rest all shuddered at me.

(24.762–75)

It is no coincidence that the two men she singles out so conspicuously as *not* blaming her are those we have seen responding affectionately to her remorseful self-presentation.

The price Helen pays for her success with powerful men is their denial of her responsibility and thus her agency—explicitly, in Priam's case. But the payoff is her safety, and this result is something that she achieves for herself through discourse. The self-blame that guarantees her guilt thus works to her advantage, neutralizing her transgression and ensuring her protection. It is an exercise of power, albeit within the extremely limited sphere of action available to women in the *Iliad*. This skill with words—particularly her skill in manipulating the discourse of "good" womanhood—betrays obliquely the dangerous power that seductive women exercise over men. The very decorum of her self-reproach renders her more dangerous. It is the verbal counterpart of her modest yet tantalizing veil.

The discourse of self-blame also empowers Helen in a different way, by allowing her to reclaim the agency denied to her by men. She could have collaborated in her own objectification by representing herself as a plundered object. Instead, she blames herself in a way that implicitly asserts her own past agency. This forms part of a coherent perspective on the original elopement. Where others blame only Paris, Helen links herself with him as jointly responsible (6.356–58). When she tells Priam that she wished death had been her pleasure instead of following Paris (3.173–74), she implies that she derived her pleasure from a different source, in other words, that she was impelled by her own desire. She is the only mortal in the *Iliad* to use active verbs for her part in the elopement, saying that she "followed" Paris, "leaving" her family (3.174), "went away" and "departed" from Greece (24.766). Though such language does not strictly entail willing agency—one may "leave," "go," and even "follow" under duress— it stands out in sharp relief against her objectification by the male characters.[2]

---

2. The only other character to employ an active verb for Helen's elopement is Athena, who uses the verb "follow" in a way that clearly implies agency (5.423).

The diction used in her self-blame reinforces this impression. The "dog" insult and the word "evil-devising" (6.344) both suggest active misbehavior, implying a self-conscious awareness of her own role in her elopement and its disastrous consequences. By engaging in the discourse of Greek misogyny she is acknowledging her own power. This enables the poet to have his cake and eat it too, making Helen a "good" woman, and thus worth fighting for, but also blameworthy; presenting her as a precious but passive object of men's desires while also allowing her a measure of subjectivity and agency; indirectly claiming both the (dis)credit and the renown that are her due.

No other Homeric character blames Helen as she blames herself. But she does claim to have been the target of blame from others at Troy who remain offstage. At Hector's funeral, as we just saw, she mentions scolding by numerous family members. She also speaks vaguely to Priam of "many shameful reproaches that are upon me" (3.242), and when Aphrodite urges her to join Paris in their bedroom she replies:

> I shall not go there—that would be worthy of blame (*nemesis*)—
> to tend to that man's bed. All the Trojan women
> will reproach me afterward.
>
> (3.410–12)

Her tone here suggests a pattern of reproach, the future tense conveying a confidence presumably based on past experience.

Such reports of hostility complement Helen's self-blame, reinforcing her self-presentation as a chastened woman. They also suggest that if we look beyond Homer's cast of speaking characters she is indeed held responsible by the Trojans, but more especially by the Trojan women, whom she mentions here specifically. Her lament for Hector (quoted earlier) includes his brothers among those who scold her, but they are far outweighed rhetorically by the plethora of reproachful female relatives. Hecuba's hostility provides the climax, in vivid contrast with Priam's constant kindness, and of course, the kindness of Hector himself. There is a sharply gendered distinction between the two friendly men on the one hand, both of whom we have seen charmed by Helen's presence, and the scolding of the rest of the extended family, represented predominantly by women, on the other.

The Trojan women's reported blame implies that they, too, perceive Helen as a subject with the power to make choices and the obligation to take responsibility for those choices. Women, who understand the limitations under which other women labor as "objects" in men's eyes, are willing to blame each other for the actions they take within these limits. The Trojan women understand the circumscribed world in which Helen operates, and within that world, as women, they hold her accountable. Paris, by contrast—a man who charms women—is blamed only by men (with the important exception of Helen herself). Hector and others reproach him not only for actively causing the war but for failing in the proper performance of masculine prowess. Like women, men understand the obligations that construct and constrain their gender.

Helen makes no attempt to overcome such female disapproval by exercising her personal charm. That charm is, in its essence, both erotic and heterosexual; it has no leverage with the other Trojan women and gives them no inclination to exonerate her. Though she misses her female age-mates at Sparta (3.175), we are made privy to no personal interactions between her and other women at Troy, in marked contrast to her affectionate relationships with men. The closest thing to such an interaction is her visit from the goddess Iris, who is impersonating one of Helen's sisters-in-law (3.121–24), but this only underlines her isolation from real women. Andromache, by contrast, frequents the homes of her sisters-in-law and participates in rituals with the other Trojan women (6.377–80). The poet describes one such communal act of female worship, led by Hecuba (6.286–96), during which Helen is at home with Paris. Even her relationship with Aphrodite implies competitiveness and jealousy on the goddess's part, with Helen suggesting bitterly that the goddess really wants Paris for herself (3.406–9).

The Trojan women also lack their men's other major incentive to exculpate Helen, since their gender gives them little stake in the heroic enterprise. Women are typically victims of the pursuit of glory on the battlefield, not its beneficiaries. Andromache does not celebrate her husband as a warrior, but tries instead to keep him out of battle. When Hector responds by explaining why he must fight, he speaks of winning renown for himself and his father; for Andromache herself he foresees only suffering and degradation, sharpened by the humiliation of being known as another man's slave-concubine instead of Hector's wife (6.444–63). Under these circumstances, the reported hostility of other women toward Helen is scarcely surprising. Unlike the men, they have no reason to perceive a single woman—even this one—as an object of such transcendent beauty that she transforms this terrible war into a glorious struggle.

Helen herself has a different kind of relationship to heroic renown, one that is unique for a woman. Insofar as her own reputation, and her identity, depend on her function as an occasion for male glory, to question her own value as an object of heroic struggle is to flirt with self-annihilation. She seems aware of this when she wishes, in a speech to Hector, that she had indeed been annihilated at birth:

> How I wish that on the day my mother first bore me
> an evil storm of wind had carried me up and away
> to a mountain or to the waves of the much-resounding sea,
> where a wave could have swept me off before these deeds took place!
>
> (6.345–48)

Her words suggest a desire not so much to have acted differently as never to have existed—or at least never to have existed as Helen, whose birth was ordained to give rise to "these deeds." She lives or dies *as* Helen, however, along with the glory of the Trojan War. As a result, she is unique among the women of the *Iliad* in urging her husband back into battle, albeit with considerable ambivalence in light of his prospects there (3.432–36; cf. 6.337–38). Nor, unlike Andromache, does she make any effort to keep Hector safe from the fighting, despite their warm relationship. She invites him to rest, but not to desist from the heroic "labor" that has overcome him on her account—labor that will result in poetic immortality not only for him but for herself and Paris, on whom

> Zeus has laid an evil destiny, so that in the future too
> we may be a subject of song for people yet to come.
>
> (6.357–58)

Like her blood-red weaving, these words display a distinctive self-awareness about her role in causing such a terrible war, without eschewing the fame that cannot—for better or worse—be detached from it.

The *Iliad* thus offers several divergent perspectives on Helen's role in causing the Trojan War. Yet it is her own that seems to be endorsed by the epic overall. Her weaving of the war story aligns her with the poet himself, whose narrative echoes hers (compare 3.127 with 131). As we just saw, she is well aware that this story will live on through poetic song. In the course of the epic she controls the form that story will take, weaving many modes of speech (conversation, lament, invective) into a discourse that is both unusually authoritative for a woman and unusually independent of her husband. (Andromache, by contrast, is seen in conversation only with Hector.) Her account of herself is thus inserted into the masculine narrative of the war, ensuring its survival as long as the epic itself survives. In collaboration with the narrator, Helen has been extraordinarily successful in disarming not only the men of Troy but the epic's external audience, winning over nearly every reader with the charm of her voice.

The narrative vouches, in particular, for the sincerity of the self-blame that is the most distinctive aspect of this voice. Helen's self-loathing, while useful to her and artfully deployed, is not presented as fundamentally deceptive. In Book 3 her tearful nostalgia for Menelaus and her old home is divinely induced, which indicates sincerity (3.139–42). The self-disparagement in her speech to Aphrodite (3.411) can serve no manipulative purpose, since her only witness is an all-knowing divinity. Nor is there any reason to doubt the veracity of her reports of such reproach from others, given their public nature (notably at Hector's funeral). Yet the poet refrains from corroborating these reports by means of other voices (in marked contrast with his treatment of Paris, who is roundly blamed by all and sundry). This suggests that the sympathy for Helen induced by her self-blame is not only Helen's strategy, but Homer's. Overt blame by others would risk undermining that sympathy by inviting us to adopt the blamer's point of view.

Helen's confrontation with Aphrodite also provides a poetic endorsement of Helen's perspective on her own agency, by opening an extraordinary window into her past and present subjectivity. Within the epic present, Helen's actions are severely constrained. There is no suggestion, for example, that she has the power to end the war by leaving Troy, even if she wanted to (something she never actually asserts, despite her nostalgia for Greece). Regardless of her role in the original elopement, it is clearly Paris who is to blame for perpetuating the war, which he could end at any time by returning her. Yet Helen is given one significant opportunity to exercise moral choice. When Aphrodite visits her in book 3, to lure her to Paris's bed, the goddess offers her, ten years on, the same kind of opportunity for action that greeted her in her prior life as Menelaus's wife.

These early books of the epic are rich in incidents reenacting earlier stages in the story, such as the duel and Helen's identification of the Greek heroes (both of which we would expect to occur near the beginning of the war). The Aphrodite scene forms part of this retrospective series. When the goddess summons Helen on Paris's behalf, she is recapitulating her role in rewarding Paris for the Judgment by assigning Helen to his bed. It is true that Helen's opinion of Paris seems to have changed for the worse since that first meeting. She bitterly recalls him boasting that he was stronger than Menelaus (3.430–31)—a boast more plausibly attributed to the time of the original seduction than the more recent past. Nevertheless, the scene clearly reenacts the original seduction, in which Aphrodite "led" Helen to Paris as she does here. It thus provides our best Homeric "evidence" for Helen's state of mind at that time.

Using her characteristic methods, Aphrodite "arouses the heart in Helen's breast" (3.395) with a description of Paris's physical charms that makes the cause of her original infidelity palpably obvious (quoted above, p. 56). Helen's reaction replays vividly the internal dynamics of a moment in which *erōs* overpowers moral judgment. Upon recognizing the goddess she accuses her angrily of deceiving her (3.399, 3.405). In its immediate context, this refers to the goddess's disguise as an old woman. But that disguise (which serves no obvious purpose) stands for Aphrodite's deeper association with deception. In keeping with her amoral mission, the goddess is trying to beguile Helen into acting against her better judgment. On the original occasion, Helen was, of course, married to another man, and might therefore be expected to resist. This time she is Paris's wife. Yet she is ashamed of their sexual relationship, which constitutes the essence of their past and present failures. Her fear of reproach from other women for persisting in that relationship conveys not only a proper sensitivity to public opinion but a clear sense of herself as a re-sponsible agent: she sees herself through the eyes of others as a potential object of blame. Hence her anger at the goddess, as her better judgment resists.

Yet Helen ends up, nonetheless, following Aphrodite to Paris's bed. She is clearly responsible for this action in her own eyes, just as she was for her part in the original elopement. Even in declaring "I shall not go" (3.410) she is claiming a subjectivity that is not so much negated, as affirmed, when she does go after all. These words confirm that when she changes her mind she is making a choice, albeit a reprehensible one. Helen's poignancy as a character derives in part from the fact that, unlike so many of Aphrodite's victims, she remains fully conscious of the conflict between her desires and her better judg-ment. The confrontation with Aphrodite lets us know that she knows what she is doing. Her good judgment is defeated by the power of desire, but—in con-trast to the "wits" of Paris, or even Zeus—it is not shrouded, deceived, or "per-suaded." In this respect she is more successful than most male characters in resisting Aphrodite's power. Yet this awareness also enhances the culpability of her choice.

By attempting such resistance Helen strives to sustain the identity of a good woman, one who feels remorse for her prior weakness and maintains the sensitivity to shame and *nemesis* that she berates Paris for lacking (6.350–51). But this self-presentation, so effective with human males, serves only to pro-voke the goddess who embodies gloriously amoral sexual self-assertion. It is a rejection of Aphrodite, and hence of Helen's own special status as the goddess's protégée. The goddess therefore reacts by threatening to withdraw that special status and abandon her:

> Don't provoke me, rash woman, or I may get angry and abandon you,
> and hate you to the same astonishing degree as I now love you,
> and devise against you lamentable hatred, between both sides,
> Trojans and Greeks, and an evil doom destroy you!

> (3.414–17)

Given the awe-inspiring power of erotic desire, as manifested in the figure of the angry goddess, it is scarcely surprising that this should prevail, inducing Helen to abandon her efforts at self-control at the command of the divinity that makes her who she is.

Yet the emphasis, at this moment of submission, is not on desire but on fear:

> Thus she spoke, and Helen the offspring of Zeus was afraid.
> Wrapping herself in her bright, shining veil she silently went;
> none of the Trojan women noticed her; the goddess led the way.

> (3.418–20)

What exactly is Helen afraid of? Aphrodite has threatened to withhold her love, but how would this result in her protégée's doom? Thus far Helen has been protected by her divinely bestowed beauty. But as Paris defensively tells Hector, such gifts do not lie under mortal control:

> Do not hold against me the lovely gifts of golden Aphrodite!
> The glorious gifts of the gods are not to be cast aside;
> gifts that they give themselves—no one could choose them on purpose.
>
> (3.64–66)

Helen's beauty is equally dependent on the goddess's whim. If Aphrodite strips her of seductive charm, neither Greeks nor Trojans will be restrained by its power from killing her. She therefore cannot afford to lose this mark of divine favor. But Aphrodite's gifts are not limited to beauty: they also comprise sexual desire. Both kinds of gift have been lavished upon Helen, as on Paris. Her existence *as* Helen therefore requires her to keep acting as she acted in the past. In order to remain who she is—and to remain protected by that fact from hatred and death—she must embrace the shame and transgression that are inseparable from the beauty that defines her.

The poet's powerful presentation of this encounter, the exceptional character of Helen's resistance, and the inner turmoil it provokes, understandably tempt many modern readers to perceive Helen as a blameless victim of divine coercion. But this interpretation depends on a misleading view of the Greek gods. Priam is unique in the *Iliad* in implying that Helen is excused by divine causation. He has his reasons for this, as we saw. But his view is not the judgment of the epic as a whole. Nor is it Helen's own view. If divine involvement exculpated her, she could not in a single breath blame herself and Paris and attribute the whole mess to Zeus (6.355–57; cf. 6.349). Her recognition that it was Aphrodite who "led" her to Troy is accompanied, similarly, by self-loathing in regard to her own role (3.400–405). Her failure to resist the goddess betrays not the absence of human agency but the presence of moral weakness. If she is coerced, it is by her own passions, and she is responsible for acquiescing. Indeed, such acquiescence is precisely the fault for which she blames herself. The goddess's physical presence does not make Helen's own erotic impulse irrelevant, but, on the contrary, underlines its reality and power. This is clear from the parallel case of Paris. No one denies that he too was instigated by Aphrodite, or excuses him on that account.

Helen makes a choice, then, and goes with Aphrodite, the verb ("she went") (3.419) evoking her own account of going to Troy with Paris ("I went") (24.766). On reaching their bedroom, she begins by averting her eyes (3.427), an avoidance of eroticism that may replay an original moment of modesty or resistance (compare figure 2.3a, above, p. 34). She wishes he would fight Menelaus again and die, but then abruptly reverses course and tells him, instead, to keep away from Menelaus for fear that he will be killed—a shift powerfully expressive of mingled contempt and desire (3.428–36). Paris then invites her to bed, using verb forms that indicate mutuality and affection: "Come, let us enjoy our love, the two of us in bed together" (3.441). Helen responds by "following" him to bed (3.447), just as she once "followed" him to Troy (3.174), and they lie down together, the Greek again implying mutuality (3.448). Her desire is not mentioned explicitly at this culminating moment, but Aphrodite's role makes it clear that this was the impulse that set the encounter in motion, just as it first did ten years earlier.

Helen's remorse at abandoning Menelaus gave the impression that she was a new woman, who realized what a mistake she had made and would not show such weakness in the future. But her willingness, however reluctant, to reenact her original deed, even when its horrible consequences are clear, may make us wonder whether she has learned her lesson after all. Faced with the awe-inspiring power of Aphrodite, she would do what she did all over again, despite the harsh reproaches of her better judgment. Her continuing inability to resist her desire for Paris, after ten long years, underlines the inability of marriage to any one man to contain the danger posed by such extraordinary beauty and the passions, both male and female, that it engenders. Despite her domestication as Paris's wife, this sense of marital instability is enhanced by Helen's remorseful longing for Menelaus (would she be on the move again if she could?), and her subtle flirtation with Hector (if only he were available!).

In contrast to the men who objectify her, then, Helen takes responsibility for her own role in her original elopement and implies, by replaying it, that the impulse leading to it has not been quenched. Her acquiescence to Aphrodite is, in the end, an acknowledgment by the poet—and by Helen herself—both of her power to initiate the war's devastation and of her culpability for so doing. The reenactment of her sexual transgression with Paris is embedded in an epic of bloodshed, suffering, and loss of which these characters and their eroticism were the originating cause. While they make love, the fighting continues to rage outside the walls (6.448–50). This larger context constitutes an implicit judgment of Helen. By the same token, however, it enshrines her amid the glory of heroic warfare as well as its terrible costs. It was her transgression that gave these men the chance for glory, while she herself is glorified by their choice to continue suffering for her sake. The *Iliad* is, after all, the story of Helen's beauty as well as the wrath of Achilles.

4

Happily Ever After? The *Odyssey*

> It makes you blind, it does you in;
> It makes you think you're pretty tough;
> It makes you prone to crime and sin;
> It makes you say things off the cuff.
>
> You just get out what they put in,
> And they never put in enough.
> Love is like a bottle of gin,
> But a bottle of gin is not like love.
> —The Magnetic Fields

The Helen of the *Odyssey* is discreetly excised from most popular retellings of this epic. The romantic imagination seems to recoil from the prospect of Helen and Menelaus living comfortably at home together in Sparta after the war. This is, however, where we find them in *Odyssey* book 4, in an elegant if uneasy and passionless alliance where husband and wife both fulfill their roles with due decorum but no sign of affection.

We encounter Sparta through the eyes of Odysseus's son, Telemachus. He and his companion Peisistratus, the son of Nestor, are traveling in search of Odysseus, who has been missing since the fall of Troy. They arrive at a splendid palace, radiant with the gleam of precious metals, which Telemachus, overcome with awe, likens to the palace of Zeus himself (4.39–59, 4.71–75). The narrator identifies it, however, as the house of Menelaus (4.1), eliding the fact that he obtained it only by marrying Helen. As the mistress of her husband's household, Helen herself plays the part of the perfect royal wife, passing her time in wool working and acting as a gracious hostess to his guests. Proper hierarchies are maintained, with the patriarch duly established at the apex. Helen orders the servants to make up beds for their visitors (4.296), and she herself (with the female servants) receives orders from Menelaus to prepare a feast for them (15.93–94).

Helen's presence at Sparta betokens Menelaus's victory in the male struggle to possess her, as an object to be regained regardless of her own desires. Though

the *Odyssey* does not do Helen the indignity of portraying her as an overtly contested object, she takes her place, with her beautiful hair and cheeks (15.58,
15.123), among her husband's countless beautiful possessions (cf. 15.75–76,
15.114), many of them gathered, like her, on the expedition to Troy. Wealth accumulation seems to be Menelaus's speciality—the one skill at which he surpasses
other heroes. According to other sources, it was this that allowed him to obtain
Helen in the first place (above, p. 31). The Trojan War has now reaffirmed her
status as the ultimate treasure, installed at the heart of Menelaus's opulent home.

Helen acknowledges the propriety of her return to Sparta, blaming herself
for her past transgression in language that evokes the *Iliad*. Once again she
calls herself "dog-eyed" (4.145), and speaks of the remorse she felt during the
war. On one occasion, she says, after Odysseus had killed many Trojans,

> the other Trojan women wailed shrilly, but my spirit
> rejoiced, since my heart had already turned toward going
> back home, and I lamented the madness (*atē*) that Aphrodite
> gave me, when she led me there, away from my dear fatherland,
> abandoning my daughter, my bedroom and my husband,
> a man by no means lacking in either wits or beauty.
>
> (4.259–64)

These words align Helen, as in the *Iliad*, with the sympathies and interests of
her male audience, and distance her—this time explicitly—from the other
women at Troy. She goes further than in the *Iliad*, however, claiming positive joy
at the slaughter of Trojans (in stark contrast with the grief of the other Trojan
women) and an active desire to return home. She betrays no hint of wrestling
with her desire for Paris, and her polite praise of Menelaus adds a new dimension to her expressed preference for him in the wartime epic. This self-serving
speech functions, like her regrets in the *Iliad*, to deflect male anger by presenting the persona of a good because repentant woman. It implies not only that she
is back in her proper place, but that she embraces her redomestication. Her
impulse to break the bounds of normative domesticity—the impulse that defines
her essence as a mythic character—appears to have been extinguished.

Decorous and resplendent as it is, however, the house of Menelaus is shad-
owed by Helen's transgression and its consequences. Memories of the war suf-
fuse its occupants with melancholy, reminding us of the price that was paid to
regain her. The *Odyssey's* Spartan scenes are, moreover, replete with hints of
her extraordinary nature, hints suggesting the reasons why Menelaus was
willing to pay such a price, the folly of doing so, and the threat she continues
to pose to masculine control.

Marriage—the problem embodied in Helen's very person—is thematized strikingly at the outset of Telemachus's sojourn in Sparta. When he arrives, a double wedding is in progress. One couple consists of Achilles' son (so identified) and Hermione, the daughter of Helen and Menelaus, who is endowed with "the beauty of golden Aphrodite" (4.14). The second bridegroom is Menelaus's illegitimate son, Megapenthes, who is marrying a local Spartan girl. The first couple evokes Achilles' shadowy relationship with Helen, here consummated in the next generation. As for Hermione, her likeness to Aphrodite is an obvious reminder of her mother, and the poet goes out of his way to note that she is Helen's only child. It is even hinted that his wife's failure to produce a son may be the reason Menelaus conceived Megapenthes with a slave woman (4.10–14)—unless it was simply because of her absence at Troy.

Either way, Megapenthes' conspicuous role in Menelaus's ménage underlines the deficiencies in his marriage. An illegitimate son may be beloved, as this one clearly is, and in the absence of legitimate sons may serve as an heir. But his status is still secondary and his well-being precarious (cf. 14.200–210). Megapenthes' name, which means "great grief," underlines Menelaus's most salient trait in this epic, his constant grieving, in a way that ties this sorrow to the failings—reproductive and otherwise—in his marriage to Helen. Nor is there any evidence that Megapenthes (of whom we know virtually nothing else) carried on his father's line. He seems to have been invented specially for the occasion, to create a poignant contrast with Telemachus, Odysseus's legitimate son and heir. As Helen herself will remark, Telemachus looks exactly like his father, but has grown up deprived of him thanks to her "dog-eyed" self (4.141–46). The *Odyssey*, then, like the *Iliad*, is predicated upon Helen and the failure of marriage that she represents, and thus upon the threat she poses to the kind of prosperous domesticity here presented for the admiration of a young and impressionable male visitor.

Menelaus welcomes the visitors, and soon reduces Telemachus to tears by speaking of his grief over the war, especially the loss of Odysseus. At this moment Helen emerges from her bedroom and takes her seat among the accoutrements that mark her domestication: a golden distaff and a silver wool basket trimmed with gold (4.130–32). Her beauty is conveyed, as in the *Iliad*, through standard epithets. She is "glorious among women" (4.305), with white arms (22.227), beautiful hair and cheeks (15.58, 15.123), and a long gown (4.305, 15.171). In keeping with the youth's awestruck reaction to the palace, she is likened once again to a goddess. This time, however, it is a specific divinity. She makes her entrance looking like "Artemis of the golden distaff" (4.122), the divine embodiment of the supremely desirable *parthenos*. Wool working associates her with scenes of nubile beauty (cf. above, p. 20, and figure 2.9, p. 51), and her special equipment, like the house itself, glimmers with the aura of the divine parentage that makes her so extraordinary. By juxtaposing this vision with Hermione's wedding the poet collapses the generations, underlining Helen's timelessness.

This description of Helen's arrival creates a tableau for Telemachus's (and our) admiration. The young man's reaction is not recorded. But the palace is described from his point of view, inviting us to imagine Helen through his eyes and prompting us, perhaps, to recall her impact upon a different young male guest many years ago. Sparta is, at any rate, a place where the social norms of hospitality seem to require constant reaffirmation. Those norms call for traveling strangers to be welcomed into the house immediately and without discussion, but in this case the question of whether to take in the unknown youths is—atypically—foregrounded, if only to be dismissed (4.26–36). When the guests prepare to depart, Menelaus will again place a curious emphasis on the behavior proper to a host (15.64–74). If anyone should know the rules of guest-friendship, he should.

Helen received her remarkable distaff and workbasket from their hostesses in Egypt on the journey home from Troy. They were given specifically to her, as distinct from Menelaus, who received his own gifts from the king (4.125–32). Like Homeric men (especially the men of the *Odyssey*), she has accumulated precious objects by traveling, obtaining gifts of hospitality in the process. She is not merely a treasure herself, but an active participant in the economy of gift exchange, with the power—unique among Homeric women—to enhance the splendor of her husband's household by acquiring precious items of her own. Greek women typically have two ways of contributing to men's wealth: garnering courtship gifts, which attest to their value as objects of exchange, and producing precious fabrics through their own labor. Helen adds value in both these ways, but her own travels, disreputable as they are, have allowed her to supplement these feminine economic interventions by importing gifts from outside the household, via a network of guest-friends of a kind that is normally limited to men.

She also plays an unusually active role, for a woman, in bestowing gifts of guest-friendship upon others. At his departure Telemachus receives rich gifts from Menelaus, but also a women's garment made by Helen (15.104–5). It is not unusual for Homeric women to give clothing to visiting men, as a component of their husbands' hospitality, but Helen seems to have exceptional authority to disburse gifts from Menelaus's store in her own right. When he orders her, along with the serving women, to make a feast (15.93), there is no sign that she obeys. Instead, while the food is being prepared, she goes unprompted with Menelaus to the inner chamber that also serves as a storeroom (15.99–100). They both emerge with gifts that are "most beautiful." Helen selected a garment that "was most beautiful in its patterning, and biggest, / and shone like a star" (15.107–8), while Menelaus contributed a "most precious" mixing bowl, "the work of Hephaestus," made of silver and trimmed with gold (15.114–17).

These gifts are gendered as products of weaving and metalwork respectively. They are also gendered in their provenance and function. Menelaus's bowl has a lineage derived from the traditional practices of guest-friendship. It was acquired during the voyage home from Troy as a gift from a king (15.117–19). This kind of gift typically passes from man to man in consolidation of aristocratic friendship ties—a function reflected in its use, as a wine bowl for convivial gatherings. Helen's gift is a feminine complement to such objects. It is intended for Telemachus's future bride, but is to be kept meanwhile by his mother, Penelope:

> I, too, give you this gift, dear child, as a memorial
> from Helen's hands, for your wife to wear when the time arrives
> for your much-desired marriage; until then let your
> dear mother keep it stored away in the palace.
>
> (15.125–28)

Like the treasures that Helen received in Egypt, the garment contributes to an extraordinary female network of guest-friendship consolidated through the circulation of gifts.

Helen also diverges from other female gift givers by explicitly stating that the gift is her own work and naming herself as its maker. By declaring it a "memorial" of her own hands she lays claim not only to future recognition but to the authorship of her work and the right to its disposal. This kind of emphatic self-naming is standard practice for male heroes—who are prone to proud proclamations of their name and lineage—but it is exceptional for a woman. This is, moreover, the only explicitly commemorative garment in the poem, and the only such "memorial" to commemorate a woman. As the work of Helen's hands it fulfills this function in two ways, since she is both the skilled artisan who made it and the owner who disposes of it. Again, this makes her role extraordinary, since aristocratic men do not typically make the gifts they pass on to other men. Helen's gift is thus a self-promoting gesture of a highly unusual kind.

The purpose of this garment, as a gift for Telemachus's bride, may remind us of the divine Helen's function as a wedding goddess (above, p. 44). It also recalls the decorative accessories that Aphrodite sometimes bestows on favored women. Such gifts are a sign of beauty and may be given even to the most virtuous of brides, like Andromache (*Il.* 22.470–72). But they are also potentially dangerous. One anecdote, for example, tells of a necklace given by Aphrodite to Helen herself. After she left Menelaus he dedicated it in a temple; other women quarreled over it, and it ended up in the hands of a beautiful, lustful woman who echoed Helen's behavior by falling in love with a young man and running away with him (Athen. 6.232e–233a). Necklaces (which were often made of twisted metal) are a frequent token of erotic treachery in myth, but clothing can be dangerous as well. Helen's gift recalls, in particular, the ill-omened garment that the Trojan women offer to Athena in the *Iliad*. It too "was most beautiful in its patterning, and biggest, / and shone like a star" (*Il.* 6.294–95). This gift—spurned by the goddess—was acquired by Paris on his ill-fated expedition to Sparta (*Il.* 6.289–92), making it a metonym for the transgressive Helen. The star simile applied to both garments is also sinister in effect. Stars can convey the light of erotic beauty, but they can also signify destruction. As such they are linked especially with the devastating might of Achilles.

There is danger, then, as well as allure in Helen's gift, reflecting the risks inherent in the circulation of beautiful women. Weddings are "much-desired," as Helen puts it (15.126), in part because of the beauty of the bride, but the more desirable the bride in question, the greater the potential for disaster, as the history of the much-desired Helen makes all too clear. A girl's wedding marks the dangerous, liminal moment in her life that Helen was notoriously unable to negotiate successfully, and seems, as a result, to inhabit permanently—a failure whose consequences are lamented throughout Telemachus's visit. The Spartan episode thus ends, as it began, with marriage imagery that, while ostensibly happy, has disturbing undertones associated with Helen's erotic power and independence.

Helen's assertiveness in disposing of her own handiwork is matched by other aspects of her character. She is more talkative than other Odyssean women, more assertive, and more independent of her husband, whom she outshines in insight and decisiveness. Menelaus comes across as slow-witted and hesitant in comparison. It takes some time for him to recognize Telemachus, and when he finally does so, he deliberates whether to identify him out loud (4.117–19). Helen, by contrast, recognizes the youth instantly from his resemblance to his father, and speaks out both "immediately" (4.137) and as her "heart (*thumos*) urges" (4.140). When she has "another idea"—to drug the wine at dinner—she once more acts on it "immediately" and independently (4.219), without reflecting or consulting her husband as to the advisability of serving narcotics to their guests. The pattern is repeated at the end of Telemachus's visit, when an eagle swoops down and carries off a tame goose. While Menelaus stops to think about how to interpret the omen and respond, Helen butts in:

> Listen to me! I shall prophesy as the immortal gods
> put it in my heart (*thumos*), and as I think it shall be accomplished.
>
> (15.172–73)

She goes on to interpret the omen, with perfect accuracy, as a sign that Odysseus will return and take vengeance on the suitors preying on his faithful wife, Penelope (15.169–78).

It is not unusual for Homeric characters to speak as their *thumos* bids them, but such speakers are nearly always male. Helen's outspokenness as compared with her husband suggests the stereotypical representation of women—especially beautiful women—as lacking in self-control of all kinds. It was this that made her susceptible to the "madness" (*atē*) that Aphrodite put into her *thumos*, causing her to elope with Paris (23.223–24; cf. 4.261–62). In the scene at Telemachus's departure, however, Helen's lack of self-restraint is innocuous enough. Her prophecy of Odysseus's return is presumably influenced by some other, more benign divinity. Her interpretation is, in any case, characteristically adroit, giving her the last word and inspiring warm appreciation in her audience. Telemachus tells her that if she is right (as we know she is) he will glorify her as a goddess (15.180–81). By the end of the young man's visit, then, Helen seems to have displaced Menelaus as the quasi-divine object of his admiration (cf. 4.160). Our last view of Sparta is dominated not by the master of the house but by his extraordinary wife.

Telemachus's parting words gain further resonance from Helen's special ties to divinity, which are much more noticeable in the *Odyssey* than in the *Iliad*. Such associations lie close to the surface throughout the Spartan episode, aligning her with superhuman females who appear elsewhere in the *Odyssey*, such as Circe, a sorceress who ensnares Odysseus's men; Calypso, a nymph who offers him immortality if he will stay with her; and the Sirens, who lure ships onto the rocks with their singing. These are all figures of a type that scholars have labeled "dread goddesses," that is, dangerous females with the power to speak falsehood or divinely sanctioned truth, who exercise magical and/or erotic power over men in a way that threatens to emasculate them, but can be beneficial if successfully resisted. Such figures are central to the larger plot of the *Odyssey*, since they embody the feminine powers of seduction, manipulative language, and crafty intelligence, all of which create obstacles to Odysseus's return.

Helen's prophetic skill is one of several ways in which she resembles such supernatural figures. Her most striking manifestation of such power is, however, the drug with which she doctors the wine, providing the company with a temporary reprieve from the emotional burdens of the human condition:

> It erases grief and anger, and makes one forget all evils.
> Whoever should swallow it, mixed into the wine,
> would not shed a tear down his cheeks for that day,
> not if his mother should die, and his father,
> not if men slaughtered his brother or his dear son with bronze
> in front of him, and he saw it happen with his own eyes.
>
> (4.221–26)

A fortiori, such a drug should assuage Telemachus's sorrow about the missing Odysseus, Peisistratus's tears for his brother, dead in the Trojan War (4.186–202), and Menelaus's grief for his friends lost at Troy and his brother's murder back home in Greece.

Like her exotic wool-working tools, Helen's drug comes from Egypt. It was a gift from the Egyptian queen Polydamna, whose name, appropriately, means "much-subduing" (4.228).[1] To the Greeks, Egypt was an exotic land of mysterious wisdom. In the *Odyssey*, this takes the form of skill at medicine, thanks to the abundant drugs that grow there (4.229–32). Homer's Helen thus anticipates the many philosophers and sages who were reputed, in classical times, to have traveled to Egypt to acquire its wisdom and then returned to Greece. Egypt produces many negative or "mournful" drugs, however, mixed up with the beneficial ones (4.230), reflecting a Greek suspicion of drugs in general as deeply ambiguous in their power. In this respect they resemble Zeus himself, who, as Helen rather enigmatically remarks after doctoring the wine, has the power to allot both good and evil (4.236–37). Helen's drug, in particular, seems to evoke her father's power. "The daughter of Zeus," we are told, possessed drugs "full of craftiness (*mētis*)" (4.227)—an expression used elsewhere in early poetry only of Zeus himself.

Helen's Egyptian drug is, we are assured, of the beneficial variety (4.228). Nevertheless, the way its effects are described suggests negative implications inseparable from its positive effects. The *Odyssey* is much concerned with memory and its moral dimension, which is often threatened by erotic desire. A fickle woman is one who "no longer remembers" her husband and children (15.21–23), and Calypso's goal is to make Odysseus "forget" his home by means of soft seductive words (1.56–57). Drugs and magic may be used to similar effect. The Lotus-Eaters, for example, feed Odysseus's men a mysterious plant that makes them forget about home (9.92–102). Such passages refer less to the literal forgetting of facts than to emotional "forgetting," that is, erasure of the emotions that drive proper behavior. The dehumanizing implications of such "forgetting" are clearest in the case of Circe, who gives "mournful drugs" to Odysseus's men to make them forget their home, then turns them into pigs, though their minds remain intact (10.235–40). Helen's drug has a similar power to dehumanize, insofar as it eliminates the emotional fuel that powers morality. By erasing sorrow it serves as an antidote to grief, but also undermines the affectionate kinship ties that inspire loyalty and the tears and lamentation due to the dead (cf. 4.195–98). By erasing anger it eliminates destructive wrath, but also the righteous revenge that is the foundation of archaic justice.

Through this kind of emotional manipulation Helen's drug mimics the destructive effect upon the rational mind of *erōs* (itself often likened to drugs or magic). Its mechanism is, to be sure, the opposite—her drug neutralizes strong

---

1. Her name, like those of most of the Egyptians in this story, is transparently Greek. Yet Egyptologists suspect a connection with the Egyptian queen Tausret, who reigned at roughly the time of the Trojan War (Callender 2012:25–26).

emotion instead of producing it—but the ethical impact is comparable. Helen's drug mimics, in the first place, her own subjection to *erōs*. If it makes one immune to the death of a son, presumably (a fortiori) it removes any qualms about abandoning one's daughter and husband. By defusing the emotions that drive moral judgment, it also mimics the impact of Helen's beauty on men, as exemplified most notoriously at the sack of Troy, when Menelaus dropped his sword. The dinner party in Sparta, long after the war, is itself a consequence of the power of erotic beauty to overcome vengeful anger. The immediate function of Helen's superhuman drug is, of course, to soothe the grief that she brought her husband and his friends, but it may also be expected to foster domestic harmony by erasing a resentment whose most obvious potential target, in the present context, is herself. As a symbolic equivalent of *erōs*, the drug not only explains Helen's transgression but undermines the impulse to hold her accountable.

The drug is thus the pharmaceutical equivalent of the persuasive discourse with which the Homeric Helen, in both epics, disarms blame. It has, in fact, been equated with her eloquence since ancient times. Its effect resembles that of Helen's divine half sisters, the Muses (who have much in common with the *Odyssey*'s "dread goddesses"). As Hesiod tells us, the Muses make possible the pleasure of poetry, which causes people to forget their evils and cease from cares (*Theog.* 55, 98–103). The Muses also warn Hesiod that they can speak at will either truth or "many falsehoods resembling the truth" (*Theog.* 27–28). Helen's likeness to them in this respect, too, is hinted at early in the Spartan episode, when she asks, before identifying Telemachus, "Shall I speak falsely or truly?" (4.140). This rather odd question, which has no obvious purpose in its context, draws attention to her Muse-like capacity for deception. The Muses also share Helen's ambiguity in a further sense, since their gifts can come at a high cost. The Muse that favored the bard Demodocus, for example, gave him "both good and evil": she gave him "sweet song," but took away his eyesight (8.62–64).

By immunizing her audience against the painful emotions caused by memories of the Trojan War, Helen's drug, like the Muses, makes possible the pleasure of storytelling, freeing the company to enjoy the evocation of such memories through discourse. It thereby lays them open to the power of her voice. Upon serving the drug she invites everyone to enjoy the speeches that are to follow (4.238–39), and proceeds to deliver the first such speech herself. In so doing she takes on the role, uniquely for a woman, of bard at the Homeric feast. Menelaus then responds with a speech of equal length. The result is a semiformal debate over Helen's role in the last days of the Trojan War.

The debate is couched in the form of two anecdotes about Helen's relationship to Odysseus, thus integrating her into the *Odyssey*'s larger narrative of the hero's journey home to Ithaca. Central to that narrative is the definition of Odysseus's heroism through his response to the threat of the feminine, as embodied in the many female figures, divine and mortal, who threaten his return. That threat inheres, in many cases, in the power of the manipulative female voice, which turns out to be central to both anecdotes recounted in book 4. Since the voice in question belongs to Helen, her discourse is self-reflexive, while Menelaus's provides a retrospective lens through which to reassess her self-presentation. The stories are told ostensibly for the pleasure and edification of their guests, but Helen addresses the men who fought at Troy (4.243), represented here solely by Menelaus, and he rather pointedly addresses Helen herself (4.274, etc.). The twin speeches are a conversation between husband and wife, coded and filtered through the social context in which they are performed.

Helen's story concerns an incident near the end of the war when Odysseus entered Troy on a spying mission, dressed as a beggar. She was, so she tells us, the only person to see through his disguise (4.249–50). This accords with the perceptiveness shown by her speedy recognition of Telemachus (4.137–46), and, in the *Iliad*, by her ability to see through Aphrodite's disguise as an old woman (3.96). She shares this trait with Odysseus himself, who is known for his crafty intelligence. When Helen recognized and questioned him, at first, she says, he was cunningly evasive:

> But after I bathed him and anointed him with olive oil,
> put clothing upon him, and swore a mighty oath
> not to reveal Odysseus's presence to the Trojans
> before he could get back to the swift ships and the huts,
> then he told me all the Achaeans' intentions.
>
> (4.252–56)

Under the circumstances, stripping Odysseus of his disguise makes no sense whatsoever. The effect, however, is to posit Helen as a seductive hostess who neutralizes Odysseus's craftiness through manipulations of her own, specifically feminine, species of cunning. This makes Helen the first, chronologically, in the sequence of seductive or threatening females who obstruct the hero's journey home. Her physical attentions have strong erotic overtones implying, if not seduction, at least questionably appropriate intimacy. The bath also renders a man physically vulnerable to women (as Agamemnon was to discover). Their similar character reinforces the erotic tension by suggesting that they might make a well-matched pair, especially if one recalls that Odysseus was one of Helen's original suitors (above, p. 31).

Undoing Odysseus's disguise gives Helen complete power over him. He is, of course, protected by her oath, but the oath serves Helen's interests, too. It assists her in obtaining information (for unspecified purposes) and promotes her self-presentation as loyal to the Achaeans—a picture intended not only for Odysseus but for Menelaus and his guests at Sparta. The oath is, moreover, rather artfully limited. Helen swears only that she will not reveal Odysseus's presence before he gets back to the Greek camp. One might expect the cunning Odysseus to require something more comprehensive. But he accepts this oath as proof of her good faith and divulges all the Achaeans' plans. By so doing, he puts the Achaean army into Helen's power, gambling quite unnecessarily with their lives. She has succeeded in inducing the cleverest of the Greeks to put the outcome of the entire war in jeopardy by entrusting it to the woman whose untrustworthiness caused it in the first place.

Helen concludes her speech by affirming her remorse and renewed loyalty to the Greeks in general and Menelaus in particular (4.259–64). If her audience—or Homer's—retained doubts nonetheless about the wisdom of entrusting her with Achaean secrets, those doubts would have been confirmed by the story Menelaus tells in response. He rebuts Helen's repentant, loyal, and flattering self-presentation by describing a fickle, treacherous Helen, whose nostalgia for home could by no means be counted on to outweigh her erotic weakness. Though he begins by praising his wife for speaking "appropriately" (4.266)—presumably in reference to her expressed remorse—he will go on to expose her voice as untrustworthy and manipulative.

Menelaus's competing anecdote takes place just before the fall of Troy, when the wooden horse was already inside the city walls, full of Greek warriors, including himself and the great hero Diomedes. Since the horse was obviously central to the plans Odysseus divulged to Helen, Greek lives again depend on her silence, as a result of his indiscretion. While the men were waiting to emerge, Helen approached the horse, influenced (so Menelaus speculates) by an unnamed pro-Trojan divinity, who can only be Aphrodite (4.274–75). Then, he says,

> three times you circled the hollow ambush, feeling it all around;
> you named the Greeks' best men, calling to each by name,
> making your voice like the voices of all the Achaeans' wives.
>
> (4.277–79)

This strange treatment of the Trojan Horse lies securely in the mingled spheres of the erotic, the divine, and the magical. Gods in general, and Aphrodite in particular, are skilled at deceiving mortals through impersonation. (We may also recall the shape-shifting of Helen's mother Nemesis.) Magical overtones are provided by the number three (used frequently in magic), the naming of the men (often vital to the power of spells), and the caressing of the horse, which evokes magical forms of touch as well as intimate physical contact. The passage attests, again, to Helen's ability to penetrate disguises, and above all to the spellbinding power of the female voice. Like the Muses, who can tell falsehoods "resembling the truth," Helen displays the deceptiveness associated with the female from Pandora onward. Reproducing the voice of each man's wife in turn, she exercises the seductive power of every woman, magically becoming the embodiment of female desirability as such. The story finesses the tension between the abstract notion of a perfectly objective female beauty and the fact that in reality, different women are desirable to different men. As the ultimate object of desire, Helen is every woman and no woman.

Helen's voice impairs men's intellectual and emotional functioning beyond even her drug or her beauty. At the sound of it, Menelaus tells us, he and Diomedes, along with a minor character named Anticlus, wanted to leap out of the horse or answer her call. They were apparently bewitched into thinking that their wives were at Troy, or else, just as absurdly, that they themselves were safely back home with their families. Fortunately, Odysseus saw (or heard) through Helen's vocal disguise, as she earlier saw through his physical one. He restrained the delusional men—forcibly, in the case of Anticlus—and saved the day for the Achaeans (4.280–88). His patron goddess, Athena, also played her part by "leading" Helen away (4.289).

If Aphrodite signifies Helen's treacherous desire, the goddess of wisdom indicates the rather tardy prudence that motivates her remorse. By the same token, however, the involvement of these two divinities suggests the instability of Helen's intentions. The scene provides a further reminder of her erotic lability in the person of Deiphobus, her husband at the time of the incident, who, Menelaus tells us, "followed" Helen to the horse (4.276). This detail not only sharpens the treacherous implications of her bizarre behavior but associates her betrayal of the Greeks with her career as a serial monogamist. It reminds us, too, of her emasculating impact, since it is Deiphobus, the man, who "follows" his wife, reversing the normal structure of marital authority. Odysseus saves the Greeks not only from discovery by the Trojans but from the emasculating power of Helen's uncanny presence.

The paired stories both present Helen as clever, seductive, and in control, dwelling in the first case on her power for good and in the second on her capacity for harm. Which, if either, should we believe? Menelaus's account trumps Helen's rhetorically through its placement, which gives him the last word. The veracity of his tale is also endorsed dramatically by Helen's drugging of the wine, which chimes with her supernatural manipulation of the men in the horse and links her quasi-magical powers with the use of her voice. Her Muse-like power to speak falsely if she chooses further prepares for the possibility that her tale is a deceptive enchantment. This does not mean her story is simply untrue. We know from the *Iliad* that she vacillated in her loyalties, and Menelaus's tale confirms that Odysseus put the Greeks at risk by telling her about the horse. But her use of discourse remains open to suspicion. Her flattery of her husband, for example, may give us pause (4.263–64). Menelaus's negative portrait is thus consistent with what we see of Helen in the epic present.

At the same time, Menelaus's story backfires by making him and the other Greeks inside the horse, except Odysseus, look like putty in Helen's hands. Unlike the rest of the men Menelaus is not literally delusional, since the "wife" whose voice she "imitates" is, of course, herself. Yet he is obviously still "deceived" by erotic passion. His desire to leap from the horse makes it clear that Helen retains her power over him, foreshadowing his notorious failure of will when they are, eventually, reunited. The story thus discloses not only her duplicity but his own weakness. If she is as treacherous as his story indicates, why bring her home to Sparta instead of killing her at the sack of Troy?

Death is, in fact, the fate meted out to other unfaithful women in the *Odyssey*. Like Helen, the unchaste, disloyal maidservants at Ithaca fell under the influence of Aphrodite (22.444–45) and are repeatedly called "dogs" (18.338, 19.91, 154, 372). Unlike her, however, they meet a painful and degrading end, hanged by their avenging master (22.465–73). The *Odyssey*'s chief paradigm of disloyal womanhood is Helen's sister, the equally doglike Clytemnestra (11.424, 11.427). When Menelaus refers to his brother's "destructive wife" (4.92), the phrase could just as well apply to his own, who, like her sister, performed a "shocking deed" (23.222–23; cf. 11.429). Like the maidservants, however, Clytemnestra was killed for the deed in question. The woman whose disloyalty created the conditions for these and many other misfortunes is, in striking contrast, spared the censure directed at other promiscuous women—not to mention their grisly fate. Helen stands outside the strong moral framework of the epic as a whole.

This places her on the same footing as her divine patron, Aphrodite, who enjoys an adulterous escapade of her own in the *Odyssey*. While Odysseus is a guest at the home of Alcinous in Phaeacia—another palace of godlike splendor—the blind bard Demodocus sings of an erotic triangle among the beautiful but "dog-eyed" Aphrodite, her husband Hephaestus—a second-rate male who foolishly leaves her unattended—and Ares, her beautiful lover (8.266–367). The structural similarity to Helen's story is obvious. But Hephaestus, the Menelaus of this tale, also bears a resemblance to the crafty Odysseus. When he found out that his wife was having an affair, the craftsman god forged an ingenious golden net, trapped the lovers in bed, and displayed them in flagrante to the assembled gods. Like Menelaus's dinner story, the bard's tale implies that the only way to control female beauty is by a combination of crafty intelligence and physical coercion—the combination used by Odysseus to protect his comrades in the horse from Helen's voice.

Like Helen, Aphrodite suffers no further consequences for her misbehavior. After being caught in adultery and publicly shamed, she simply retires to one of her sanctuaries to restore her looks with a bath, perfume, and clothing that is, characteristically, "a wonder to behold" (8.362–66). Nor does the prospect of such egregious humiliation deter her male admirers. As Hermes declares to Apollo, when he sees the divine lovers in bed:

> I wish that would happen to me, lord far-shooter Apollo!
> Three times as many seamless bonds could surround us,
> you gods and all the goddesses could look on,
> but I would sleep with golden Aphrodite!
>
> (8.339–42)

The utter shamelessness of this proposal is underlined by Hermes' inclusion of "all the goddesses," who, we were told earlier, stayed away from the spectacle out of modesty (8.324). Despite her husband's best efforts at reimposing moral and social order, a would-be adulterous lover cannot be deterred from sex with Aphrodite. The goddess's human protégée lacks her divine freedom and insouciance, yet she too eludes the sanctions imposed by men on errant women. Menelaus may be granted the last word in their debate, but the fact that Helen is alive and well and living in Sparta is conclusive evidence of her disarming power.

The morning after the banquet Menelaus makes another attempt to reassert narrative control over his wife. Leaving Helen in bed, he regales Telemachus with an extended account of his visit to Egypt on the way home from Troy. He makes no mention at all of Helen's presence on this voyage, or even of the Egyptian hosts who supplied her with such extraordinary gifts. His narrative does, however, reiterate the contrast between his own dull-wittedness and the cleverness of a crafty and beautiful female endowed with supernatural resources. He was rescued on the coast of Egypt, after a storm, by the sea nymph Eidothea ("divine beauty"). She told him that her father, the shape-shifting sea god Proteus, could inform him what "good and bad" things might be happening at his home in Sparta (4.392). First, however, Proteus had to be wrestled into submission, despite his ability to assume various monstrous forms. Eidothea solved this problem for Menelaus by employing, in a humorous and degrading way, the feminine skill at imitation and disguise. She had him hide in the skin of a freshly slaughtered seal—thoughtfully protecting him from the foul odor with divine ambrosia (4.440–46)—so that he could surprise the sleeping Proteus and defeat him, thus obtaining the information that he sought.

The sea god provides Menelaus with extensive revelations, at the end of which he finally mentions Helen's name. He explains that Menelaus will never die but will live on in the paradise of Elysium, "because you have Helen and are the son-in-law of Zeus" (4.569). The book began by underlining Helen's failure to give her husband an heir to continue his name. Thanks to her paternity, it now seems, she will provide him instead with literal immortality. This prophecy is the most unambiguous statement of Helen's special significance anywhere in Homeric epic. That significance is presented, however, from a strictly masculine perspective, affirming Menelaus's exalted family status and blessed future without mentioning hers. Proteus's prophecy posits Helen as a mere conduit for patriarchal power, assigning her the role of the bride as a precious object circulated among men with no acknowledgment of her subjectivity. Proteus, or Menelaus, who reports the story, thus provides a face-saving perspective on the latter's marriage. Yet the prophecy also underlines the degree to which his privileged status depends on his wife, belying the way he elides her from his narrative.

Despite her redomestication, then, Helen appears both more superhuman and more dangerous in the *Odyssey* than in the *Iliad*. Even though she is confined to the role of repentant wife, we are repeatedly reminded of her ability to transgress the limitations of that role and to provoke transgression in others. It is therefore scarcely surprising to find her subjected to a more extensive battery of narrative controls. To begin with, she is blamed more than in the *Iliad*, and held more accountable by others for the Trojan War—at least by those who are not exposed to her presence, or her drug. Odysseus's faithful swineherd Eumaeus, for example, wishes that Helen's whole "tribe" had perished because she "loosed the knees" of many men in death—an expression equating her destructive agency with that of a warrior (14.69). Penelope, too, is emphatic in disapproving of her cousin's "shocking deed" (23.222).

Such noncombatants, like the women on the margins of the *Iliad*, might be expected to blame Helen freely, since they lack a personal stake in the manly, aristocratic heroism for which she served as the occasion. But this time the epic hero concurs. Odysseus tells Alcinous that the war was fought because of "an evil woman" (11.384), and couples Clytemnestra and Helen as twin causes of men's destruction. On his visit to the underworld, he laments to the shade of Agamemnon:

> Alas, what astonishing hatred far-seeing Zeus showed from the start
> for the offspring of Atreus, through plans involving women;
> on account of Helen many of us were destroyed,
> and Clytemnestra schemed against you while you were gone.
> (11.436–39)

The phrase "plans involving women" is ambiguous. It refers most obviously to the plans of Zeus, who used both sisters as his instruments, but the Greek also suggests that, like Pandora, they served his hostile purposes by devising reprehensible schemes of their own.

Heightened blame of Helen goes hand in hand with a general reassessment, in the aftermath of the Trojan War, of the glory acquired through combat. The *Iliad* is well aware of the high cost of such glory yet ultimately embraces it. In the *Odyssey*, however, even Achilles challenges the heroic values that underpin the *Iliad*. In the underworld Agamemnon declares that by dying at Troy

Achilles won "noble glory [*kleos*] forever among all people" (24.93–94), and Odysseus calls him the most blessed of all men because of his high status in life and death (11.482–86). But Achilles replies:

> Don't try to console me for dying, splendid Odysseus!
> I would prefer to be a farmhand laboring for hire,
> for some impoverished master with only a little to live on,
> than rule as lord over all the perished dead.

(11.488–91)

Achilles' reassessment of the values of the *Iliad* is also an implicit reassessment of Helen as an object of heroic quest. His posthumous perspective on the glory of warfare dovetails with the *Odyssey*'s increased willingness to acknowledge Helen's agency, and to blame her. If she is no longer emblematic of a glorious enterprise, then there is no need to evade her culpability; conversely, acknowledgment of her agency calls for increased social control in the form of blame.

This shift in attitude toward Helen in the *Odyssey*, as compared with the *Iliad*, forms part of a broader realignment of perspectives. The postwar poem values responsibility across a broader spectrum of social roles. Marriage, the household, and the community are at stake, and depend on the loyalty and prudence of all their members, male and female. Judged by these criteria, the marriage of Helen and Menelaus is an abject failure. Helen is, of course, the essence of the irresponsible wife, but Menelaus is also at fault. After losing control of his wife he chose to reacquire her at incalculable cost in lives and property, and in so doing, as he puts it himself, "destroyed" a prosperous household (4.95–96). His material prosperity has, to be sure, been rebuilt to Olympian levels. But this is not enough, he acknowledges, to compensate for the human cost of the war (4.97–99), and thus for his colossal overvaluation of Helen as an object to be resecured regardless of both her failings and her own desires.

The tense and problematic relationship between Menelaus and Helen serves as a foil to the ideal partnership of Odysseus and Penelope, which challenges the underlying attitude toward marriage that led to the Trojan War. Menelaus's susceptibility to female beauty—which caused the war and then almost derailed its conclusion—is a weakness shared by Odysseus, who must learn to resist it in order to reach home. Faced with a series of "dread goddesses," who control and emasculate men through magic, drugs, sex, or some combination thereof, he does not resist their allure immediately or with ease. It takes him considerable time to reject both Circe, with whom he stays for a year, and Calypso, with whom he spends seven. In each case he succumbs, at first, to their feminine wiles, but eventually repudiates them in favor of returning home. The two encounters with Helen recounted over dinner at Sparta initiate this pattern. The first puts Odysseus in Helen's power and endangers all the Greeks; the second thwarts her and saves them. Odysseus demonstrates, inside the wooden horse, the need for men to gain and retain control over the threat posed by feminine seduction. In contrast to Menelaus, who will pay any price to hold on to Helen, he shows that the truly heroic male can learn to resist her sway.

As for Odysseus's wife, Penelope, her relationship to her husband contrasts with Helen's not only in fidelity but in fertility, affection, and the "like-mindedness" that is central to the *Odyssey*'s marital ideal (cf. 6.180–85). Where Helen is mobile, fickle, and destructive of men's lives and property, Penelope is stable, loyal, protective of property, and productive of life. Unlike the uxorilocal Helen, who bears only a daughter and then abandons her, she relocates to her husband's household at marriage, then bears him a son whom she nurses and raises to manhood. That son, Telemachus, looks exactly like his father (4.140–50) and even resembles him in behavior. At Sparta he, too, faces the temptation of beguiling discourse and awe-inspiring beauty in a context redolent of divinity. But he remains self-controlled and sensitive to blame, cautious and sensible (4.158–60). Despite Helen's drug, he keeps his wits about him and does not lose the grief that drives his quest (cf. 4.290–93). He resists, too, Menelaus's emphasis on conspicuous wealth, requesting a more humble and practical gift than the splendid chariot and horses that Menelaus offers (4.589–608), and declining a proposed wealth-accumulation tour, which would cause a risky delay (15.80–91). When he bids farewell to Helen, saying he will glorify her as a goddess, his words echo Odysseus's farewell to Nausicaa, the Phaeacian princess who offered the prospect of marriage to a lovely young *parthenos* (8.467). Like his father, Telemachus knows how to acknowledge the hospitality of an alluring woman graciously, and move on.

Meanwhile, Penelope waits at home, through ten years of war and the ten that follow it, fending off the suitors who are preying on her husband's property as she attempts to mitigate the damage caused by his absence. Like her son, however, she does not overvalue wealth for its own sake. While Telemachus is dallying at Sparta, Athena raises in him the fear that Penelope may marry one of her suitors—under pressure from her father and brothers—because he is offering the most courtship gifts (15.16–19; cf. 16.73–77). This approach to marriage threatens Odysseus's successful return, since it would allow a lesser man to win by means of sheer wealth—as Menelaus won Helen. Such an outcome is prevented, however, by Penelope herself, who resists the pressure of her natal male relatives, preferring instead to set up a contest among the suitors to see who can draw Odysseus's mighty bow—a contest that will win her back Odysseus, or his equal. It is this that makes the epic's successful outcome possible, an outcome suggesting that the commodification of women—even, or especially, as supremely precious objects—is a mistaken way to approach the business of marriage.

Despite these marked contrasts with Helen, Penelope shares many of her "feminine" qualities—intelligence, deception, and even seductive beauty. She uses them, however, not to destroy, but to preserve the stability and prosperity of her husband's household. Her signature feature as a heroine is her intelligence, both practical and moral, as indicated by the insistence on her unimpeachable "wits" (*phrenes*) (e.g., 2.117, 18.248–49, 24.194–95). As one suitor remarks, it is her mind that brings her renown (*kleos*) (2.124–26). His tone here is resentful, since the suitors have just discovered the trick she was using to keep them at bay, refusing to remarry until she has finished weaving a shroud for her father-in-law, but secretly unraveling it at night. In keeping with the ambivalence attached in Greek thinking to this quintessential female activity, Penelope's skill at weaving enhances her charm in the eyes of the suitors, but also enables her to dupe them. The effect of her ruse is enhanced by her virtuous insistence on avoiding reproach from other women, who would cast blame (*nemesis*) if she failed in this duty to her father-in-law (2.101–2). Like Helen, Penelope is a weaver of feminine wiles, both literally and figuratively. But she employs these powers strictly with a view to preserving her chastity, her marriage, and as far as she can, the integrity of her husband's property.

Unlike the outspoken Helen, who instantly identifies Telemachus through his resemblance to Odysseus, Penelope's use of her intelligence is marked by an extraordinary caution and restraint, especially when it comes to identifying the stranger who so much resembles Odysseus as her husband. The two women react quite differently to similar omens predicting the hero's return. As we saw earlier, Helen unhesitatingly interprets an omen in which an eagle carries off a tame goose (above, p. 78). Shortly before Penelope's reunion with her husband she reports an almost identical omen, a dream in which an eagle kills twenty geese that are eating grain in her house (19.535–40). Like Helen's omen, this clearly refers to Odysseus's destruction of the suitors, but Penelope first asks Odysseus to interpret it for her (19.535), then disbelieves him when he does so (19.559–69). It is impossible to tell whether she lacks Helen's confident—and accurate—prophetic skill, is simply more cautious about leaping to conclusions, or is using the omen—whose meaning is perfectly obvious—as a way of testing the stranger. Unlike Helen, Penelope characteristically plays her cards close to her chest.

In further contrast with Helen, Penelope's intellect is properly subordinate to that of her husband. Helen outsmarted Odysseus himself, when she saw through his disguise as a beggar inside Troy, but Penelope is taken in when he appears in Ithaca wearing exactly the same kind of disguise. She does, to be sure, play a famous trick on Odysseus, when she claims, in a final test of his identity, to have moved the bed that only they two know is unmovable, implying that she has given another man access to her bedroom and thus her body (23.173–204). This turns the tables and puts her back on an equal footing with her husband, but only after he successfully deceived her first. In Troy

Helen got the better of Odysseus at first through her perceptiveness and charm; this obliged him later to suppress the dangerous consequences. In Ithaca Odysseus successfully deceives Penelope at first; only then is she allowed to show herself his equal in a way that affirms, once more, her fidelity. Their marriage may be based on "like-mindedness," but Odysseus, the husband, remains in control.

Penelope's attitude toward her own beauty also accords with Greek ideals of feminine virtue. She disavows it in the absence of her husband, to whose presence both her looks and her reputation are, in her own mind, bound (18.180–81, 251–55, 19.124–28). According to one of her suitors, however, she surpasses other women in beauty as well as "wits" (18.248–49). He is reacting to an appearance that she makes before the assembled company with the specific intention of further inflaming the heart (*thumos*) of the suitors and enhancing her own value in the eyes of her husband and son (18.158–65). Since her beauty has been worn by time and grief, it requires restoration to produce this effect, but she does not pay attention, like a vain woman, to her own toilette. She rejects a servant's suggestion that she wash and anoint her face since it is marred by tears (18.171–84). Instead, Athena magically beautifies Penelope in her sleep (18.187–96). The effect on her suitors is dramatic. Despite her age and marital status her appearance has the impact of a nubile *parthenos*. She "loosens their knees" and enchants their hearts with *erōs*, making them all want to go to bed with her (18.206–13) and eliciting an impressive array of courtship gifts (18.274–303). Odysseus rightly sees this as a consciously deceptive strategy on Penelope's part, designed to replenish his plundered household (18.274–83). She knows how to make use of her own erotic appeal, to her husband's benefit, without succumbing to an improper vanity.

Nor does Penelope evince the sexual weakness that typically accompanies female beauty. Her heart remains remarkably stubborn, even at the moment of her reunion with the longed-for Odysseus (23.100, 168, 215–17, 230). When she does at last accept him, her heart and knees alike are "loosened" (23.205), an expression of erotic submission that echoes her own impact on the suitors (18.212). Even so, she wishes to repair to bed only when it pleases Odysseus's own heart (*thumos*), and even postpones the moment until she has heard all he has to tell (23.254–62). She controls herself, as she has done for the past twenty years, thus obviating the need for control by men.

Penelope thus surpasses Helen in the appropriate use of both beauty and intelligence. Yet this depends, paradoxically, on her inferiority to the superhuman Helen in both respects. Her beauty is mortal and transient, not divine and permanent. She arouses the suitors' desire only after it has been divinely enhanced in a way that Helen's never requires. This makes her a fitting partner for Odysseus. The gods, as Penelope poignantly puts it, have begrudged them the pleasure of enjoying their youth together (23.210–12). In contrast to Helen's timeless beauty, they have both been worn by time and suffering during the twenty years since Odysseus left home. Like his wife, Odysseus has aged (8.179–83); he correctly attributes his own godlike beauty to divine intervention (16.202–12). As for Penelope's intelligence, she controls her own situation, despite its difficulties, through her own wits. Helen elicits desire through her uncanny mimetic abilities and erases unpleasant emotions through the doubtful cleverness of exotic drugs, but in Ithaca different methods are recommended. When Penelope is overcome with sorrow by tales of the Greek heroes, her own son advocates either a heart that can endure or her swift removal from the company of men (1.353–59). There are, it seems, alternatives to Helen's drug.

Helen's superhuman qualities carry with them the promise of immortality for her husband, but this is something else that the *Odyssey* suggests is not worth having for its own sake, and certainly not at the expense of the right kind of marriage. Odysseus insists pointedly on his own mortality (7.208–10, 16.187), and declines Calypso's offer of an immortal life together even though her beauty, being divine, outstrips Penelope's (5.215–20). He rejects her in favor of his mortal marriage, which is defined in part by subjection to time and change. This loyalty to his human wife—and his humanity—spares him the emasculation of marriage to a divinely beautiful woman. Menelaus embraces the beautiful evil that is Helen, and with it immortality in Elysium, but Odysseus chooses a different, and superior, combination of good and evil fortune: his uniquely harmonious marriage to Penelope, beset as it is by the limitations of mortality. Helen is devalued, finally, by the implication that what sets her above all other women does not make her worth having in the eyes of the epic hero. The only truly desirable form of immortality for a man is replacement by a son and heir who resembles him—an immortality secured for Odysseus by his perfect wife.

This subtle and compelling portrait of Penelope counters the threat of infidelity embodied in Helen and challenges the Hesiodic view of women as intrinsically a "beautiful evil." Nevertheless, the *Odyssey* remains haunted by the fear that *no* woman is free of suspicion. The idea that an innate susceptibility to sexual pleasure can lead astray even a woman who is worthwhile in other ways is a recurrent theme (cf. 11.432–34, 15.420–22, 24.199–202). Clytemnestra herself is said to have had sound "wits" before Aegisthus seduced her; as in Helen's case, the problem was the absence of her designated guardian (3.263–72). According to the shade of the murdered Agamemnon her misdeeds have soiled the reputation of all women, even the good ones (24.192–202). He therefore warns Odysseus to be surreptitious upon his return (11.441–56). He makes it clear that Clytemnestra is the rule, Penelope the exception, but the latter is not exempt from suspicion.

Odysseus takes this advice to heart. When he finally reaches Ithaca he intentionally deceives his wife and leaves her out of the crucial plotting at the denouement. Penelope's own son distrusts her too. Early in the epic Telemachus declares her word insufficient proof of his paternity (1.215–16), and when he lingers at Sparta, Athena nudges him into action by casting doubt on his mother's loyalty (15.20–23). Even the narrator gives Penelope an aura of ambivalence. In her dream about the geese and the eagle she looks with pleasure on the geese—which obviously represent the suitors—and weeps and laments when the eagle slaughters them (19.537, 542–43). Her motivation for expressing such feelings to the disguised Odysseus is, as we saw, characteristically opaque. Nevertheless, the dream leaves open the possibility that her suitors' attentions were not entirely unwelcome.

Be that as it may, at the climactic moment when she finally acknowledges her husband, Penelope voices the fear that even she might have been susceptible to the deceptive blandishments of some ill-intentioned visiting stranger (23.215–17). She implies that such a risk could be posed in her case only by someone indistinguishable from her husband—a disguised god, perhaps. She thus avoids any suggestion that she could knowingly desire another man. But the idea of being seduced by a clever imitator recalls Menelaus's tale of Helen and the Trojan Horse, and with it the intrinsically deceptive power of *erōs*. One aspect of Penelope's vaunted prudence is, it seems, the ability to protect herself from herself. She treats attractive newcomers with a suspicion that is justified not only by male malevolence but by the fragility of female virtue.

In her next breath, Penelope names Helen:

> Nor would Argive Helen, the offspring of Zeus,
> have mingled in love in bed with a man from another land,
> if she had known that the warlike sons of the Achaeans
> meant to take her home again to her own dear fatherland.
> It was a god that drove her to perform such a shocking deed;
> never before then did she put into her heart lamentable
> madness (*atē*), which was the source of grief for us as well.
>
> (23.218–24)

Penelope is more explicit here than any other Homeric character in identifying Helen's own desire as the cause of her transgression, and the elopement as a "shocking deed" for which Helen is actively responsible. She makes it clear not only that Helen *acted* out of her *own* desire, but that in her view Helen could have done otherwise—the very essence of moral responsibility. At the same time, she evinces a remarkable degree of sympathy with her errant cousin, who (like her sister Clytemnestra) had never suffered from such "madness" in the past.

As Penelope tells it, this uncharacteristic "madness" impaired Helen's judgment in such a way that she failed to foresee the consequences of her actions. Her mistake, apparently, was to think she could get away with it. Penelope seems to be suggesting that Helen underestimated her own value in men's eyes. She thus makes Helen's dilemma, and her deed, hinge on intellect, which happens to be the distinctive heroic excellence of the *Odyssey* for both genders. If only Helen had had the right information or judged correctly, Penelope implies, she would have resisted Aphrodite rather than bring on such dire consequences. This is highly implausible, given that rational judgment is precisely the faculty that Aphrodite impairs. But phrasing the issue in intellectual terms allows Penelope to underline Helen's weakness in contrast to herself. She explains Helen's action as, in essence, the predictably foolish and irrational behavior of a previously well-behaved woman in the face of *erōs*—a backhanded defense that relies on female erotic susceptibility and the discourse of female self-deprecation, implying women's need for masculine control.

The context of Penelope's words—she is explaining her own caution in accepting Odysseus—suggests that her sympathy for Helen is grounded in a fear that she herself might make the same kind of mistake. Despite the crucial differences between the two women, the passage insinuates Helen into the reunion of husband and wife in a way that reminds us that women can never be trusted, even by themselves. Even "perfect Penelope," as she is repeatedly called, cannot entirely escape her cousin's shadow. Like Helen, she resembles Aphrodite as well as the virgin goddess Artemis (17.37, 19.54). She is, to be sure, a model of the virtuous, self-controlled wife, but the appearance of such propriety is always potentially deceptive (hence Odysseus's caution). Worse still, modesty is itself erotically appealing. It is her modesty, in part, that makes Penelope so intensely desirable to the suitors who threaten Odysseus's marriage. When she appears before them and arouses their *erōs* she is, like Helen on the walls of Troy, chaperoned by attendants and wearing a shining veil that she modestly holds before her face in a gesture evocative of a bride (18.206–13).

The erotic impact that furnishes the requisite evidence of Penelope's beauty also introduces such beauty's inevitable risk. The scene with the suitors shows her manipulating men in an actively seductive manner, for devious reasons, in a way that even Helen never does in Homer. It is an acknowledgment that any beautiful woman—even the most virtuous—has the power to control men to their detriment. Where her suitors are concerned, Penelope's beauty is palpably destructive. It is worth bearing in mind that their wooing is not, under the circumstances, intrinsically objectionable, though their methods are. And even their methods are corrected by the proper provision of courtship gifts at her behest. They can scarcely be blamed for resenting the way she has been stringing them along (2.87–92, 24.125–28). From their perspective, Penelope's deceptions and her beauty are as deadly as Helen's. Like Helen, she "loosens the knees" of men with desire (18.238), and as in Helen's case, the end result is death for the men in question. When the time comes for Odysseus to attack the suitors, Athena urges him to display the same vigor and courage that he did fighting "for white-armed Helen of noble paternity" (22.226–30). The epic thus culminates in a miniature replay of the Trojan War, marked as such by a reference to none other than Helen.

Penelope's final test of Odysseus—the test of the bed—reminds us (and him) that she retains the capacity to deceive even her husband, and the power, if not the inclination, to betray him. She may be an exception to the rule embodied in Tyndareus's deadly daughters, but this is not something that can ever be taken for granted. The destructive power of female beauty, and of the desire it engenders in men and women alike, is not only eternal and divine but ineliminable from human life. As such it cannot be controlled, as Menelaus attempted to control it, through violence. The *Odyssey* suggests that the Trojan War was a very expensive failure. In the ideal marriage, men and women alike must take responsibility for self-control and the exercise of prudent judgment. Men have no choice, ultimately, but to trust women to control themselves.

5

The Many Faces of Helen: Archaic Lyric

> I may crack but I'll never shatter.
> Tested, wasted, over and over,
> I may crack but it doesn't matter,
> Cuz I still have a secret.
> In the dark I keep it close.
> I still have a secret no one knows.
> —Meredith Brooks

Life in ancient Greece was pervaded by formal and informal poetry and song, much of it now classed under the loose rubric of "lyric." Archaic lyric, our earliest Greek poetry besides epic, embraces works of diverse styles and subjects composed for public and private occasions of many kinds. Many of these poems were probably performed at symposia, private drinking parties where groups of aristocratic men entertained each other with music and song. Lyric frequently engages with the Homeric tradition, and symposiastic poetry, in particular, is much preoccupied with *erōs* and beauty. Helen seems tailor-made for such concerns, and judging from our rather meager surviving fragments, the lyric poets viewed her with particular interest.

One species of lyric poetry (often called "iambic" because of its association with iambic meters) was the poetry of blame, for which Helen might seem like a natural target. The most substantial surviving specimen of this genre is the crude, colorful poem by Semonides equating different kinds of women with various animals (above, p. 23). As it happens, this seventh-century poem also includes our earliest surviving lyric treatment of Helen. There is a suggestion of the problem she poses in the glamorous, frisky mare woman with her long hair, vanity, and propensity for trouble. In an echo of the Hesiodic "beautiful evil," Semonides describes the mare woman as a beautiful sight (*kalon*) for others, but an evil (*kakon*) for the man who "has" her—unless he is a king (7.67–70). The last lines of the poem allude to Helen more explicitly. After declaring even the most virtuous-seeming woman a sham, the poet tells his audience:

Zeus made [women] as the greatest evil,
and shackled us with this unbreakable fetter,
ever since the time when Hades received
those who fought on account of a woman.

(7.115–18)

Though Helen is not named she is called irresistibly to mind, providing this misogynistic diatribe with a fitting climax. As the most destructive woman of all, she transcends the various species of woman to encompass women as such, marking, like Pandora, the beginning of male misery.

It may be no accident that Helen goes unnamed here, since mythic heroines (and heroes) are not typically subjected to such invective in our admittedly scanty surviving iambic texts. She is named, however, in a number of noniambic lyric fragments, very different in form and style from Semonides' invective. Several of these poems originate from Lesbos, in the eastern Aegean, whose poets had further reasons for interest in Helen. Their island had a reputation for female beauty, luxury, and uninhibited eroticism (though not for lesbianism in a modern sense). It also had special connections with Achilles, with whom Helen, as we have seen, is intimately associated. In the *Iliad* it is Achilles who conquers Lesbos (9.128–30), and the Lesbians retained a patriotic interest in Achilles because of his nearby tomb, an important cult site on the coast not far from Troy. Several surviving poems link Achilles with Helen, two of them by the Lesbian Alcaeus.

Alcaeus

Alcaeus, who wrote around 600 BCE, was an active participant in the lively and violent politics of contemporary Lesbos. Like other Greek writers, he used the epic tradition to define himself as a poet and the Trojan War as a vehicle for examining warfare, masculinity, and heroism. He seems to have had a special interest in Achilles, as a heroic model for brotherhood within his political faction. There is some ambivalence, however, in his appropriation of epic heroism for the struggles of his own time. The surviving fragments suggest that this may stem in part from the nature of the epic cause, as embodied in Helen.

Alcaeus 42 parses the factors that produced Achilles' heroism by systematically opposing the character of his mother, the sea nymph Thetis, to that of Helen. Such oppositional pairing is typical of the poetry of praise and blame, especially where women are concerned. The stage had already been set for this particular pairing in the *Cypria*, in which Momos advises Zeus to cause the Trojan War by begetting "a beautiful daughter" and marrying Thetis to a mortal man (fr. 1). This fragment does not expressly blame any of Zeus's human instruments, but it does introduce Helen and Thetis as two female figures with divergent yet complementary roles to play in the divine plan. Alcaeus 42 draws on this tradition but polarizes the two females, turning them into exemplars of the good woman and the bad.

The opposition between Helen and Thetis is structured primarily through their relationships to their husbands—Paris and Peleus respectively:[1]

> As the story goes, [because of evil deeds,]
> to Priam and his children [there once came, Helen,]
> bitter grief from you, and [Zeus destroyed with fire]
> sacred Troy.
>
> Not of such a kind was she whom Aeacus's [noble] son,   5
> [inviting] all the blessed gods to the wedding,
> led in marriage, taking (helōn) her from Nereus's [halls],
> a delicate virgin,
>
> to the home of Chiron; he loosened the [pure]
> virgin's sash, and love [flourished]   10
> between Peleus and the best of Nereus's daughters;
> within a year
>
> she bore a son, the [finest] of demigods,
> a prosperous driver of tawny [horses].
> But they perished over [Helen—the Trojans]   15
> and their city.

The core of the poem is devoted to celebrating Thetis, her marriage, and her reproductive triumph in giving birth to Achilles, but it is framed by the repeated name of Helen.[2] The opening apostrophe is particularly striking. The poet uses it to make Helen notionally present at the all-male symposium without allowing her to speak—or to be visible. This enables him to translate her to his own world and reproach her "face-to-face"—something that Homer's characters seem unable to do.

The distance bridged by the apostrophe is acknowledged in the opening phrase ("as the story goes"). The men of Alcaeus's day, and of his symposiastic cohort, can—in their fantasies—look Helen in the eye, thus casting themselves as superior to the heroes of the past in their ability to resist the impact of her beauty. There is, however, no mention of that beauty—the attribute that posits

---

1. Unlike much surviving early lyric this poem is probably complete, but many individual words are missing or uncertain. Phrases in square brackets translate scholarly supplements, often completing partial words in the original.

2. Both instances of her name are supplements widely (though not universally) accepted by scholars.

Helen as a worthwhile object of struggle—or of the divine lineage that engendered it. The poet does not celebrate, or even acknowledge, the distinctive ground of Helen's renown. Since this is not his fight, he has no compelling need either to celebrate her beauty or to treat her as a precious object of struggle. She is simply a source of "bitter grief," with no hint as to how or why that grief came about.

Helen's agency seems at first to be obscured along with her renown. The perpetrator of the "evil deeds" in the first line is unclear. These "deeds" could theoretically belong to Helen, Paris, or both (cf. *Il.* 6.348), and are, in any case, a supplement. The phrase "from you" is neutral about agency. Helen could be a source of "bitter grief" merely as a contested object, leaving agency in the hands of men. It soon becomes clear, however, that the origin of the destruction lies in Helen's character (and thus her actions), when we hear that Thetis, by contrast, was "not of such a kind" (5). Troy fell, it is implied, because of the *kind* of woman that Helen was. In *Iliad* book 3, being "of such a kind" was precisely what made Helen worth fighting for in the eyes of the Trojan elders (above, p. 55). Alcaeus transforms their awe at the quality of her beauty into a hostile judgment on the quality of her character.

The specifics of that character must, however, be extrapolated from the detailed account of her polar opposite. Helen receives not a single descriptive noun or epithet, but Thetis is granted three in the fragment as it stands—"virgin" (*parthenos*) (8), "delicate" (*habros*) (8), "best of Nereus's daughters" (11)—and if the text has been properly reconstructed, a fourth, "pure" (9). Helen's beauty goes unmentioned, but Thetis's is demurely signaled. As a *parthenos* and "best" of the Nereids she is presumptively beautiful, and the adjective *habros* (8) suggests an elegant, aristocratic eroticism. (It is used, for example, for Semonides' mare woman, and often denotes a desirable bride.) Unlike Helen, however, Thetis remains decorously unnamed, identified only via her father and husband (7, 11). She is, above all, passive: she was a *parthenos* whom her husband *took*, and *led* in marriage, before he *loosened* the sash of her virginity (7–10).

Helen's character and behavior are specified only as "not like" Thetis, and so, by implication, as nonvirginal, erotically active, impure, and bad. Her active, transgressive desire is obliquely but clearly conveyed through systematic opposition with the passive Thetis. The contrast is underlined by the pun on Helen's name in line 7, where the verb *helōn* is used for "taking" Thetis in marriage. The ambivalences embodied in the figure of Homer's Helen—desirable but destructive, object but agent—are thus polarized into two diametrically opposed but complementary female figures, one dangerous and active, the other desirable and passive.

This polarization depends on a simplification of Thetis, no less than of Helen. Thetis often appears as a paradigmatic bride (for example, in wedding scenes on vases). But she acquired this status in part, paradoxically, because of a notorious reluctance to be married. Like Helen's mother Nemesis, she attempts to escape her designated groom by turning into a lion, a snake, and other monsters. Despite these strenuous efforts she is eventually forced into marriage, but her initial resistance betokens both a proper virginal purity and the absence of any untoward eroticism. The taming of the reluctant bride also signifies masculine control of a threatening, divinely powerful female force. In Alcaeus's rendition, however, there is no trace of these complexities. Thetis's persona as a shape-shifting monster is pointedly overwritten in order to present her as a normative *parthenos*.

Nor is there any hint, in our fragment, of Thetis's rather checkered career as a wife. In Homer she abandons Peleus after Achilles is born and goes back to live with Nereus in the sea. Like Helen, then, but in a diametrically opposed fashion, she departs from wifely decorum by asserting her independence from her husband. She rejects sex instead of pursuing it, and returns to her father instead of leaving her husband for a lover. This behavior is far less heinous than Helen's, since it signifies both chastity and a proper loyalty to the patriarchal family (albeit her natal family). Nevertheless, Alcaeus's poem shows no trace of such willfulness. Thetis's marriage is characterized simply by the flourishing of "love" (*philotēs*)—a word indicating affectionate conjugal sex—which results in the timely birth of a son (10–13), without any sign of subsequent marital discord. To portray Thetis abandoning her husband for any reason would blur the sharp contrast between the passive, virtuous bride and the fickle, independent Helen. Alcaeus therefore ends her story at Achilles' birth, allowing him to present her as a normative married woman who outdoes Helen as a wife as well as a bride.

She also outdoes her as a mother. Helen produces no children in this poem, but only "bitter grief" (3). Thetis, by contrast, bore "the finest of demigods" (13),[3] a description that echoes and confirms her status as "best of Nereus's daughters" (11). It is no accident that "bore" (13) is the only verb of which Thetis is the grammatical subject, since it denotes the proper reproductive activity of a good wife. The best woman is the one who bears the best son. This emphasis on Thetis's maternity accords with other mythological sources, which are unanimous in presenting her as an exceptionally devoted mother. Even here, however, Alcaeus has elided a salient feature of the broader tradition. Thetis is often portrayed, notably in the *Iliad*, as grieving constantly over the prospect of Achilles' premature death. In Alcaeus's poem such "bitter grief" is mentioned, to be sure, but only as something that "came from" Helen. It is not connected with Thetis in any way that might detract from her presentation as an exemplary, blessed bride and mother.

Achilles, too, is presented in a way that eliminates his epic ambiguity. The poem focuses neither on his untimely death nor on his bloody exploits. He is

---

3. "Finest" translates a supplement, but some kind of superlative is likely.

simply "the finest of demigods" and a "prosperous driver of tawny horses" (14). By Alcaeus's time chariots were militarily archaic, associated less with contemporary warfare than with the aristocratic glamour of athletic competition. They also had well-developed erotic overtones. Horses were traditionally associated with luxury and eroticism (as exemplified in Semonides' mare woman), and horse taming is a frequent metaphor for sexual conquest. "Tawny" (*xanthos*) is, moreover, a hair color associated with aristocracy and divinity. The prosperous hero's tawny chariot horses thus evoke the splendor and aggression of the epic battlefield, without direct reference to the negative consequences for their driver or his victims. This splendid, semidivine Achilles trumps the Helen whose splendor and semidivinity were elided along with her erotic allure, leaving her only the bad character that set the scene for this display of glorious masculinity. The splendor is all his, the destruction all hers.

In the closing lines Helen is named a second time: the Trojans and their city "perished over Helen" (15–16). The second-person address is abandoned, along with any indication of Helen's character or agency. She has been dismissed from the symposiastic setting, to be presented strictly from a heroic male perspective as an object of struggle. Yet there is still no explanation of why those heroes valued her so highly. Nor is any agent specified in the destruction of Troy. Just as grief simply "came" to Troy from Helen (2–3), the Trojans simply "perished" over her (15). Troy's destruction by fire is a divine punishment for "evil deeds" (1–4)—no more and no less, with no special value attached to Helen and no moral ambiguity to the men who carried out that punishment. This elision of male agency has the effect of assigning sole causation to Helen. Despite the objectification inherent in the phrase "over Helen," it is as if she somehow destroyed the Trojans on her own and the Greek men played no part in it.

This effect is enhanced by focusing exclusively on the destruction of Troy, with no mention of the Achaeans' sufferings. To insist on the latter would raise uncomfortable questions about the advisability of pursuing such an apparently worthless object as this Helen at such great cost. As it is, the negative consequences—and any imputation of folly or wrongdoing—are confined to the Trojans. In consequence, male splendor is detached not only from female splendor but from the ambiguities of the heroic battlefield. The justice of the Greeks' cause as instruments of Zeus's vengeance is left unsullied by the troubling implications of the countless Achaean deaths, and specifically the death of the magnificent Achilles, in the slaughter of the Trojan War.

It is impossible, however, to insulate such a highly selective account of a well-known story from the freight of tradition on which it draws and depends for its meaning. Merely by introducing the major players in this most familiar of tales, Alcaeus situates his Trojan War miniature in the context of the larger epic tradition. Yet specific poetic choices determine the degree to which any such rewriting reaffirms, questions, or complicates the larger picture to which it contributes. In this case, a striking Homeric allusion serves to challenge the deceptively simple dichotomy upon which the poem is built, drawing us back into the ambiguities of the Trojan War and hence of its human causes. The word *xanthos* evokes Achilles' famous chariot horses in the *Iliad*, one of whom was actually named Xanthos. These horses are mentioned several times in Homer, and in one extraordinary incident Xanthos miraculously speaks, predicting his master's death. Achilles responds, addressing the horse by name, and affirms his knowledge of his own impending death before driving the horses back into battle (19.404–24). Alcaeus's "tawny horses" thus allude not only to Achilles' heroic exceptionalism but also to his premature death. They alert us, moreover, to a more subtle Homeric resonance in the poem's blunt conclusion: the Trojans and their city perished "over Helen" (15). That same phrase is used in the *Iliad* to denote Helen's status as an object of male struggle, most notably in the duel of Paris and Menelaus, the scene above all others at which her beauty is on display (3.70, 3.91; cf. 3.157, 3.254).

These allusions suggest that neither the "good" and "bad" women nor their products—so starkly differentiated at the outset—can be separated as easily as the poem's structure might initially suggest. All three characters— Helen, Achilles, and Thetis—are essential players in Troy's destruction. Helen could not have engendered "bitter grief" for Troy without Achilles' agency, or without the marriage that produced him. Conversely, Achilles needs Helen's transgression to certify him as "finest" of the demigods while excusing him from blame for the devastation that underwrites his masculine heroism. The feminine superiority of his mother is likewise dependent on her destructive counterpart. Helen is not merely a foil who allows Thetis's virtues to be illuminated by opposition. Through her reproductive power—predicated here on passivity—the good woman becomes the indirect avenger of the bad woman's active transgression. That transgression is essential if Achilles is to display his supremacy, which in turn confirms Thetis's superiority as a mother. Nor would the Achaeans have fought "over Helen" had they not deemed her a worthy object of struggle. Thetis and Helen are thus mutually implicated in the glorification of Achilles. The poem that began by making Helen into a (mere) object of blame by eliding her beauty does not, in the end, deny her inextricable role in the production of male heroism.

Alcaeus wrote at least one other poem about Helen, of which we have only a fragment (fr. 283). The beginning and end are both lost, and there are many additional gaps and uncertainties:

> . . . .
> . . . .
> . . . and [Eros?] excited in her breast

the heart of Argive Helen; and driven mad
by the Trojan man, the host-deceiver, she followed him   5
over the sea in his ship,

leaving in her home her child [abandoned?]
and her husband's richly covered bed,
[since] her heart persuaded her [to yield?] to *erōs*
[through the daughter of Dione?] and Zeus . . .   10

. . . .
many of his brothers [the dark earth?]
holds, laid low on the plain of the Trojans
for that woman's sake,

and many chariots [crashed?] in the dust,   15
and many dark-eyed [Achaeans?]
were trampled, and the slaughter . . .
. . . [Achilles] . . .

This time Helen and Paris are both clearly to blame. The terms in which their roles are characterized are gender specific, as are the consequences. Paris violates the (masculine) social codes governing guest-friendship, which leads to the death of his brothers—to whom a man's loyalty should be paramount—whereas Helen violates her (female) obligations as wife and mother, betraying those to whom, above all, a woman should remain faithful.

Unlike poem 42, this fragment focuses on Helen's own role in the elopement. In contrast to the single reproachful epithet aimed at Paris, the "host-deceiver" (5), there is a detailed parsing of the complex of causal factors generating her action. This includes remarkably precise verbal echoes of Helen's own self-presentation in the *Iliad*, including the use of the active verbs "follow" and "leave," which in the epic, as we saw, are peculiar to her own voice (above, p. 65). The poet thus endorses Helen's Iliadic perspective on her own elopement, along with its implications for responsibility and blame. He has, however, appropriated her voice for himself, thereby denying her both the self-assertion of the epic and the remorseful context in which she locates her acceptance of responsibility. Nor, in contrast to the Homeric scene on the walls of Troy, is there any mention of her beauty or its impact (even on Paris). As in poem 42, there is no explanation of why men thought Helen worth fighting for. She is eroticized, this time, as a desiring agent, but not as an object of desire. Unlike Homer, then, Alcaeus refrains from displaying the power of Helen's beauty or of her voice. Unlike Homer's male characters, on the other hand, he does not hesitate to blame her.

This fragment also dwells far more graphically than poem 42 on the horrors of the war. After a few unintelligible words, we read of the destruction of

Greeks and Trojans alike. The noun described by the adjective "dark-eyed" (16) is missing, but in Homer this particular epithet is used exclusively for the Achaeans. It thus seems likely that, in contrast to poem 42, Greek warriors were specified along with Trojans as victims of the slaughter. This would suggest that all men, regardless of their differences, are victims of the lethal combination of Paris's treachery and Helen's infidelity.

Among these victims only Achilles is named (if, as many scholars think, his name should be supplied in line 18). Perhaps the complete poem picked him out from the anonymous mass of male dead and enshrined him as the hero whose life, as well as death, acquired special meaning through the Trojan War. But we cannot know this, since the text we have is so deficient. The proximity of his (reconstructed) name to the word "slaughter" is particularly tantalizing, since his precise relationship to that slaughter remains unclear. In any case, he is implicated somehow in the destruction. This may suggest a more Iliadic view of gendered causation and responsibility for the war than we saw in poem 42. In contrast to the *Iliad*, however, there is no indication, in the admittedly poor remains of our poem, of any compensating glory. If Helen's beauty is absent—as far as we can tell—from the fragment, so is the magnificence of heroic warfare.

One reason for this may perhaps be hinted at by a distinctive detail in this account of the war, namely the mention of Paris's brothers as victims. Alcaeus writes as a warrior-poet whose first allegiance is to his political "brothers." As in the case of Paris, the group of comrades with and for whom he fights is clan-based, and his literal brothers will have been prominent members of the group. This solidarity colors Alcaeus's relationship to the epic past. However eager he may have been to endow his own exploits with epic splendor, he could not accept a woman for whom a man betrayed his brothers as embodying the glory of that fight. More than this we unfortunately cannot say, given the state of the text.

Ibycus

Both of Alcaeus's Helen fragments tacitly acknowledge Helen's destructive power by holding her responsible for her actions, but remain silent on the extraordinary beauty that underwrites it. Her beauty does get mentioned, however, in a fragment attributed to Ibycus (S151). Ibycus was a south Italian poet who moved to the Aegean island of Samos some time in the early to mid-sixth century, probably during the youth of the Samian ruler Polycrates, to whom this poem is addressed. Ibycus was known for his erotic (especially homoerotic) poetry, which often included mythic elements. As we might expect, he seems to have found Helen a useful vehicle for this intertwining of erotic and legendary themes. Though most of his poetry is lost, we know that it included both Menelaus's loss of his sword at the sight of Helen (fr. 296) and the dispute over her that followed Paris's death (fr. 297).

The surviving portion of the Polycrates fragment—of which we have the end but not the beginning—opens in the midst of an account of the Trojan War:

> ... destroyed the great, most renowned, prosperous city
> of Priam, son of Dardanus,
> setting off from [Greece]
> by the plans of great [Zeus],
>
> enduring much-sung strife   5
> over the beauty (*eidos*) of tawny-haired Helen
> in tearful war;
> and ruin mounted long-suffering Troy
> through golden-haired Aphrodite.

Since the formal structure is of a kind typically used for choral poetry (with stanzas arranged in groups of three), some scholars have inferred that this song was intended for public performance by a group. But the structural argument is not conclusive, and the content suggests that it would be equally if not more at home at a symposium, especially the content of the final lines, as we shall see.

There is no way to determine how long the complete poem was, or how much was said about the war before our fragment opens. We simply come in on the Greeks destroying Troy in a war over "tawny-haired" (*xanthos*) Helen's beauty (5). This hair color—the same as that of Achilles' horses in Alcaeus 42—is associated in general with divine and noble characters. It gives Helen a touch of epic glamour and links her with "golden-haired" Aphrodite (9), specified here as the cause of Troy's "ruin" (*atē*). The word *atē* is often used for the erotic "madness" inflicted by Aphrodite on Helen and Paris, which may be hinted at here. In the next stanza Ibycus will blame Paris as a "host-deceiver" (11)—possibly in imitation of Alcaeus—but he ascribes neither blame nor action of any kind to Helen, who is simply identified with her beauty and objectified as the prize of male struggle.

By glorifying the war as "much-sung" (5) the author positions himself as a potential heir of—or rival to—the traditions of epic poetry. In keeping with this posture, the fragment's opening lines have a strongly Iliadic tone, which is sustained in the account of the war that follows—despite the poet's claim that this is not, in fact, his subject:

> But it is not [now] my heart's wish   10
> to sing of Paris, deceiver of his host,
> or of slender-ankled Cassandra
> and Priam's other children,

and the unmentionable day
of the capture of high-gated Troy;   15
nor shall I recount the extraordinary
excellence of the heroes whom hollow,

many-bolted [ships] brought
to be an evil for Troy—fine heroes.
They were led by lord Agamemnon,   20
descendant of Pleisthenes, king, leader of men,
fine son born to Atreus.

On these the skilled Muses
of Helicon might embark in story,
but no mortal man   25
. . . could tell each detail,

the [great] number of ships that came from Aulis
across the Aegean sea from Greece
to horse-rearing [Troy],
with men on board,   30

bronze-shielded, sons of the Achaeans;
among them foremost with the spear
[was] swift-footed Achilles
and great, valiant [Ajax] son of Telamon . . .
. . . .   35

The Trojan War is presented as an occasion of pride for those who undertook it, those "fine heroes" to whose "extraordinary excellence (aretē)" it gave rise (16–19). Agamemnon receives three lines of honorific description and the two greatest Iliadic heroes—Achilles and Ajax son of Telamon—are also specifically feted. The homage to the Muses and the heavily Homeric language, meter, and style help conjure a world in which Helen's beauty is indeed a worthy object of struggle and only the treacherous Paris is to blame.

The earlier insistence on the sufferings of "tearful" war (7) is equally Homeric, in its recognition of the high costs of heroic glory. It is the Trojans, however, who bear the brunt of those costs. The Greeks simply "endure strife" (6), but Troy suffers "ruin" (8), "capture" (15), and "evil" (19). A poignant note is introduced with the name of Priam's daughter Cassandra, who was famous both for her beauty—acknowledged here with the epithet "slender-ankled" (12)—and for her violent rape by the other Ajax, the son of Oileus. Both of the two exceptionally beautiful women named thus far—one Greek, one Trojan— are referred to in a manner suggesting that such beauty is problematic less because of women's own actions than because of the criminal male responses, whether Trojan or Greek, that it instigates.

Ibycus's celebration of Greek heroism is further complicated by its peculiar frame. The poet's claim that he does *not* want to sing about the war—in the middle of doing so—ironizes his relationship to the poetic renown of which he is an instrument. His tribute to the Muses is also notoriously difficult to interpret, thanks in part to a corrupt text. Is Ibycus saying, like the poet of the *Iliad*, that he sings with the Muses' help (thus equating himself with Homer and embracing the role of epic singer)? Or is he declaring that he cannot treat such grand themes because only the Muses are capable of doing so (thus distancing himself from epic practice)? Many scholars have taken the latter view, using the passage to interpret the whole elaborate opening as a rejection of heroic verse. But in Greek thinking, a need for help from the Muses is no reflection on the poet's own skill; on the contrary, the Muses' favor is a sign of his excellence. The structure of the poem, too, suggests not inferiority to Homer but a playfully competitive relationship. The poet demonstrates his ability to sing of epic themes in an epic style should he choose to do so, but eschews the role of epic poet for the moment in pursuit of rather different interests.

The nature of those interests emerges in the final triad, where the subject shifts from the Greek warriors' military prowess to their personal beauty:

> [With them also went] from Greece
> to Troy Cyanippus,
> the most [beautiful] . . .
> [and Zeuxippus, whom the nymph],
>
> . . . . golden-sashed   40
> Hyllis, bore [to Apollo?]; and to him
> they likened Troilus as gold
> already thrice-refined to orichalc,
>
> both Trojans and Greeks,
> judging him very similar in desirable form.   45
> Along with them you too, Polycrates,
> will always have imperishable renown for your beauty,
> just as my renown too will exist through song.

For Homer, Achilles was simultaneously the mightiest and the most beautiful of the Greeks. But Ibycus polarizes masculine beauty and military prowess in a movement that takes us out of the world of the *Iliad*. He bifurcates the excellence of the supremely heroic and beautiful Achilles, sharing it between the mightiest warrior (Achilles himself) and three exceptionally beautiful youths: two Greeks, named Cyanippus and Zeuxippus, and a Trojan, Priam's famously beautiful son Troilus.

The beauty embodied in these young men is decoupled from the heroic physical achievement of Achilles on the one hand, and from the destructive, "feminine" beauty of Paris on the other. Troilus is mentioned once, in passing, in the *Iliad* (24.257), but neither of the Greek youths is named in epic or is significant in our other surviving sources. The "most beautiful" Cyanippus (37) was a son (or grandson) of a king of Argos named Acastus. Of him the fragment has no more to divulge. Zeuxippus was a son of Apollo—the divine model of youthful male beauty—and of the "golden-sashed" nymph Hyllis. With Hyllis female beauty reappears, but this time harmlessly. There is nothing to suggest that Apollo's coupling with the nymph—unlike the notorious misdeeds of Paris and Ajax son of Oileus—is in any way problematic. As an embodiment of divine female beauty, Hyllis also provides an apparently innocent alternative to the troublesome Aphrodite of the fragment's opening. Her positive value as an object of male desire is further affirmed—as with Thetis in Alcaeus 42—through the production of an extraordinary son. In this case, however, that son is exceptional not for his valor but for the extraordinary beauty derived from his divine parents.

This successful coupling of two divinities paves the way, through the beauty of their offspring, for a poetic transition to a different kind of *erōs*. Zeuxippus's beauty is lauded by comparing him to Troilus. The Greek youth was not, it seems, *quite* as handsome as Priam's son, since he was like orichalc ("mountain-bronze") as compared to Troilus's 24-carat gold (41–45). Orichalc was precious and much admired, and often appears in the company of gold. Still, it is hard to believe that it was on the same level as "thrice-refined" gold, given gold's associations with royalty, beauty, and divinity. These associations have already been activated by references to "golden-haired" Aphrodite and the "golden-sashed" nymph Hyllis. Where erotic beauty is concerned, however, a young man, Troilus, turns out to be the gold standard. Nonetheless, Zeuxippus was definitely in Troilus's league: Greeks and Trojans alike judged the two youths "very similar in desirable form" (45). Like Helen in line 6, they are presented as beautiful objects to whom no action is ascribed. Their beauty seems to have been somehow on display at Troy for scrutiny, evaluation, and praise by warriors on both sides.

In a Trojan War context this public assessment of erotic beauty calls to mind both the Judgment of Paris and the Trojan elders' awestruck reaction to Helen when she appears on the walls of Troy to watch the duel, episodes demonstrating the destruction caused by the most beautiful females, divine and human respectively. The former led, of course, to the war, while the latter dramatizes the dispute between men that lies at its heart. Ibycus presents male beauty, by contrast, as a source not of conflict, but of congeniality. The assessment of the two youths' looks results in an apparently innocuous rivalry across army lines, as Greeks and Trojans alike assess the beauty of a Trojan and a Greek. The Greeks are even content to acknowledge that the ultimate standard of such beauty is Troilus, a Trojan. Helen's beauty, the cause of heroic but "tearful" warfare, is displaced in favor of an appreciation of male beauty that transcends hostilities, uniting Greeks and Trojans in harmonious admiration. No doubt Trojans and Greeks would also agree on the supremacy of Helen's beauty where women are in question, but in her case such universal admiration leads to carnage on both sides. Yet the struggle to possess her also provides, in Ibycus's poem, an occasion not for the possession but for the display and admiration of a beauty that is, if not more perfect, at least more worthy of poetic praise.

Viewed in its broader legendary context, however, a shadow lies over this universal admiration for Troilus's beauty. Achilles, mentioned just a few lines earlier, was presumably one of those who rated the youth so highly. Within the fragment as we have it these two characters are kept apart, standing as they do for two different kinds of manly excellence. Yet their stories were intimately linked. Our only reference to Troilus in the *Iliad* finds Priam lamenting the wartime death of his "most excellent sons," of whom Troilus is one (24.255–57). But as Ibycus's audience were well aware, the youth was killed by none other than Achilles, in a sanctuary of Apollo, thus angering the god. We are primed to recall this famous incident by the poem's earlier emphasis on the deaths of Priam's children (13), and probably also by a mention of Apollo, as the father of Zeuxippus, in the lines immediately preceding Troilus's name (41–42).

A tradition making Troilus a love object of Achilles is of particular interest here. It seems that the youth resisted Achilles' advances and died in his embrace. This creates a close parallel with the rape of the equally innocent Cassandra, Troilus's sister, which also took place in a sanctuary and incurred the wrath of the god in question (in her case Athena). We do not know whether the erotic aspect of Troilus's death was current as early as Ibycus, but we do know that Ibycus composed a poem about Troilus's death that included praise for the young man's beauty (S224). It may also be significant that in the Polycrates poem the beauty of the two young men (unlike Helen's) is explicitly eroticized, through the adjective "desirable" (44). And Achilles' absence from the catalogue of male beauties leaves him available to play the active role of lover.[4] The story is thus entirely consistent with the poem as we have it. If Ibycus's audience did indeed recall that Priam's famously beautiful son suffered a fate similar to that of his beautiful daughter, this would complicate the apparent transition from destructive heterosexual *erōs* to homoerotic camaraderie.

Regardless of whether the story of Troilus's death had already been eroticized in Ibycus's time, the fact that it occurred in Apollo's sanctuary at Achilles' hands was certainly well-known. Images of the scene show the youth essentially unarmed, and often attempting to escape. The incident, which cut short

---

4. Because of the asymmetrical structure of Greek homoerotic relationships, a focus on Achilles' beauty would posit him, instead, as a sexually passive love object (cf. Pl. *Symp.* 180a).

a potentially heroic career, was, by any account, one of Achilles' least glorious moments. By celebrating Troilus's beauty, however—even if that beauty led directly to his death—Ibycus rescues Priam's son from his truncated role in the *Iliad* and allows him to live on forever through the renown bestowed by poetry. In the earlier part of the fragment the poet showed his facility with Homeric themes and style; now he bestows "imperishable renown" (47) both on Troilus—whose beauty goes unmentioned by Homer—and on two otherwise obscure figures whom Homer neglected to mention altogether, suggesting that the epic has deficiencies that he is able to supply in his capacity as a homoerotic Homer.

This leads directly into the final anchoring of the poem in the present moment—the moment of performance—as the poet ranks the beauty of the young Polycrates with that of the three mythical youths. Thanks to the performer's song Polycrates too will win "imperishable renown" (*kleos aphthiton*) for his beauty (47). The phrase *kleos aphthiton* evokes the *Iliad*—specifically, Achilles' famous choice between "imperishable renown" and a safe journey home from Troy (9.411–16), which is the only place in Homer where this phrase appears. In Ibycus's poem Achilles is replaced by Polycrates, as the subject of immortalizing song, and Homer himself by Ibycus, whose poem will bring him poetic glory. By including his addressee alongside those whose beauty Homer unaccountably overlooked, Ibycus elevates him to epic status, tethering the present moment to the war not through glorious exploits but through shared appreciation of the male body.

By now Helen's beauty has been long forgotten, swiftly set aside after serving its purpose as an occasion for the display of male valor and male beauty alike. It serves these two purposes in rather different ways, however. The fragment's epic opening acknowledges the function of female beauty as the ground for heroic warfare. Such beauty also provides the occasion for the display of male beauty at Troy. Yet Helen is, in the end, irrelevant to the renown a man may acquire because of his own beauty, since this can equally be manifested in more peaceful contexts. The fantasy of homoerotic admiration under the walls of Troy is, in fact, especially well suited to the convivial environment of the symposium. At the court of Polycrates, which was notable for its homoerotic ambiance, the relative merits of beautiful boys would be a natural topic of conversation. In this kind of context the display of youthful male beauty has no life-or-death consequences. The poem's movement away from the epic battlefield thus looks like an implicit rejection of the more problematic arena for masculine glory that is symbolized by Helen.

As an agent of renown, however, the poet has more than one string to his bow. His own *kleos* is earned through his skill with verse (48), and much of the fragment shows him employing that skill to immortalize both the Achaeans and the "most renowned" city of Troy (2). It may not *now* be his wish—at Polycrates' symposium—to devote himself to a song about heroic exploits, but that does not prevent him from doing so in the future. In contrast to Helen or Cassandra, Polycrates' status as a beautiful object does not exclude him from heroic action. Even if he is still a lovely youth, he is not merely an object of desire but a budding ruler. If he resembles men whose beauty was displayed on the Trojan battlefield, then he is already of fighting age. And if he resembles Troilus, he may hope for a more fortunate future than Achilles' beautiful victim; indeed, he may aspire to exploits as splendid as those of the epic hero himself. The various warriors conjured at Troy leave open an array of possible futures for Ibycus's noble addressee. The recording of such exploits lies, however, in the hands of the poet, who ends the song with an emphatic affirmation of his *own* glory.

Sappho

Alcaeus holds Helen responsible for her actions but elides the beauty that might suggest she is worth fighting for. Ibycus makes her beauty the prize of heroic struggle but attributes no agency to Helen herself and ends up displacing her beauty in favor of that of men. Helen's beauty makes a more prominent appearance, however, in a poem by Sappho, Alcaeus's contemporary and fellow Lesbian. A number of Sappho's fragments draw on Iliadic or Helenic themes, including the marriage of Hector and Andromache (fr. 44), Leda discovering an egg (fr. 166)—presumably laid by Nemesis—and a tantalizing mention of Hermione and Helen, which seems to posit Helen as the ultimate standard of female beauty (fr. 23). This interest in Helen is hardly surprising, since Sappho's poetry is characterized by an intense focus on Aphrodite, beauty, and female eroticism. Though her poems were composed for various settings (including weddings, for example), many were probably intended for performance at the closest female equivalent of the symposium: a single-sex gathering where women of various ages constructed and celebrated an idealized formation of their gender, class, and way of life, in part through exclusion of the other gender.

The poet's most substantial fragment dealing with Helen is Sappho 16. It is probably a complete poem, though there are several small gaps and a larger one in the middle:

> Some say an army of cavalry, others of infantry,
> and others of ships, is the most beautiful thing
> on the black earth, but I say it is whatever
> one passionately desires.[5]

5. The verb is *eratai*, cognate with *erōs*.

It is perfectly easy to make this understood   5
by everyone; for she who far surpassed
humankind in beauty, Helen, leaving
her most [excellent[6]] husband

went (*eba*) sailing to Troy;
she gave no mind at all to her child   10
or dear parents, but [*erōs*? Aphrodite?] led her astray . . .
. . . .

. . . .
lightly . . . [and she?] . . . .
puts me in mind of Anactoria   15
who is not here;

I would rather see her lovely walk (*bama*)
and the bright sparkle of her face
than the Lydians' chariots and infantry
in their armor.   20

This poem resembles Alcaeus 42, structurally as well as thematically. It begins
and ends with images of military splendor, which the speaker rejects but which
frame the central account of Helen's transgression. Alcaeus 42 likewise begins
and ends with warfare, this time linked with Helen, who is disparaged in favor
of Thetis and her son, celebrated at the center of the poem. And just as Alcaeus's praise of Thetis and Achilles depends ultimately on the Helen, whom he
rejects, so too Sappho's preference for Anactoria turns out to be harder to disentangle from warfare than may be apparent at first glance. This is in large part
due to Helen's presence, as we shall see.

The poem's opening stanza seems to challenge the typical Greek view of
beauty as an objective quality, by denying that it can be measured by an impersonal standard. Yet Sappho goes on to affirm the supremacy of Helen's
beauty among all mortals. Helen is used, however, to exemplify not the power
of (her own) beauty over men, but the power of Paris's beauty, and thus of
erōs, over her. Her exemplary role thus depends only indirectly on her own
beauty. Just as Paris's personal beauty qualified him to judge the three goddesses, Helen too is an expert, needing no credentials to illustrate Sappho's
novel definition beyond her own supreme possession of the quality in question. That supremacy is stated, however, without qualification, creating a certain tension with the initial denial of objectivity.

Yet that denial is not as simple as it looks. It cannot *simply* mean that (physical, erotic) beauty is in the eye of the beholder, since Sappho exemplifies the

---

6. The text of this line is uncertain, but some superlative is indicated.

point by means of mythic figures whose exceptional beauty is universally acknowledged. The problem is eased, if not exactly solved, if we bear in mind the ancient presumption that *erōs* is in its very essence a response to beauty (itself conceived of as an objective phenomenon). To say that what is most beautiful is whatever one desires is not to deny that there may be certain objects that are desired by (almost) everyone, thus attesting to their superior beauty. By using the supremely beautiful Helen to make her point, Sappho reinstates the view that some people are more beautiful than others because more desired. Even while she avoids using Helen as an absolute standard of beauty, then, she exploits the fact that she is precisely this. If Helen had been beautiful only to one personal lover, the image would lose its point. Since she is, however, the most desired of all women, then by this Sapphic logic she is indeed the most beautiful of all.

From this perspective, to say that what is most beautiful to any one person is whatever she or he desires is a truism or even a tautology. Since no one in life (as opposed to legend) is perfectly beautiful, disputes will naturally arise about the relative beauty of particular love objects. But that does not rule out independent assessment of who is, in fact, more beautiful. The most beautiful is, objectively speaking, the one who inspires the most intense *erōs* in the largest number. Most assessors will, of course, claim the superiority of their own love object, but they will typically do so by invoking conventional tropes to enumerate her or his charms. What is it, after all, that arouses *erōs* on Sappho's account, if not the presence of objectively specifiable qualities? The absent Anactoria's "lovely walk and the bright sparkle of her face" (17–18)—her movement and flashing eyes—are familiar signifiers of erotic beauty, for which Helen is an archetype. Though the text of the fourth stanza is sadly shredded, it may be Helen herself who moves "lightly" and brings Anactoria to mind (15). Anactoria's movement, in any case, evokes Helen's through a distinct verbal echo. Helen's signature verb "she went" (*eba*) (9) is picked up by Anactoria's "walk" (*bama*) (17). It is by participating in Helen's iconic beauty that Anactoria arouses *erōs* in the poem's speaker, which in turn makes her, in the latter's judgment, "the most beautiful thing on the black earth."

In contrast to Helen, however, Anactoria has only one person (as far as we know) who desires her and thus finds her most beautiful. Exalting the subjectivity of beauty therefore works to her disadvantage—and to the disadvantage of any real person as compared with Helen. This is where Sappho's assertion of Helen's supreme beauty plays an essential role, allowing her to exploit objective as well as subjective notions of beauty and thus imply that her praise for Anactoria is more than mere personal preference. Anactoria—a particular human love object, otherwise unknown to us—benefits from her implied likeness to Helen, famed as the most beautiful of all. Like Ibycus, though more subtly, Sappho enhances the splendor of a desirable contemporary by equating her with the mythical gold standard of beauty for her gender. This strategy collapses if Helen's absolute beauty is called into question. Her legendary status allows her to occupy a paradoxical position as *the* most beautiful woman, while at the same time symbolizing the impact of different embodiments of female beauty on individual lovers. Where women are concerned, Helen *is* the Sapphic "whatever one desires."

Despite Anactoria's likeness to Helen, the speaker of this poem also implicitly identifies herself with Helen, as a desiring agent, and Anactoria with Paris, as the "most beautiful thing" that she desires. Yet the alignment is not a straightforward one. The poet shows no sign of following her absent beloved over the sea. It is not only Anactoria's beauty but her departure from her lover that makes her the Helen of this tale, leaving the speaker to play the role of the abandoned Menelaus. As such she evinces a loyalty that distances her from the fickle Helen. Whereas Helen "gave no mind at all" to her loved ones (10–11), something—perhaps Helen herself—puts the speaker "in mind" of Anactoria (15–16). Her praise of the "most excellent" Menelaus underscores her own impeccable innocence in this role. But since she has no fleets or armies at her disposal (not to mention the social and ethical firepower to launch them), she has no choice but to remain a Penelope, a woman who— unlike Helen—does not forget. However much she may identify with Helen as a desiring subject, she eschews the transgressive behavior provoked by that desire.

Is it really true, however, that Helen's act is presented with disapproval in this poem? Many scholars have argued, to the contrary, that Sappho is celebrating the active assertion of female desire. Certainly, the poem emphasizes Helen's erotic agency to an unprecedented degree. Like Alcaeus in his fragment 283, it does so in part by appropriating aspects of Helen's own voice from the *Iliad*. Line 11, damaged though it is, clearly states that something—probably Eros or Aphrodite—"led [Helen] astray," the verb evoking her Homeric relationship with the goddess (cf. *Il.* 3.400–401, *Od.* 4.261–62). As in Alcaeus, the active participle "leaving" (7) echoes Helen's "leaving" in the *Iliad* (3.174). Sappho's "went" (9) echoes, in addition, the Homeric Helen's "I went" (*Il.* 24.766). And like Alcaeus, Sappho mentions the child and husband that Helen left behind (8, 10), adding for good measure the parents for whom Homer's Helen is filled with longing (11; cf. *Il.* 3.140). The poem thus resembles Alcaeus 283 in drawing upon Helen's own perspective in the *Iliad*, by acknowledging her transgression while ascribing it to a combination of divine influence and her own agency.

In comparison with Alcaeus, however, Sappho puts considerably more emphasis on the latter. She does so largely by demoting Paris from Alcaeus's active "deceiver of his host" to the nameless object of Helen's desire. Alcaeus's Helen "followed" Paris "in his ship" (283.5–6), but Sappho's simply "went sailing to Troy" (9). Both of them suffer the intellectual and ethical impairment caused by erotic passion, but whereas Alcaeus's Helen was (with a passive verb) "driven mad" by Paris (283.4), Sappho's simply "gave no mind" to her child and parents (10–11). Sappho focuses on the abandoned former husband, not the irresponsible new one. Paris is the man that Helen desired and thus, for her, the "most beautiful thing," but he is not explicitly identified as such. Nor is there any trace of the contempt she expresses for him in the *Iliad*, which would imply active responsibility on his part. He goes unnamed—and unblamed—in the fragment as it stands.

Sappho's choice of the grammatical neuter for the love object in line 4 ("whatever" one desires, not "whomever") contributes to the implied objectification of Paris, who, as the object of Helen's desire, sets her in motion without any indication of agency on his part. It was (probably) not Paris but Aphrodite or Eros who "led her astray" (11), presumably by holding out an alluring vision of Paris's beauty, as Aphrodite does in Homer (*Il.* 3.390–94). Paris thus exercises the passive power that beautiful women wield so often, with or without their consent—the kind of power the Trojan elders attribute to Helen in the *Iliad*. The declaration of Helen's own surpassing beauty opens her to the prospect of objectification in her own right, but this prospect is left unacknowledged. Unlike Alcaeus or Ibycus, Sappho insists in the strongest terms on Helen's beauty, but she conveys its erotic power only obliquely, by asserting the beauty of anything that arouses *erōs*. She ostentatiously avoids presenting Helen as a (destructive) object of male desire, instead allowing her to retain both her beauty and her agency.

Despite this clarity of focus where Helen's agency is concerned, the poem nowhere blames her for the devastation of the Trojan War. Where Alcaeus suppressed the power of her face and presence, listing only the destructive consequences of her behavior, Sappho underlines her beauty while eschewing any mention of the war. To focus on the domestic dimension of Helen's transgression without mentioning the military consequences is not, however, to excuse it. The voice Sappho borrows from Homer is Helen's own, that is, the Homeric voice most strongly associated with blame. Her enhanced emphasis on Helen's (sole) agency increases the burden of that blame. The verb "led astray" (11) clearly indicates wrongdoing on her part. And abandoning one's husband, home, and family is intrinsically blameworthy, a fact underlined both by the Homeric reminiscences and by the parallels with the accusing Alcaeus.

Helen's guilt is, in fact, enhanced by subtle departures from the Homeric subtext. In the *Iliad*, Iris makes Helen miss her "former husband, city, and parents" (3.139–40), and she herself speaks of her bedroom, relatives, child, and female companions (3.174–75). But Sappho goes further. She omits the Homeric Helen's reference to her "city," adds the intensifying adjective "dear" for her parents, and even includes a superlative adjective for Menelaus qua husband. In the *Odyssey*, Helen complimented her husband as "by no means lacking in either wits or beauty" (4.264), but Sappho is more positive in her praise. That praise is, moreover, granted the authority of the narrative voice, in contrast to the *Odyssey*, where Helen's self-serving words stand in tension with the larger epic picture of Menelaus as a less-than-superlative hero. Sappho's adaptation of Homer thus casts Helen's actions in a distinctly negative light, creating a sharp disjunction between beauty and manly excellence and informing us that the beautiful Helen, desiring the beautiful Paris, gave excellence short shrift.

There are subtle differences, too, between Sappho's presentation of Helen's offense and its portrayal by Alcaeus. Whereas Alcaeus emphasizes home and marital sex (the husband's bed) as the site of Helen's offense (283.7–8), Sappho stresses the quality of the man she left and the larger familial community, natal as well as marital. She focuses, that is, on factors that exacerbate the transgression from a female point of view. Alcaeus, by contrast, has no interest in her natal family and no compliments for Menelaus. Men despise men who cannot control their own wives.

If Sappho's poem does not excuse Helen for violating the bonds of family, however, it does not on that account endorse men's use of that violation as a ground for war. It begins by rejecting military splendor—the beauty of armies and ships—and ends by declaring the poet's beloved more desirable than chariots and armed men. These military references are not tied explicitly to the Trojan War, but both of them evoke it, especially considering Helen's presence in their midst. The Trojan War was, of course, renowned for the size of its army and the number of its ships, and chariots have an epic grandeur, enhanced here by the association with Lydia, a wealthy, non-Greek land near Troy. The immediate effect of rejecting these symbols of male glory is not only to avoid coupling Helen's deed with the war but to repudiate heroic warfare as an object of desire.

The speaker does not deny, of course, that for those who do desire such things, a splendid army is indeed "most beautiful." The same internal logic explains the Achaean pursuit of Helen, insofar as she is the object of their collective desire. It was *erōs* for the surpassingly beautiful Helen that set in motion the very ships, chariots, and armies repudiated at the opening of the poem and again at its close, making these rejected comparanda themselves proof of her beauty's supremacy. But if Helen found Paris too beautiful, perhaps men find both Helen and the war that she stands for too beautiful as well. Alcaeus, whose reference to chariots in fragment 283 echoes (or is echoed by) Sappho, blames both Paris and Helen for the consequences of their desire, but does not seem to call into question the resulting male desire for Helen or for "chariots"— chariots that end up crashing in the dust (283.15–16). Sappho, who focuses exclusively on Helen's agency in the elopement, nevertheless avoids blaming her for the male response. If men chose to retrieve her at any cost, that is not, perhaps, a consequence for which she should be held accountable.

☙

Stesichorus

Like Ibycus, Stesichorus came from the Greek west, in his case Sicily. He lived around the same time as the Lesbian poets, but in contrast to their short lyrics he composed long narrative poems, probably for public performance. His poetry was apparently a kind of lyric epic; that is, it treated epic themes in extended lyric form.

Almost all Stesichorus's work has been lost, but it seems to have covered most of Helen's story, including the oath of the suitors, her marriage to Menelaus, and her abduction by Paris. One fragment, in which a group of men drop the stones with which they had intended to kill her (fr. 201), suggests that he extended Menelaus's failure to kill her at the sack of Troy to all the Greeks. Another striking fragment maintains that Aphrodite punished Tyndareus for a failure to sacrifice by making his daughters "twice-married and thrice-married and husband-leavers" (fr. 223). It is hard to map these epithets precisely onto Tyndareus's various daughters, but any or all of them could apply to Helen. A fascinating anecdote reports, however, that after Helen became a goddess she blinded Stesichorus in punishment of such "abuse" or "slander." Blinding is an emasculating gesture, often inflicted on mortal men by wrathful goddesses, but it seems particularly apt to Helen, given the intimate and powerful associations between *erōs*, beauty, and vision.

Even though this incident was famous in antiquity, the surviving evidence for it is inconsistent, obscure, and tenuous. The most detailed account comes from Plato's *Phaedrus*, where Socrates asserts:

> For those who err in telling stories there is an ancient purification, of which Homer was not aware but Stesichorus was. When deprived of his eyesight because of his slander of Helen he did not fail to understand the cause, like Homer, but because he was favored by the Muses (*mousikos*) understood it and immediately composed these lines:
>
> > That story is not true;
> > you did not go in the well-benched ships;
> > you did not reach the citadel of Troy.
>
> After composing the whole of the Palinode, as it is called, he at once regained his sight.
>
> (243ab)

Judging from this story, Stesichorus is the first author we know of to make an explicit project of defending Helen. The means by which he does so is quite striking. He does not argue that she was an innocent victim of abduction, or that her elopement was justified, but denies, in his "recantation" (the literal meaning of the word "palinode") that she went to Troy at all. One may blame Helen, it seems, simply by attesting to her traditional actions, for which she is presumed to be both responsible and culpable. Stesichorus therefore "defends" her by repudiating those actions altogether. The newly virtuous Helen is defined in negative terms, by denying her Homeric self's transgressive agency ("You did *not* go, you did *not* sail"). By demanding a retraction of the deed that made her infamous, the goddess underlines the importance of erotic agency to the epic Helen's identity, since this is the key factor that must be denied. Her reputation can be saved only by refusing her an active role in her own story. Such is the price she pays for Stesichorus's defense.

It might seem to follow that the Trojan War did not take place, but interestingly, this is not the case. It is apparently impossible to deny that the war occurred at all, or even that it was fought over Helen. This creates an obvious problem for Stesichorus, which he seems to have solved by introducing an *eidōlon*, a visible image or double of Helen created by the gods to fulfill her traditional function.

Helen is not the only mythological character to be replaced, on occasion, by a divinely fabricated *eidōlon*. Such doubles are, among other things, a time-honored device for protecting the honor of a goddess by preserving her from the shame of rape by a mortal. They are typically made by Zeus, and his usual construction material is "cloud." When the impious Ixion tried to have sex with Hera, for example, Zeus replaced the goddess with an *eidōlon*, described by the poet Pindar as a "cloud," a "sweet falsehood," and a "beautiful disaster," which resembled the goddess in *eidos*—"appearance" or "beauty" (*Pyth.* 2.36–40). Despite their fictitiousness, such images succeed in deceiving the man in question, and are, as one scholar delicately puts it, "physiologically functional." After Ixion has sex with Hera's double, it actually gives birth to a monstrous offspring named Centauros (the ancestor of the centaurs). Stesichorus uses Helen's double, similarly, to preserve her reputation.

The motif of the double seems especially appropriate in Helen's case. Her story is replete with doubling, from her two fathers to her twin brothers to her two principal husbands to the two sons of Atreus who went in pursuit when she eloped. She is also, at times, an emblem of illusion, and her signature feature, her beauty, is itself a form of potentially delusive mirage. The word *eidōlon* is closely related to *eidos*, which means "appearance" or physical beauty (as in the Pindar passage just quoted). When Ibycus speaks of the warriors at Troy fighting over Helen's beauty, *eidos* is the word he uses (S151.5). It is a short step from conceiving of that beauty as the cause of war to the notion of fighting over an *eidōlon* identical in appearance. As the linguistic connection suggests, visible beauty is the essence of Helen's double, enabling it to fulfill the purpose for which Zeus traditionally created her. Conversely, the beautiful Helen is herself an illusion, insofar as she embodies not a real woman but an idea—the idea of the most beautiful woman in the world. There is a sense, then, in which even the "real" Helen is essentially an *eidōlon*, since she stands for something that no flesh-and-blood woman can ever be. As later writers would see, it is not difficult to interpret the Trojan War as a battle over a mirage.

By shifting the burden of the Trojan War onto the double's inhuman shoulders, Stesichorus left the "real" Helen's beauty unsullied by misbehavior, thus satisfying the indignant goddess. This kind of rehabilitation was not required by the dictates of Greek religion. Gods and heroes alike were well-known for shocking misdeeds of every kind. But the gods are not exempt from moral judgment, and human anxiety about their misbehavior was increasing in the archaic period. Moreover, sexually transgressive *female* divinities had always been a matter for concern. Aphrodite, for example, dallies with various lovers, blithely disregarding her marriage to Hephaestus, but that does not stop him from reproaching her as a "dog-eyed" adulteress and doing his best to control her behavior (*Od.* 8.306–20). Goddesses do have more power and freedom than mortal women, but there is still a definite sexual double standard on Mount Olympus. Stesichorus's tale makes the goddess Helen complicit in this policing of the divine female.

If Helen did not go to Troy, where did she go? Obviously, she could not be left in full view at Sparta while her husband sailed off after her double. The evidence is tenuous, but it seems most likely that Stesichorus had the gods transport her to Egypt. He must have done *something* with her, and this is the most plausible solution. Egypt was a mysterious, marginal land, already linked with Helen through the *Odyssey*. What better place for her to wait out the Trojan War while her traditional story was on hold? There she presumably remained until Menelaus could pick her up on his way home after the war. Subsequently she was immortalized, to reappear as the goddess of Stesichorus's tale. Freed both from her role in human narrative and from the constraints imposed on mortal women, she can now take active control of her poetic reputation by supernatural means.

The substance and structure of Stesichorus's Palinode are almost entirely lost to us. Plato's brief quotation is the only certain fragment, and other sources that mention the poem are both confused and confusing. It seems likely, however, that the poet's encounter with the goddess was originally reported within the Palinode itself, with Stesichorus first recounting and then recanting Helen's traditional tale. If so the poem's very form enshrined her ambiguity, articulating the dual urge to blame and exonerate her by literally splitting her in two and allowing her to serve as her own foil. Regardless of the Palinode's form and content, however, the story *about* it—which may have been better known than the poem itself even in antiquity—exposes many aspects of Helen and her myth to scrutiny.

Plato's anecdote makes explicit, to begin with, the widespread impulse to use Helen as a vehicle for articulating an author's relationship to Homer. That relationship was particularly intimate in Stesichorus's case. He was known in antiquity as "most Homeric," and an epigram even fetes him as Homer's reincarnation (*Anth. Pal.* 7.75). The stance of the Palinode story is confrontational, however, reflecting the competitive spirit that marked Greek literary and intellectual traditions from the outset. Plato's Socrates frames the tale as a demonstration of Stesichorus's superior insight and poetic skill (he is, by implication, more "favored by the Muses" than the benighted Homer). And when the poet concedes to the goddess, "You did not go," he is directly contradicting Homer's Helen, who used the same verb to declare, "I went" (*Il.* 24.766). By denying that the "real" Helen ever spoke such words, he exposes the epic Helen as a Homeric fiction—a poetic double. The authority for this exposure is Helen herself, who appropriates the role of epic Muse both by guaranteeing the "truth" of the poet's words and by striking him blind, as the Muses did Demodocus (*Od.* 8.62–64). It is this that allows Stesichorus to reject Homer's Muse-sanctioned version of events.

By choosing Helen as the ground on which to negotiate his relationship to Homer, Stesichorus underlines her centrality to the epic tradition. As we saw, he makes her elopement *the* defining event of the Trojan War—the event that must be repudiated in order to assert his own poetic superiority. Yet there is also a sense in which he leaves the epic intact. The Palinode story changes nothing about Homer's account of the Trojan War besides Helen's ontological status. Unfortunately, we know nothing specific about Stesichorus's treatment of the *eidōlon.* But in order to fulfill its function it presumably looked and behaved exactly as Helen always did. If we are to believe the Palinode, none of these behaviors was—despite appearances—an expression of human agency. But the Helen who spent the war in Egypt ends up exercising superhuman agency as a goddess. Stesichorus transmutes the threat and allure of the beautiful but transgressive woman into a different kind of double-edged power, the power of a retributive divinity to control mortals at her pleasure.

The bonds that contained Homer's human Helen, as an object with highly circumscribed agency who yet has supernatural power over men, have thus ruptured to reveal its component parts: a powerless object, created by gods and fought over by men, and a mighty goddess who controls their lives. These two Helens oppose each other on multiple axes: they are not only divine and mortal but active and passive, virtuous and transgressive, beneficial and destructive, powerful and powerless, avenger and victim. Both of them derive from aspects of the epic Helen, yet both are utterly different from her—not least because neither is human, and neither is to blame for the war.

The story also implies the existence of a third Helen, the human wife of Menelaus, who sat out the war in Egypt while remaining faithful to her husband. This virtuous Helen is present in the Palinode anecdote only through her absence, as the negation of the Helen who went to Troy. But she probably played a more substantial role in the Palinode itself, which seems to have been quite lengthy and may have had much to say of the human Helen's adventures. Based on what little we know of it, however, the only action that can be plausibly attributed to this Helen is her marriage to Menelaus, an event that was presumably central to establishing her character as a "good" woman. The meager evidence for this scene (frr. 187, 188) has nothing to say about the bride, but its tone—fruit, flowers, luxury—is similar to that of other wedding poetry. We saw in Alcaeus 42 how a woman's wedding may be used to define her as "good," and may perhaps imagine the wedding of the Palinode in similar terms.

There remains an unresolved tension, however, between the faithful wife of Menelaus and the divinity that she becomes. Nowhere in our sources is the goddess who punishes Stesichorus presented as the apotheosis of a virtuous wife. There is no mention of Menelaus in any surviving version of the story, and in one account her anger is actually reported to the poet by a messenger from White Island, where she is living with Achilles after his death (Paus. 3.19.11–13). This version underscores Helen's serial polyandry at the precise moment when she is objecting to its immortalization in epic. Another of our sources, a speech by the fourth-century rhetorician Isocrates, takes it for granted that Helen *did* go to Troy with Paris. Isocrates does not treat the goddess's wrath as grounds for rejecting Homer, but goes on to report a competing anecdote in which, far from objecting to the *Iliad*, she herself commands Homer to compose it (below, pp. 242–3).

At this point we may be starting to wonder whether Helen the goddess protests too much. It would certainly not be out of character for her to manipulate the poetic tradition in her favor. A concern with her own reputation is already visible in the Homeric Helen, who "weaves" her own story in the *Iliad*, does her best to present herself in a good light, and displays, in the *Odyssey*, an uncanny skill at deceptive imitation that evokes her half sisters, the Muses. As a full-fledged goddess, she has acquired a Muse-like divine power that allows her to control her story more effectively. But the Muses are known for their ability to inspire falsehood as well as truth. In other words, we need not take Stesichorus too literally when he declares Homer's story to be untrue. Like the epic poet himself, he is presenting us with an artfully constructed Helen on whom we may or may not choose to rely.

Be that as it may, the story of the double that went to Troy remains parasitic on the Homeric original, which it leaves intact as a story, thus reinscribing what it would deny: the Trojan War was caused by the gods, using an embodiment of extraordinary female beauty created for that purpose. The Helen whose beauty overpowers and destroys men persists in the person of the double, to whom the epic heroine's well-known adventures must be attributed. Even though, superficially, the Palinode story declares this transgressive woman an illusion, the good wife the reality, in this fundamental respect the virtuous Helen is a mere fantasy and the *eidōlon* the "real" Helen of Troy.

Yet the anecdote also implies that there is no such thing as the "real" Helen. Homer's Helen is exposed as a fiction, making the double, as a fabricated object, an analogue for the poet's own production. Meanwhile, the goddess Helen provides Stesichorus with a convenient divine cover for his bravura reinvention of tradition. It is no coincidence that the story illustrating her power demonstrates, at the same time, his own superior insight and poetic skill. He outdoes Homer not only by realizing what he must do to cure his blindness, but also by creating a new and better Helen. If the gods can construct Helens at their whim, so can Stesichorus, along with Homer and every other poet, create and re-create new Helens for purposes of his own.

The disparate nature of the poems grouped under the rubric of "lyric," dispersed as they are in place, time, poetic type, and social function, precludes any neat summary of Helen's role, attesting rather to her flexibility as a vehicle for an array of artistic and cultural concerns. She makes her next major appearance in a more cohesive genre, one that, though broad, rich, and varied, is nevertheless tied closely to a particular place, period, and mode of performance, and engages, in consequence, with a specific set of historical and cultural circumstances: Athenian tragedy.

6

Behind the Scenes: The *Oresteia*

> When you start out as a kid, sin just doesn't seem like that big
> of a deal. It looks kind of cute, in fact. Warm and fuzzy. But
> sin is designed to destroy you. And you feed this baby long
> enough and he's gonna grow in your life until you got yourself
> a tiger by the tail, and you don't know which end is up. And
> what used to seem very innocent now controls your life.
>
> —*Jesus Camp*

Helen enjoys a varied and extensive presence in Greek tragedy, thanks largely
to the playwrights' continuing engagement with the Trojan War as a paradigm
for heroism and a source of Greek identity. In contrast to Panhellenic epic,
however, and the disparate fragments of lyric, tragedy was the distinctive product of fifth-century democratic Athens, and as such a highly culturally specific
art form.

Athenian tragedy was not an elite mode of entertainment but a spectacle
for the citizenry at large. Audiences were engaged and enthusiastic, and participation in the chorus was an important civic obligation. Most of our surviving
plays were presented at the Greater Dionysia, a festival in honor of Dionysus,
god of wine, masking, and shifting identities. Dramatic performances in the
Theater of Dionysus were preceded by ceremonies celebrating the *polis* and
promoting the ideology of Athenian democracy, especially the solidarity of the
democratic citizen army (in contrast to the individual pursuit of *kleos* found in
Homer). The names of civic benefactors, to be honored by the city with the
award of a golden crown, were announced in the theater to encourage public
service in others, and the sons of men who had died in battle were paraded
wearing armor granted to them by the *polis*.

Drama offered its audiences a new way—literally—of viewing legendary
figures. In contrast to epic and lyric poetry, which are mediated by a single
performer, theatrical characters are physically present on the stage and address
each other face-to-face. The playwright and director still control the story, of

course, deciding who is to speak, sing, or move, and how. They are also free to privilege, undermine, or withhold particular points of view. Nevertheless, the characters have become "people" present to our eyes and ears. Drama thus presents itself as less mediated than other genres, providing the illusion of direct access to figures from the past.

At the same time, drama is always, by definition, an imitation of something else, leaving the audience well aware that the characters are fabricated objects and they themselves not "really" seeing the events before their eyes. This awareness was reinforced, in Greek drama, by conspicuous stylization in every aspect of the performance. Theatrical masks (which covered the whole head, with hair attached) were not grotesque, but they were simple and conventional. Characters were not differentiated by subtle "realistic" details. Rather, broad traits such as age, social status, and gender could be read from basic markers that would be clearly visible in the enormous theater—primarily hair length and color, skin color, and dress. The actors, who were all male, used stylized gestures and performed in counterpoint with a singing, dancing chorus, which was also made up of men. The poetic script, especially the lyric portions, departed from the language of ordinary life through meter and elevated diction. Such conventions inform the spectators that they are in the world of legend, and underline the nonreality of events on stage.

Tragedy thus conveys a sense of unmediated "reality" while simultaneously raising questions about the relationship between the seen and the unseen, the real and the imaginary. This epistemological tension lies at the heart of theater as an artistic form. As a result, drama more than any other genre obliges us to confront the paradox of female subjectivity as a product of male-authored discourse. "Female" figures as well as male could be seen moving and speaking on the Greek stage. Yet they were created by male actors speaking a male-authored script to a notional audience of other men.[1] Every masked and costumed female represented on stage is a kind of Pandora: an artificial woman constructed by males to serve a male agenda.

Classical Athens shared the pervasive Greek preoccupation with gender and warfare that gives Helen her perennial allure. It is, indeed, at Athens that these concerns are most visible to us, since it is the source of so many of our surviving texts. But they are refracted in those texts, including tragedy, through the historical circumstances—political, military, intellectual, and artistic—that shaped Athenian ideology in the fifth century BCE. That century was dominated, at Athens, by two great wars. The Persian Wars, in its early decades, constituted an encounter between Greeks and non-Greeks, or "barbarians," for which the Trojan War provided a ready-made template. The last thirty years of

---

1. The notional audience is the audience to whom a work appears to be addressed by the implied author, in this case the male Athenian citizen body. The actual audience for tragedy may also have included others, such as women, foreigners, and slaves.

the fifth century were consumed by the Peloponnesian War, between Athens and Sparta, which Athens finally lost—like Troy in the Trojan War—after a long and grueling struggle. In contrast to epic, where the Trojan War is a heroic struggle confined to the distant past, Athenian treatments of the legendary war are always filtered through this contemporary lens, giving a visceral immediacy to the old questions about warfare and heroism. These questions are also fundamental to masculine identity, a subject with which tragedy is much preoccupied, especially since the rise of democracy for male citizens meant—paradoxically—increased anxiety about the visibility and sexual power of women. It is therefore hardly surprising to find tragedy, as a genre, distinctly hostile toward Helen.[2]

To the best of our knowledge, Helen did not appear on the tragic stage in propria persona until 415 BCE, in Euripides' *Trojan Women* (below, chapter 9). Prior to that date, however, the playwrights were happy to give the stage to her detractors. This does not mean men are excused for their role in the Trojan War. In tragedy, there is plenty of blame to go around. The problematic decision to go to war over Helen, played down in Homer, is highlighted in tragedy, often by focusing on the sacrifice of Iphigenia. Many plays also insist on the brutality of what followed, especially the ruthlessness of the final sack of Troy. But such blame does not detract from Helen's culpability. The Greek atrocities are rendered all the more despicable by the oft-lamented fact that the war was fought "just for a woman." This dismissive phrase, while it demeans Helen as casus belli, also draws attention to the huge gulf in magnitude between cause and effect, and with it to male responsibility. Blackening Helen makes the men who desired her still more culpable; conversely, the more one blames them, the less reason one has to affirm her worth.

The earliest tragedy dealing with Helen to survive, and one of the most powerful and disturbing, is Aeschylus's *Agamemnon*, which was produced in 458 BCE as the first play in his trilogy, the *Oresteia*. The basic plot is simple. Agamemnon returns home to Argos victorious from the Trojan War, only to be killed by his wife, Clytemnestra, in revenge for the sacrifice of Iphigenia (an event recalled for us by the chorus, which is composed of old men loyal to the king). Clytemnestra's lover, Aegisthus, assists in the planning of the murder, but it is she who wields the sword. She also kills Cassandra, Priam's daughter, whom Agamemnon has brought home as his slave-concubine. At the heart of the play lies Clytemnestra's hypocritical welcome of her returning husband, whom she persuades, against his better judgment, to enter the house walking on the kind of fragile, precious fabrics that should be reserved for honoring the gods. There he meets his end, ignominiously, in the bath, where Clytemnestra

---

2. The sole exception is the subject of chapter 10.

stabs him after first disabling him with an enveloping garment. At the dramatic climax she reemerges from the house with the corpses, her husband's dead body still tangled in the fabric used to trap him.

In the *Oresteia*'s second tragedy, *Libation Bearers*, Agamemnon's son Orestes returns from exile and avenges his father's death by killing both his mother and Aegisthus. The play ends with his incipient pursuit by the Furies, demonic female divinities who punish mortal crimes, especially the shedding of kindred blood. In *Libation Bearers* the Furies are visible only to Orestes, but in the final tragedy, *Eumenides*, they appear in person as the dramatic chorus. In the course of this play, they pursue Orestes to Athens where he is defended by Apollo, his protector, at the hallowed Athenian court of the Areopagus. His trial, which takes place under the auspices of Athena herself, inaugurates the institution of trial by jury—one of the proud achievements of democratic Athens and a distinctive aspect of its political culture. The human vote is split down the middle, but Athena casts a deciding vote for mercy. In the denouement of the entire trilogy, the goddess convinces the Furies to abandon their wrath at losing their case and become incorporated into Athenian cult as beneficent divinities. Their new role is reflected in the title attached to the play, *Eumenides*, which means "kindly ones." The trilogy ends with a celebration of Athens, which the newly benevolent Furies shower with blessings.

The overarching theme of the *Oresteia* is justice, human and divine. Clytemnestra's murder of her husband is the first stage in a development that takes place, in the course of all three plays, from the justice of personal revenge to the climactic institution of legal justice. The chain of crime and punishment haunting the house of Atreus reaches an end only when justice is taken out of the hands of the injured parties and entrusted to the impersonal process of trial by jury. This central theme is placed in a grand metaphysical, ethical, and theological framework, especially in *Agamemnon*, by the complex and extensive ruminations of the chorus. The sequence of crimes is portrayed as the work of a family curse, transmitted from one generation to the next quasi-genetically, of fate, or of an evil spirit that dogs the house. The impact of these superhuman forces is powerfully conveyed through layers of interconnected imagery, especially the persistent symbolism of trapping and constraining fabrics. Nevertheless, as usual in Greek thinking, the human beings who commit these crimes remain responsible for their own actions.

Helen is a persistent background presence in *Agamemnon*, evoked compellingly by the chorus in their songs. But she does not appear as a character, nor do we hear her voice. Menelaus, we are informed, has disappeared in a storm on the way home from Troy, presumably taking her with him. Though doubtless still alive, she is nowhere mentioned in the real time of the drama. Deprived of a dramatic presence, this Helen is also deprived of the opportunity to seduce or mollify those who would blame her—including the theatrical audience—thus leaving the field open for her enemies and rendering the audience receptive to their point of view. Clytemnestra dominates the drama with her extraordinarily powerful voice and presence, but her sister remains a mysterious background presence, a creature of the imagination whose power consists in her elusiveness. Clytemnestra is a visible embodiment of female evil, Helen a sinister shadow lying behind—and inseparably linked with—her half sister.

Clytemnestra is introduced—though not named—by the watchman who speaks the prologue, who informs us that he was set at his post by "the ruling of a woman's man-planning heart" (10–11). Helen is first mentioned some fifty lines later, equally namelessly: Zeus sent the army to Troy "over a many-manned woman" (62). These pithy descriptions echo each other verbally, pairing the sisters while contrasting them as two different kinds of threat to the Greek gender system: one woman who thinks like a man, another who marries many men instead of one. Clytemnestra disrupts the order of things by exercising political power ("ruling"), Helen by making herself a source of male dispute. The sisters thus represent two different types of dangerous female: the aggressive, violent woman with a "manly" heart, and the elusive, fickle, but beautiful one with the traditionally feminine power of erotic allure. Their complementary roles are summed up by the chorus after Agamemnon's death: "He endured much for the sake of a woman, and at a woman's hand he lost his life" (1453–54).

Despite the obvious differences between them, the two sisters are assimilated to each other in many ways. Even their destructive methods are not as divergent as they may at first appear. The chorus equate the "feminine" Helen with her violent sister, as we shall see, and Clytemnestra herself is far from simply "masculine." She is not only prone, like Helen, to unbridled sexual desire, but highly adept at exercising certain forms of "feminine" power. She uses textiles to entrap Agamemnon, both literally (in the bath) and figuratively (by luring him to walk on the precious tapestries), and her speech of welcome is a masterpiece of mendacity. She assures her returning husband that she is a good wife, a "watchdog" of his house, loyal and sexually faithful (606–10)—the converse of her sister. But since we know full well that she is lying, this self-description serves the opposite of its superficial purpose, assimilating her to Helen instead of distancing her. When the chorus call her a "duplicitous keeper of the house" (155), the phrase could just as well apply to Helen.

Most fundamentally, both sisters act independently of men, whom they treat as replaceable and dispensable, refusing to allow their own desires to be subjected to male constraint. Instead, they turn the tables and control their husbands in ways that are tailored to the men's characters as well as their own. Like their wives, Menelaus and Agamemnon are a closely linked yet divergent pair. Agamemnon, as the elder brother, takes responsibility for the expedition to Troy, but they are characterized as "yokemates" (44) and even live together as joint kings (apparently an innovation by Aeschylus). As with the sisters, however, one brother is central to the dramatic action while the other remains a shadow in the background, his absence strongly marked (617–33, 674–79). Like the women, too, the brothers who married them represent different but related models of gender failure. Each in his way is symbolically emasculated by his troublesome wife. The manly man married the manly woman, whom he leaves at home to make mischief; when he returns, his wife reduces him to what he himself objects is a womanly status by persuading him to walk on the tapestries against his better judgment (918–19, 927–28). Clytemnestra visibly controls the stage, specifically the threshold of the palace and with it Agamemnon's movement to his death. Meanwhile the softer brother married the "feminine" woman with even more disastrous results.

Menelaus's inability to control his wife leads to Helen's abduction, which links the criminal history of the house of Atreus with the Trojan War. The offense of Paris is presented as a violation of guest-friendship through "theft" (402, 534), which has incurred the wrath of Zeus and is justly punished by the assault on Troy. The abducted Helen is, however, no mere plundered object but an emphatically transgressive agent. The chorus use a whole series of active verbs for her departure, including the recurrent three that seem to convey the essence of her transgression: "leaving," she "went," and "sailed away" (403, 407, 691). In contrast to most of the characters she seems unrestricted by the entanglements of fate, as symbolized by constraining fabrics. She simply slips away on the breeze through delicate veils, undeterred by the "curtain" of modesty (690–92). She is a dream or a winged creature that her husband cannot hold (420–26). As such she just "goes," without deliberation or compulsion, stepping "lightly" through the gates of his house (407–8). Even Paris is a boy chasing a flying bird (394).

When Helen arrived at Troy, as the chorus tell it, the Trojans, like the elders in the *Iliad*, looked upon her with delight and awe—at least in the beginning:

> At first I would say there came
> to the city of Troy a temper
> of windless calm,
> a gentle treasure (*agalma*) of wealth,
> a soft arrow cast from the eyes,
> a flower of *erōs* to pierce the heart.
>
> (738–43)

The effect of this passage is brilliantly conveyed by the great German scholar, Eduard Fraenkel, in his magisterial commentary:

> The important thing here is the avoidance of the person. The
> contour of the human figure is effaced, the bounds of her personality
> seem to be widened while first a mood, then a delight, then the arrow

of the eyes, and lastly the fullness of the charm living in the flower take her place. . . . The individual traits combine to form a figure whose many-coloured bewitchingness, gentle and at the same time powerful, lays the hearer under its spell. The air of impersonality, of super-personality, raises Helen above the merely human, removes her from among her kind, and brings her close to unknown Powers.

The flower that pierces the heart and the dangerous glance of the eye, two species of oxymoronic "soft weapon," are metonyms for Helen. Though her paternity is not mentioned anywhere in the trilogy, her deadly eyes evoke no less a power than her divine father, Zeus. In describing the sack of Troy, the chorus affirmed earlier that Zeus himself shot an unerring arrow at Paris (362–66). Later they sang of the thunderbolt flashing from his eyes, which destroys the high and mighty (468–70). As for the piercing flower of *erōs*, they will echo this image after the murders, declaring that the bloodshed has given Helen a wreath of flowers with which to adorn herself (1458–60; quoted below, p. 131). Her beauty does not merely bring men disaster, it seems, but actively thrives on their destruction.

This combination of beauty, power, and bloody slaughter is expressed memorably through a graphic image offered by the chorus just prior to describing Helen's arrival at Troy:

> A man once reared within his house
> the offspring of a lion, deprived
> of milk but longing for the breast,
> at the beginning of its life
> tame, loved by children,
> and bringing joy to the old.
> . . . .
> But it showed in time the character
> passed down by its parents;
> repaying its nurturers with gratitude
> it made, unbidden, a feast,
> along with sheep-slaughtering ruin (*atē*);
> the house was soaked with blood,
> an insurmountable grief for the household,
> a great calamity, murdering many;
> through a god a sacrificial priest of Madness (*atē*)
> had been reared within the house.
>
> (717–22, 727–36)

This disturbing picture forms part of a pattern of lion imagery running through the drama. In their account of the sacrifice of Iphigenia, the chorus mention lion cubs among the wild young creatures loved by Artemis (141). These cubs symbolize the dangerous wildness of the *parthenos*, who lies under this goddess's protection and must be tamed through marriage. The subsequent image of Helen, as a charming cub that seems tame at first but grows up and runs amok, conveys vividly the threat to a man's household of taking in such a creature as a bride. She is another Pandora, or Trojan Horse, who becomes, in the chorus's image, a priest of Madness or Ruin (*atē*). The *atē* from Aphrodite that took Helen to Troy, rupturing her husband's household, is transformed into the mindless savagery of a wild beast that tears a household to pieces quite literally. Later the lion appears as a symbol of war and even of victory over Troy, when Agamemnon portrays the Greeks sacking the city as a lion lapping up "the blood of kings" (825–28). This echo of the slaughter perpetrated by the lion in the house reinforces Helen's responsibility for the bloodshed at Troy. At the same time, it clearly anticipates Clytemnestra's act of domestic slaughter. Cassandra will actually characterize Clytemnestra as a "two-footed lioness," who sleeps with a wolf while the lion, her proper mate, is absent (1258–60), intertwining lion imagery with sexual infidelity in a manner that evokes, once again, the "lion cub" Helen.

Helen's alleged responsibility for the entire war is powerfully expressed in another choral passage, where the destruction of ships and cities is designated as the meaning of her very name. In a dazzling series of neologisms Aeschylus puns on the similarity between "Helen" and the Greek verb *helein*. This word means "take," but can also signify "capture" or "kill." It is often used for the overwhelming power of erotic desire, such as the *erōs* that overcomes Anchises at the sight of Aphrodite (*HH* 5.91), or Paris at the sight of Helen in the *Iliad* (3.446). Aeschylus's chorus extend that power beyond such erotic "capturing" to the literal destruction of the Trojan War. Dwelling on the ominous correctness of the name "Helen" (*Helenan*), they say it must have been assigned by a god, since she was *helenaus helandros heleptolis*: "taker of ships, taker of men, taker of cities" (681–90). The threefold sequence of epithets provides an interpretation of Helen as actively destructive in her very essence. It also has incantatory force, since name play and the number three are often used in magic (cf. above, p. 83). The effect is to present Helen as a superhuman force for destruction.

At the climax of the drama, when Clytemnestra emerges from the house with the bodies of her victims, the chorus seem to attribute to Helen not only active agency but sole responsibility in causing the countless deaths at Troy and even the death of Agamemnon, with which she might be thought to have very little to do:

> Woe! Woe! Demented Helen,
> who alone destroyed the many,
> so very many lives at Troy!

Now you have adorned yourself with the ultimate flower-garland,
   unforgettable,
through blood that cannot be washed out.
Truly there was then in the house
a force for strife, a husband's lamentation.

(1455–61)

Although Helen's behavior is just one of many threads in the web of causation that generates the drama's horrors, no blame is voiced here for any of the male participants. She is presented not as a disputed object of male strife but as the essence of strife itself.

By holding her responsible for the entire sequence of events, Aeschylus's chorus treat Helen as the fundamental initiating force of destruction, linking all the events of the Trojan War and its aftermath into one tidy causal chain. Clytemnestra responds by defending her sister:

Do not turn your wrath against Helen
as a man-killer, saying that she alone
destroyed the lives of many Greek men
and brought about their pain.

(1464–67)

This moment of female solidarity is intriguingly reminiscent of Penelope's "defense" of Helen in the *Odyssey* (above, p. 93). It presumably serves here as a way of insisting, albeit obliquely, on the Greek men's own share of responsibility for the slaughter, in particular Agamemnon's murder of their daughter. The chorus ignore her objection, however, and respond by pairing the sisters as actively murderous agents. The evil spirit oppressing the house exercised its power, they say, through both women alike, who are each other's equal in destructive, "ruling" temperament (1468–71). Their equation of the sisters makes Clytemnestra into a visible manifestation of the abstract, superhuman force for evil betokened by very the name of Helen.

This privileging of Helen's role seems disproportionate, to say the least. Yet it does have a certain logic. Her elopement is the only offense in the sequence that is in no way reactive or vengeful. She is therefore, in a significant sense, the beginning of the chain of crime and punishment that led up to Agamemnon's death. Even Clytemnestra can legitimately claim to be an instrument of divine justice (1432–33), but no such argument is available to Helen. Yet it takes two to elope. Unlike Helen, Paris is assigned virtually no explicit blame for the bloodshed of the war or its aftermath (as opposed to the "theft" that began it). Willful, destructive agency is projected not onto the man who actively seduced a married woman, but exclusively onto the woman who responded by "leaving" her husband's house. The chorus transform this departure into the slaughter of thousands, as if Helen had personally fought at Troy, then go even further, to hold her responsible for the deed of her sword-wielding sister. By blaming the adulterous wife for the murderous wife's act, they imply that killing a husband is less heinous than abandoning him.

These choral lyrics, with their dense, complex diction and imagery, paint a surreal picture of Helen as an evil and horrifying yet enchanting figure who transcends the limitations of human life. Her absence from the stage facilitates this imaginative hyperbole, allowing Aeschylus to use the very concreteness of theater to express the idea of Helen as an elusive, magnetic force. Despite the shocking nature of Clytemnestra's murders, her violence is limited by its literalness, its consequences displayed visibly on stage. Helen committed no such act of violence. Since we neither see nor hear her, however, Aeschylus is free to exploit and reinterpret the supernatural penumbra that clings to her mythic persona, portraying her as an abstract force for evil that transcends the boundaries of a single embodied person. Like the mysterious charm from which it is inextricable, the horror of Helen is conveyed through a poetic allusiveness that depends for effect on her absence.

The specific character of that superhuman power is conveyed through its impact on her husband. Menelaus is presented, for the first time in our surviving texts, not only as a victim of Paris's violation of guest-friendship but as a specifically *erotic* victim of Helen herself. As such he is thoroughly emasculated. The effect of the light-footed Helen on her husband is a kind of paralysis. When the chorus describe his condition after her departure, they use the words of certain unnamed "spokesmen" of the house—presumably because Menelaus is unable to speak for himself, or unwilling to emerge and speak in public:

> Woe, woe for the house, for the house and its rulers!
> Woe for the marriage-bed and the man-loving footsteps!
> We can see the dishonored silence of one
> abandoned, not reviling, not beseeching.
> Out of longing for her who is beyond the sea,
> an apparition will seem to rule the house.
>
> (410–15)

The focus here is exclusively on the pathetically abandoned husband, who has suffered a deeply personal loss. We hear nothing of Helen's child, her parents, her other relatives, or friends. In contrast to the two adulterous women, and even Agamemnon with his concubine, Menelaus treats his wife as a unique and irreplaceable treasure. He sits at home, in the female domain, consumed by longing, silent and passive. It is Agamemnon who subsequently takes action and mounts the expedition to Troy "on account of Helen" (800).

As the chorus continue, they eroticize Menelaus's longing for Helen more explicitly:

> And the charm of her graceful statues
> is hateful to her husband;
> in the absence of her eyes,
> all Aphrodite has departed.
>
> (416–19)

The palace is apparently decorated with statues of Helen, presumably in tribute to her beauty and her husband's devotion. Yet such lifeless images cannot
supply her absence, since they lack the glancing eyes where Aphrodite dwells.
Unlike these dead, immobile artifacts the living Helen has departed, taking
Aphrodite with her and leaving Menelaus himself as motionless and silent as
a statue. The Helen he desires is the Helen who can reciprocate his glance and
with it his desire. Such reciprocity, in happier times, is conveyed by describing
Helen's footsteps as "man-loving" (*philanores*) (411). Since the word "man" in
Greek can also mean "husband," the phrase may allude to a bride's arrival at
her bridegroom's house or a wife approaching her husband's bed. In either
case, it conveys Helen's active desire. That desire is, in this report, directed at
Menelaus, but the word "man-loving" is general enough to hint at the risk of
infidelity.

Dreams provide another inadequate substitute for Helen's presence. In
his dreams, Menelaus sees his wife "lamenting" (420)—suggesting perhaps,
that in his wishful imagination she has repented and misses him, as in Homer.
But this brings him only "empty delight," a false vision that eludes his grasp
and "is gone" (420–26), the verb echoing Helen's own departure (407). Even
as an "apparition" (*phasma*), however, Helen still seems to rule over his house
(415). The word *phasma* often indicates a powerful supernatural presence,
notably that of a god or hero appearing in human form (cf. below, pp. 160,
229). Helen's "apparition" exists only in her husband's mind, yet its enchanting
spectral power seems to be even more spellbinding than her physical presence. This experience is replicated in the audience, insofar as our desire to
see Helen's ineffable beauty and hear her seductive voice remains, like his,
unsatisfied.

It is this desire for Helen's presence that drives the Trojan War. Despite the
drama's heavy emphasis on justice, there is no doubt that the war is also fought
"for the sake of a woman" (62, 823, 1453). From the perspective of the kings'
subjects, this makes their royal masters' motivation both personal and trivial,
and Menelaus's desire for the absent Helen as ignoble as the passion of Paris
and Helen itself. The chorus's account of his misery is pointedly juxtaposed
with the suffering that the war has brought to every house in the "land of
Greece" (*Hellanos aias*) (429–31). The word *Hellanos* resonates with Helen's
name, and *aias* evokes the sound *aiai*, an extremely common exclamation of
inarticulate grief. Their wording thus underlines through soundplay the intimate link between Helen and the sorrows of Greece as a whole. They go on to

report the people's bitter resentment that so many died "for another man's woman" (448–49), a phrase indicting not only the woman in question but the men who thought her worth pursuing at such enormous cost in other people's lives.

The Greek kings' quest is thus motivated not only by justice but by uncontrolled passion. Menelaus's passion is his demeaning desire for Helen, but the leaders collectively are driven by an equally ruinous passion for warfare and plunder. Both the death of Iphigenia and the appalling slaughter at Troy are equated, through patterns of repeated imagery, with the erotic transgression of Paris and Helen. The lion cub image, in particular, links Helen's elopement with the carnage at Troy, and the characterization of Paris's offense as "theft" (402, 534) of a precious treasure (*agalma*) (741) assimilates it to the killing of Iphigenia, who was likewise a "treasure (*agalma*) of the house" (208). Clytemnestra herself, speculating about the sack of Troy, warns that the Greeks should not yield to the lust (*erōs*) to violate what should not be violated, "conquered" by a desire for gain (341–42). Needless to say, no such warnings are heeded. The excessive violence that does eventuate at Troy is a manifestation of the evil spirit hanging over the house, to which Clytemnestra attributes an *erōs* of its own for "lapping blood" (1478)

Aeschylus further undermines the splendor of the Trojan War by providing a "democratic" perspective on the doings of the aristocratic characters. We have already seen the general resentment reported by the chorus. This is complemented by the herald bringing the news of Troy's fall, who prefaces his celebration of Greek victory with a detailed account of the miseries of war from an ordinary soldier's point of view: wretched shelters and bedding, rain, dew, lice, cold, heat (551–66). The kings' lust for warfare, and for Helen, is challenged, implicitly, by the humble herald's *erōs* for his homeland (540)—a longing reciprocated by his fellow citizens (544). This places the pursuit of Helen—the ultimate aristocratic treasure—into a class framework that would resonate with Aeschylus's theatrical audience, the citizens of democratic Athens. It is no accident that the resolution of these destructive passions, in the final play of the trilogy, will be closely bound up with the institutions of Athenian democracy.

According to the prophet Cassandra, even the most successful mortals are but shadows, the others easily erased (*Ag.* 1327–29). The shadowy Helen seems, in *Agamemnon*, an exception to this rule, her absence heightening her power over events in which she takes no physical part. As the trilogy progresses, however, that power is undermined and displaced by a very different symbol of female power and its ambiguities: the Furies.

Furies are demonic underworld goddesses of revenge. They pursue and punish human beings for certain crimes, especially kin-murder, visiting offenders with madness and horrible disfigurement. Aeschylus portrays them as ghastly hounds tracking the scent of human blood, who eat their victims alive and drink their blood. This makes them a sinister embodiment of the "blood-lapping" spirit that hangs over the house of Atreus (*Ag.* 1478). As such they are emblematic of— and instrumental in—the entire sequence of vengeful murderers that runs through the trilogy (cf. *LB* 283–84, 402–4, 577–78). But they are identified primarily with female revenge. At the end of *Agamemnon*, Clytemnestra asserts that she slaughtered Agamemnon as a sacrifice to a Fury (1433), and Aegisthus calls her entrapping fabric "the Furies' woven snare" (1580–81); in *Libation Bearers* the chorus identify her with a Fury herself (652); Orestes, caught between the vengeful wrath of both parents, fears the Furies of both, but after he kills his mother they become strongly associated with her cause.

In *Agamemnon* Helen, too, is likened to a Fury (*Ag.* 749). This is in keeping with the way the Furies' destructive effect is described, which parallels that of *erōs* in general and Helen in particular. Their archenemy Apollo sneers that they belong in the den of a blood-drinking lion (*Eum.* 193–94), linking them not only with the "blood-lapping" *erōs* of the family curse but with the lion cub that stands for Helen. Like *erōs* they inflict psychological blindness or "madness" (*atē*) (*Eum.* 376) and cast a spell of mindlessness that damages the wits (*phrenes*) (*LB* 1023–24, 1056; *Eum.* 328–33, 341–46, 377). And like Helen they wander unconstrained over land and sea, inducing men to do the same (*Eum.* 75–77, 250–51). In other ways, however, their effect is the inverse of erotic. They disfigure their victims' flesh with a foul disease (*LB* 278–82), blight them with infertility (*Eum.* 785, 815), shroud them in darkness (*Eum.* 378–80), and drain them of joy and vigor (*Eum.* 299–302, 422–23). Their own appearance is equally devoid of Helenic charm. Like a beautiful woman, they are a "wonder" to look upon (*Eum.* 407; cf. 46), but this is because of the terror they inspire (*Eum.* 34). According to a famous anecdote, during the play's first performance pregnant women in the audience suffered miscarriages at the sight of them. Regardless of the truth of this improbable claim, it attests to the Furies' extraordinary theatrical impact.

How was that impact achieved? As ancient goddesses the Furies are repeatedly described as "old," but this was probably not reflected in their appearance (divinities do not typically age). Their faces, like other theatrical masks, were probably simple and stylized, awe-inspiring but dignified and neutral in expression, like the stern-looking Furies represented in figure 6.1. Such neutrality allows the playwright to use the script to convey aspects of the characters— such as facial expressions—that would be imperceptible to the audience because of the size of the theater and inflexibility of the mask. Greek dramatic texts regularly appeal to the imagination in this way, telling us what we are looking at even if it is not actually visible. Conversely, we see what we are told to see. Cues in the script, including the reactions of other characters, prompt us to project emotions such as joy or sorrow, arrogance or fear, onto the neutral and unchanging mask. This synergy between the verbal and the visible allows the spectators' perception of the characters to be shaped by the text, and if necessary to shift as their role develops—something that will turn out to be important in the case of the Furies.

Despite the simplicity of their masks, however, the overall appearance of Aeschylus's Furies was clearly unusual. Athena herself says they look unlike "any kind of thing that is begotten," whether god or mortal (*Eum.* 410–12). They lack, in particular, the normal signs of femininity. They have dark skin (*Eum.* 52), which is typically a feature of male masks, in contrast to the lighter complexion associated with women. They may also be wearing short outfits suitable to their role as hunters (like the first Fury in figure 6.1), which would, again, mark them as "masculine." Though virginal (*Eum.* 68–73, 213–16), they lack the charm of the *parthenos*. They are described paradoxically as "aged girls," "ancient children" (*Eum.* 69), and "children who are not children" (*Eum.* 1033), the last of which could also be translated "childless children." This repeated use of oxymoron vividly conveys the Furies' asexual nature. They embody childhood and old age at once, without the eroticism of the bride or the fertility of the mature woman that should lie between. Their strange appearance

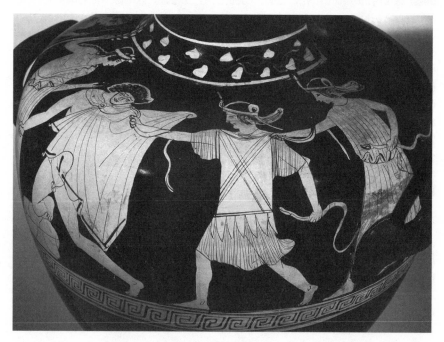

FIGURE 6.1 Two Furies pursuing Orestes, who takes refuge with Apollo on the left. The first wears a short, cross-belted hunting outfit, and the second a long tunic of a kind worn by women. Attic red-figure hydria, mid-fifth century BCE. Berlin, Antikensammlung, Staatliche Museen F 2380; *ARV*² 1121.16; BAD 214834. pbk, Berlin/Johannes Laurentius/Art Resource, NY.

negates the standard conventions of female beauty, depriving them of erotic allure and removing them from the realms of sex and reproduction. As Apollo puts it, with characteristic spite, there is no one—god, mortal, or beast—who "mingles" with them (*Eum.* 69–70).

The Furies are not supposed to be merely asexual or unfeminine, however, but viscerally repulsive. We are prepared even before their entrance for the horror their appearance is intended to elicit. In *Libation Bearers* Orestes, the only person who can see them, describes them as a terrifying vision. His words are echoed and reinforced in the prologue of *Eumenides*, when Apollo's priestess, the Pythia, describes the Furies sleeping inside his temple. After finding them there (offstage), she reenters crawling on her hands and knees, so shocked is she at the sight:

> They are black, and completely repulsive;
> they are snoring with unapproachable blasts;
> from their eyes a loathsome liquid drips;
> their adornment (*kosmos*) is of a kind not rightly brought
> near images of the gods or into human homes.
>
> (*Eum.* 52–56)

These particulars provided by the Pythia, and reiterated throughout the text, focus primarily on features associated with female erotic beauty, which also happen to be the most conspicuous aspects of any theatrical figure: eyes, cheeks and hair, clothing, movement, and voice. Their "black" skin is the opposite of the fair complexion associated with such beauty. Their eyes ooze a foul liquid, probably blood (cf. *LB* 1058). They produce inarticulate, animal-istic snores, grunts, and whines (cf. *Eum.* 117–32). They are "adorned" with dark clothing (cf. *LB* 1049, *Eum.* 370), which betokens mourning and death and hence should not be brought into temples or homes. They themselves declare that they eschew white garments (*Eum.* 352), which connote, in con-trast, rejoicing and festivity. Their accessories are not golden wreaths or bracelets but snakes (*LB* 1049–50), twined either in their hair or around their arms (as in figure 6.1). Their singing and dancing are not erotic or charming but angry and terrifying (*Eum.* 328–33, 341–46, 370–76). In sum, they embody the polar opposite of feminine beauty.

Despite this horrifying appearance, however, the Furies have the potential to bring great benefit. Their mandate, as they see it, is to enforce justice (*Eum.* 538–65)—the theme of the trilogy as a whole. They are concerned, more specif-ically, with the three fundamentals of traditional Greek morality: respect for gods, parents, and guest-friendship (*Eum.* 269–72). The fear they inspire is fear of punishment for violating these sacred norms, a fear that is, as they rightly insist, essential to an orderly and prosperous society (*Eum.* 517–37). Avenging such violations makes them a force for good. This is affirmed at the end of the trilogy when Athena, who agrees on the importance of fear, estab-lishes the court of the Areopagus for this very purpose (*Eum.* 696–706). By doing so she embeds the Furies' central function into the institutions of dem-ocratic Athens. In recognition of this role they are transformed into benevolent Eumenides, or "Kindly Ones," and duly installed in Athenian cult. They are to wander no more, but live henceforth in a sacred cave, where they will sit on shining thrones receiving honors from the citizenry (*Eum.* 804–7). The play ends with a procession of the united Athenian people escorting the Furies to their new home (*Eum.* 1038, 1045).

The events of the trilogy, initiated by Helen, thus end with the embrace of a very different kind of "beautiful evil." The Furies are externally repulsive, but when their power is properly harnessed it serves the purposes of moral "beauty." In an inversion of the pattern exemplified by both Helen and Pan-dora, whose physical beauty brings disaster by arousing men's desire, the Furies' production of moral "beauty" depends on their physical repulsiveness and the terror it inspires. They thus retain the ambiguity associated with female power. They can still curse as well as bless, give joyful songs to some and tears to others (*Eum.* 953–55). But that power is now turned to beneficial ends. Athena commands them to keep destructive forces down below, while sending up benefits for her city (*Eum.* 1006–9). Prosperity will ensue, provided the Athenians abide by the values the Furies are entrusted with policing.

The transformation of the Furies into Kindly Ones is conveyed visually on stage by giving them dark-red garments to wear for the final procession (*Eum.* 1028–29). This honorific clothing evokes the wearing of red tunics by resident aliens at the great Athenian festival of the Panathenaea. It thus marks the Furies' incorporation into the fabric of civic life. Their new garments, which are probably long enough to cover their dark, "masculine" attire (like the tunic of the second Fury in figure 6.1), serve to reverse Clytemnestra's destructive use of woven fabric in a manner befitting their new status as dig-nified female divinities. The Furies' masks, however, remain unchanged. Their faces are still frightening, as they must be if they are to fulfill their ben-eficial function (*Eum.* 990–91). But the simple stylization of the theatrical mask lets the playwright guide the audience to perceive them in a new way. The Furies do not, of course, become erotically beautiful, but we hear no more of the revolting language used for them earlier. They are addressed in digni-fied terms (*Eum.* 951) and invoked, at the trilogy's conclusion, as "august goddesses" (*Eum.* 1041)—one of their honorific titles in Athenian cult. In vivid contrast to the revulsion conveyed at the outset by the Pythia's crawling entrance, the final procession escorting the Furies offstage dramatizes their embrace by the people of Athens.

In the course of the trilogy, then, the two sisters likened to Furies for their ruinous power fade from view to be replaced by actual Furies, visible on stage. Clytemnestra is reduced, in *Libation Bearers*, from a murderous dramatic force into a frightened woman who has lost control and ends up as a murder victim herself. In *Eumenides* she fades further, into a ghostly presence who speaks only a few plaintive lines. At the beginning of the play she scolds her Furies into action (*Eum.* 94–116), but in the end her authority over them is trumped by Athena. Abandoning their loyalty to Clytemnestra, her Furies submit to Athena's persuasive offer of special honors and a home at Athens. That offer is backed by a discreet threat of force, available to Athena from her father, Zeus (*Eum.* 826–28). Zeus is Helen's father too, of course, but we hear nothing of that in the *Oresteia*. Athena is Helen's opposite, an eternal virgin who remains loyal to the male. She casts her vote in favor of Orestes because she has no mother (having been born from her father's head) and therefore favors the male in all things (*Eum.* 735–40). In the denouement of the trilogy she co-opts Clytemnestra's Furies and replaces her as the acceptable face of the authoritative "masculine" female, a role made possible by her divinity.

Helen, too, is displaced dramatically. Though she never appears on stage, in *Agamemnon* her nonpresence is exploited, as we saw, to endow her with a disturbing degree of supernatural power. The Furies supersede her, however, as the trilogy progresses. In *Libation Bearers* she is mentioned nowhere, not even in the chorus's extended denunciation of women's *erōs* (*LB* 594–630). In the final scene of this second play the Furies, visible only to their maddened victim, Orestes, take on Helen's role as a mysterious, terrifying offstage force that drives men insane. In *Eumenides* she goes unmentioned once again, while the Furies emerge onto the stage, appropriating her spellbinding superhuman power along with Clytemnestra's impressive voice and presence.

The Furies who displace both sisters embody, in their own way, the threat of female power. But their rehabilitation reverses the destruction that has pervaded the trilogy. Their collaboration with Athena puts a stop to the sequence of evils begun by Helen and continued by Clytemnestra, neutralizing the threat that each, in her way, represents, and restoring the norms of marriage, family, household, and society. Helen ruined the house of Atreus, while continuing to rule over it as an emasculating "apparition," but the Furies punish the overthrow of houses (*Eum.* 354–59), and in the future no house will prosper without them (*Eum.* 895). Helen's lack of self-control destroyed men's minds and lives, but the Furies, through the fear that teaches self-control, promote the healthy "wits" that bring prosperity (*Eum.* 517–21, 536). The slaughter wrought by the lion cub is replaced, in the trilogy's closing scene, with life and fertility of plants, animals, and people. These gifts are bestowed by blessings from the rehabilitated Furies (*Eum.* 903–12, 922–26, 938–48), including a blessing on marriage between men and "desirable" young women (*Eum.* 956–60). The honors they receive in return will include sacrifices before marriage and childbirth (*Eum.* 834–36). Only now that these repulsive creatures have been incorporated into Athens is the threat of female beauty contained and the institution of marriage turned to its civic function of fertility.

The principal object of *erōs* is henceforth to be Athens itself. Athena insists that even the Furies, if they chose not to stay, would miss this land and suffer *erōs* for it (*Eum.* 852), reminding us of the herald's nostalgia for home while away at Troy (*Ag.* 540, cf. 544). Her words anticipate Pericles' famous exhortation to the Athenians, in the funeral speech ascribed to him by Thucydides, to "fall in love" with their own city (Thuc. 2.43.1). This patriotic *erōs* supersedes not only the deadly passion of Paris and Helen but the *erōs* for blood attributed to the demonic spirit of the house (*Ag.* 1478). In the men of Athens, such passion for self-destructive strife is henceforth to be replaced by a "terrible *erōs* for glorious renown" (*Eum.* 865)—that is, for the glory of warfare, now untainted by sexual transgression, child-murder, or revenge beyond the call of justice. The martial goddess Athena will grant her people victory in war (*Eum.* 913–15), and the Furies will endow them with heroic manly excellence (*Eum.* 1031). The masculine glory so severely compromised by the circumstances of the Trojan War is finally recuperated.

The Furies reverse Helen's transgression in another way too, by enacting proper feminine behavior. Like Helen they begin as footloose females who wander of their own volition to a foreign land; unlike her, however, they bring only benefit to the city that takes them in. In a reversal of the image of the lion cub (or the Trojan Horse), where a beautiful creature is embraced but brings disaster, in their case a loathsome object is welcomed and brings great good. This benefit is incurred, moreover, through a successful exercise of self-control, the most fundamental feminine virtue and the one in which Helen so notoriously failed. The Furies do not, of course, require sexual self-control, since they are not susceptible to *erōs*. In order to be honored and rewarded, however, they must learn to control a passion of their own—the passion of anger (*Eum.* 832–33, 900). This will make them an instrument, in turn, of Athenian self-restraint (*sōphrosunē*) (*Eum.* 1000). When they put aside their anger they also voluntarily give up their independence (cf. *Eum.* 900), becoming not only beholden to Athena but subject to her authority (*Eum.* 897, 902). Instead of roaming freely they will henceforth be safely ensconced in their underground cave.

In thus subordinating themselves, the Furies are also accepting the patriarchal government of Zeus, Athena's father, whose interests she serves. They are, moreover, embracing the patriarchal social structures in place in Aeschylus's Athens. In the course of the trilogy, the exercise of political power shifts from the aristocracy of legend, where women (in the person of Clytemnestra) play a significant and visible role, to democratic Athens, where women are excluded from the exercise of public power and stringently sheltered from any temptation to sexual misconduct. This is also the ideology of Athena, the "masculine" goddess and patron of Athens, who votes to acquit Orestes in part because the husband is the proper guardian of the house (*Eum.* 740). The threatened violence of the vengeful female is redirected into legal justice administered by men on the Areopagus—the very place, we are told, where the Amazons, the ultimate emblem of female independence, were defeated (*Eum.* 685–90). The foundation of the court on this particular spot marks the fact that classical Athens, with its democratic institutions and its noble victories, is founded on the suppression of such independence—the threat embodied not only in the Amazons but in Clytemnestra and her sister, Helen.

7

Spartan Woman and Spartan Goddess: Herodotus

> They had you crying but you came up smiling;
> They had you crawling and you came up flying;
> They had you crying and you came up smiling;
> And the last laugh, baby is yours.
>
> —Mark Knopfler

It may seem surprising to meet a creature of myth like Helen in the pages of the first Greek historian, Herodotus of Halicarnassus, whose subject—the Persian Wars—occurred early in his own lifetime. Herodotus's conception of history was, however, a capacious one. His own term for it—*historiē*, or "inquiry"—embraces all kinds of material, including legend, ethnography, and travelers' tales. We should bear in mind, too, that he and his contemporaries thought of the Homeric heroes as historical persons (albeit from the very distant past). The Trojan War was both the most important war of legendary times and, as an epochal clash between east and west, a direct antecedent to Herodotus's own theme. Even for a fifth-century prose author, moreover, Homeric epic, with its enormous cultural authority, remained a predecessor to emulate, subsume, and surpass. Herodotus eschews the Muses, to be sure. In general, he takes a skeptical, rationalizing view of legendary characters, treating them as exceptional people but relieving them of most of their more exotic mythological baggage. Yet he also gives history the weight of legend, presenting the Persian Wars as a Trojan War for his own time. Like his poetic predecessors the historian was acutely aware of his relationship with epic, and like them he used Helen's story in part as a vehicle for defining that relationship.

Helen makes three appearances in the *Histories*, in three widely separated and seemingly disconnected accounts told from three different perspectives and serving three agendas. In the course of these diverse narratives Herodotus picks up and reshuffles the cards that Stesichorus had dealt. He, too, has a human Helen who spends the war in Egypt, a powerful goddess, and an illusory Helen who is fought over at Troy. Since the *Histories* is concerned, ultimately, not with legend but with recent events, Helen is removed as a historical actor. Yet she takes her place, nonetheless, among the forces that drive history, as an emblem of the *erōs* aroused by female beauty and of its weighty consequences.

Prologue

Herodotus opens his monumental work with a proclamation redolent of epic. His purpose is to record for posterity the great and wondrous works of Greeks and non-Greeks alike, including the reason why they fought, so that they will not lack renown (*kleos*). His audience might have expected the question about causes to be answered with the abduction of Helen, or failing that some more recent antecedent to the Persian invasions. Instead we are a treated to a humorously specific account of a kidnapping long ago, which is derived, so Herodotus tells us, from certain Persian storytellers (1.1.1).[1] These Persians claim that some Phoenician merchants visiting Argos—the most prominent Greek city at the time—abducted the king's daughter and carried her off to Egypt. This potentially heroic opening is transposed into the distinctly unheroic register of the marketplace: the princess was shopping the merchants' wares with a lot of other women; they came toward the end and were picking out what they liked from the remaining goods; they clustered around the stern of the ship; some got away but others were taken with the princess; and so on.

The anonymity and plurality of the abductors and most of the women contribute to the mundane atmosphere. The king's daughter is, however, named as Io, daughter of Inachus (1.1.3). To a Greek audience this identification would be quite startling. As Herodotus mentions—just in passing—this is "not how" the Greeks tell Io's story (1.2.1). That is something of an understatement. In Greek myth Inachus was an Argive river god whose daughter, Io, was seduced by Zeus; when the jealous Hera caught them together Zeus turned Io into a cow. The Persian account is thus an unequivocal opening salvo in the demythologizing of Greek traditions about the past.

The Io incident (the Persians say) began a string of tit-for-tat abductions between Greeks and non-Greeks, or "barbarians," which ranged, geographically, over much of the Mediterranean world. Io's loss was followed by the abduction of the Phoenician king's daughter, Europa, by some nameless Greeks who were probably Cretan (1.2.1). Europa is another well-known figure from Greek myth, who was seduced by Zeus in the form of a bull, but there is no mention of that here. According to Herodotus's sources, her abduction cleaned

---

1. The authenticity of Herodotus's various sources is much debated by scholars. In this case the "Persians" are probably a Greek construct, since their narrative clearly reflects Greek traditions and concerns.

the slate, since "equal" had been exchanged for "equal" (1.2.1). But the Greeks went on to upset this balance by abducting yet another king's daughter, from a different (and far distant) part of the non-Greek world: Medea from Colchis (1.2.2). In Greek myth Jason acquired Medea in the course of stealing her father's Golden Fleece. As with Io, this incident is alluded to without being spelled out. (Herodotus merely mentions that the Greeks had sailed to Colchis on "other business.") The shock of demythologization is, however, less severe in this case, given that no divine seductions or bovine transformations are involved.

The Colchian king demanded Medea's return plus compensation (1.2.3), thus raising the ante from tit-for-tat substitution to restoration of the status quo with reparations (a more complex notion of justice). The Greeks refused, on the ground that Io had not been returned—even though that was an unrelated incident and in any case already balanced, according to the Persian view, by the theft of the non-Greek princess Europa. This is the first hint that the Greeks value their own women more highly than the women of foreigners. But it also opens the door for another non-Greek, Paris, in yet another completely different barbarian location, to decide, "when he heard these things," that he wanted to abduct "a woman" from Greece, knowing (supposedly) that he would get away with it, since the Greeks got away with taking Medea (1.3.1). He therefore abducted Helen (1.3.2).

Why did Paris want a Greek wife? We are not told. Nor is his selection of Helen explained. The mythic infrastructure binding them together has disappeared without trace, to be replaced only by the suggestion that Paris thought he could get something for nothing. That suits the generally calculative tone of this whole introductory series of stories, but does not explain Paris's desire for a *Greek* wife, or for Helen. As in myth, however, his deed does involve a willful disregard for the fundamental social values of Herodotus's world. That world, as presented in the *Histories*, is structured around personal ties of reciprocity, both positive (in the form of friendship) and negative (in the form of revenge). This Paris belittles the norms of positive reciprocity by evading the bride-price payable in the case of legitimate marriage, and negative reciprocity by discounting the possibility of vengeance. There is no mention, though, of guest-friendship, the fundamental social norm that he violated in Greek tradition.

This time, we are informed, the Greeks reacted very differently. They did not simply steal another woman in exchange. Instead, like Medea's father (whose claims they had earlier dismissed), they sent emissaries to demand Helen's restoration plus compensation for the injustice (1.3.2). The Trojans refused, on the grounds that the Greeks had refused in the case of Medea (1.3.2). Unwilling to accept this, the Greeks made war on Troy and destroyed the city.

Helen thus enters Herodotus's narrative, via the "Persians," in her traditional role as the cause of the Trojan War. As such, however, she is utterly trivialized. Her Homeric significance as "the beginning of the quarrel" (*Il.* 22.116) is usurped by Io, who serves as a vulgar, semicomic Helen substitute. Helen herself becomes just another link in a chain of stolen women. The Greeks' willingness to fight over her suggests that her value far outweighs that of the other women in the series, but the Persian storytellers say nothing to set her apart from the other abductees. They make it sound as though any Greek woman would have served Paris's purpose, and go on to dismiss the object of the great Achaean expedition as just "a Spartan woman" (1.4.3). Helen is demythologized even more surely than Io or Medea, without the slightest nod toward the more miraculous aspects of her story (daughter of Zeus, swan, egg). Nor is there anything special about her even on a strictly human level. The Persians have nothing to say about her appearance, her courtship, the suitors' oath, or any aspect of tradition relating to her beauty and its power. Herodotus is, as his opening sentence declares, fascinated by "wonders," that is, by things exceptional for their beauty and rarity (cf. 3.116), but there is nothing wonderful about this Helen.

In depriving Helen of her extraordinary status the Persian storytellers strip the Trojan War, too, of extraordinary significance. The mythical notion that one woman could legitimately serve as the cause of a mighty conflict is treated as absurd. The war is not a terrible-yet-glorious adventure, launched in the name of justice, but a ludicrous overreaction. The Greeks are, in these Persians' view, "greatly to blame," since they were the first to cross the boundary between Europe and Asia with hostile intent (1.4.1). This claim has implications for Herodotus's larger project, since it implicitly justifies the subsequent Persian invasion of Greece as a retaliatory act. More fundamentally, it draws the line between east and west that ultimately lies behind the Persian Wars. It was from this time onward, the storytellers say, that enmity and warfare were established between Greeks and non-Greeks (1.4.4–1.5.1). These "Persians"—themselves a projection of Greek concerns—use the Trojan War to define a world in which they are differentiated from Greeks by their values.

The war thus marks not, as in legend, the beginning of the end of the age of heroes, but the beginning of cultural distinction between Greeks and barbarians. This distinction is grounded in the valuation and control of women. Since the Persians admit that stealing women is unjust (1.4.2), one might expect them to denounce the Greek response not as revenge per se (a pervasive mode of justice in the ancient world) but as excessive revenge (something castigated as early as the *Iliad*). Such a claim would locate Herodotus's Persians in the mainstream of Greek moral thinking. Instead they decouple reason from morality, placing prudent pragmatism above the demands of justice and belittling the very notion of vengeance in such a case:

> Abducting women is a deed of unjust men. To care greatly about
> taking revenge for women who have been abducted is, however, a
> mark of mindlessness, and not to care about abducted women a
> mark of self-control. (1.4.2)

When they call the kind of men who take such revenge "mindless," the Persians are implying that their wits have been damaged by the erotic spell of the woman in question; those who stay home instead are "self-controlled" because they are immune to that spell. The implication for cultural difference emerges clearly when the Persians observe that they themselves did not make such a fuss when the non-Greek women were abducted (1.4.3).

The reason it is "mindless" to care about revenge in such cases is, the Persians go on to explain, because "women would not be abducted if they did not want to be" (1.4.2). In other words, one should refrain from vengeance because all female abductees are complicit in their own abduction. The underlying reasoning is presumably that by departing a woman has revealed her lustfulness, which makes her damaged goods. The very fact of abduction automatically impairs a woman's worth, marking a man who still desires her as devoid of proper self-control. The point at issue here is not just the (pragmatic) value of retrieving such a woman, but the (moral) goal of vengeance. These two factors coalesce, however, if revenge should properly be proportionate to the value of the woman in question. The Persians imply that no woman whose value is impaired in this way can be precious enough to justify an expensive revenge on her account. In any case, whether the focus is on retrieval or revenge, the argument depends on treating women as more or less precious objects. The merits of the Trojan War are assessed through a crude calculation of value that is in keeping with the mercantile tone of the preface as a whole. The Persians implicitly reassert the propriety of the more limited Greek reaction to Io's abduction, reinstating that initial picture of women as fungible objects, of strictly limited value, which can and should be exchanged for each other to restore equilibrium.

Yet the argument also depends crucially on acknowledging women's subjectivity, since it is the abductee's own erotic agency that impairs her value. The Persians imply that women's desires, and consequently their behavior, cannot ultimately be controlled by men, rendering any effort to retrieve an errant woman futile. This provides a convenient explanation for viewing *no* abducted woman as worth reclaiming (let alone avenging), regardless of circumstances. Io and the others who seemed, in their earlier narrative, to be taken against their will, are themselves tarred with the brush of complicity. This becomes explicit in an alternate version of Io's story, appended by Herodotus, which supposedly derives from the Phoenicians themselves (and is, not coincidentally, less detrimental to the reputation of Phoenician traders). In this account Io was not kidnapped, but went voluntarily with the sea captain because she had slept with him and wanted to conceal her pregnancy (1.5.2). Despite the variation in tawdry narrative detail, this version corroborates the Persian view of abducted women in general, producing a unified non-Greek perspective regarding the misadventures of Greek and non-Greek women alike.

This "barbarian" perspective is, in its essence, an unmasking of the Greeks' own anxiety about female eroticism. The Persian storytellers imply that the abduction of a woman, which testifies to her desirability, is an index of her own desire. In the *Iliad*, as we saw, the male characters avoid acknowledging this complicity in Helen's case, thus sustaining her value as an emblem of male glory. But Herodotus's pragmatic Persians oblige his Greek audience to confront the fact that the great heroic adventure of the Trojan War was indeed fought over a voluntary abductee, and use this fact to deny Helen's value and hence the legitimacy of both "official" motives for the resulting war (revenge and retrieval). If Helen is no more than "a Spartan woman" who ran off with a foreign sea captain, then she is either insignificant, outrageous, or both. The Trojan War is reduced to a foolish dispute over a slut.

We hear nothing of the Greeks' perspective on all this—nothing to explain why they might have considered Helen worth retrieving or such extreme revenge justified. By eliding her beauty the Persians eliminate the possibility of construing the war as a splendid quest for an extraordinarily precious object. They also suppress the moral ground for the Greek reaction by omitting the two factors that set Helen's abduction apart from that of the other women with whom she is artificially linked in the preface: her distinct status as the only abducted wife in the series and Paris's violation of guest-friendship. The Greek values that can be extrapolated from the "Persian" view are, in contrast, far from complimentary. These storytellers construct a world that is polarized between Greeks and non-Greeks, but reverse the typical Hellenocentric perspective to place the former at a distinct disadvantage. Rational self-control was central to classical Greek conceptions of masculinity, in contrast to the "effeminate" emotional lability of women and foreigners, but Herodotus's Persians claim this Hellenic high ground for themselves. It is Greeks, not barbarians, who are "mindless" and devoid of erotic self-control.

Such apparently anti-Greek sentiments roused the ire of those who considered Herodotus unpatriotic even in antiquity. But Herodotus does not, in general, endorse the accounts of his various sources, which come from all over the Greek and non-Greek world and, not surprisingly, tend to cast the group from which they derive in a positive light. The self-serving nature of the Persian account—especially when juxtaposed with the Phoenician variant—makes this very clear. Far from approving either version, Herodotus concludes his preface by explicitly refusing to take a stand: "This is what the Persians and the Phoenicians say. But about these matters I am not going to state that they happened either one way or the other" (1.5.3). Nevertheless, the demythologizing approach of these supposedly barbarian sources is true to his own. The preface thus leaves vital questions hanging in the air. Who was really at fault for the Trojan War? How could the Greeks have launched such a war just for "a Spartan woman"? Was its extremity really defensible in the name of justice? These are not merely Persian questions—if indeed they are Persian questions at all—but Greek ones, as we have seen. They are questions, regardless, that any competing account will have to address.

We must wait for such an account, however, until well into Herodotus's larger narrative. After reaching the threshold of the Trojan War he turns his back on the uncertainties of the distant past to recommence with something that he says he *knows*, namely that Croesus, king of Lydia, was the first non-Greek man to "initiate unjust deeds," by subjecting certain Greeks to his own rule (1.5.3, 1.6.2). The prologue's messy sequence of disputes over women is simplified into straightforward political aggression, uncomplicated by doubts about female virtue, with Croesus replacing Paris and Helen nowhere to be seen.

Having launched into this alternative story of beginnings, however, Herodotus immediately backtracks to the remarkable tale of Croesus's ancestor Gyges. The themes of female beauty and power, so markedly absent from the preface, now move to the foreground of historical explanation. Candaules, an early king of Lydia, conceived a passionate desire (*erōs*) for his own wife; being thus in love with her, he thought her "by far the most beautiful of all women," and used to praise her beauty excessively to his favorite bodyguard, Gyges (1.8.1). Candaules seems to have thought he was married to Helen. In any case, he behaved even more foolishly than Menelaus, not merely leaving his wife unattended but virtually pushing her into another man's arms. Thinking his bodyguard did not believe his exorbitant praise, he insisted that Gyges hide in their bedroom so that he could see her naked (1.8.2).

Such improper viewing is analogous to sexual violation, since, as Gyges himself puts it, a woman "removes her modesty with her clothing"; he therefore protested this "sick" idea (1.8.3). But Candaules insisted, and so the plan proceeded. The wife, who remains nameless, noticed Gyges spying on her, realized who was responsible, and planned her revenge (1.10.2). In a remarkable feat of self-discipline she kept quiet during the incident itself. She saw herself being seen but chose not to reveal that awareness, using it instead to turn the tables on her husband and transform male objectification into a source of female power. The following day she gave Gyges the choice of either dying himself or killing Candaules and becoming king (1.11.1–2). He chose, as Herodotus drily puts it, "to survive" (1.11.4), thus obtaining both queen and kingdom.

The tale of Candaules' wife rewrites the story of Helen, whose status as "by far the most beautiful of all women" was elided from the preface. Unlike the "Persian" account of the Trojan War, Herodotus's narrative of the Persian Wars begins with the disastrous consequences of male subjection to female beauty, which does, it turns out after all, have the power to topple kings and change the course of history. Like Helen, the wife of Candaules acquires a second husband by betraying the first, but she does so in a way that protects her sexual honor instead of besmirching it. She does not violate the Greek (and non-Greek) norm prohibiting any man but her husband from seeing a woman naked, but acts to sustain it by forcing the man who sees her to marry her or die. Despite her exceptional beauty, there is no sign of active eroticism on her part. She thus defies Greek stereotype by decoupling female beauty from female desire. Yet she also refuses to remain a passively violated object, using not only "feminine" ingenuity but self-control, her royal status, and a modicum of ruthlessness to defend her honor and obtain revenge. Female self-assertion remains a cause of male destruction, but only as a complement to and consequence of male erotic weakness. This opening incident in Herodotus's postlegendary narrative is fundamentally a tale not of female misbehavior but of male folly.

The form that folly takes is, moreover, subtly different from Paris's wrongdoing. Like Paris, Candaules is a non-Greek man who violates the respect due to a married woman, driven by *erōs* for her beauty. His wife is not described, however, as objectively the most beautiful of all women (a notion belonging to the realm of myth), but rather as a woman whose husband *thinks* she is. Candaules' downfall results not from the power of supreme female beauty as such, but from being so enamored of a particular woman that he both makes this judgment about her and requires (as only a tyrant can) that others endorse it. As an explanation of his fall, the tale parallels Sappho's account of the Trojan War, demonstrating the power of "whatever one desires" to provoke misdeeds because it seems supremely beautiful. Herodotus's rewriting of the Helen story affirms the danger of male erotic folly embedded in that story, but radically revises the figure of Helen herself by making a woman's standing as "the most beautiful in the world" into the subjective judgment of a foolish man.

The tale of Candaules and his wife initiates a Herodotean theme. Throughout the *Histories*, *erōs* is linked with tyranny and the transgression of boundaries of all kinds. This kind of behavior is attributed primarily to non-Greek kings, who exhibit sexual *erōs* and lust for empire alike, both leading to disaster. Such tyrants are feminized, by Greek standards, through their failure to control both their women and their own desires. This provides a new lens through which to view the Persian storytellers' contempt for the allegedly overreactive Greeks of the preface. Candaules, the first non-Greek king we meet, is guilty of just the kind of overvaluing of the desirable female that these Persians attribute to the Greeks. Their claim to superior erotic self-control among barbarians will be further undermined by the representation of other non-Greek kings throughout the *Histories*, most notably at its conclusion. The work ends with a complex narrative about the downfall of the Persian king Xerxes, which results from his subjection to *erōs* and consequently to female power (9.108–13).

Like her husband, Candaules' wife is the first example of a Herodotean type, the powerful non-Greek royal woman or "barbarian queen." As we might expect, these women who control or dominate men are portrayed as "masculine" in many respects. They are assertive, intelligent, and often shockingly violent (usually in revenge). In addition, they show little of the sexual weakness that Greek culture associates with women. The cynical Persians of the preface, with their assumption of complicity in all abducted women (Greek and barbarian alike), seem to share this aspect of Greek gender ideology. Here too, therefore, the story of Candaules' wife initiates a larger pattern that will challenge their outlook. Yet the storytellers also lay the groundwork for the extraordinary power of the barbarian queens, by opining that abducted women should not be pursued but let go. The *Histories* as a whole will suggest that only tyrannies fail thus in their responsibility to control unruly women. Thanks to Candaules and his wife, then, the attitudes and values of the Persians in the preface, concerning both gender and the values behind the Trojan War, have been called into question by the time Helen's story is resumed.

Helen in Egypt

The second book of the *Histories* consists of a detailed account of Egyptian history, customs, and beliefs, derived from a journey that Herodotus made there personally. It is the longest of several excursuses in which he explores the culture of various regions invaded by the Persians. Egypt was, like Persia, a paradigmatic non-Greek or "barbarian" land. But even though Herodotus's work reflects the Greek-barbarian dichotomy in many respects, his attitude toward it is far from uncritical or simplistic. As a historian he places particular faith in Egyptian sources, owing to the antiquity of their traditions, and traces to Egypt many significant aspects of the Greeks' own culture. Since Helen's story is *the* legendary link between Greece and Egypt, it is only natural that in the course of his visit he should investigate that link. Once again, he uses non-Greek sources to defamiliarize Greek legend by presenting it from an outsider's perspective. As we shall see, however, this perspective diverges markedly from that of the Persians in the preface.

Herodotus's history of Egypt's rulers includes a number of intriguing "barbarian queens," including Nitocris, the sole Egyptian queen (2.100), and the nameless wife of King Sesostris (2.107). Both these powerful women exemplify the kind of ruthless self-assertion, in admittedly difficult circumstances, that we saw in the case of Candaules' wife, but neither beauty nor sex plays a role in their stories. Female sexual misbehavior does occur, however, under the rule of Sesostris's son Pheros, who is notable for setting fire to a large number of women—including his wife—for infidelity to their husbands (2.111). The next ruler is none other than Proteus, the shape-shifting sea god of the *Odyssey*, now transformed into an Egyptian king. This Proteus is devoid of supernatural features but does enjoy a cult after his death, as indicated by a sacred precinct in his honor (2.112.1). Within that precinct is a shrine dedicated to "the foreign Aphrodite," a title that could also, thanks to the ambiguity of the Greek word *xenos*, be translated "Aphrodite the stranger" or "Aphrodite our guest" (2.112.2). The shrine in question—which Herodotus seems to have visited personally—was probably the temple of Astarte, the Phoenician equivalent of Aphrodite, called "foreign" in Egypt to distinguish her from her local counterpart Hathor.[2] But Herodotus believes this goddess to be Helen, based on two pieces of evidence: first, the legend of her stay in Egypt (he is alluding to the *Odyssey* and perhaps also Stesichorus); and second, the fact that this is the only Egyptian shrine to Aphrodite where the goddess is titled "foreign."

When Herodotus made inquiries of the Egyptian priests, they picked up Helen's story where the Persians left it in the preface. Sailing back to Troy after the abduction, Paris and Helen were blown off course to Egypt. They landed near a shrine of Heracles, where Paris's slaves took refuge and denounced him, telling "the whole story about Helen and the injustice to Menelaus" (2.113.3). Like the Persians, the Egyptians view Helen as complicit in her own abduction. The messenger who reports the shipwreck to Proteus declares that Paris "deceived" her (2.114.2)—a reference to the "deception" of seduction—and Proteus himself accuses Paris of having "excited" her, or "made her flighty" (2.115.4). Yet no one chastises her. The focus is less on her transgression than on the "injustice" done to her husband by another man. It is Paris, the "most evil of men" (2.115.4), who takes all the blame. In contrast to the way female volition is deployed in the preface, Helen's complicity is used less to indict her than to increase the enormity of Paris's offense. As Proteus puts it, by "going to" his host's wife Paris committed "a most impious deed," and as if that wasn't enough, he "got her excited" and took her away (2.115.4). The argument recalls a famous passage in a speech by the orator Lysias, where he argues that seducing a married woman is a worse crime than raping her because it transfers her affection from her husband to her lover (Lysias 1.32–33).

Unlike most of Herodotus's Egyptian rulers, Proteus, who is Greek in both name and legendary origin, is no tyrant but a virtuous king along traditional Greek lines. As such he is a "good barbarian," who enables Herodotus to co-opt the ancient wisdom of Egypt in affirmation of Hellenic values. Proteus's respect for guest-friendship, in particular, is emphatically hammered home. By showing extraordinary hospitality to visiting strangers he exemplifies precisely the values that Paris flouted. Via Egypt, then, we are finally offered a "Greek" version of Helen's story to challenge the narrative supplied by the self-interested Persians of the preface.

According to those Persians, the Phoenicians started the trouble by stealing Io, or the Greeks by invading Asia. The Egyptians of book 2 "correct" this account by making Paris the first offender, ignoring the extraneous stories of Io, Europa, and Medea, and giving Helen's abduction the primacy that is its due.

2. The exact location has not been determined, but it was probably close to the temple of Ptah, the patron god of Memphis.

The pro-Greek Proteus also emphasizes the two crucial differences between Helen and the other abductees of the prologue: she was a married woman, and Paris was a guest in her husband's house. Helen's abduction was, as a result, not just another "theft" of a woman but an assault on the most sacred of Greek values. The Persians failed to understand that Helen was not just a piece of shopworn stolen property but an emblem of those values. The negative reciprocity of revenge, which they belittled, was a proper response to Paris's heinous violation of the positive reciprocity enshrined in guest-friendship. Like Paris himself (in their own version of the story), they gave neither form of reciprocity its due.

The Egyptian narrative fills out the preface in a further way by referring repeatedly to Paris's accompanying theft of Menelaus's property (2.114.2, 115.1, 118.3, 119.1). The Persians ignored this, perhaps because the property could not be said to have left of its own volition (the linchpin of their argument against vengeance). In Proteus's view, however, the theft of the property exacerbates Paris's offense against guest-friendship still further. After reproving Paris for "exciting" his own host's wife and taking her away with him, the king exclaims, "Not even *that* was enough for you, but you came here after plundering the household of your host (*xenos*) as well!" (2.115.4–5). This slightly disconcerting emphasis on the property de-eroticizes the offense, reinforcing the impression that Helen was barely more than an object, and Paris (whose own *erōs* is not mentioned) no more than a vulgar thief. The theft of the property is, nonetheless, climactic because the victim was his host, a fact underlined by insistent repetition of the word *xenos*.

Luckily for Paris, however, the hospitable Proteus is opposed on principle to killing a stranger (*xenos*) (2.115.4, 6). He therefore dismisses him from Egypt with no more than a scolding. As for Helen, he declares that he will "guard" her along with the stolen goods until "the Greek *xenos*," Menelaus, can come to retrieve her (2.115.6). Like Homer's Priam this Proteus is a benevolent, protective foreign king, who shows no sign of blaming Helen despite her complicity. In contrast to the *Iliad*, however, this is not explained or justified by positing any kind of personal relationship between them. Helen has no voice or dramatic presence in Herodotus's Egyptian narrative. She appears to be no more than a piece of property that Proteus has undertaken to protect on behalf of its rightful owner.

This picture of Helen's elopement recalls the Greek men's perspective in the *Iliad*, both in its emphasis on the stolen goods and in its minimizing of Helen's agency. The *Iliad*'s male speakers often mention the property, mostly in the context of the duel where Helen is at her most objectified (above, p. 59). As for Helen's agency, Homer's Greeks do not dispute or deny it, but they do avoid acknowledging it in such a way as to assign her the blame due to a responsible agent, thus reinforcing the righteousness of their cause. Herodotus's Proteus goes further, however. He links the property with Helen still more closely, and even though, unlike the Greeks of the *Iliad*, he mentions her desire for Paris, he does not treat it as something for whose consequences she should be held responsible. The difference between this Helen and the women described just prior to her arrival in Egypt is quite striking. In contrast to the assertive "barbarian queens" she is presented as no more than a passive object. As such she is not held responsible for her infidelity, unlike the unfortunate women whom King Pheros burned alive.

This objectification of Helen and minimizing of her agency are of a piece with Proteus's assumption that Menelaus still values Helen, despite her unfortunate excitability, and will sooner or later come to reclaim her. When Menelaus does indeed show up in Egypt, he finds that Helen has "suffered no harm" and retrieves her along with his property, which is likewise intact (2.119.1). The value she is accorded here seems to have nothing to do with her own feelings. She is simply passed unceremoniously from one man's control to another's. Again, this evokes the Greek male values of the *Iliad*. In contrast to the epic, however, this objectifying perspective is not complicated by the larger dramatic context. Helen is denied her Homeric voice and presence, and with them both her impact on others and her own assertions of agency. Herodotus's Egyptians may speak in the voice of Iliadic Greeks, but they do so without the broader perspective supplied for Homer's audience by the epic narrator.

Proteus's attitude obliquely challenges the Persian argument that women who stray should not be retrieved, thus affirming Greek gender norms in face of the female independence and gender reversal that tends to characterize non-Greeks (including Egyptians). The fact that her flighty desires can be aroused by a visiting stranger is not treated as a reason to let her go, or to replace her with some other stolen woman. It is, rather, a reason to return her to her husband's control. In one respect, however, the Egyptian narrative does not challenge but corroborates the Persian version. There is nothing in either of these accounts comparable to the reaction of Homer's Trojan elders, which might suggest that Helen has special beauty or significance. Proteus assumes that she remains valuable to her rightful husband, but the reasons for this are not explained. The Egyptian narrative focuses exclusively on the values violated by Paris, especially the sanctity of guest-friendship; there is no suggestion that Helen is worth fighting for in herself. This pro-Greek perspective occludes awkward questions about the value placed on Helen by Greek men, and specifically about the desire that she arouses. This reinforces the function of the Trojan War as an antecedent for the war with which Herodotus is directly concerned, which was lost by the Persians in part because of the barbarian susceptibility to *erōs* that distinguishes them from Greeks.

Having entrusted Helen to Proteus's safekeeping for the duration of the Trojan War, Herodotus, like Stesichorus, must find some other way to account for that war. His cautious empiricism eschews such supernatural gimmicks as Helen's double. He therefore proposes another possibility—one rarely entertained in our sources—namely that the traditional Greek story is simply "nonsense" (2.118.1). He goes on to reject this hypothesis, but only after further consultation with the Egyptian priests, who supply him with an explanation supposedly derived from Menelaus during his postwar visit (2.118.1). According to this impeccable source a huge Greek army did indeed sail off to Troy in his support (2.118.2). As we heard in the preface, they first demanded the return of Helen and the stolen property, plus compensation for Paris's injustice (2.118.3). When the Trojans swore that both she and the property were in Egypt, however, they did not believe them and thought they were being "laughed at" (2.118.3–4). The rejection of their demands, exacerbated by this perceived mockery, induced them to go ahead and besiege the city. Only after sacking Troy did they discover that Helen was not there.

Herodotus explains the discrepancy with epic tradition by opining that Homer knew the Egyptian version of Helen's story but did not judge it "seemly" for epic (2.116.1). What exactly Herodotus means by this we are not told, but the Greek word (*euprepēs*) denotes a superficially fine appearance that may be specious. Its use here suggests that if the Trojan War had been fought not over Helen but over a mistake it would be devoid of heroic significance and unsuitable for epic commemoration. Had Homer's audience known that Helen was in Egypt all along, they would not have viewed his warriors, despite their feats in battle, as worthy candidates for such renown. A properly heroic undertaking must, it seems, be justified by the value of its object, and, at least in this case, vengeance alone would not have sufficed for such purposes. Herodotus is declaring, in his own way, that Homer's story "is not true," while affirming that Helen's presence in Troy is essential to epic as a genre.

Whether or not Herodotus was engaging with Stesichorus intentionally, his explanation of the Trojan War betrays the underlying "truth" behind the idea of Helen's *eidōlon*: the war was literally fought over nothing. The Helen who is reputed to have been at Troy is no more than an illusion created by poets. As a result, his account has much in common with the Palinode story. Both authors absent Helen from the scene, attribute the war to a misperception, and use Helen to assert their superiority over epic, especially in regard to truthfulness. Both criticize and correct Homer, though for different reasons and in different ways. Herodotus's interpretation goes far beyond Stesichorus, however, in dismantling the epic. Stesichorus left Homer's account intact (though founded on an illusion), but Herodotus's Egyptians reject, by implication, the historicity of all the scenes in Homer where Helen plays a part, and revise many others in consequence.

Despite these radical implications, Herodotus firmly believes the Egyptians are right. Their version is more plausible, he declares, because there is no way the Trojans would have failed to give Helen back rather than endure a ten-year war on her behalf. To do otherwise, just so that Paris could continue cohabiting with Helen, would be insane, or "damaged in the wits" (2.120.1–2).

Even if they did not return her at first, once the deaths mounted up Priam would have done so—even if he had been sleeping with her himself! (2.120.3). Paris, to be sure, might have wanted to keep on fighting (brain damage being a familiar symptom of erotic passion), but he could not have had that much authority over the rest of the Trojans, since he was not the heir to the throne, and Hector, who was, would never have put up with it (2.120.4). In other words, it is impossible that any woman could have been valued so highly. Paris was no doubt driven crazy by her beauty, but its power stops with a single man. As with Candaules, the judgment of supreme beauty results from the infatuation of a foolish individual.

To speak rationally like this about Helen is to show oneself immune to the idea of her beauty as a transcendent force. Such rationalization depends on treating epic figures as historical persons, whose behavior can be understood as if they were real, tolerably sensible people. This approach, like that of the Persians and Proteus, eviscerates Helen's special significance. The more she is demoted into a mere mortal, a specific woman, the more we are obliged to face up to the impossibility of her mythic power. The Persians of the preface disapproved of the Greeks going to war over "a Spartan woman"; Herodotus goes further in his own voice, rejecting as absurd the idea that their opponents would have been willing to sustain such a war. The Egyptian account enables him to answer a question that the pragmatic, probarbarian Persians left unaddressed: Why did the *Trojans*—who, as non-Greeks, should, by the Persian account, have been "self-controlled"—not give Helen back to Menelaus? The Egyptian version resolves this tension, aligning the Trojans with their fellow non-Greeks as practical people who do not overvalue promiscuous women. Ironically, this assessment supports the Persians' claim to rational self-control among barbarians.

After explaining that the Greeks did not believe the Trojans about Helen's whereabouts, "even though they spoke the truth," Herodotus goes on:

> To give my own opinion, this was because divine power was arranging things so that by being utterly destroyed the Trojans should make this conspicuously clear to human beings: that the punishments from the gods for great injustices are also great. (2.120.5)

The "great injustice" was, clearly, Paris's violation of guest-friendship by the theft of a wife, the offense against Zeus that sets him apart from the preface's other woman-stealers. The enormity of this transgression stands, regardless of Helen's actual whereabouts during the war. The truth about those whereabouts, which places her in Egypt rather than Troy, may not be enough to underwrite the glory of epic heroism, but it does not alter the fact that the war was motivated by the fundamental values of reciprocity and justice. By letting Troy fall, the gods themselves make it clear that the Persians of the preface were mistaken in their presentation of the whole affair as petty and unworthy of punishment, and give divine endorsement to the Greek values of guest-friendship and revenge.

This interpretation of the Trojan War accords with Herodotus's use of the war elsewhere in the *Histories* as an antecedent for Panhellenic revenge on barbarians. The Trojan War foreshadows the moral conflict of the Persian Wars, in which the Greeks, despite all their differences and the myriad complications in their alliances, ultimately have right on their side. This is most strikingly exemplified in a specific evocation of the Trojan War at the end of the *Histories*. After expelling the Persians, the Greeks severely punish a Persian named Artayktes for plundering and having sex with women in the shrine of the cult hero Protesilaus—a shrine that the criminal himself disingenuously refers to as "the house of a Greek man" (9.116.3). Protesilaus, whose special significance lay in his role as the first Greek warrior in the Trojan War to set foot on non-Greek land, thus crossing the boundary between west and east, was buried at the very spot where the Greeks first landed. Artayktes' punishment for violating his shrine bridges the temporal gap between the Trojan and Persian Wars, uniting them through a shared pattern of retribution for plundering and sexually desecrating a Greek man's "house."

Menelaus is, of course, the archetypal victim of such barbaric treatment. He is also the beneficiary, twice over, of Proteus's reverence for guest-friendship. The Egyptian king not only retained the stolen Helen on his behalf, but treated him with "great hospitality" when the Greeks dispatched him to retrieve Helen after the war (2.119.1). Yet he turns out—as we discover in a strange coda to the Egyptian narrative—to be a remarkably inept standard-bearer for the all-important institution of guest-friendship. When he tried to leave Egypt, he was detained by contrary winds and therefore "devised an impious deed": he sacrificed two Egyptian children in order to obtain a favorable wind (2.119.2–3). This "impious deed" of an "unjust man" (2.119.2), shocking enough in itself, is compounded by the affront to Egyptian hospitality. This makes it comparable to Paris's original crime, which was likewise an "injustice" (2.113.3) and an "impious deed" (2.114.2). By evoking the sacrifice of Iphigenia, Menelaus's murders also remind us of the dubious moral foundations of the Trojan War itself.

The Egyptians gave chase but eventually lost track of Menelaus and his ships (2.119.3). Their pursuit endorses the idea that violations of guest-friendship should be avenged—but only up to a point. Proteus, we may recall, affirmed the propriety of punishing Paris with death, but refrained from executing him out of hospitality, which was, for him, a higher value than revenge (2.115.6). Nor did he explicitly approve the Trojan War as a response to Paris's crime. Even now, when the Egyptians' own hospitality has been so sorely abused, their reaction is limited. Like the Greeks, they are willing to sail off and (presumably) fight for vengeance, but they do not mount an expedition to Greece, wage a ten-year war, and destroy Menelaus's city. Egypt under

Proteus thus sets a standard by which not only barbarian but Greek misbehavior can be judged and found wanting. Such failures include violations of
guest-friendship, exemplified equally by Paris and Menelaus, but also, by implication, excessive vengeance in response.

This implicit criticism of the Trojan War is not affected by the fact that
Herodotus identifies the war as an instrument of divine punishment. When
he explains the Greek failure to believe the Trojans regarding Helen's whereabouts by saying that the gods were "arranging things" to make their justice
"conspicuously clear," this does not, of itself, exonerate the Greeks or explain
their motives. The gods have a distinct tendency to "arrange things" by
driving humans to foolish and even criminal behavior—such as the sacrifice
of Iphigenia—in the service of the divine agenda. The Greeks' refusal to
believe the Trojans has a strong whiff of the irrational, which often accompanies such divine manipulations. Clearly they did not apply the same kind
of rational analysis that Herodotus did. Instead, they rejected a perfectly reasonable explanation that would have allowed them to retrieve Helen without
bloodshed. The Egyptians' relatively restrained response to Menelaus's appalling behavior suggests, in contrast, that extreme vengeance is not, in fact,
required by strictly human norms of justice, bringing them closer to the position of their fellow non-Greeks, the Persians, than was initially apparent.

If the Greek reaction to Helen's abduction went beyond the require-
ments of justice—at least by the standards of these unimpeachably virtuous
Egyptians—perhaps the Trojan War had other motives after all. In the preface, the Persians implied that the war should be attributed to the Greeks'
"mindless" lack of self-restraint (1.4.2). The Egyptian account endorsed by
Herodotus overwrites this with the ethical case for revenge. Yet traces of less
admirable motivation remain detectable even in book 2. As we have just
seen, the Greeks react irrationally to the Trojan explanation, inflamed by an
imaginary insult to their honor. Despite Helen's susceptibility to seduction,
moreover, she somehow seems to escape the category of damaged goods.
Proteus assumes that Menelaus will want her back, and after the war the
Greeks collectively "send" him all the way to Egypt to get her (2.118.4). Retrieving her is clearly important in its own right, despite her flightiness.
Mainstream gender ideology, was, of course, less indulgent toward adulterous wives, a fact underlined by juxtaposing Helen's story with that of Pheros, who killed his unfaithful wife (along with many others).

The Egyptian narrative thus implies that Helen does indeed have special
value of some kind. As we saw, this implication is not cashed out in terms of
beauty or desire. Herodotus protects the Greeks, in general, from the Persian
charge that they lack self-control, maintaining a broad distinction throughout
the *Histories* between erotically susceptible foreigners and virtuously vengeful
Greeks. If Menelaus is a Greek, however, he is also a Spartan. Spartans in
Herodotus often display the finest of Greek qualities (notably courage). But the

fact that Sparta was ruled by kings—albeit dual kings—brings it dangerously close to the perils of monarchy that beset barbarians. Accordingly, Spartan kings, like non-Greek tyrants, have a tendency to erotic weakness and misbehavior. Menelaus's shocking murder of the Egyptian children betrays this kinship, since human sacrifice was considered quintessentially barbarian and tyrannical. As a violation of guest-friendship it also makes him a doublet of his barbarian enemy, Paris, the mythic archetype of irresponsible male eroticism. Given such royal male susceptibility to erotic passion, perhaps the Persians were not wrong, after all, to attribute the Trojan War to the Spartan Menelaus's lack of self-control.

This possibility is confined to Herodotus's subtext, excavated via the coda to the Egyptian version of Helen's story. It is reinforced, however, by his introduction to that story. The tale told to Herodotus by the Egyptian priests is that of an epic heroine, albeit one whose role in her own adventures has been diminished almost to the vanishing point. But it began with a question about "Aphrodite, our guest." Though Herodotus never spells this out, his identification of this goddess with Helen is obviously based on her exceptional beauty as well as the time she spent as a "guest" in Egypt. He must have assumed that the Egyptians, back in legendary times, were as impressed by that beauty as the Trojan elders in the *Iliad* who liken her to an immortal goddess. This time the equation is more than a simile, since the temple in question actually existed. But if Helen's beauty was great enough to equate her with Aphrodite herself, why should it not suffice to cause the Trojan War? The effacement of Helen by Egyptians and Persians alike is challenged by the implication that she did indeed embody something so glorious that it might inspire men to worship her, or even, perhaps, lose their collective mind. Herodotus supplies the leaders of the Trojan War with motives that displace Helen's beauty from his narrative, but her temple remains as a reminder that this may not be the whole story.

The Goddess of Therapne

If the goddess Helen is a "guest" in Egypt, Sparta is her home, and it is as a Spartan goddess that she makes her third appearance in the *Histories*. The goddess in question is a far cry from either the "Spartan woman" of Herodotus's preface or the object of theft in his Egyptian narrative. Read in light of her previous appearances, this final narrative suggests that the silenced and objectified Helen, transformed into a powerful and independent goddess, got the last laugh.

As we saw in chapter 2, Helen had several cult sites in Sparta, including the Menelaion at Therapne. Such husband-and-wife cults were not uncommon, but this one is exceptional, since the evidence suggests that Helen was more important there than her husband (above, pp. 45–46). Archaeologists have found numerous votive offerings at Therapne, some of them inscribed specifically "to Helen." This site is the location of a fascinating anecdote in Herodotus book 6, which suggests the kind of reason why one might dedicate such an offering. The shrine presumably honored Helen's (re)marriage to Menelaus, but he goes unmentioned in Herodotus's tale, which suggests, rather, that even here Helen was worshipped as a patron of girls' transition to marriage, with the instability and threat that this brings in its train.

The goddess of Therapne appears during an excursus explaining the family background of Demaratus, an important Spartan king (6.61). Demaratus's father, King Ariston, had been married to two different women but was still childless; he therefore took a third wife who, Herodotus informs us, was "by far the most beautiful of the women in Sparta." As an infant this woman had been extraordinarily ugly, something her wealthy parents viewed as a "calamity." Her nurse therefore carried her every day to Helen's shrine at Therapne, set her down by the cult statue (*agalma*), and prayed to the goddess to free the baby from ugliness. One day "a woman" appeared—obviously Helen in person—and insisted on seeing the infant. The nurse resisted, because the embarrassed parents had forbidden her to show anyone the child, but finally gave in. The mysterious woman touched the baby's head, declaring that she would be "the most beautiful of all the women in Sparta," and from that day on the infant's appearance was transformed.

This description of Ariston's third wife (who remains unnamed) recalls the wife of Candaules, the only other woman in the *Histories* of whom the expression "most beautiful" is used. In a Spartan context the superlative also evokes, still more obviously, Helen herself. When she beautifies the baby, the goddess is evidently reproducing herself in mortal form. She is also assuming the role of her own divine patron, Aphrodite, well-known for her ability to bestow the gift of beauty. Unlike the gifts of Aphrodite, the divine Helen's gift does not seem to be accompanied by an untoward lust in its recipient. Nevertheless, like Aphrodite's gifts it will prove both socially and ethically disruptive thanks to the desire that her protégée will inspire in men. The impact of the reincarnated human Helen is not, to be sure, as cataclysmic as that of the original, but it turns out to be remarkably similar in several respects (6.62.1–2).

When the beautiful baby grew up, she was married to a man called Agetus. Agetus also happened to be King Ariston's best friend, but this did not stop the king from "itching" with *erōs* for his friend's wife. He therefore hatched a nefarious scheme to take her for himself, getting Agetus to agree to an exchange of gifts, with each gift to be chosen by the recipient. Agetus knew that his wife might in theory count as one of the "gifts" but did not worry, because Ariston was already married. He worked on the "Greek" assumption that a woman, once married, stays with her husband. But this did not stop the tyrannical Ariston from demanding her. Despite his Greek identity, he behaved like a barbarian. More specifically, he behaved like Paris, violating both male friendship and existing marriage ties by sneakily stealing the wife of another man.

Agetus, of course, had no choice but to hand over his wife. After Ariston married her she gave birth to a son, Demaratus, suspiciously soon, giving rise to rumors about his paternity. Ariston put aside the concern this aroused and raised Demaratus as his heir. The destructive spell cast by the divine Helen's gift persisted, however, into the next generation. Demaratus grew up to be a Paris figure, like his father before him, incurring the enmity of another man by plotting to "abduct" his betrothed wife (6.65.1–2).

Unlike the human Helen, Demaratus's mother changes husbands not as a victim of seduction but as an entirely innocent pawn in Ariston's game. Yet her subsequent history suggests that she is neither a mere object nor entirely beyond suspicion. When her son asks her about rumors of her infidelity to Ariston, she uses a storytelling skill worthy of Helen herself to maintain her reputation. She declares, under oath, that she cheated on her husband only with a cult hero named Astrabacus, who came to her, a few days after her marriage to Ariston, in the form of an "apparition" (*phasma*) impersonating Ariston himself (6.69.1). This supernatural explanation allows Demaratus's mother to hint at infidelity on her part—tacitly justified by Ariston's infertility—without shaming either her husband or her son. It is also a form of self-glorification, putting her beauty on a par with that of mythic women seduced by gods. Her account evokes, especially, Alcmene, mother of the Spartan hero Heracles, whose husband Zeus impersonated in order to sleep with her. Like her miraculous beautification, it reinserts the supernatural power of female beauty into the human narrative of the *Histories*.

The beautification of Demaratus's mother forms the climax of Helen's three appearances in the *Histories*, in each of which the quasi-divine power of her beauty becomes more manifest. In the preface her beauty as a mortal heroine is entirely suppressed; in Egypt it is enough to make people mistake her for a goddess; in Sparta she lives on as a powerful divinity. The awe-inspiring nature of that beauty is evident from the shrines that honor it (in Egypt as well as Sparta), its desirability from the distress of the parents who regard their baby's lack of this fundamental female asset as a "calamity." Yet it also, predictably, brings calamity in its train, causing disputes among men, the untoward circulation of women, and suspicion of female eroticism. The extraordinary power of female beauty, for both good and ill, that was so conspicuously absent from Herodotus's account of the Trojan War, is restored to Helen in the role of goddess.

Nor is this power confined to the distant past. The incident at Therapne and its consequences take place on the eve of the battle of Marathon, a pivotal moment in the Persian Wars. Like the story of Artayktes and Protesilaus, Helen's miracle bridges the gap between the legendary past and Herodotus's own day, bringing her power into the present in a way that invites us to reconsider the influence of her beauty in the past. The book 6 anecdote retrospectively qualifies both the tendentious Persian narrative in the preface and the heavily moralized pro-Greek version of book 2. The Persian storytellers elided her supernatural significance completely, and the Egyptian narrative presented a sharp dichotomy between the human Helen and the goddess: the temple that testified to her superhuman impact remained disconnected from the heroine's own story. Book 6 reconnects the divine power of her beauty with the human realm, and more specifically with Sparta, whose kings display a dangerous barbarian susceptibility to *erōs* in face of the goddess Helen's influence. Even among Herodotus's contemporary Greeks, Spartan kings represent a point of vulnerability, a tendency toward both excessive eroticism and the tyranny with which it is linked throughout the *Histories*. This retrospectively supports the hints of erotic susceptibility in the Spartan Menelaus in book 2, inviting us, once more, to reinscribe Helen's beauty as a force behind the Trojan War.

Despite the cynicism about abducted women voiced by the Persians of the preface, in both of Helen's subsequent appearances blame for the destructive impact of female beauty is placed squarely at the door of the men who succumb to it. As in the case of Candaules' wife, the *Histories* diverge markedly from the usual Greek habit of attributing culpable lust to beautiful women themselves. Helen's desire for Paris is neither blamed nor taken seriously by any of the men, and in the story of Demaratus's mother female desire plays essentially no role. It is the Spartan kings associated with Helen, in both myth and history, who transgress in response to female beauty, following the pattern more broadly associated with non-Greek monarchs. Unlike these male monarchs, the "barbarian queens" are for the most part sexually virtuous, contributing to barbarian gender reversal by asserting themselves in other ways. This, too, is echoed at Sparta. The human Helen shows no such assertiveness, to be sure, but she compensates for this in her divine persona and through her reincarnation as Demaratus's resourceful mother.

Compared to queens, nonroyal women are much less visible in Herodotus. Since Greeks are less prone to monarchy than barbarians, this means that many fewer Greek women play a prominent role (Demaratus's royal mother being a notable exception). We might expect to see evidence of more "normal"—that is, lustful—female behavior among such ordinary women as do appear. Yet they too are, in general, rather well behaved sexually. (There is nothing, for example, to compare with the rampant female promiscuity in the story of King Pheros.) The Persians of the preface turn out to be wrong, in particular, in their attribution of promiscuity to all abductees. The most notable abduction story in the *Histories*, besides those already discussed, occurs later in book 6. It involves a group of Athenian women who are first violently raped (6.137.3) and later abducted (6.138.1) by some Pelasgians (a name Herodotus gives the pre-Greek inhabitants of Greece). Far from being complicit in their abduction, these women's reluctance is made clear not only by the vio-lence of the initial rape but by their subsequent passive resistance. After bearing their abductors' children, they raise them to speak Greek and follow Athenian ways (6.138.2). These children grow up to embody the outlook that underpinned the assault on Troy. When one of them was injured, "they all helped him and took vengeance on each other's behalf" (6.138.2).

This episode attests to the superiority of Greek culture and values, which in turn help explain and justify Greek victory in the Persian Wars. Despite the shared theme of Greek solidarity, however, it paints a picture that diverges con-siderably from the way the Greeks behaved in the Trojan War. The Athenians do not pursue the Pelasgians, as the Greeks pursued Helen. In fact, when the women are first raped, the Athenian men explicitly refrain from killing the rapists, merely exiling them from Attica, a restraint that, in their own view, shows they are "better men" (6.137). This attitude is more evocative of Prote-us's limited response to moral outrage than of Menelaus's intemperance. Nor is the women's own agency belittled. Without asserting themselves in the vio-lent, "masculine" fashion of "barbarian queens," they actively preserve Athe-nian culture and values for themselves, demonstrating a capacity for virtuous agency even under the most trying circumstances.

The story of the raped Athenian women unveils Proteus's "Greek" view of Helen, as a mere object despite her excitable desires, for what it is—a belittling of female agency that goes hand in hand with a dangerous male overvaluation of beautiful women as erotic objects. This same pattern is visible in postleg-endary times, in both the barbarian Candaules' treatment of his wife, whom he thought "the most beautiful of all women," and the Spartan Ariston's of his third wife, the divine Helen's "most beautiful" protégée. The threat of Helen thus lives on among the Greeks, posed not—remarkably—by beautiful wom-en's own excessive desires, but only by the desire they arouse in men, and more specifically in Spartan kings. Their Greekness notwithstanding, these kings' tendency toward tyranny and erotic weakness aligns them with the barbarian enemy, and lures them into treating women as mere objects, without regard for their capacity for responsible agency.

This looks at first sight like an anti-Spartan perspective on the past and pre-sent alike. Yet there are hints in the Egyptian narrative that Menelaus exem-plifies not only Sparta but Greece more generally. Proteus, for one, speaks of him as if he were an emblematic Greek, referring to him not by name but as "the Greek man" or "the Greek foreigner (xenos)" (2.115.4, 6). Agamemnon is, more-over, strikingly absent. The other Greeks, we are simply told, were "helping" Menelaus (2.118.2). This suggests that their motive was a kind of solidarity. But that solidarity is underwritten, traditionally, by the oath of the suitors, which implicates the Greeks collectively in desire for Helen. In Herodotus's view, keeping her at Troy would have been evidence of Trojan insanity, but as we saw, the same might be said of the Greeks' willingness to pursue her.

One last mention of Helen suggests that subjection to female beauty, with its tyrannical implications, is indeed a danger that threatens all Greeks, not just Spartans. At the end of the *Histories*—just prior to recounting the downfall of Xerxes through untoward *erōs* of his own—Herodotus briefly mentions Helen's abduction by the Athenian hero Theseus (9.73). He identifies the incident as a cause of dissent within Attica and of military conflict between Athens and Sparta. This makes it a legendary antecedent to the Peloponnesian War, which, as Herodotus spells out, was in progress at the time of writing. That war in turn contained the potential for tyranny by Athens, which was in the process of extending the reach of its empire. The Trojan War, though led by the Spartan Menelaus, is thus a cautionary tale for Greece as a whole—and Athens in particular—against the barbarian *erōs* aroused by women and tyranny. All Greek men must remain vigilant, and not fall into complacency about their superiority to non-Greek tyrants in resisting the power of female beauty. The Persians in the preface may, after all, have identified the Greeks' Achilles' heel.

8

Playing Defense: Gorgias's *Encomium of Helen*

> With one wave of your hand,
> I'm your slave to command,
> And I gladly obey.
> Anything you say, I'm like a hunk of clay.
> I'm just like putty, putty in your hands, uh huh!
> —The Shirelles

Among all the finely calibrated attitudes toward Helen encountered so far, we have as yet seen no attempt to defend her for eloping with Paris (as opposed to simply denying that she did so). That changes with the *Encomium of Helen* by Gorgias of Leontini, a fifth-century Sicilian Greek orator who plucks Helen out of legend, sets her down in an imaginary courtroom, and appoints himself her advocate.

Gorgias was one of the most famous and successful of the sophists, a loose movement of intellectual entrepreneurs who traveled the Greek world offering a highly priced education to ambitious and wealthy young men. Different sophists had different interests, ranging from mathematics to ethics to anthropology to linguistics. Despite this intellectual diversity, however, they shared a common fascination with rhetoric. The teaching of oratory was also their bread and butter since it could command high fees, especially in democratic Athens where persuasive speaking was essential to political success. The power of language is a central theme of Gorgias's *Helen*, along with other sophistic concerns, including human nature, the psyche, and causation.

Much sophistic thinking betrays a skepticism about established traditions that was on the rise in the fifth century (as we have already seen in the case of Herodotus). Some sophists questioned conventional assumptions about ethics and epistemology in ways that aroused considerable anxiety and hostility. Their enthusiasm for rhetoric caused particular concern, especially the idea, which they promoted, that it gives one the skill to argue on either side—or both sides—of any case. A related charge by their enemies was that sophists cared nothing for truth, only for persuasive technique, which could be used to defend any claim—true or false, right or wrong—glossing over unpalatable facts with specious rhetorical charm and thus "making the weaker argument defeat the stronger." In his comedy the *Clouds*, Aristophanes brought the Weaker and Stronger Arguments on stage in personified form to debate each other. Needless to say, the amoral and sophistic Weaker Argument is victorious over his conservative opponent. The young man who is sent to school with him ends up abandoning traditional morality in a way that utterly scandalizes his old-fashioned father, arguing that it is acceptable for a son to beat his parents and that Zeus no longer exists.

Such concerns did not prevent the sophists from thriving. Gorgias, in particular, acquired an enormous reputation and with it great wealth. The first time he visited Athens, in 427 BCE, he gave a public speech on behalf of his native city that stunned the Athenians with its verbal pyrotechnics. He advertised his quick wit, dexterity, and analytical skill, including the ability to improvise and answer any question on the spot, and fostered the same skills in his students. We hear of him giving rhetorical displays, at Athens, in private houses and public places such as theaters. He and other sophists also performed at the great Panhellenic festivals, where they dressed in splendid outfits and competed in theatrical style for the applause of large audiences from all over Greece. Gorgias was honored for a speech at the Pythian Games, in Delphi, with a golden statue of himself, which he may have dedicated personally. He was especially renowned for his epideictic or "display" speeches, which focused primarily on Panhellenic themes, urging unity among the often-fractious Greek city-states in face of the "barbarians" to the east.

Gorgias's *Helen* was probably composed sometime in the last quarter of the fifth century. It may have circulated in written form, but oral performance seems more appropriate. This was still the primary mode of delivery for most kinds of writing, especially oratory, and the style of *Helen*—a jingly, poetical style for which Gorgias became famous—is highly aural, rich in soundplay that must be heard to be fully appreciated. The speech may have been delivered in more than one place, and in various performance contexts, but it seems particularly well suited to Athens, where Gorgias became a well-known figure after his famous first visit. It is written in Attic Greek (the dialect of Athens), alludes to the distinctively Athenian literary genres of tragedy and public oratory, and has a central theme—the power of persuasion—that was of special interest in democratic Athens. It seems reasonable, therefore, to conceive of the speech as composed and performed for an Athenian audience.

Since epideictic oratory includes speeches of praise, Gorgias's *Helen* can be viewed as a specimen of this genre. It is, however, a peculiar one. Though nominally an encomium, his *Helen* is, in its substance, a defense speech. As such it is the first, as far as we can tell, in a rich history of playful speeches designed to display the orator's skill and creativity either by praising something trivial (mice, pebbles, bumblebees, salt) or defending the indefensible (Thersites, Clytemnestra, death). It is also the first such speech that we know of to be composed for a mythical or imaginary context. Sophists often employed myth in quite traditional ways. Prodicus, for example, is said to have made a lot of money presenting his *Choice of Heracles* as a morally improving discourse. But Gorgias, who was known for his love of paradox, thumbs his nose at such conventional uses of myth by purporting to "praise" a notorious adulteress. The result is—perhaps literally—a textbook case of "making the weaker argument defeat the stronger." Gorgias's speech is, then, intentionally provocative.

The choice of such an improbable mythic topic serves several purposes for Gorgias. It allows him to show off his ingenuity and rhetorical skill, by defending the most indefensible of "clients," without the inconvenience of concrete human circumstances. He is not representing a real person, with real friends and enemies in the audience, in a real trial that will have real (and potentially scandalous) consequences. This frees him to use Helen to explore more abstract ideas, for which she makes a natural focus, surrounding human agency, moral responsibility, and the power of persuasive discourse. In democratic Athens, oratory had taken over from the Homeric battlefield as the central arena for competitive masculine display. Helen remains an object and pretext for such display, but the weapons are now those of eloquence and intellect.

Like Herodotus, another pioneering prose author, Gorgias is interested in challenging and appropriating the prestige and cultural authority of poetry. He therefore prefaces his defense of Helen by taking on the poetic tradition en masse. He reproaches "the poets" for erroneously and (he claims) unanimously blaming Helen, and using "the message of her name" as a "reminder of disaster" (2). The Homeric Helen's self-blame, though not mentioned explicitly, is implicitly delegitimized. The idea of misplaced blame might also recall the "abuse" that the goddess Helen forced Stesichorus to retract. The phrase "the message of her name" alludes to the frequent puns on Helen's name, and perhaps specifically to Aeschylus's remarkable wordplay in *Agamemnon*. In opposition to such authors, Gorgias will, he implies, provide Helen with the praise that is her due.

An encomium typically focuses on heroic or praiseworthy deeds. Helen's defining action is, of course, diametrically opposed to the fidelity and self-sacrifice that normally supply such material in the case of women. The only attributes that provide uncontroversial grounds for praise are her birth and her beauty. Accordingly, Gorgias starts by paying brief homage to her godlike beauty and her lineage, both human and divine (3–4). Even these traits are, however, inseparable from her misbehavior, since her divine father begot her specifically to make trouble through her beauty. Praise of Helen is thus bound to devolve into exculpation, encomium into a speech for the defense.

Gorgias therefore moves quickly to the language of the courtroom. He promises to use "reasoning" (*logismos*) to remove blame from Helen, show that those who accuse her speak falsely, demonstrate the "truth" of her innocence, and put a stop to "ignorance" (2).

Unlike Stesichorus, Gorgias does not revisit the familiar "facts" of Helen's case. He is more interested in reinterpreting than rejecting or even reporting them. He does mention the courtship, as evidence for the exceptional beauty by which she "brought together" so many fine suitors, each distinguished for wealth, birth, strength, or wisdom (4). But he dispenses with further narration, passing over the specifics of the wooing and in particular Menelaus's success (something better left unemphasized, under the circumstances). He omits these things, he says, not because the story is untrue but because it is already well-known (5). This insistence on novelty tacitly justifies him in bypassing the rest of the Trojan War story (not the best terrain for praising Helen), and turning his attention to what really interests him, namely Helen's role in her own abduction.

The rest of the speech consists of a neatly structured case for the defense. Gorgias claims that there are just four possible explanations for Helen's conduct, any of which, he alleges, renders her departure for Troy "plausible," that is to say, excusable (5):

> She did what she did either because of the wishes of Chance and the plans of the gods and decrees of Necessity, or abducted by force, or persuaded by speech (*logos*), or captured by *erōs*. (6)

The suggestion that Paris might have abducted Helen violently, as opposed to seducing her, is unprecedented and remains strictly hypothetical.[1] But Gorgias's other three causes were all traditional factors in her elopement. In *Iliad* book 3, for example, which replays the original seduction (above, p. 69), the *divine* Aphrodite uses *speech* to inspire Helen with *erōs* by describing Paris's beautiful appearance. Gorgias addresses these three causes in distinct arguments, but the separation is an artificial one, since they are not mutually exclusive. As the speech proceeds they are interlaced, especially through the recurrent and overlapping themes of persuasion, magic, drugs, and divine power, all of which we have already seen associated with Helen.

Gorgias spends little time on the force argument, whose main purpose is to provide a template for a cast-iron defense. Even among the suspicious, misogynistic Greeks, forcible abduction normally exculpates its victim, provided there is no whiff of complicity in the abductee before, during, or after the event. Ex hypothesi, Helen's abduction is a case of such a kind. This allows Gorgias to

---

1. The only possible antecedent is an ambiguous line in the *Iliad* (above, pp. 62–63).

draw a sharp line between the agent, or "doer," and victim, or "sufferer." As he puts it, in such cases it is the abductor who does wrong, whereas it is both "plausible" and just for the victim to be pitied, not blamed (7). Paris therefore deserves both blame and punishment, but Helen is innocent, her victimization conveyed via a flurry of passive verbs: she "was abducted, was forced, was violated, was deprived, was bereaved," and in sum, "suffered"; Paris, on the other hand, "abducted, violated, did wrong, undertook," and in sum, "acted" (7). Gorgias's basic approach, in the remainder of the speech, is to assimilate the other three causes to this one.

The argument from divine power is also dealt with swiftly. Gorgias argues that it is "natural" for the weaker to be "ruled" and "led" by the stronger, and a god is stronger than a mortal, therefore Helen is not at fault (6). The germ of this approach can be found in the *Iliad*, when Priam reassures Helen that it is the gods who are responsible for the war. But Gorgias decontextualizes this paternalistic defense, which, as we saw, is a face-saving maneuver for everyone concerned, and as such depends on a larger framework in which Helen herself takes responsibility for her actions (above, pp. 61, 63–64). Even in Homer, divine power is not a legitimate means of defense, and in the classical period this kind of argument was strongly linked with the sophists. In Aristophanes' *Clouds*, for example, the sophistic Weaker Argument instructs his student:

If you're caught committing adultery, this is what you'll tell the husband:
That you've done nothing wrong. Then transfer the blame to Zeus,
saying that even *he's* defeated by *erōs* and by women,
and how could you, a mortal, be stronger than a god?

(1079–82)

The argument is not quite the same as Gorgias's, since the youth is not advised to claim that he was defeated by a god himself. But the tone, themes, and basic approach are similar, with the argument depending on the superhuman power of *erōs* to conquer even the mightiest of the gods, and hence, a fortiori, any mortal.

Gorgias gives his third hypothesis more attention. Speech (*logos*), he declares, can induce or remove positive or negative emotions: joy, sorrow, fear, courage, pity, longing, pleasure (8–9, 14). It has the power to "mold" the *psuchē*—the soul or psyche—which it affects like a drug that can kill or cure (13, 14). The molding image posits the mind as a passive, lifeless substance like clay. *Logos* itself, in contrast, is a "powerful ruler" that accomplishes "most divine deeds" (8). As such it exercises an irresistible compulsion on the hearer, regardless of the truth or probity of its content. If Helen was persuaded by speech to go to Troy, this was, according to Gorgias, the moral equivalent of violent abduction (12). As with the argument from force, Helen, qua passive hearer, is not guilty; the "persuader" is guilty, having actively exercised compulsion. Her elopement was not a misdeed, but a "mischance" (15)—merely an unfortunate accident.

Gorgias supports this limb of the argument by pointing to various examples of the power of speech. The first is poetry, whose well-known influence on the emotions he appropriates for speech more broadly:

> Into those hearing it there comes frightening fear and tearful pity
> and mournful longing, and through speeches the *psuchē* experiences
> its own suffering at the good and ill fortune of other people's doings
> and persons. (9)

The next example is magic spells (10), which were likewise associated with emotional manipulation, particularly of the erotic variety. But Gorgias's conception of "speech" also embraces such rational modes of discourse as astronomy and philosophy (13). He mentions, in addition, competitive public oratory (13), the very genre that he is in the process of exploiting. All forms of discourse are thus subsumed under the larger umbrella of Gorgianic *logos*. Despite the inclusion of rational argument, however, it is speech's anticognitive impact that excuses Helen, since it expelled her "mind" (12). Gorgias thus appropriates for speech the kind of irrational power traditionally attributed to Helen's own beauty and the *erōs* it inspires, along with the magic and drugs with which such forces are so often equated.

Speech has this power because humans are fallible and ignorant, lacking sure knowledge of past, present, and future and relying, in consequence, on mere opinions (11). This is why Helen, like the rest of us, could be "deceived" by it (8). There has been much scholarly discussion about Gorgias's notion of "deception," mostly focused on whether he views discourse as intrinsically deceptive in some sense. In the context of a speech about Helen, however, the audience would surely think first of the erotic "deception" that typifies Aphrodite's operations. What, exactly, Paris may have said to Helen is left to our imaginations (we may perhaps recall his seductive speech to her in the *Iliad*). But it is hard to imagine a truly deceptive speech on his part—even outright lies—that would, in ordinary terms, exonerate her. If Helen was "ignorant," her ignorance was surely the moral "ignorance" that does not excuse but convicts. By equating this quasi-metaphorical "ignorance" and "deception" with physical violence Gorgias erases the line between persuasion and force, a distinction that may sometimes be fuzzy, but is nonetheless fundamental to moral responsibility and with it to human civilization.

The fourth and final argument concerns the power of *erōs*. In Gorgias's telling this works very much like *logos*, but operates, not surprisingly, through the sense of sight instead of hearing. Like persuasive speech, powerful sights "mold the psyche in its character" (15), and "engrave" or "paint" images of what is seen upon the mind (17). As with speech the results may be strongly negative, both emotionally and ethically. Soldiers in battle are often terrified when they see heavily armed enemies, and run away, because the sight disturbs their psyches, drives them out of their minds, and banishes rational thought (15–17). Like speech—which can kill as well as cure—such sights can even inflict "terrible diseases," by inducing an insanity not easily healed (17; cf. 19). As with the speech argument, Gorgias conflates the mental disturbance of powerful emotions with the kind of derangement that really does exculpate its sufferers, typically replacing blame with pity—the emotion Gorgias claims we should feel for Helen (7).

The impact of terrifying sights is strongly emphasized, indeed exaggerated, by Gorgias, in order to assimilate the power of vision to other forms of coercion. It also serves to prepare us for his attribution of an equally irresistible force to attractive visual phenomena, which "compel" the viewer toward them instead of away. The latter are first exemplified by beautiful paintings and sculptures, which likewise provide a "disease for the eyes" (albeit a "sweet" one) (18).[2] This probably refers to the ability of illusionistic art objects to deceive us by their appearance, which may suggest that the eyes are somehow defective. But even if this is the phrase's overt meaning, in the present context it evokes inescapably the familiar metaphor of the "disease" of *erōs*, which Gorgias uses explicitly just a few lines later (19). Artistic images are, of course, traditional comparanda for beautiful people. By employing the word "disease" for the visual impact of such images the sophist blurs the line between the beauty of a work of art and that of a living person, whose effect tends to be far more consequential.

Gorgias blurs that boundary still further by presenting such objects as actively affecting the receiving mind, which itself becomes a passive object, a work of art "molded" (15) or "painted" (17) by external forces. These metaphors evoke the paralyzing effect sometimes attributed to great beauty, reinforcing the helplessness of its victim. The "deception" or "ignorance" suffered by such a victim is, however, of a very different kind from that produced by an illusionistic artwork. The effect is not visual confusion, but moral blindness. Such was the effect on Helen of the sight of Paris, which induced in her an "enthusiasm and striving of *erōs*" (19). Since *erōs*, Gorgias says, is either a god (with the overwhelming divine power discussed earlier) or a "disease" that induces "ignorance in the psyche," her behavior should be attributed to "necessity" and therefore not blamed, but viewed, once more, as a "mischance" (19).

In both of his sustained arguments—the arguments from speech and vision—Gorgias erases the ambiguities inherent in poetic and traditional discourse in order to undermine the standard view that the "deception," "violence," and "madness" of erotic passion explain sexual transgression without excusing it. This strategy parallels his sophistic treatment of the power of the gods. Gorgias blithely ignores the complexities embedded in mainstream views not only

---

2. The word "disease" (*noson*) is an emendation, but widely accepted by scholars.

of divine influence but also of *erōs* and even persuasion, which do not, normally, draw this kind of bright line between agent and object in order to excuse the latter. The divine excuse is, in fact, interwoven with the other three causes: the gods' power is equivalent to violence, *logos* is divine in its power, and *erōs* can be personified as a god.

Thanks to its Homeric background, the argument from divine power also underwrites the speech and *erōs* arguments in another way. Both of the latter depend on treating strong emotions as induced by overwhelmingly powerful external forces. This is just how the gods function in epic, where they are presented as external powers that yet influence human action through the internal processes of the psyche. This conception of the gods introduces the rhetorical possibility of denying human responsibility on the basis of divine involvement (exemplified by Priam's defense of Helen in the *Iliad*). Gorgias exploits this possibility, specious though it is, by extending the paradigm of divine intervention to other kinds of external stimuli that generate a powerful feeling or drive. It is this that enables him to treat Helen as a mere object without responsibility for acting in response to her feelings, whether those feelings are inspired by the gods, words, or the sight of the beautiful Paris.

The result, as critics have complained since antiquity, is not much of an encomium—at least of Helen. What is actually praised in Gorgias's speech is, in the end, not Helen herself but the art of rhetoric that rides gallantly to her defense. As an encomiastic object Helen is merely noble, beautiful, and not guilty—somewhat faint praise! Speech, by contrast, is granted a full measure of personified agency, as "a powerful ruler" performing deeds that are "most divine" (8). But speech is not, of course, really an agent, any more than an artwork is. Before it can "mold" the psyche of its audience, it must first be "fabricated" by a skillful writer (11, 13). It is the writer or sculptor who is empowered by Gorgias's argument, and the writer, and metaphorical sculptor, is himself.

The sophist's praise of speech is obviously self-referential, referring to his own stock-in-trade and to this work in particular. In the final summary of what he has allegedly achieved the word *logos* occurs no less than three times, interlaced with a strenuous insistence on the author's agency:

> I removed by my speech a woman's bad reputation; I kept to the
> purpose I set myself at the beginning of the speech; I set out to
> dispel unjust blame and ignorant opinion; I wished to write the
> speech as an encomium of Helen and an amusement for myself. (21)

Gorgias was not a self-effacing man. In performance there can have been no doubt that the event was about *him*, the power of *his* speech, and what *he* is doing to manipulate his audience. In denying Helen's agency he is asserting his own. In silencing her, he is ensuring that the only voice we hear is his. He makes himself the center of attention at Helen's expense, standing literally at center stage while she remains invisible and unheard.

Other writers had, of course, deprived Helen of a voice, but Gorgias goes further, inverting her relationship to language by making her its victim. In Homer Helen is an active persuader, a "poet" and weaver of spells and stories who controls her own story and as far as possible her life. Gorgias appropriates these qualities for speech itself, which arouses the kind of powerful emotions typically associated with Helen—delight, fear, pleasure, grief, desire. He exploits, in addition, the traditional interconnections between verbal persuasion, *erōs*, and magic, all of which are linked with Helen, attributing them to speech as the medium of his own power. He himself is the "Helen" praised in this speech, the enchanting verbal manipulator who captures the eye and ear as he administers the drug of discourse taken from her hands. Helen remains an emblem of the power of language, but only as a tool for the sophist's use—a prop for his own display of rhetorical magic.

The silencing of Helen places Gorgias's speech in conformity with Greek gender norms, especially at Athens, where a woman involved in a trial had to be represented by her male guardian. As a Sicilian, the sophist could not speak in a real Athenian court, but he creates for himself a courtroom of the imagination, taking on the dramatic role of Helen's protector and advocate. This fictional setting is complemented by aspects of his argument, which takes advantage at several points of conventional gender ideology. When Gorgias declares it "natural," for example, for the weaker to be "ruled" and "led" by the stronger (6), he is evoking the power dynamic of Greek marriage. The molding image, which posits the *psuchē* as a malleable substance like clay, recalls both the creation of Hesiod's Pandora and the soft, impressionable nature of female flesh (cf. above, pp. 10 and 15). And in the speech argument, where *logos* is the "persuader" of the *psuchē* (12), Gorgias takes advantage of the fact that the word *logos* is grammatically gendered as masculine, and *psuchē* as feminine. The resulting ambiguities allow him to equate the active power of speech with the male and the passive psyche with the female. The feminine weakness of Helen's *psuchē* implicitly explains her supposedly helpless submission to the authoritative, masculine power of verbal persuasion.

Such weakness was conventionally used to justify subjecting women to male control and suppressing their public voice and presence, just as Helen's is suppressed in this imaginary courtroom. In an elegant trick, however, Gorgias uses Helen's submission to the power of persuasion not as evidence for reprehensible feminine weakness but as grounds for excusing the most scandalous behavior. His argument highlights the tension inherent in the conventional view of women as objects who are nonetheless responsible for their actions. By declaring Helen *no more than* a passive object, Gorgias cuts this Gordian knot. But the price is a high one: the exoneration of lustful, adulterous women.

This soon leads into even more alarming territory. Exploiting the gender binary in such an extreme form backfires to undermine not only Helen's guilt but all moral responsibility. To start with, the dichotomy between Paris and Helen as agent and victim, upon which the argument is built, cannot withstand scrutiny. Gorgias's audience, who knew the familiar story, were well aware that Paris's behavior was caused by the same combination of divine power, *erōs*, and persuasion as Helen's: the divine Aphrodite, with her stunning appearance at the Judgment of Paris and her (verbal) offer of Helen, followed by the sight of Helen herself. By insisting so strongly on the power of such external forces Gorgias implies, contrary to his own premise, that the abductor is, in fact, as innocent as the abducted. In Paris's case, however, the sophist slices the knot a different way, declaring *this* object of external forces a responsible agent. The disparity in his treatment of the two transgressors falls, predictably, along gender lines, with parallel and complementary oversimplification in both cases: men act and women are acted upon.

Perhaps we should infer that Gorgias's argument rests on an unstated but "obvious" assumption of feminine weakness, differentiating Helen from Paris by means of the standard dichotomy of gender. Yet that dichotomy is not sustained throughout the speech. Other men—and much more "manly" men than Paris—are implicitly excused, like Helen, for the most disgraceful behavior. Gorgias's first example of the power of vision concerns terrifying sights on the battlefield. Resistance to fear, especially in battle, is central to the distinctively masculine virtue of courage or "manliness." Yet the sight of armed enemies, Gorgias says, makes men turn tail in defiance of "law," "(moral) beauty," "goodness," and "justice" (16). This string of terms, all laden with normative cultural weight, underlines the ethical consequences of Gorgias's line of argument: it erases the criteria for judging not only Helen's elopement but honorable Greek masculinity. Nor is his example restricted to exceptional cowards. Men "often" flee in panic, "many" become insane out of fear, and "many" other frightening sights have a similar impact (16–17). Gorgias's overt agenda gave him no compelling need to draw examples from the masculine realm of warfare, or indeed to mention the power of any negative sights. The sight of beauty would have sufficed for his immediate purpose. Instead, he defends Helen in a way that excuses the worst possible behavior in men as well as women.

Gorgias's second set of visual examples, concerning beautiful sights, is more attuned to the female sphere insofar as it concerns erotic weakness. Yet he does not gender such susceptibility as feminine, situating it, rather, in a context that once again includes and even emphasizes male behavior. His examples, which as we saw are drawn from the visual arts, embrace all kinds of pleasing artistic images. Some art objects in Greek life were designed to be viewed by women, but the sophist's diction evokes primarily the kind of public art whose notional audience was made up of men. When he speaks of statues of human figures, cult images, and paintings (18), he is referring to items that were made almost exclusively by men, primarily for other men to view. The argument is presented, too, in very general terms: "Many things create in many people *erōs* and desire for many things and bodies" (18). This not only broadens the range of those affected by beauty, but generalizes the resulting desire for beautiful things beyond the realm of the strictly erotic to include as its objects not just works of art but anything at all that could be considered beautiful. Helen's elopement—caused by the delight her eye took in the sight of Paris's body (19)—takes its place as just one example of a generalized human susceptibility to the emotional power of visual phenomena.

The *logos* argument is likewise supported by largely masculine examples with serious implications for Gorgias's audience. Magical speech, to be sure, has feminine associations, since it gives women the ability to manipulate men, but many practitioners of magic (as well as its victims) were male. Poetry, too, is linked conceptually with femininity (for example, through the Muses), but virtually all the well-known poets and their audiences were men. Gorgias presents the power of poetry in a way that emphasizes audience identification with its characters (9), a phenomenon associated with the power of performance and thus with the histrionic public genres of drama and epic, whose primary audience was the male citizenry. He also mentions the exclusively masculine discourses of astronomy, philosophy, and oratory (13). Broadly speaking, the world of speech was the world of men, especially in Athens, with its strong ideology of female silence and public male discourse. The art of verbal persuasion touted by Gorgias was integral to the functioning of democracy and its institutions. Thucydides' Pericles, for example, presents the Athenian skill at reasoning, deliberation, and the judging of speeches as the foundation of their distinctive political system (2.40.2–3). Gorgias's argument thus applies to every Athenian male who has voted in the Assembly or cast his vote in a jury trial. As he exclaims, in terms suggestive of an epidemic, "How many people have persuaded and do persuade how many about how many things!" (11). In order to excuse Helen he denies agency, and with it moral responsibility, to every democratic citizen.

Between them, then, the speech and vision arguments embrace the broad array of activities open to male citizens in classical Athens—artistic, military, political, intellectual—from most of which women were barred. In case anything slips through the cracks, however, Gorgias presents divine power in a way that eliminates any remaining opportunities for human responsibility. He speaks of supernatural forces in an impersonal, abstract fashion that makes them apply not just to "many" actions but to human action as such. He allows that *erōs* may be divine, but treats it less as a personal agent than as a quasiscientific power: if it is not a god, he remarks, it is a disease (19). The argument from divine power itself does not focus on Aphrodite—who would have sufficed where Helen is concerned—or any other anthropomorphic divinity. Gorgias speaks only of "the gods" (or "the god"—an abstract locution), grouping them with Chance and Necessity (6). These last two were sometimes thought of as divine, but do not normally appear as mythic personalities. They are, rather, abstract forces governing any and all aspects of human life. Hence their use to reinforce Gorgias's other arguments. Both speech and *erōs* work by "necessity" (12, 19), and the result is a "mischance" (15, 19). This kind of language was also used in medical inquiry and natural philosophy, where it is linked with ideas about impersonal materialist causation.

The argument overall thus implies not only that Helen is innocent but that no human being can be blamed for anything whatsoever. As a corollary, it also erases responsibility for virtuous action. Gorgias's praise for Helen's suitors (4) is rendered meaningless, as is the Trojan War as an arena for defining admirable masculinity, since the Greeks were (by Gorgias's own account) acting in response to Helen's beauty, as she was to Paris's (4, 19). Nor are these implications limited to the legendary past. The Athenian citizens who cast their votes in the Assembly or lawcourts, after listening to various orators make their case, are deprived of credit as well as criticism for their decisions. The same applies to those who "fall in love" with their city and perform deeds of virtue and courage on its behalf, as Pericles urged them to do (Thuc. 2.43.1–2). If *erōs* for "things" as well as people eliminates moral responsibility, such patriots deserve no more praise than Helen does blame. Gorgias has not only defended the most notorious of mythic adulterers, but done so using arguments that undermine all moral judgment.

This is not the speech's only radical implication. Gorgias's examples, as we saw, are drawn almost exclusively from the world of men. Traditionally, the gendered realms of warfare and *erōs* are used to define and complicate each other. The erotic impact of beauty is often likened to violent assault, for example, while the realm of warfare is eroticized. But Gorgias makes these connections more than metaphorical. The impact of beauty on the eyes works in *exactly the same way* as the impact of the terrifying sight of armed enemies. Nor is there any indication that men are better able than women to resist the forces of *erōs*, speech, or divine power, which are equated and aligned through overlapping diction. A notorious case of "feminine" weakness is explained by behavioral patterns that apply equally to men, and, moreover, to every sphere of masculine life. The application of such models to Helen implies that a woman's psyche is not intrinsically different from that of a man. By the same token, the argument equates male psychological processes with those of a woman.

This equation is reinforced by the fact that the speech draws no distinction between the male and female psyche or nature. References to feminine weakness, or female erotic susceptibility, are conspicuous by their absence, in a context that might seem to cry out for them. Gorgias mentions no woman besides Helen and says nothing at all about women or female nature as such. By avoiding overt attention to gender, and at the same time analyzing and explaining Helen's action through a broad spectrum of human (and predominantly male) activities, Gorgias makes her a vehicle for understanding the forces that bear upon all human beings. In so doing he challenges the gender binary by offering a female psychology indistinguishable from that of the male. He abandons the traditional Greek perception of women as a different "race," physiologically and psychologically different in kind from men, making Helen's act exemplary not just of feminine behavior, but of human behavior as such.

Gorgias's other surviving works betray no hint of radical determinism or rejection of the gender binary. The evidence suggests that, on the contrary, he shared the conventional moral values of his time. Nor would it be in his interest, as a teacher of oratory, to promote such notions. Aside from anything else, the argument undermines his own agency along with Helen's, and with it any claim to praise for his own no doubt bravura performance. It is equally contrary to his interests to insult potential clients by denying them the possibility of agency. If his male audience took him seriously, they would be not only outraged by the denial of Helen's guilt but grievously insulted at being reduced to mindless putty by orators wielding the power of the *logos*, and, worse, feminized as a psychic weakling by assimilation to the notorious Helen. Gorgias therefore assures his audience, in his final words, that the speech is not serious—it is only a "plaything" or "amusement" for himself (21).

These words flag Gorgias's "encomium" of Helen as a rhetorical jeu d'esprit, a defense of the indefensible, of a kind that was strongly associated with the sophists, especially by the disapproving Plato. In Plato's *Symposium*, for example, the sophistic Agathon argues that Eros, of all people, is "most self-controlled" (196b), in a speech that he himself calls partly playful and partly serious (197e) and that Socrates jokingly characterizes as Gorgianic (198c). In *Phaedrus* the orator Lysias argues that a love object should yield to the one who does not love him rather than the one who does (227c), and in *Euthydemus*, a sophist "proves" that his interlocutor's father is his dog, and hence that he beats his own father (298de). All these "amusements" reach obviously unacceptable conclusions. No one expects you to be talked into believing that your father is a dog. The point is not to convince people of such absurdities, but to make a novel and ingenious case for an improbable point of view. Similarly, Gorgias's goal is not really to convince us that Helen is innocent. Like the sophistic arguments parodied by Plato, his speech has a specious rationality that entertains but does not convince. A joke is not really *meant* to convince anyone, only to amuse.

Gorgias provides his final phrase as a safety net, just in case anyone took him at his word, to reassure them that he is not, after all, personally endorsing the "weaker" cause. But the majority of his audience would not require any such caveat. Greek authors catered to a sophisticated and critical audience, especially at Athens, where, as we just saw, a love of rhetorical argument was central to democratic ideology. The reason Gorgias made such an impact on his first visit to the city was, we are told, because the Athenians are "naturally talented" and "lovers of *logos*" (DK 82 A4). Plato tells essentially the same story, despite elements of caricature. He presents Phaedrus as enraptured by Lysias's "cleverness" (*Phdr.* 228a, 236b) and the sophists' audience in *Euthydemus* as applauding and laughing with delight (303b). Gorgias's *Helen* is addressed, likewise, to an audience of connoisseurs. As he makes clear at the outset, he is speaking to people who know the familiar old stories and will enjoy something novel (5)—an audience that will appreciate his games.

Despite the speech's imaginary setting, then, Gorgias's relationship to his audience is not governed by the serious concerns of the courtroom. Nor are his arguments those that a real Athenian defendant would employ. He informs us explicitly that he intends to privilege enjoyment over persuasiveness. He is omitting the details of Helen's story, he says, not because they are untrue but because "telling people what they already know carries conviction, but does not bring delight" (5). This lack of interest in what "carries conviction" makes Gorgias a very bad advocate for the defense. We are invited to judge not the "defendant" but the speaker himself, for his wit and cleverness, and the success of his performance for its entertainment value, not its ability to convince. The speech is, in fact, enjoyable as an "amusement" in part *because* no one would buy the arguments if they were subjected to rational scrutiny. Enjoying its ingenuity actually depends on finding it unconvincing—otherwise the proper response would be outrage at the shocking view of the world that it implies.

Given his glorification of persuasive speech, however—not to mention his interest in attracting ambitious clients—why would Gorgias produce, even in play, a speech that was not intended to persuade them of the case for which it argues? What educational function could it serve for the budding democratic politician? Speeches like *Helen* were certainly not in any literal sense exemplary for the practical orator. Nevertheless, they did demonstrate highly marketable skills. Besides their ability to delight an audience—itself a precious commodity—they provided a valuable exercise in quick wit. Arguing absurdities or defending trivia could be considered a useful training ground for addressing weightier topics. Gorgias's student Isocrates was to scoff at this notion, but in doing so he confirms the prevalence of such views. People who make speeches defending trivial, paradoxical positions, he says,

> use this as proof that, if they have something to say about worthless matters, they will easily find a lot to say about things that are good and noble. What seems to me most ridiculous of all is that they seek to persuade people by these speeches that they have knowledge about the business of politics. (10.8–9)

Isocrates is referring here to the practice of defending the indefensible that Gorgias initiated with his *Helen*. It seems reasonable to assume that in the fifth century this kind of rhetorical play was already being justified along such lines.

The use of paradoxical argument for training in wit and ingenuity does not, however, exclude an interest in serious ideas for their own sake, in either the speaker or his intended audience. As with some of the arguments drama- tized by Plato—himself a master of "serious play"—the very absurdity of Gor- gias's conclusions (both expressed and implied) challenges the audience to scrutinize the quality of his arguments. The sophist declares at the outset that his particular contribution to Helen's story will be "reasoning" (*logismos*) and that one of his goals is to free people from "ignorance" (2)—a goal he claims, at the end, to have achieved (21). Such language provokes his audience, even as they enjoy the playful arguments that follow, to reflect on their cogency and apply "reasoning" of their own.

If we do so, we will find clues enabling the thoughtful reader to rebut the speech's shocking claims and still more shocking implications. The funda- mental weakness in its deterministic psychology is the simple equation of external influences on the psyche with violence done to the body. The "molding" of Helen's psyche by such forces as speech and vision does not, in fact, excuse her for acting on the resulting impulses. If her action was driven by her own desire, then it is an act for which she is responsible. In the argument from force Paris is indeed the agent or "doer," Helen the object (7). In all the others, however, despite the sophist's use of the passive voice, Helen herself is an agent. Gorgias is clear about this when announcing his own agenda. He will explain why Helen "*did* what she *did*" (6). The same words recur at the end of the speech, when he summarizes what he has supposedly proved (20). This seemingly innocent phrase, strategically placed to introduce the four argu- ments and then conclude them, is juxtaposed provocatively, on both occasions, with a string of passive verbs rendering Helen a mere victim. Gorgias under- cuts his own assertions of Helen's agency by allowing the passive verb forms to prevail, but the tension generated by his wording can just as well be taken as a challenge to the active/passive binary on which the speech ostensibly insists.

If we dismiss Gorgias's deterministic conclusions, his account is, rather, an analysis of weakness of will, the very lack of self-control that was Helen's traditional fault. As such it is an analysis of agency under particular circumstances—of *acting* against one's better judgment, as *erōs* notoriously makes one do. Helen's behavior is in this respect no different from that of Paris, the "doer," who was equally influenced by external forces but is yet held responsible for his actions. Viewed in this way, as an examination of agency in the face of both external and internal (psychological) forces, the speech pro- vides the most detailed analysis of Helen's subjectivity that we have encoun- tered. This is most evident in the vision argument, where Gorgias focuses on her own motivation. Paris is the beautiful object, the equivalent of a statue or picture, she the onlooker who responds. The active character of this response is highlighted by the rather tortured description of her desire as an "enthusiasm and striving" of *erōs* (19). The Greek word translated as "striving" (*hamilla*) sounds odd here, since it typically denotes competitive struggle (often in masculine arenas such as athletic contests or competition for a bride). It makes Helen's desire sound like the "victory-loving" *erōs* that drove her own suitors (4), reinstating her *erōs* for Paris as a force for active self-assertion on her part.

The involvement of Helen's will is also implicit in the speech argument. As Gorgias puts it, speech "compels" the psyche by "necessity" not only "to obey what is said" but "to approve of what is done" (12). According to Plato, Gorgias distinguished between violence and verbal persuasion by saying the latter "makes all things its slaves not through violence but because they are willing" (*Phlb.* 58b). In other Greek texts such acquiescence likewise marks submission to the "compulsion" of beauty and *erōs*, as distinct, for example, from physical coercion (Pl. *Symp.* 196bc; Isoc. 10.57). It is this element of approval that makes one responsible for acting on one's own desires, as Helen did, unlike a kidnapping victim who is taken against her will.

If voluntary submission to such forces is culpable, however, then resistance must somehow lie within our power. Even though "many" people "often" panic in response to fearful sights, not *every* solider *always* runs away (16–17). How, then, does the virtuous agent resist the impact of such feelings? Here again Gorgias's speech provides clues. As the physician who administers the "drug" of speech, a skilled orator has the power to affect human behavior for better as well as for worse. Sights may induce fear, but Gorgias himself declares that speech can "stop fear" and induce boldness (8, 14)—we may think, perhaps, of a rousing exhortation on the battlefield. The means by which *logos* produces such results include not only emotional manipulation but also the power of reason. Gorgias's argument depends on viewing the psyche as completely passive, never rational or purposeful in face of emotional influences. Yet he himself signals the importance of reason from the outset, when he declares "wisdom" to be the "ornament" (*kosmos*) of the psyche. Some of Helen's suitors, too, are distinguished for their "wisdom," which is deemed both praiseworthy and a source of power (4). It is also, significantly, described as something that can be acquired, presumably by means of education or rational inquiry.

Wisdom is, in fact, the source of Gorgias's own power, which his students may in turn "acquire" from him. The sophist insists, as we saw, that his own contribution is "reasoning" and that he will put a stop to "ignorance" (2). Gorgianic *logos* includes the discourse of astronomers and philosophers, which, he explicitly tells us, can change people's considered judgment (13). In this case, at least, the power of speech must depend in part on its rational content and logical cogency. He also alludes to the power of rhetorical "skill" (*technē*) (13), a term that implies rational understanding of a craft. Such skill enables the orator to arouse emotion but also, where appropriate, to appeal to reason. The orator's own art, as Gorgias portrays it, therefore undermines the deterministic implications of the argument by exalting the ability of reason to affect action, both by empowering the orator and by enabling him to influence the opinions and feelings of his audience.

If Gorgias's *Helen* was successful on its own terms—that is, as an intellectually provocative "amusement"—those implications will have been further undermined in performance through the response of his audience. The desired effect depends, as we saw, on refusing to take Gorgias's arguments at face value. The sophist thus relies on his audience's capacity for rational resistance to the mighty power of speech, even as he harnesses that power to his own end. By rejecting his conclusions and the reasoning by which he reaches them, we are not only condemning Helen for failing to resist Paris's words but demonstrating, through our own resistance, the falsehood of Gorgias's claim that it was impossible for her to do so. Speech may be a powerful ruler, but it is not an irresistible force.

The speech's other scandalous implication, its challenge to the gender binary, is not undermined so directly. In order to reject Gorgias's implied assumption of gender equality, his audience would have to supply from their own experience the "evidence" of male rational superiority provided by their own civic and military activities. Once again, however, this would become clear in performance. As we saw earlier, *logos* is a masculine force, and not merely because it is masculine grammatically. Although it can be used for any kind of speech, this word has strong ties, in particular, to rational discourse. (It is no accident that the word for reasoning, *logismos*, is derived from it.) Such discourse was, of course, coded as masculine in Greek culture. The rational activities referred to within the speech are also activities of men. Since, therefore, the performer and implied audience are both male, the experience of resistance in Gorgias's audience implicitly reinstates the gender binary by enacting male superiority. Helen, the only female present even nominally in the speech, shows no sign of rational activity or of resisting, rationally or otherwise, the forces arrayed against her psyche. The men in the audience are invited, in consequence, to see themselves as her intellectual and moral superiors. By appealing to reason, then offering his outrageous speech as a target for critique, Gorgias reaffirms conventional gender ideology by flattering the rational capacity of the male. The ability to reinstate blame of Helen in face of his arguments allows his male audience—threatened with rhetorical emasculation by those arguments—to reinstate praise of themselves. The equation of the male and female *psuchē* seems, after all, to be part of the joke.

Yet Gorgias's "amusement" remains a kind of intellectual Trojan Horse. In the reassuring guise of a mere joke it raises acute ethical and psychological issues that are still under discussion today. At the time when he was writing, Greek thinkers—not only sophists, but philosophers, orators, scientific and medical writers—were becoming ever more fascinated with questions surrounding the conditions of responsible human action, voluntariness, and blame, questions that would be taken up in the next century by Plato, Aristotle, and their successors. Gorgias's most distinctive contribution to this intellectual ferment was his argument for a radical, or "hard," determinism. Determinism is a defensible position, intuitively plausible to many, which requires sophisticated thought to rebut. The sophist's "amusement" raised questions about causation and responsibility that were destined to have a long philosophical history—a history that is not yet at an end.

The conventional wisdom stipulating that men and women are essentially different was also starting to come under scrutiny in Gorgias's day, albeit more tentatively. Plato's Socrates challenges the mainstream views of a character named Meno (a student, interestingly, of Gorgias), by asserting that excellence is the same for men and women, and indeed that all human beings are excellent in the same way (*Meno* 72c–73c). Such themes are also found in drama—both tragedy and comedy—notably Euripides' *Medea*, where the heroine complains at length about the subordinate status of women in Athenian society (214–66). Dramatic form enables Euripides to distance himself from such controversial notions, and air a novel perspective on the sexual double standard without taking up a position in his own voice. Regardless of his personal views, however, his script put these ideas into play, where they have been ever since. By equating the male and female psyche Gorgias too, in his perverse way, is contributing to the "new" thinking about gender. His designation of his own work as an "amusement" serves, like Euripides' dramatic context, as a shield from behind which to air such intellectual provocations without committing himself to them personally.

The potential significance of this implied challenge to the gender binary may be seen from its reappearance—more fully and consistently developed— in Plato's *Republic*, where Socrates claims that the psyche of a woman is no different in kind from a man's, and female nature no different, fundamentally, from that of the male (452e–456b). It follows that women should be educated like men and participate with them in government at every level. In contrast to Gorgias, Socrates emphasizes his seriousness, but he does so in part—we should note—by portraying his proposals as something that ordinary people will find hilariously funny. Though the "feminist" credentials of Plato's argument are a matter of heated dispute, it is enormously important for the history of gender. But Gorgias foreshadowed that argument by a generation, when he used human nature and the psyche as such to explain Helen's behavior without gendering it as a consequence of "feminine" weakness. Despite Helen's erasure as an agent from Gorgias's *Helen*, then, the speech uses her notorious action to explore the nature of human action as such. In the process, the woman who served, traditionally, as the very model of the emotional, moral, and psychological weakness that differentiates women from men becomes a vehicle for challenging that difference. A joke is never *just* a joke, and this one is no exception.

9

Enter Helen: Euripides' *Trojan Women*

You flick your mane and click your fingers again,
And from your bed you call my name,
And like a fool I run right back to you,
And dance along to your latest tune.
And when the land slides,
And when the planets die,
That's when I come back, when I come back to you.
—Brett Anderson

Deprived of her Homeric eloquence by Aeschylus, Gorgias, and many others, Helen's voice was restored to her by the playwright Euripides. She was a natural choice for him. Even in his own time Euripides was known for his interest in transgressive women; the Trojan War is central to many of his plays, most of which were produced in the shadow of the Peloponnesian War; and he was influenced by fifth-century intellectual developments, including the fascination with problems of agency and responsibility exemplified in Gorgias's *Helen* (above, chapter 8). These strands come together in his tragedy *Trojan Women*, first produced in 415 BCE, which presents the most prominent female characters from inside Troy, with a chorus of female captives, lamenting their city's destruction and their own fate as slaves to the victorious Greeks. The drama consists of a series of scenes between Hecuba and three other women, first Cassandra, then Andromache (accompanied by her infant son Astyanax), and finally Helen, who enters about two-thirds of the way into the play and defends herself in Gorgianic style.

When Helen made her entrance in 415 BCE, this may well have been her first appearance on the tragic stage. To the best of our knowledge, earlier Trojan War tragedies kept her offstage, constructing her entirely through the voices of other, mostly hostile, characters. In *Trojan Women*, however, she became a physical presence, confronting the audience with the living impact of a moving, speaking body and eyes that returned their gaze. Euripides thus grants her a dramatically presented subjectivity, and with it the possibility of audience identification and sympathy. Thanks to the kind of emotional identification that we saw emphasized by Gorgias (above, p. 169), classical Greeks worried a good deal about the psychological impact of such dramatic "impersonations." If we are to believe Aristophanes, Euripides in particular was criticized for staging "bad" women who might set other women a bad example (*Frogs* 1043–56). Helen's appearance must therefore have been quite a coup de théâtre.

What did she look like? Unlike modern casting directors, Euripides did not confront the impossible task of selecting an actor who supposedly embodies in her person a beauty that is in its very nature unrepresentable. The stylization of Greek theater defused from the outset any such expectation of "realism." Helen would be portrayed on stage not by a particular real woman (whose beauty the audience might assess by comparing it to others), but by a masked male actor. As we saw earlier, masks were not realistic portraits of a specific individual, but simple, conventional, and neutral in feature and expression. The mask of the actor playing Helen does not have to resemble a unique person named Helen, or anyone's particular conception of "the most beautiful woman in the world"; it only has to declare, "These are the signifiers of female beauty." The neutrality of the mask also assists in conveying beauty, since idiosyncrasy and even extreme facial expressions would depart from the generic character of Greek aesthetic ideals. Helen's beauty would therefore be shown, like that of any other female figure, by basic, easily visible features such as long wavy hair and light skin. The conventional nature of such signs makes them an effective, culturally coded means of expression, and their simplicity serves to prompt the imagination rather than confining it to the contours of an individual "real" person. The stylization of theater thus assists in conveying the imaginary, nonliteral quality of Helen's beauty.

The special power of Helen's beauty, as distinct from other women's, is, however, expressed by means of textual cues and the larger dramatic context, which "instruct" the reactions of the audience. Like Aeschylus with his Furies, Euripides frames Helen's appearance as exceptional and her beauty as awe-inspiring in its power long before she actually enters, beginning with the staging.[1]

The set represents one or more huts where some of the Trojan prisoners, including Helen, are being held. Behind it is the city of Troy, described by Poseidon in the prologue as a smoldering ruin filled with the wails of captive

---

1. Since *Trojan Women* is the third play of a trilogy this framing began in the two earlier plays, but they are unfortunately almost entirely lost.

women (8–9, 28–29). The audience cannot literally see or hear what he describes, but the scene is conveyed to the eyes—and ears—of the imagination through this verbal "scene painting," which is sustained throughout the drama. Behind the performance space, however, the audience seated on the slopes of the acropolis could see their own city, which thus became an extension of the stage set, inviting them to perceive Athens itself in the role of Troy and in consequence to empathize viscerally with the Trojans. This identification is enhanced by the appearance of Athena herself in the prologue, and by references to her temple and statue (69–70, 599). It is, however, a complex one. The Athenians took pride in their leading role against "barbarians" in the Persian Wars, for which the Trojan War was a legendary paradigm. Yet the leaders of the expedition to Troy came from Sparta, the enemy of Athens in the Peloponnesian War, which was under way at the time the drama was first produced. When Euripides' audience projected the ruins of Troy onto their own splendidly built city, they may have thought of the burning of Athens by non-Greeks in the Persian Wars (a crisis that haunted Athenian memory), but equally of the present threat posed by their Spartan enemies.

Euripides' staging thus manifests from the outset the terrible consequences for Troy of Helen's elopement. His script insists on her personal responsibility for those consequences, preparing us for her entrance by means of a torrent of abuse directed at her by other characters. Hecuba, Cassandra, and Andromache, along with the chorus, build up a damning cumulative picture, insisting on Helen's willing agency in the elopement (373), her metaphorical agency in the slaughter of the war (134–37), and her singularity (*one* woman) (368, 498–99, 780–81)—which takes on new significance in a play whose dramatis personae consists almost entirely of women of a very different kind. The women affirm, above all, their own unremitting hatred, which reaches its climax in an apostrophe to Helen by Andromache, after hearing that her son Astyanax is to be killed:

> Offspring of Tyndareus, you were never born from Zeus!
> I say you were begotten by many fathers,
> first of all by a Curse, then Envy, Murder,
> Death, and all the evils nourished by the earth.
> For I declare that Zeus never begot you,
> who were doom to so many Greeks and non-Greeks alike.
> Death to you! With your most beautiful eyes
> you hideously destroyed the Trojans' glorious plains.
>
> (766–73)

The adjective "most beautiful" (*kallistos*) stands out, since it is rarely used in tragedy for erotic beauty, drawing special attention to the power of Helen's eyes. Andromache seems to be denying the divine paternity that underwrites this power, but her denial is only symbolic. Zeus's paternity of Helen is taken for granted throughout the play (398, 1109). When Andromache replaces him rhetorically with Curse, Envy, Murder, Death, and all the evils of the earth, she is not denying but underlining Helen's superhuman power.

By staging the Trojan women's hatred, Euripides places before our eyes, and in our ears, a dimension of Helen's story that was merely hinted at in epic and left unaddressed in other works we have looked at thus far, namely her vexed relationship to other women. In *Trojan Women* Helen's sisters-in-law and Hecuba, whose hostility was mentioned in passing in Homer (*Il.* 24.768–70), replace the affectionate and paternalistic men of the *Iliad* as the characters whose perspective guides our response. Unlike Homer's characters, moreover, these women can be *seen* on stage—as miserable, degraded creatures who have paid the price for Helen's adultery. Hecuba, in particular—Helen's primary dramatic antagonist—is an iconic image of suffering, debased by age, appearance, and her fall from privilege, a queen reduced to the cropped hair and wretched clothing of slavery and mourning. The drama opens with her prostrate on the ground in misery, and she remains on stage until the bitter end, inviting the audience to perceive the entire action through her eyes.

After Andromache has been led away, and Astyanax taken to his death, the chorus sing a bleak ode about the destructive consequences of erotic passion for Troy. This is followed by the entrance of a jarringly cheerful Menelaus:

> Oh beautiful bright light of day! This is the day
> on which I shall lay hands upon my wife!
>
> (860–61)

The verb "lay hands upon" is a violent one, but in light of Menelaus's palpable excitement and delight it may also hint at sexual conquest. He goes on to declare, however, that he did not come to Troy "on account of a woman" (as people think), but to exact justice from the *man* who betrayed guest-friendship and "plundered" his wife from home (864–68). Now he has got "the Spartan woman"—whom he would rather not name—safely confined in a "prison house" and come to "lead her away"; as the injured party he has the choice of killing her or "leading" her home, and plans to do both: he will "lead" her back to Greece and kill her there in punishment (869–79). The emphatically repeated verb "lead" evokes the language of weddings, thus hinting at remarriage, but postponing the execution allows Menelaus, for now, to avoid the choice between "leading" and killing.

Before Helen is brought onto the stage, Hecuba gives Menelaus a warning that will inevitably make her, at the moment of her entrance, the cynosure of all eyes onstage and off:

> Avoid looking at her, Menelaus, or she may capture you with longing!
> She captures the eyes of men, captures cities and burns
> down houses; such are the magic charms that she possesses.
>
> (891–93)

Hecuba spells out the visual power of erotic beauty, which she equates with "magic charms" like those on Aphrodite's magic breast band (above, p. 5). "Capture" translates the Greek verb *helein*, evoking Aeschylus's famous three-fold pun and with it the suggestion that Helen's very name exercises some kind of supernatural power (above, p. 130). Fear of such "charms" may also help explain Menelaus's confessed reluctance to speak the "Spartan woman's" name (869–70). Her destructive power, conveyed through imagery of "capture" and of fire, is literalized by the fact that Troy is smoldering in the background. Hecuba's invocation of Helen's erotic "fire" thus forms part of the pattern of verbal "scene painting" that draws our imaginative attention to the burning city. Conversely, her warning makes the ruined city itself a manifestation of the power of Helen's beauty.

That warning is the culmination of nearly nine hundred lines of verbal preparation for Helen's entrance. Belying the expectations that it raises, however, the manner of that entrance is both humiliating and seriously threatening. Unlike the other women, Helen has not cropped her hair in mourning, a fact that becomes apparent when Menelaus orders his men to drag her out from the prison-hut by her "most murderous hair" (880–82). The menace this implies is shown by a passage in Euripides' *Orestes* where the hero grabs Helen by her hair with intent to murder her (1469–74). Similarly, images of the rape of Cassandra routinely depict Ajax seizing her by the hair (see figure 1.3, above, p. 13). It is hardly surprising, then, that when Helen is dragged onto the stage by Menelaus's henchmen her first words are of fear (895–97). But this moment of abjection will not last.

Violent as it is, the manner of Helen's entrance draws attention via a striking synecdoche ("most murderous hair") to one of her chief erotic assets. Menelaus seems to be holding her hair responsible for the entire war. Flowing locks—an important component of female beauty—are a prominent aspect of Helen's traditional persona. (In epic, she is said to have "lovely hair" more often than any other goddess or heroine.) Euripides uses staging, together with the script, to focus our attention on that hair. The long wig attached to Helen's mask creates a sharp visual contrast with the other women who, as slaves and mourners, have their hair cropped short. The other women have also been scratching their cheeks in lamentation (cf. 279–80), another standard mourning practice, which, like haircutting, defaces a conspicuous site of erotic beauty (cf. below, p. 213). But Helen's cheeks presumably remain unmarked. The contrast in costume is equally vivid. The other captives wear drab rags, but Helen, as Hecuba will comment bitterly, has dressed and groomed her body carefully—or more literally, "polished it up" like a fine statue (1022–23). Her outfit may also reflect the extravagant tastes upon which Hecuba acerbically comments (991–97).

This remarkable entrance is the prelude to a scene in which, for the only time in our ancient Greek sources, Helen defends herself in her own voice for eloping with Paris. She begins by asking Menelaus, in a humble tone, whether she may argue against the death sentence he has pronounced against her. He replies that he has come not to talk, but to kill her (903–5). It is Hecuba who then insists that Helen have her day in "court"—provided that she herself gets a chance to respond. Since Menelaus has not, presumably, heeded the old woman's advice to avert his gaze, argument is her only weapon against the visual power of Helen's beauty. Her own warning notwithstanding, Hecuba insists that if Menelaus *listens* to his wife—and allows herself to respond— then Helen's death will be inevitable (906–10). Helen therefore wins her first victory over Menelaus, ironically, with Hecuba's help—a victory already suggesting, on his part, a certain weakness of resolve.

Like Gorgias's *Encomium*, Helen's speech evokes a defense at an Athenian trial. Her arguments also parallel the sophist's, as we shall see.[2] There are, however, some important dramatic differences. Helen is speaking on her own behalf, and this time it is not merely her reputation but her life that is on the line. Unlike Gorgias's speech, this is not a one-sided display, but the opening salvo in a debate. And in contrast to Gorgias's performance, the theatrical audience is not the fictional target of the speech, which is aimed specifically at Menelaus (914–18). In dramatic terms, the Athenian spectators are merely eavesdropping, spying on the mythic characters' interactions. That said, however, the agonistic format constitutes Euripides' audience as a kind of democratic "jury," inviting them to evaluate Helen's defense and Hecuba's response as if they were, indeed, competing speakers in an Athenian courtroom.

The charge against Helen is that she intentionally wronged her husband by leaving him for another man (cf. 916–18, 938–39). She rebuts it much as Gorgias did on her behalf, by presenting herself as an object with no will of her own, a mere victim of mortals and gods alike. She blames everyone who was involved in the events that caused the Trojan War, except herself. She blames Hecuba, who bore Paris (919–20); she blames the old man who was supposed to kill the infant Paris but did not do so, thereby "destroying" Troy (920–22);[3] she blames Paris himself—calling him the "beginning of the evils" (919), the firebrand that burned down Troy (922), and Hecuba's "curse" (941)—who

2. Our evidence does not allow us to determine whether either author influenced the other directly.

3. I agree with those who interpret the "old man" as the shepherd entrusted with exposing Paris at birth because Hecuba dreamed she would bear a firebrand. But he could also be Priam.

chose Aphrodite at the Judgment, then married Helen allegedly "by force" (963); she blames Menelaus, whom she calls *kakistos*, "most evil," for being stupid enough to leave town while Paris was visiting (943–44); she blames Deiphobus, her second Trojan husband, who supposedly "abducted" her and kept her "by force" after Paris died (959–60); above all, she blames Aphrodite, who promised her to Paris as a gift (929–30), accompanied him to Sparta as his ally (940), and overpowered Helen's mind so that she "followed" Paris and "betrayed" Menelaus (946–50). Despite these active verbs she herself is to be excused as a completely passive victim of circumstances, "destroyed" by the old man (920–21), "sold" by Aphrodite for her beauty (936), married to Paris and then Deiphobus "by force" (959, 963), and "enslaved" at Troy (963–64).

In the *Iliad*, no one explicitly blames Helen but Helen herself. In *Trojan Women* Euripides reverses that pattern: everyone *except* Helen blames Helen in the bitterest terms, while she blames everybody but herself, including many whose role might seem far more incidental or passive than her own. The resulting effect is likewise the opposite of the *Iliad*. In the epic she is convinced of her guilt and therefore seems less guilty; in *Trojan Women* she claims innocence and therefore seems less innocent. There, her self-blame allowed Priam to save face for her, but here her blame of others comes across as a shameless and opportunistic evasion of responsibility. This is in large part because of the sophistic character of her arguments. Centuries later, a moralizing Plutarch would warn his readers against admiring Helen's blame of Hecuba as witty and ingenious (*Mor.* 28a). In the same passage, Plutarch disapproves of another Euripidean character who blames her husband for her own infidelity. Helen employs this tactic too, when she calls Menelaus "most evil" (*kakistos*) for leaving her with Paris (943). She ends her speech by calling him a fool, for good measure (965).

In both these cases, the theatrical context betrays the flimsiness of Helen's arguments by allowing Euripides to show her blaming her targets face-to-face. In performance, Hecuba's helplessness and degraded appearance—in contrast to the well-dressed Helen—make it absurd to see her as anything other than a victim. In the case of Menelaus, however, the direct confrontation made possible by drama has a different effect. *Kakistos* is a very strong word, conveying a degree of contempt that is quite remarkable, under the circumstances. Not only does Menelaus hold Helen's life in his hands, but she is actually scolding him for his failure to keep her under control, thus impugning his masculinity as a husband. In so doing she draws on the language of Menelaus's bitterest enemies elsewhere in Euripides. In *Andromache*, for example, Peleus twice calls Menelaus *kakistos* and not a real man, both times in connection with his weakness regarding Helen. In one case he is referring to erotic weakness (631), but in the other he, too, disparages Menelaus for leaving Helen unguarded when Paris came to call (590–95). Peleus, however, is far from viewing Menelaus's folly as exculpating Helen. On the contrary, he calls her, too, "most evil" (*kakistē*) of all women, because of her lack of sexual self-control (594–96), underlining the symmetry in the couple's joint failure to live up to appropriately gendered standards of behavior. Helen's attempt to evade responsibility by blaming her husband is thus entirely specious.

Despite the lavishness with which she blames other mortals, however, another kind of sophistic argument lies at the heart of Helen's self-defense. Like the bona fide sophist Gorgias, she rejects the fundamental principle that human beings are responsible for their actions even if they are influenced by a god. She is not guilty, she says, because "Paris arrived bringing with him no trivial goddess" (940). She goes on to address the matter of her own mentality at the time:

> Why, if I was in my right mind, did I leave our house and
> follow the stranger, betraying my fatherland and home?
> Punish the goddess and become stronger than Zeus,
> who has power over the other divinities
> yet is [Aphrodite's] slave! For me, forgiveness!
>
> (946–50)

Helen does not deny her own agency—she never claims to have been literally kidnapped—but like Gorgias she equates divine influence on her mental state with external "force" (963). As we have seen, this kind of argument only works as a face-saver if one accepts personal responsibility. But Helen employs it for the opposite purpose, adopting the techniques of sophistry at their most disreputable. She transfers blame to the gods in just the way recommended by the sophistic Weaker Argument in Aristophanes' *Clouds* (above, p. 168).

The drama as a whole denies the validity of this maneuver. Since powerful gods were behind the Trojan War, Helen's argument might in theory be used to excuse all the horrible actions performed in this very play—from rape to child-murder to the sacrifice of Hecuba's virginal daughter, Polyxena, on Achilles' tomb. But no character, divine or human, treats the gods' involvement in the destruction of Troy as a reason for excusing their human instruments. The play starts with the literal appearance of two gods in the prologue, who have no hesitation in blaming humans, including Helen, for their actions. Poseidon, who remarks that Helen is held captive "justly" (34–35), also declares that it was Athena who destroyed Troy (45–47). The Trojan women likewise attribute their own suffering to the gods (e.g., 775–76), but this in no way detracts from their passionate loathing for Helen.

Even Hecuba, Helen's bitterest enemy, acknowledges the gods' role in ruining Troy (612). Yet in her rebuttal she provides a withering critique of Helen's account of divine involvement. She denies that the beauty contest took place as Helen described it, or that Aphrodite "accompanied" Paris, an idea she calls "laughable" (983). Rather, she says, *seeing* the exceedingly beautiful Paris drove Helen out of her mind: "Aphrodite" is just a name that mortals give to their own folly (987–92). Despite this combative stance, her focus is less on challenging Helen's facts than on reinterpreting them in a way that reinstates personal responsibility. They both agree on the essential point that Helen "betrayed" Menelaus (947, 1032). The only question is whether she should be held accountable. The point is thus not whether the beauty contest (literally) took place, or Aphrodite (literally) accompanied Paris. By any interpretation, Paris did in some sense bring Aphrodite's power with him to Sparta. The goddess might even truthfully be said, as Hecuba sarcastically puts it, to have conveyed Helen to Troy without leaving her divine home (985–86). The important point, as she makes clear, is that Helen's erotic "insanity" is not an excuse, but a condemnation.

Hecuba reinforces Helen's responsibility in strictly human terms by insisting vehemently on her agency in the elopement. She sketches the encounter as an erotic role reversal, with Paris the desirable object and Helen the lustful pursuer. In a lavish development of the *Iliad*, where Paris "shines with beauty and clothing" (3.392), Hecuba portrays her son as "most outstanding in beauty" (987), barbarized and eroticized with exotic clothes and golden ornaments of the kind traditionally associated with feminine allure (991–92). She goes on to equate Helen's desire for him with greed for such riches, claiming that Menelaus was not wealthy enough for her extravagant tastes (993–97)—a claim that may have been corroborated on stage by Helen's costume. She renders Helen an agent who seeks out precious objects for herself, instead of a passive object pursued and disposed of by men. This enables her, like Homer's Priam, to avoid blaming her own son. Unlike Priam, however, she transfers the blame to Helen, making her actively responsible for the entire war. It was Helen, she tells Menelaus, who "slaughtered" his friends (1044).

Hecuba also challenges Helen's account of what went on within wartime Troy. In a prejudicial rewriting of Helen's divided feelings in *Iliad* book 3, she alleges that Helen rooted for whichever side happened to be winning at the time (1002–9). If Helen had really missed Menelaus and was held at Troy against her will, says Hecuba, she should have killed herself (1010–14). She agrees, however, that Helen ought to have left Troy of her own volition. Helen said she tried to do so, even claiming to have witnesses to her escape attempts (955–58), but Hecuba replies that, on the contrary, Helen spurned both her advice to leave and her offers of help in doing so (1015–19). We do not know, of course, what "really" happened inside Troy. But both women imply that Helen had the power to end the war by returning to Menelaus, making her both more powerful and potentially more culpable than she is in Homer.

Hecuba's insistence on Helen's agency, even under such constrained conditions, is reinforced by the larger dramatic context, which challenges her claims to helplessness by asserting the possibility of virtuous female agency regardless of circumstances. The play presents us with a world in which women are responsible for their actions, capable both of controlling their desires and of exercising virtuous, rational agency. Andromache appears, as in Homer, as a picture of wifely virtue in implicit contrast to the unfaithful Helen. Since going outside is enough to bring even an innocent woman into disrepute, she says,

> letting go my desire to do so I stayed inside the house,
> nor did I admit within my walls the clever words
> of women, but my own mind was enough for me
> as a good teacher, from inside myself,
> and in my husband's presence I maintained
> a quiet tongue and peaceful eye.
>
> (650–55)

The virtuous wife presents herself as a rational, self-controlled agent who voluntarily embraces the confines of what is, in essence, a classical Athenian marriage. Andromache is an anti-Helen who, by voluntarily accepting the physical limitations of her domestic role (650), undermines in advance Helen's claim to have been a slave "at home" in Troy (963–64).

Now that Andromache is to be a real slave in the house of her husband's killers (660), those limitations are obviously greater still. As enslaved women, she and the rest of the captives have a thorough understanding of the meaning of constrained choice. Helen speaks as if she had been treated like a piece of baggage by those with power over her—human as well as divine—but the other women demonstrate that there is always room for ethical agency. Despite the overwhelming restrictions on their freedom, the play is, nonetheless, a drama of female self-assertion, especially through speech. The women can and do take responsibility for what little action is available to them, even if that is only to speak or keep silent. Hecuba advises Andromache to win over her captor by behaving affectionately, in order to save her son from death, thus providing the family with descendants who may rebuild Troy (699–705). When the noose tightens further (Astyanax is condemned to die), Talthybius, the Greek herald, tells the helpless Andromache to stay silent in face of her son's murder—yet even this is proposed as a strategic choice, to ensure that the child will at least get a decent burial (726–39). After Andromache and Astyanax are taken away, Hecuba insists that she still retains control over the gestures of mourning (792–95). In the final scene she exercises the limited agency that is left to her by arranging her grandson's funeral.

Even Cassandra asserts her own agency, in a characteristically unhinged fashion. Despite the passivity of her role in the story of Agamemnon's death (which she foresees prophetically), she claims credit for his eventual murder by Clytemnestra, claiming it as an act of revenge for Troy (359–60). She declares, "I shall kill him" (359), appropriating for herself the kind of "agency" assigned to Helen by so many of her enemies and to others by Helen herself, namely the mere fact of being a link in the causal chain. She even draws an analogy between her own destructive "marriage" to Agamemnon and Helen's to Paris (357). By highlighting the demented consequences of the idea that *any* causal involvement entails responsibility, these bizarre arguments prepare us to see the absurdity of Helen's logic.

All these women underscore the helplessness of victims who, unlike Helen, are truly coerced and objectified, while demonstrating that resistance—if only mental resistance—always lies within one's power. By conjuring vividly the prospect of enforced and degrading "marriage" to a Greek captor, both Cassandra and Andromache demonstrate the illegitimacy of Helen's assimilation of Aphrodite's power to physical violence. The brute force to which the slaves are subject is emphasized over and over again, especially in the case of Cassandra. Ajax dragged her away "by force" from Athena's temple (70), she is torn from her mother "by force" (617), and Agamemnon will "marry her forcibly" (44). If Helen is to be excused because of Aphrodite's power, Agamemnon should equally be forgiven for this treatment of Cassandra, since he too has been attacked by *erōs* (255, 413–15). This prepares us, before Helen even appears, to see through her self-justifying assimilation of Aphrodite's power to violence. When she does appear, the manner of her own entrance demonstrates yet again what it is really like to be subjected to force (897), to be passed from one man to another to kill if he so chooses (901–2).

Against this background, Helen's claim to have been married to Paris "by force" (963) rings hollow indeed. The point is brought out by Hecuba in her rebuttal, when she challenges this particular claim by asking who, if force was in question, heard Helen cry out as she was taken from Sparta (998–1001). She is not perversely misunderstanding Helen's argument about the "force" of Aphrodite (as some critics think), so much as literalizing Helen's implication that erotic passion is as exculpatory as physical violence, thereby highlighting its speciousness. Real violence is something that does indeed make its victims cry out for help, as we see over and over again. Helen, by contrast, shows no sign of having struggled against the "force" supposedly applied by Paris. This deprives her of the kind of sympathy aroused by Helen in the *Iliad*, when she tries but fails to resist the power of Aphrodite.

Despite Helen's alleged passivity in the past, moreover, in the drama we see her, like the other women, doing what she can to control her destiny. Indeed, her very insistence on past passivity is part of an active strategy in her own defense. That strategy parallels Gorgias's, but it takes on a different coloring now that Helen is the one to use it. Gorgias's defense is reinforced by silencing Helen, in keeping with her presentation as a powerless object. He "defends" her by erasing her as a speaker and an agent. In *Trojan Women*, however, Helen herself is the speaker who defends herself by disempowering herself, drawing on stereotypes of female weakness and passivity to the point where she denies that her own agency has any significance at all. By *voicing* her own lack of agency, however, using the power of language to assert her power-lessness, she renders her argument rhetorically self-defeating. What was, in Gorgias's hands, a semihumorous defense of Helen becomes an attack, by the simple expedient of placing it in her own mouth.

Helen's self-defense is undermined in a different way by the fact that she is a female character who appropriates the role and status of a male citizen by speaking on her own behalf. In contrast to her role as Gorgias's mute "client," here she acts as her own guardian, defending herself in a distinctively mascu-line arena. Women are, to be sure, far more visible and audible in drama than they were in Athenian life. Many female characters participate on stage in the "masculine" agonistic modes of public oratory. But the audience's response to such speeches depends on how they are dramatically framed in each instance. Hecuba, for example, delivers a long, rhetorical speech in the role of prosecutor at Helen's "trial." But her pitiful status as a downtrodden victim helps protect her from the negative associations aroused by the spectacle of a woman exer-cising a man's prerogatives. Helen's performance, in contrast, is undermined by her luxurious appearance, insulting language, and self-serving agenda.

Helen's assumption of this manly role adds a further dimension to the self-defeating character of her rhetorical performance. Her gender, which helps the male sophist Gorgias's argument by making it easier for him to pre-sent her as a mere object, damages her defense by undermining the presump-tion of feminine passivity and weakness on which her case is built. By speaking on her own behalf she positions herself as her own guardian, with the right and authority to speak for herself, thus belying the implication that she was not competent to think or act without Menelaus to protect her from herself. If she can perform effectively in this masculine domain, why should she not be held responsible for her actions as a man would be?

As if all this were not enough, Helen has also taken on the role of sophistic performer. No longer a passive object of Gorgianic entertainment, it is she who now stands at center stage, ostentatiously dressed, competing for applause. It is she who, as the purveyor of a rhetorical "amusement," presents the audience with arguments of a kind that they are primed to enjoy, but not believe (cf. above, p. 176). By thus presenting her in the guise of a sophist, Euripides updates Hesiod's notion of woman as a *kalon kakon* for contemporary Athens, giving a distinctively fifth-century twist to the age-old association of beautiful women with deceptive discourse. In the words of the chorus, she speaks "beau-tifully even though she is an evil-doer" (967–68). Or as Hecuba puts it, she uses the superficial "beauty" of rhetoric to "dress up" an evil deed (982). The word Hecuba uses for such "adornment" is *kosmos*—the same word used by Hesiod for the decorations in which Pandora takes delight (*WD* 76, *Theog.* 587). Helen's specious arguments are the intellectual counterpart of Pandora's lovely costume, and indeed of her own: they veil a morally rotten core.

Our sympathy is alienated still further by Helen's confident, even arrogant tone. This is manifested most egregiously in her account of the Judgment of Paris. As she tells it, Athena offered Paris military conquest of Greece, Hera offered kingship over Europe, and of course Aphrodite offered Helen herself to be Paris's wife. It follows, she alleges, that when Paris chose her, this benefited the whole of Greece by protecting it from "barbarian" rule. For bringing them such good fortune, she goes on, the Greeks should have "placed a crown upon my head" (932–37). On trial for her life, Helen declares that she deserves not punishment from those she is accused of harming, but a crown—a mark of honor that was given, in Euripides' Athens, to victorious athletes and public benefactors (normally male, of course). The original audience would be all too aware of the scandalous contrast, having just heard the names of such benefactors announced in the theater (above, p. 123).

The effect of this claim on an Athenian audience may be surmised from the experience of Socrates fifteen years later, at least as Plato tells it in his *Apology*. Socrates is, of course, quite unlike Helen in most respects. He is, in fact, Plato's anti-Helen, a notoriously ugly figure whose off-putting exterior conceals extraordinary beauty of character. Nevertheless, in the defense speech he gives when on trial for his life, he shares the rhetorically self-defeating arrogance of Helen in this particular play. He, too, chastises the audience that holds his life in its hands, and explicitly refuses to apologize, or to pander by making himself seem pitiful (34b–35b). After being convicted he claims that he is a benefactor to Athens and should be rewarded with free meals at public expense (36de)—an honor assigned to Olympic victors and other distinguished citizens. This wins him a larger majority in favor of his death. His tone is such that many have actually wondered whether Plato intended the *Apology* to be a serious self-defense. Helen's brash, scolding manner is even more striking, in part because of her gender.

Unlike Plato, however, or even Gorgias, Euripides does not pose as a defense attorney. He has no obligation to his client. This leaves him free to allow her to condemn herself, through the persona with which he endows her and the drama in which he embeds it. The sophists' critics—notably Plato—were less than confident about the harmlessness of "amusements" like Gorgias's *Helen*, which, they feared, encouraged a frivolous, intellectually irresponsible attitude toward matters of the utmost importance. Euripides' presentation of Helen in *Trojan Women* serves, similarly, to insist on the importance of human choice, agency, and responsibility in face of sophistic modes of argument, and to rebuke the rhetorical trivialization of such serious concerns. By framing Helen's speech in a way that renders its irresponsibility palpable, he rebuts it not just intellectually, through Hecuba's response, but dramatically, through the tragic context in which it is embedded.

At the same time, the playwright also gives the actor who plays the part of Helen a fine opportunity for sophistic self-display. His performance presumably elicited from the theatrical audience the same kind of amused intellectual appreciation sought by orators like Gorgias. Unlike Gorgias, however, neither actor nor playwright needs to reassure us that he is not really serious. The opprobrium aroused by such arguments can be safely directed at the fictional character they have created. The audience can admire the bravura of the actor playing the role of sophist-Helen, while repudiating Helen's own use of such specious arguments. They can be amused by her ingenious denials of responsibility, while sharing in the condemnation voiced by the other characters and affirmed by the drama as a whole. Euripides enables us to have our cake and eat it too.

Helen's self-defense speech is, then, an intellectually and morally vacuous tissue of sophistries, delivered in a manner that would simultaneously entertain and alienate an Athenian jury. But an Athenian jury is not her target. The only audience that matters as far as she is concerned is Menelaus—a man whose measure she has taken in the past—and the speech is aimed quite specifically at him. The contempt with which she addresses him might seem to belie this. It does, however, suggest a confidence in her ability to sway him, if not by personal praise or reasoned argument, then by other means. We may recall Helen's abuse of Paris in the *Iliad*, which in no way impaired his desire for her, suggesting that their relationship has nothing to do with moral approval or rational judgment. That confidence will be justified by Menelaus's failure—like the unmanly Paris—to be angered by her contempt.

Viewed in this light, Helen's arguments have distinct rhetorical benefits for her that go beyond the dubious claim to excusing her elopement. To begin with, her sophistic appeal to the power of Aphrodite offers Menelaus a way of saving face if he backs down. It implies not only that she was taken from him by "force" (rather than betraying him of her own volition), but that the same "force" is responsible for the terrible war he launched to retrieve her. She herself warns him that he is not stronger than *erōs* (964–65). If even Zeus is Aphrodite's "slave" (948–50), Menelaus can scarcely be blamed if he ends up abandoning his plan for revenge under the impact of Helen's godlike beauty. However specious Helen's Aphrodite argument may be, it lays the groundwork for a change of heart in Menelaus by preemptively excusing anything that he may do under the emasculating influence of her physical presence.

Helen's speech also brings the goddess's power to bear in a different way, by drawing attention, repeatedly, to the beauty of which she claims to be the victim. In recounting the Judgment of Paris she declares that Aphrodite herself was "astonished" at her beautiful appearance (929). Her verb evokes the "astonishing" love that the goddess herself expresses for Helen in the *Iliad* (3.415). Once again, however, the fact that Helen is now the speaker transforms the import of her words. By talking in such terms about herself she is failing to show a good woman's modesty, glorifying her own appearance, instead, in a way that evokes the threat of competitive female beauty manifested in the Judgment itself. But the particular way in which she does so also draws attention to the divine quality of her beauty, which so greatly impressed even the most beautiful of goddesses.

Helen goes on to mention the "lovely form" for which she was supposedly "sold," and the head that she declares should be decorated with a crown (935–37). This outrageous suggestion directs the spectators' gaze toward that head, with its long hair and powerful eyes, calling to mind not only the honoring of public benefactors but the crowns and wreaths that feature so prominently in representations of beautiful women, including brides (see figures 1.1, 1.2, 1.4, 1.5, 2.4, above, pp. 8, 9, 14, 18, 37). Later in the speech Helen points quite literally at "this very body" (958), using a word (*sōma*) that often appears as a synonym for her beauty (e.g., Gorg. *Hel.* 4). In performance, the actor who played Helen presumably employed appropriate gestures, drawing the eyes of Menelaus—and the audience—to the body in question. Despite her sophistries and insults, then, Euripides presents Helen as well aware of the nature of her particular persuasive assets.

Hecuba is obviously in no position to compete with this dimension of Helen's performance. The best she can do is scold her enemy for shamelessly flaunting her physical allure in her husband's presence:

> On top of everything, have you come out here after
> polishing up your body? Do you presume to look upon
> the same sky as your husband, you repulsive thing (*kara*)?
> You should have come here groveling, in scraps of
> clothing, trembling with fear, your head shaved,
> expressing self-restraint (*sōphrosunē*) instead of shamelessness
> after the wrongs that you committed in the past.
>
> (1022–28)

Hecuba's disgust at Helen's eroticized self-presentation may remind us of her initial warning to Menelaus about his wife's devastating visual "magic." All she can do to combat this is divest Helen verbally of the symbols and instruments of erotic power—disparaging her fine clothes, long hair, grooming, seductive body language, and confident demeanor. Her rhetorical purpose is presumably to undermine the power of Helen's body, if only in imagination, by reducing her to the state of the other women, making it easier for Menelaus to carry through his original death sentence.

This strategy backfires, however, by reemphasizing the very features to which Hecuba takes exception. She focuses on Helen's luxurious outfit, pointing to the "body" that she has "polished up" with fine dress and grooming (1022; cf. 1010). She also addresses her with the word *kara*, which I have translated as "thing," but which literally means "head" (1024). This idiomatic usage carries a strong emotional charge, whether positive or—as here—negative. Despite its valence the word draws renewed attention to Helen's head, with its compelling eyes and hair, both of which feature in Hecuba's tirade. She highlights Helen's flowing locks by insisting that they should be shaved (1026), and her eyes by condemning the direct gaze with which she "looks upon the same sky as her husband" (1023–24). Such a gaze is, as Hecuba says, a sign of shamelessness, in contrast to the "peaceful eye" maintained even in the presence of her husband by a modest woman like Andromache (654). The reason such a gaze was considered shameless, however, was precisely its power as an erotic stimulus.

In most such debates in tragedy the second speaker is considered the winner. Judging by the criteria of reason and morality, there can be no doubt that this is also true in the present case. Yet there remains an unresolved tension between Hecuba's rational victory and the inescapable dramatic impact of Helen's physical presence, which her opponent has inadvertently reinforced. The effect of this tension on the judge, Menelaus, is played out for the remainder of the scene.

Initially, Hecuba seems to prevail. She was confident that Helen's perversely unpersuasive arguments would not convince the "wise" (982), and she is right. Menelaus is not normally noted for his wisdom, but even he agrees with her on the central issue: Helen left of her own volition, and used Aphrodite in her speech "as something to brag about" (1036–39), that is, as an excuse to draw attention to her own appearance. His death sentence therefore stands. Helen is to be stoned, he says, both in retribution for all the deaths in the Trojan War and for the shame she has brought him personally (1039–41). This verdict seems to justify Hecuba's original confidence in the power of rational discourse to bring about Helen's death (909–10).

Though Hecuba wins the battle, however, Euripides makes it clear that she will lose the war. Helen, with her mesmerizing body, gorgeous clothing, powerful eyes, and seductive demeanor, will ultimately be victorious, not because of her sophistic arguments but in spite of them. If Menelaus remains a fool, as Helen called him (965), his folly does not consist in an inability to judge the merits of such speeches. It is, rather, foolishness of the well-known variety induced by Aphrodite. Hecuba herself derives the goddess's name from the word *aphrosunē*, "witlessness" (989–90). Her wordplay conveys more than she intends, however, reminding us not only of the reprehensible character of such erotic "folly," but of its immortality and divinity. Despite Hecuba's intellectual and moral victory, it is this folly that will ultimately prevail.

The drama concludes not with Helen's execution, but with intimations of her unextinguished power. The manner in which Menelaus orders her death is characteristically unassertive, leaving agency in her hands and evading personal responsibility on his part: "Go to those who will stone you!" (1039). Helen seizes the opportunity for one more appeal, grasping his knees in supplication as she reiterates her central point about the "disease" sent by the gods, which should excuse her (1042–43). This gesture adds physical contact and the appeal of female self-abasement, as well as moral and religious pressure, to her repertoire of persuasive techniques. Though Menelaus claims to pay her no mind (1046), he tacitly alters his intention. He orders his men to take Helen away to the ships, but there is no more talk of stoning (1047–48).

Hecuba, who initially warned Menelaus against looking at Helen, now warns him not to share his ship with her because of the erotic danger of physical proximity (1049–51). His immediate reaction suggests an obtuse inability to understand her concern or take it seriously. Has Helen gained weight, he asks? Is she now too heavy for his ship? (1050). This feeble joke draws our attention, one last time, to Helen's body. But Menelaus agrees that Hecuba's suggestion is a good one and affirms, yet again, his intention to kill her once they get back to Greece (1055–59). Despite this face-saving declaration, however, the outcome is not seriously in doubt. We have been repeatedly reminded of the power of *erōs* to overrule reason and moral judgment. Menelaus is notoriously susceptible to that power, and we have already seen him soften at Helen's touch. The very idea of taking her back to Greece brings to mind, unavoidably, the traditional story, familiar from the *Odyssey*, which finds her ten years later alive and well and living in Sparta.

The scene as a whole thus dramatizes the conquest of rational speech by the seductive appeal of the physical body. This confrontation between the verbal and the visual is a distinctive aspect of Euripides' reimagining of Helen's story in this drama. We might initially expect her defense speech, as the seductive equivalent of her beauty, to be genuinely persuasive and arouse our sympathy. But Euripides denies his Helen the kind of self-abasing, apologetic demeanor that served her so well in epic, replacing it with an alienating voice that stands in tension with the visual impact of her beauty. This opposition is one that is most effectively conveyed through the particular resources of theater. In Homer, where Helen is visible only to the imagination, her seductive persona is constituted primarily through the charm of her voice. Thanks to the concreteness of dramatic performance, however, Euripides can show her physical presence trumping the power of discourse. The unsympathetic and unconvincing character of Helen's speech is integral to this effect, since it makes clear that when Menelaus yields it will be against his better judgment. Her self-defense underlines her victory in part by using frivolous arguments that convince no one—not even him. The more offensive and implausible those arguments are, the worse Menelaus looks and the more effective the demonstration of Helen's nonverbal power.

That power is perfectly complemented by Menelaus's weakness, making them a perversely well-matched pair. Sparing Helen is a defeat of his rational and moral judgment, a failure of self-control leading him to contravene his own values—values that accord with those of Helen's enemies. The chorus tell him that revenge will save him from blame from the Greeks for being "feminine" (1033–35), and he agrees that Helen should die for disgracing him (1040–41). If he does not kill her, says Hecuba, he will be betraying his allies (1044)—as Helen herself betrayed him (947)—and Menelaus evidently concurs with this too, agreeing that justice calls for her execution (878–79, 902, 1040–41, 1055–56). Hecuba urges him, moreover, to make an example of Helen (1031–32), and once again he agrees, implying that her survival would serve as an encouragement to unfaithful women everywhere. As he proclaims in his final lines:

> When she reaches Greece she shall die evilly as she deserves,
> evil woman (*kakē*), and bring self-control (*sōphrosunē*)
> to all women. That is not something easy to produce;
> but her destruction will turn their folly into fear—
> even women still more shameful than she is.
>
> (1055–59)

When Menelaus exits with these disparaging words about his own wife and all women, he is himself on the point of the most notorious male act of erotic "folly" and failed self-control in myth.

The play thus condemns not merely Helen, for her infidelity and shameless sophistry, but Menelaus for the weakness that subjects him to her beauty nonetheless. This gives Euripides' predominantly male audience the opportunity to judge him and feel pleasantly superior. The detachment afforded by the stylization of drama allows them to affirm their own self-control in the presence of the most beautiful and dangerous woman of all time. This superiority was presumably made still more appealing by the fact that Menelaus is Spartan, enabling the Athenian audience to project his emotional, moral, and intellectual weakness, along with Helen's, onto their enemies in the war in which they were currently engaged. It is, moreover, under the leadership of the Spartan Menelaus and his brother, Agamemnon, who is likewise disposed to excessive *erōs*, that the Greeks commit such outrages as human sacrifice and the slaughter of an innocent baby—an act deemed "barbaric" by the non-Greek Andromache (764–65). No wonder Athens, as opposed to Sparta, is the chorus's preferred destination for their future lives as slaves (207–13, 218–19).

The sons of Atreus are, nevertheless, identified repeatedly as Greeks. Agamemnon is the leader of "all the Greeks" (413), and Menelaus, the only warrior in the play, represents the Greek cause on stage. Throughout the script, Greece and the Greeks collectively are named over and over again as having launched the war, perpetrated the slaughter, endorsed the atrocities at the sack of Troy, and taken possession of the enslaved Trojan women. The herald Talthybius tells Andromache that she should not try to resist the Greeks, since they can easily fight against one woman (731–34). But can they, if that woman is Helen? She is the quintessential Hellenic woman: the woman who brought

Greek men together, first for courtship and then for a war upon which Greek identity was built. As we are reminded repeatedly, she single-handedly brought all the Greeks to Troy (368, 498–99, 780–81). As long as she is an object of their collective desire, she remains an ineliminable symbol not only of the misguidedness of warfare but also of its inevitability—the inevitable victory of irrational passion over reason and morality.

Euripides hints at Helen's significance for Greece as a whole by framing the scene in which she appears with two striking puns linking her name with that of Hellas. Just before she enters, Menelaus declares that he has decided not to deal with Helen (*Helenēs*) at Troy, but to take her back to the Greek (*Hellēnida*) land and kill her there (876–78). In the original text, the two key words are placed at the beginning of consecutive lines, highlighting the wordplay. The second pun comes in the choral song following Menelaus's exit to the ships with Helen. The chorus pray that his vessel may be struck by lightning and sink, so that he never gets home,

> after recapturing (*helōn*) her whose disastrous marriage
> brought disgrace upon mighty Greece (*Helladi*).
>
> (1114–15)

In the Greek, the words *helōn* and *Helladi* are contiguous, linking the destruction caused by Helen, through the familiar verb *helein*, to Greece itself. This time Menelaus, not Helen, is the "capturer," but the irony of the pun is palpable, especially in light of the play on the verb *helein* in Hecuba's original warning (891–93; above, p. 186).

The same choral passage provides one more foreshadowing of Menelaus's weakness. The chorus imagine Helen sailing home on his ship—contrary to Hecuba's advice and Menelaus's expressed intention. As they picture the scene,

> the daughter of Zeus is actually holding a golden mirror,
> the delight (*charis*) of adolescent girls (*parthenoi*).
>
> (1107–8)

As we have seen, the mirror is an emblem of female beauty, luxury, and vanity, indicating a self-conscious awareness of one's erotic power (above, p. 7). When the chorus refer to Helen's mirror as the "charm" or "delight" of *parthenoi*, they are evoking the association of mirrors with the seductive beauty of lovely young brides, including the eternally nubile Helen (see figures 2.8 and 2.9 above, pp. 50 and 51). The image is thus in keeping with the erotic and nuptial coloring of many representations of Menelaus reclaiming Helen after the war (above, p. 40). The chorus also underline her beauty's supernatural power by mentioning her divine paternity. In their imagination—and that of the audience—she is already turning into the Helen of the *Odyssey*, a figure of godlike, ageless beauty, surrounded by the golden accessories of a lovely *parthenos*, in the company of a resentful but nonpunitive husband.

The larger consequences of Helen's erotic power are reiterated dramatically in the final scenes. After the chorus end their song, the body of Astyanax is brought in for burial. Like the Athenian orphans who paraded in the theater prior to the performance, Astyanax was a hero's son, but his fate is very different. The Athenian youths wore armor granted by the *polis*, marking their ascension to manhood; Hecuba calls for burial garments for a dead baby:

> Come, bring adornment (*kosmos*) for the wretched corpse—
> as far as these circumstances allow. For our fate
> gives us no chance for a display of beauty (*kallos*).
>
> (1200–1202)

The child is then dressed in decorative clothing (*kosmos*) and precious ornaments (1208, 1212, 1220), demonstrating the significance of fine clothing, its ritual and emotional power, in bitter contrast to its earlier use by Helen. The contrast is marked, particularly, by the choice of the abstract noun *kallos*, "beauty," to refer to the dead child's funeral regalia, and the word *kosmos*, which echoes the sophistic "dressing up" of Helen's evil character (982). It is sharpened still further when Hecuba declares, addressing the corpse, that such clothing would have been fitting for his wedding (1218–20), in pathetic contrast with the preceding choral image of Helen sailing away with Menelaus like a bride.

The scene also provides Hecuba with a last opportunity to take action, as far as lies within her power, by arranging her grandson's funeral. While doing so she declares, using once again a form of the verb *helein*, that "god-hated Helen" has "taken everything" (*apheileto*) and destroyed their entire house (1213–15). As the child's body is carried away, and the slave women are assigned to their various masters, the city of Troy goes up in flames and then collapses into rubble. In the Greek theater such effects were not literally visible to the spectators, but verbal "scene painting" presents them to the eye of the imagination, through a last antiphonal lament by Hecuba and the chorus:

> CHORUS. The great city has perished,
>   a city no longer. Troy is no more!
> HECUBA. Oh woe!
>   The buildings and parapets
>   of Ilium and its citadel
>   are ablaze with fire!
>
> (1291–96)

The drama concludes with this culminating proof of the devastation wrought by Helen's beauty.

10

Most Beautiful and Best: Euripides' *Helen*

> I wish I had an evil twin,
> Running round doing people in.
> I wish I had a very bad
> And evil twin to do my will,
> To cull and conquer, cut and kill,
> Just like I would
> If I weren't good,
> And if I knew where to begin.
> —The Magnetic Fields

The story of Helen's *eidōlon* cried out for dramatic treatment. Insofar as every stage figure is a kind of double, the tension between illusion and reality encoded in that story is the essence of theatrical mimesis. Euripides' plays are, in general, highly self-conscious about such matters. In his *Helen*, however, they take center stage. Produced three years after *Trojan Women*, in 412 BCE, *Helen* dramatizes the fate of the virtuous human Helen who was transported by the gods to Egypt when her double went off to Troy.

The play opens on Helen in Egypt lamenting her unwarranted reputation for adultery and the perilous situation in which she finds herself. Seventeen years have passed since the Greeks sailed for Troy in pursuit of her *eidōlon*, when Hermes, under orders from Zeus, deposited her in Egypt under the protection of King Proteus. Proteus is now dead, and his nefarious son, Theoclymenus, is holding Helen captive and pressuring her to marry him. Since he wants to keep her for himself, he murders all visiting Greeks, evincing a truly barbaric contempt for hospitality. Helen remains faithful to Menelaus, despite the fact that he seems to have vanished on the way home from Troy. In the course of the drama, however, he unexpectedly appears, the bedraggled survivor of a shipwreck off the coast of Egypt. The double was on board with him—like the real Helen imagined by the chorus at the end of *Trojan Women*—but after the shipwreck Menelaus placed it under guard in a cave. When he sees the real Helen confusion naturally ensues. Eventually, however, a messenger reports that the double has revealed its own fictitiousness and vanished into thin air, clearing the way for Helen's reunion with her long-lost husband.

The rest of the play is devoted to their escape from Egypt. After winning the assistance of Proteus's wise and virtuous daughter, the priestess Theonoe, Helen hatches a plot to trick Theoclymenus by pretending that Menelaus is dead. Menelaus himself plays the part of a Greek sailor bringing the sad news. Helen then promises to marry Theoclymenus after conducting a symbolic funeral for her dead husband out at sea. The deluded king supplies for this purpose a well-appointed ship, complete with crew, and lavish offerings for the dead. After sailing out to sea with Helen on board, Menelaus and his men slaughter the ship's Egyptian crew and set sail for Greece, taking with them a substantial haul of stolen property. The journey home reenacts their original wedding, which Helen fondly recalls (639–41). Finally, the Dioscuri, Helen's divine brothers, fly in ex machina and give her remarriage a divine seal of approval. Castor goes on to prophesy that she is to be a goddess in the afterlife, while Menelaus will live forever in the Isles of the Blessed.

The device of the double satisfied Euripides' well-developed taste for paradox by enabling him to portray the notoriously beautiful but bad Helen as both beautiful and good, clinging solely to her husband despite all odds and living happily ever after. He had treated "bad" women sympathetically in several earlier dramas, but this time he contests the very notion of woman as a "beautiful evil" by presenting the ultimate embodiment of female beauty as the apogee of virtue. Other good and beautiful women, such as Penelope, had, of course, appeared previously, some of them even in tragedies (like Euripides' own *Alcestis*). But Helen's supreme beauty, along with its well-known consequences, offered a unique challenge. Euripides was setting his sights even higher than the "beautiful and good," aiming to portray a woman who was "most beautiful and best." In *Helen* he asks not just whether a beautiful woman can ever be good, but whether the *most* beautiful woman can be *perfectly* good. Can she, moreover, escape the fate of other virtuous women in tragedy and live to tell the tale?

As befits this unlikely theme, the play is set in the mythic fantasy land of Egypt. From Homer onward, as we have seen, Egypt was closely linked with Helen's story and especially its more fantastical aspects. Increasing historical contact notwithstanding, the Egypt of the fifth-century stage remained an outpost of Greek mythology, an imaginative space of weird possibility in which Greeks could scrutinize, construct, and reconstruct their own identity. As a "barbarian" land that was yet revered for its ancient wisdom, Egypt was a funhouse mirror allowing them to experiment with more or less distorted images of themselves and others. This makes it a fitting playground for Euripides' fantasy of a woman who is not only supremely beautiful but supremely good.

Helen identifies her location, in the play's first line, as the "beautiful-maiden" waters of the river Nile, using a rare compound adjective (*kalliparthe-nos*) that establishes Egypt as the natural home for beauty and virginal purity, coexisting in apparent harmony. It is also, as in Herodotus, a haven of Hellenic values. Despite the threat posed by the tyrannical Theoclymenus—which is required for the adventure plot—the upright, hospitable Proteus is still the reigning spirit of Egypt. His tomb is a prominent feature of the stage set (recall-ing his cult in Herodotus), and thanks to his daughter his values will ultimately prevail. Theonoe, who replaces him as Helen's protector, embodies in her per-son not only Hellenic justice and hospitality but the "Egyptian" coexistence of chastity and beauty. She has remained unmarried, and her virginal status is mentioned repeatedly, but her name, Helen tells us, was originally Eido (re-lated to *eidos*, "beauty"); it was changed to Theonoe ("mind of the gods") at puberty, because of her prophetic ability (10–14). That ability makes her a source of "Egyptian" wisdom, prone to vaguely mystical religious pronounce-ments. But her wisdom has, in fact, a recognizably Hellenic flavor. She is an Athena-like figure, a perpetual virgin endowed with supernatural insight who remains loyal to her father and uses her wisdom to support the values of the patriarchal status quo.

Egypt is thus established as the ideal location for a wish-fulfillment fantasy in which female beauty and virtue coincide, protected by wisdom and blessed by the gods. The Helen who embodies this fantasy is like a movie star cast against type, whose performance we enjoy in part because of its dissonance with her previous roles. Euripides plays her, in particular, against the strongly negative Helen of earlier tragedies, especially his own *Trojan Women*. The stan-dard tragic attitude toward Helen is voiced repeatedly during the play. She her-self declares that the whole world hates her for what they think she did (926; cf. 54–55), a view corroborated by the Greek hero Teucer, in a cameo appear-ance (71–74, 81, 162–63), and by the sympathetic chorus of captive Greek women (1147–48). She is anxious to replace that "ugly reputation" or "shameful renown" (*aischron kleos*, 135) with the reputation for self-control that she deserves (932), and by the end of the play she seems to have succeeded. The drama concludes with none other than the repentant Theoclymenus declaring Helen not only "best" and "most self-controlled" (1684), but the possessor of a "most noble judgment"—something, he adds, that "is not in many women" (1687). She has been transformed from the very type of erotic weakness into a marked exception to the rule of female folly.

That transformation is made possible by the existence of the *eidōlon*, which has taken on Helen's traditional misbehavior and replaced her in her own story. As we saw in the case of Stesichorus, however, the very notion of the double denatures "Helen of Troy" by stripping this legendary heroine of the deeds that define her. How, then, was Euripides to make his innocent protagonist believ-able as Helen? He addresses this problem, as we shall see, by providing her with versions of all her principal epic moments—the elopement, the war, the Recovery, remarriage at Sparta—but rewriting them in her favor. Her character, too, remains recognizable. She is still beautiful, dangerous, remorseful, quick-witted, deceptive, persuasive, and manipulative of men. She puts these traits to work, however, to preserve not only her virtue but her husband's life. At the same time, the story is handled with techniques that call into question her viability as an ideal—including parody, satire, and epistemological play— suggesting that Euripides' tongue remains securely in his cheek.

Helen's double is the key to preserving her good name. In this version, however, it is not a device intended to save her reputation but a mere side effect of the petty politics of Mount Olympus. It was the goddess Hera who created the *eidōlon* and substituted it for Helen, before Paris could claim his reward at the Judgment, in order to thwart the plans of Aphrodite. Her motive was simply pique at losing the beauty contest. But however trivial this divine quarrel may seem—and be—it nonetheless reflects the two goddesses' competing roles as patrons of legitimate marriage and dangerous eroticism respectively. Despite Hera's malevolence toward Helen, by removing her from Aphrodite's power she also saves her from infidelity. She is "stolen" not by Paris but by the gods (1672), not for adultery but to be preserved from it until Menelaus can reclaim her. This divine "abduction" sustains her traditional postmarital mobility, and even its destructive consequences (since it allows the Greeks to proceed with the Trojan War), but leaves her own behavior unimpeachable. She is, as Gorgias would put it, an object and victim instead of an agent or perpetrator. In a witty Euripidean appropriation of Priam's words in the *Iliad*, the double itself (as quoted by the messenger) declares her "not responsible" (615).

Thanks to Hera's machinations, Helen can truthfully contradict her Homeric self, echoing Stesichorus when she declares, "I did not go to Troy" (58–59; cf. 582, 1510–11). She rejects, too—albeit in paradoxical fashion—that self's admission of "leaving" Menelaus, when she tells him, "Leaving your house and bed . . . I did not leave" (696). If Helen neither "went" nor "left," however, that means she did not want to, never having fallen under Aphrodite's sway. The revised plot therefore requires the replacement of her central character trait, erotic weakness, with its opposite, the virtue of *sōphrosunē*. Though translated for convenience as "self-control" or "self-restraint," the Greek word implies, ideally, not that one resists inappropriate feelings but that one does not experience them in the first place. Helen therefore assures Menelaus that she never felt *erōs* for an unjust marriage—she was never "carried away" or "set aflutter" by the unstable movements of desire (666–68). Her Homeric regrets are developed into an unwavering lifelong devotion toward her "dearest" husband (595, 625, 899). Conversely, her Iliadic contempt for Paris, no longer complicated by erotic passion, has become a straightforward rejection of any other man.

This newfound sexual fidelity requires a radical revision of Helen's relationship to Aphrodite. Like her Homeric counterpart she reproaches her divine patron for the meddlesome, destructive *erōs* that she inspires; unlike Homer's Helen, however, she is willing to risk the goddess's enmity and take her resistance to the point of death (1097–1104). Yet an ideal wife is not devoid of all desire. Even Theonoe, despite her personal commitment to virginity, recognizes Aphrodite's importance and the need to placate her for the journey home, which symbolizes Helen's remarriage to Menelaus (1024–25). Helen herself echoes the ordinary women of many a tragic chorus when she wishes that the goddess could be "moderate," because then she is "most sweet" (1105–6). It was, of course, Helen's incapacity for a "moderate" Aphrodite that traditionally caused the Trojan War. Yet the Greek ideal of marriage incorporates the hope (if not the expectation) that women are indeed capable of such a thing—an ideal conveyed here through the improbable transformation of Aphrodite's human counterpart into a faithful yet erotically responsive wife.

Helen's conjugal eroticism is expressed discreetly, as befits a virtuous woman (who should not talk openly of such things). She speaks, however, of women's physical revulsion from an unwanted husband (296–97), and when Menelaus finally accepts her the scene culminates in an unusually extended embrace. She goes on to bathe him and dress him in fine clothes for their escape (1382–84), declaring that she will give this "stranger" the very best and most appropriate care in order to benefit her "dearest" Menelaus (1294–1300). Such treatment is erotically suggestive, recalling especially Helen's performance of such services for Odysseus in the *Odyssey* (above, p. 82). Another ambiguous moment from the epic Helen's history is turned to Menelaus's advantage.

Euripides' Egyptian plot allows Helen not merely to assure Menelaus—and us—of her fidelity but to enact it, by confronting her with a choice like that faced by her epic counterpart. Once again she is courted in her husband's absence by an amorous royal "barbarian" who cares nothing for the norms of hospitality. Theoclymenus is no rapist, despite Helen's fear that she will have to marry him "by force" (which Menelaus, in an amusing nod toward *Trojan Women*, suspects is merely a pretext on her part) (833–34). The marriage is contingent on her consent, albeit under duress (294). Theoclymenus desires her "goodwill" (1425) as a precondition of a lavish and joyful wedding (1431–35). It is, indeed, his desire to please her that leads him to equip their escape vessel so generously (1254, 1281). This time, however, she successfully resists barbarian courtship, providing living proof of her ability to police herself in her husband's absence. As a result, she is no longer complicit in an egregious violation of guest-friendship, but upholds that Hellenic institution against barbarian assault (cf. 146). She no longer brings death to thousands in the Trojan War, but saves the lives of Menelaus and his men.

By rejecting her wealthy suitor, the reformed Helen contradicts claims by the bad old Helen's enemies—notably Hecuba in the *Trojan Women*—that she was driven by greed for Paris's barbarian gold. Her marital loyalty is no doubt assisted by the fact that Theoclymenus, unlike Paris, does not come armed with Aphrodite's irresistible allure. But there are other forms of temptation. Indeed, marriage to Theoclymenus—a wealthy king to whom she is not sexually attracted—might not look so different from life at Sparta in the *Odyssey*. Theoclymenus starts out playing the part of Paris, but his grand palace affects strangers much as Menelaus's palace did in Homer (68–70, 430–32). Endowing Theoclymenus with this luxurious domain serves to romanticize, by contrast, Helen's legitimate marriage, banishing any suspicion that her husband's charms might consist in the conspicuous wealth with which he is typically endowed. On the contrary, her devotion is unshaken by the fact that he shows up in rags.

Theoclymenus has also acquired Menelaus's traditional poor judgment. This time it is he who foolishly leaves his (intended) wife unaccompanied so that she can plot to escape with a foreigner, taking with her a substantial quantity of stolen goods. At the moment of escape there is a marked emphasis on the elegant feet that take her onto the ship and away from Egypt (1528, 1570). This would not be the first time a man foolishly left those feet free to roam. But the fool in question is now a barbarian. Meanwhile Menelaus takes on the role of a new and improved Paris. Helen is, once again, a willing party to her own "abduction," stolen from under the nose of her trusting would-be husband by a visiting stranger. But this time, in a reversal of that infamous original journey, her surreptitious departure from Greece with her barbarian lover is replaced by an equally surreptitious escape back to Greece from barbarian Egypt. "Leaving" the royal palace (1526) she "sails away" (1663), but does so with her legitimate husband. Like the Helen of tradition, she is thus remarried, but not to her traditional series of mates. Her erotic mobility is not denied, but turned to Menelaus's advantage. Meanwhile Theoclymenus has conveniently taken on Menelaus's more doubtful qualities, leaving the Greek characters free to sail virtuously into the sunset.

Even while reversing Helen's defining character trait, then, Euripides provides her with a recognizably similar story. He also maintains continuity with previous Helens by allowing her to keep many other traditional traits, adapted as necessary to her newly virtuous persona. Innocent though she is, she displays an even more acute sense of responsibility than Homer's Helen for what "she" caused. She adopts her double's actions as her own, speaking, for example, of "my abduction" (50), lamenting that "my body" destroyed both Troy and the Greeks (383–85), and declaring that the city was ruined "because of me, murderer of many, / because of my lamentable name" (198–99). She not only misses her daughter, as in the *Iliad*, but is anxious about Hermione's marriage prospects, derailed by her maternal absence (282–83, 688–90). The self-pity she evinces in Homer has, understandably, become still more marked. But she also displays a sweeping pity for the victims of war, Greek and Trojan alike, and identifies especially with the suffering of women (362–74), in marked contrast with her estrangement from other women in Homeric epic and especially in *Trojan Women*. Female solidarity also plays a significant role in the success of her escape plot, which depends on winning the help of Theonoe (cf. 328, 830).

Another central trait of Helen's traditional character, which Euripides retains but adapts to his needs, is her skill with language. As in Homer, she uses this skill to resist commodification as a mere object of desire and assert her own agency in the most difficult of circumstances. She does so, however, not merely to save her skin, but rather, like Penelope in the *Odyssey*, to remain loyal to her husband, restore her reputation, and get the better of an unjust enemy. Her prologue speech, which establishes her firmly as a helpless victim of the gods, is itself an exercise in dramatic and narrative control. Later, when begging Theonoe for help, she commodifies herself strikingly as a piece of stolen property that should be returned to its proper owner (903–13). But this, too, is an *act* of persuasion, a virtuous counterpart of the manipulative self-objectification employed by her predecessor in *Trojan Women*. She also makes strategic use of the kind of self-effacement expected of good women (925, 1049). The power of deception inherent in such "feminine" skill with language, used so damagingly by Helen in the *Odyssey*, is turned to virtuous purposes through the escape plot, where Helen "most skillfully" plays the part of a bereaved wife (1528–29).

Euripides' reformed Helen thus retains nearly all the distinctive aspects of her traditional counterpart's character and story, while transforming them into indicia of virtuous womanhood. Her most fundamental feature remains, however, to be addressed: her extraordinary beauty. Euripides could not eliminate that aspect of her persona without destroying her identity as Helen, but he could reframe the threat it poses to herself and others through the way he chose to present it on stage, including the reactions it elicits from his characters.

Thanks to the generic nature of the theatrical conventions for conveying beauty, Helen's mask in this drama will have been much the same as that of her predecessor in *Trojan Women*. The text confirms, for example, that she has long, curling, golden or "tawny" (*xanthos*) hair (1087, 1224). In contrast to the earlier play there is no sign of special elegance in her attire, but she is dressed in white (1088), a color associated with festivity and sometimes with luxury. Her garments may have reminded the audience of her shimmering clothing in the *Iliad*, when she appears on the walls of Troy and the elders are awestruck by her beauty.

As in *Trojan Women*, the script and action guide us to understand this generically beautiful appearance as exceptional. But this time the only character who comments explicitly on Helen's beauty is Helen herself. She insists on its centrality to her mythic identity, dwelling on it obsessively from the prologue onward, especially in connection with the Judgment of Paris and its aftermath (23, 27–28, 236–37). In this drama the specious claim made by her counterpart in *Trojan Women* is true: she really is a victim of her own beauty. She speaks of it, accordingly, as an actively destructive force that is "responsible" for the war and has ruined herself along with Troy and the Achaeans (261, 304–5, 383–85). This idea is literalized in the *eidōlon*, whose beauty is, ex hypothesi, identical with Helen's own. The flames that destroyed Troy on account of the double (cf. 107–8, 196–97, 1162) conveys equally the power of the original.

Helen's beauty therefore becomes the primary target of the self-hatred she inherits from her character in Homer. She vehemently repudiates this "gift" of Aphrodite (364), and unlike her counterpart in *Trojan Women* neither exults in it nor takes advantage of its power. Rather, she laments and rejects it as the "most unfortunate" source of all her troubles (236–37). She even plays on the ambiguity of the word *kalos*, by suggesting that only something that brings good fortune should properly be called beautiful (27). Later she wishes she could lose her beauty like two heroines of myth, one named Callisto ("most beautiful"), whom the gods turned into a bear, and the other identified only as the daughter of Merops (otherwise unknown), who was evidently transformed into a deer (375–83). Helen equates the loss of these women's beauty with the loss of their identity as human. As the most beautiful of all, her own identity is even more intimately entwined with her appearance and its consequences.

In another striking passage, Helen plays on the ambiguity not of the word *kalos*, but of its opposite, *aischros*:

> If only I could be wiped clean, like a statue (*agalma*), and take on
> an uglier appearance instead of my beautiful one!
>
> (262–63)

Her image evokes the epic "pouring on" of beauty by the gods, which is sometimes likened to gilding a statue (above, p. 9). It refers more specifically to the ancient practice of applying paint to sculpture. Helen wishes that her beauty, like a coat of paint, could be replaced at will with an "uglier appearance." This translates the ambiguous Greek phrase *aischion eidos*, which could also mean "more shameful appearance" or "uglier beauty." If her appearance were uglier, Helen would, paradoxically, be relieved of the shameful reputation that causes her such anguish (135). By deprecating her beauty as a disastrous but superficial coating that belies her interior, Helen presents herself as a transformed Pandora, a woman whose beautiful exterior hides not an evil character but a virtuous one. As Teucer puts it, her body is like Helen's but her "wits" (*phrenes*) are not (160–61).

The hopelessness of this desire to "be wiped clean" underscores the centrality of Helen's beauty, like Pandora's, to her identity. This becomes particularly clear when we consider the image's obvious metatheatrical dimension. Spoken as it is by a masked and costumed actor, Helen's simile draws attention to the artifice of dramatic conventions for conveying beauty. In metatheatrical terms, her wish for an uglier face amounts to a wish that the actor playing her could change his mask. But the theatrical mask, though a mere covering for the actor who wears it, is integral to the dramatically constructed body. In Greek, the word for "mask" is the same as the word for "face" (pro-sōpon). The mask conceals the actor's face, of course, but as far as the character is concerned her face, and thus identity, is not covered but constituted by the mask. If Helen lost her beautiful face, how would Menelaus recognize her as the double's double? When she wishes, in effect, for a different mask, she is wishing for annihilation.

No other character is as preoccupied as Helen herself with her appearance (not even, perhaps surprisingly, Theoclymenus). Yet plot and imagery provide the audience with a different kind of perspective on its quality. Her age and married status notwithstanding, the way Helen's story is told assimilates her to a *parthenos*, an irresistibly alluring adolescent girl. Her "abduction" by Hermes occurred while she was picking flowers for the goddess Athena (244–49)—a typical pattern for abducted mythic *parthenoi*, many of whom are mentioned in the text as parallels for Helen. Her situation resembles, in particular, that of Persephone, the archetype of a virginal, flower-picking abductee. This kind of imagery is not confined to Helen's youthful past. The chorus imagine her, for example, participating in maiden dances upon her return to Sparta (1465–68). Nor is there any indication that she looks seventeen years older than when she first arrived in Egypt. Her own daughter, Hermione, is imagined turning gray with age (283), but Helen is still addressed as "young woman" by Menelaus (1288) and "child" by the chorus (1356). The light feet upon which she makes her escape are suggestive, too, of youthful beauty: they are "delicate" (*habros*), with lovely ankles (1528, 1570).

As a notional *parthenos* Helen remains a potential bride, ripe for abduction. The initial entrance of the bedraggled Menelaus evokes a famous moment in the *Odyssey*, when the shipwrecked Odysseus emerges from the sea and encounters Nausicaa, a beautiful princess of marriageable age. Nausicaa stands her ground bravely, but Helen reacts more like the princess's handmaidens, who flee in terror at the sight of the wild-looking stranger. She takes refuge at the tomb of Proteus, exclaiming:

> I must move my limbs to the tomb like a running filly
> or one of the god's bacchants! This man is savage in
> appearance and is hunting me down to seize me!
>
> (543–45)

Helen is presented here as a charming girlish fugitive of the kind whose beauty so often makes her the target of male assault, like the woman pursued by Apollo in figure 10.1. "Filly" is a frequent metaphor for a frisky *parthenos* who needs "taming" through marriage, and the "god's bacchants" are devotees of Dionysus symbolizing female wildness and freedom. In Euripides' *Bacchae*, the chorus of bacchants describe themselves in very similar terms:

> Like a filly with its mother in the pasture
> the bacchant moves her swift-footed limbs and leaps!
> (165–66)

Helen's words also evoke the cult of the divine Helen, worshipped as an ideal of beauty for the virginal bride. Our sources speak of Spartan girls dancing and running in the meadows like horses or bacchants, with Helen as their leader (Ar. *Lys.* 1303–15; cf. Theoc. 18.22–23, 30, 39–40). The scene in *Helen* thus conjures both visually and verbally a template—wild *parthenos* exposed to the threat of a strange man—that affirms Helen's youthful beauty and conjures her mythic identity as a light-footed emblem of female eroticism.

The theatrical audience also had another template ready to hand. Helen's flight to Proteus's tomb at the sight of Menelaus with his sword would certainly

FIGURE 10.1 Apollo, carrying a laurel branch, pursues a fleeing woman. Above him is inscribed *kalos*, and above the woman, *kalē*, both meaning "beautiful." Apollo's charioteer waits on the left. Attic red-figure hydria, 450–440 BCE. London, British Museum E 170; *ARV²* 1042.2; BAD 213536. © The Trustees of the British Museum.

evoke her familiar retreat to Aphrodite's protection at the sack of Troy (see fig-ure 2.6 above, p. 42). As a site of sanctuary, the tomb replaces Aphrodite's amoral protective power with a symbolic affirmation of Helen's newfound cha-stity. Thanks to the structural resemblance to that famous scene, however, the audience would no doubt be expecting Menelaus, true to form, to drop his sword under the erotic impact of Helen's beauty.

But Euripides gives the incident a surprise twist of his own. Even though this Menelaus is in general all too eager to use his sword, there is no sign that he either raises it against Helen or drops it, overwhelmed by her beauty. It is true that he is stunned and speechless at the sight of her (549)—two frequent symptoms of *erōs*—but in this case the shock seems less erotic than epistemo-logical. When Menelaus worries that his eyes are "diseased" (575) he is speaking quite literally—this apparent Helen must be some kind of optical illusion. The Recovery template is actually reversed, when Helen tries to embrace Menelaus and he backs away (566–67). He is even willing to leave without her, despite her uncanny "resemblance" to Helen (590–91). When he does finally accept her, this results not from her beauty but from new evidence that she was, after all, speaking the truth (622–24). From that point on he reciprocates her affec-tion, but never so effusively as to suggest erotic subjugation. If it is important for Euripides' reversal of Helen's myth that she remain faithful to Menelaus, it is apparently also important that he not appear subject to her beauty's emascu-lating power.

Yet Menelaus's newfound self-control is apparently not enough by itself to defuse the threat of that power. Helen, too, requires an attitude adjust-ment. Her attitude toward her beauty is, to be sure, consistently negative; nevertheless, it undergoes a perceptible shift in the course of the drama. During the earlier portion of the play, she confines herself to passively lamenting her beauty as something over which she has no control. She cannot, of course, control the antics of the double, which literally embodies the negative effects of that beauty, but her personal appearance is a different matter. As we saw in chapter 1, a woman's beauty is not simply a "natural" phenomenon. It lies in her own hands, insofar as she constructs and ma-nipulates it through clothing and accessories, voice and demeanor. Con-versely, as Hecuba pointed out in *Trojan Women*, even the most beautiful woman in the world has the power to minimize her attractions. Helen is therefore responsible for her own looks in a way of which she seems ini-tially unaware.

When she takes charge of the action, however, Helen also takes charge of her beauty. The scheme she invents to escape from Egypt, thereby erasing the bad old Helen's reputation, also fulfills the desire she expressed earlier for an uglier appearance. Before exiting to dress in mourning for Menelaus's false funeral, Helen spells out the details of her disguise (thus preparing the specta-tors for a possibly unrecognizable reappearance):

> I shall cut short my curling hair,
> exchange my white dress for a black one,
> and scratch my cheeks bloody with my fingernails.
>
> (1087–89)

When she reenters she is indeed "uglier" than before. Erotic charm is linked with life, fertility, and joy, but mourning rituals involve a symbolic embrace of death that turns its back on such charm. Cropped hair, dark clothing, and scratched cheeks are all signifiers of mourning, like that of the bereaved women at Troy, who were shown on stage in *Trojan Women* but are mentioned repeatedly in this play as well (370–74, 1122–25) (cf. figure 10.2). Thanks to the erotic charge conveyed by long hair, fair cheeks, and lovely clothing, these ritual gestures are also a renunciation of physical beauty. Even without them, tears and lamentation were thought to ruin a woman's looks (cf. above, p. 91). Not surprisingly, Theoclymenus reacts with consternation at the sight of Helen's black dress, cropped hair, and tear-stained cheeks (1186–90). He tells

FIGURE 10.2 Mourning scene. The deceased, a young woman, wears a bridal crown. She is lamented by a woman with loose hair on the left and an older woman with cropped hair on the right. The marks on the older woman's cheeks are probably wrinkles, but may be tattoos or scratches. Detail of an Attic red-figure loutrophoros, c. 460 BCE. Athens, National Archaeological Museum 1170; *ARV²* 512.13, 1657; BAD 205750. © Hellenic Ministry of Culture and Tourism/Archaeological Receipts Fund.

hernot to waste away in pointless lamentation (1285–88), and is concerned about the impact of her tears on her complexion (1419). Helen's haircutting also alludes to Spartan wedding customs (as befits her pending remarriage to Menelaus). In contrast to Athens, however, weddings in classical Sparta did not eroticize the bride. The Spartan lawgiver Lycurgus, we are told, wanted to remove "all femininity" from Spartan women (Plut. *Lyc.* 14.2). For her wedding, the bride was dressed as a young man and had her hair cut short (14.4), divesting her of conventional signifiers of feminine allure.

Helen's degraded appearance is essential to the escape plot that she herself devises, and as such a manifestation of her duplicitous "feminine" cleverness. Such deviousness is stereotypically associated with "crafty Aphrodite, murdering many (*poluktonos*)," as Helen herself calls her (238), echoing an epithet applied to the lion cub in *Agamemnon* (Aesch. *Ag.* 734). Helen, too, feels responsible for "murdering many" (198), but redeems herself through a craftiness that is not only beneficial but desexualized, and thus detached from the threat of Aphrodite. Theoclymenus, as he complains at the end, is "caught by womanly devices" (1621), but the "devices" are not those of erotic seduction. Despite her deceptiveness, Helen is an entirely passive object of Theoclymenus's desire. In contrast to her enraptured reunion with Menelaus, she resists his advances strenuously and engages in no seductive behavior toward him. Even when pretending to capitulate she avoids any suggestion of eroticism: "Let's make a truce! Be reconciled with me!" (1335). She goes on to invoke him as a "friend" (1237), falsely accept him as her "new husband" (1399), and praise him as "faultless" (1424). These are the sentiments not of a seductress but of a dutiful wife.

Most important, she uses not beauty but defacement to attain her goal, employing the deceptive feminine snares of coiffure, makeup, and clothing in the inverse of their seductive function. The "beautiful evil" has been turned inside out, a virtuous female character now veiled by a disfigured exterior. This willingness to deface herself is the final proof of Helen's rebirth as a model wife. Instead of using the divine power of her beauty, as in *Trojan Women*, to control and emasculate men, she willingly takes on the appearance of a mortal woman whose beauty is in its nature transient, like the timeworn Penelope in the *Odyssey*. This self-abnegation is implemented by means specific to the theater. The equivalence of the mask to the dramatic self enables Euripides to literalize Helen's metaphorical erasure of her own beauty, giving concrete weight to this symbolic rejection of her old identity as the most beautiful woman in the world.

That old identity took many forms, and by defacing herself Helen repudiates more than one of them, from her Homeric self, with its shimmering garments and awe-inspiring face, to the vain floozy of other Euripidean tragedies. There is a particularly striking contrast with Euripides' *Orestes*, in which Helen has a cameo role. When she comes onstage, dressed in mourning for her sister

Clytemnestra, her resentful niece Electra acerbically remarks that a person's nature does not change:

> See how she's cut off just the ends of her hair
> to preserve her beauty. She's the same as ever!
>
> (*Or.* 128–29)

Even though this play was produced four years after *Helen*, it helps clarify the significance of Helen's haircutting in the earlier play. Unlike her persona in *Orestes*, the Helen of *Helen* actively embraces the unbecoming gestures of mourning. She seems to have taken the advice of Hecuba in *Trojan Women*, who declared degrading clothing and cropped hair appropriate indicia of remorse and feminine virtue—specifically the virtue of self-control (above, p. 196).

She has also, more subtly, rejected her own identity from the first half of *Helen* itself. Despite the virtuous lamentations in which she indulges from the start, the script contains the merest hints that Helen has, in the past, (over) valued the very beauty that she deplores.[1] When she takes responsibility for the destruction caused by her beauty, she is, to be sure, displaying a good woman's sense of responsibility, but she is also accepting her beauty as fundamental to her identity. As such it remains a powerful weapon, despite the fact that she, unlike the double, has not chosen to use it for transgressive purposes. Excessive pride in her beauty is also mentioned in a mysterious choral song performed just prior to her final entrance. This baffling ode concerns some kind of offense by Helen against the goddess Demeter. Textual corruption makes it impossible to interpret clearly or in detail, but the chorus end by seeming to reproach Helen, declaring, "You gloried in your beauty alone" (1368). No such charge could be brought against the defaced Helen who reenters just as these words are sung. She has changed her attitude, not toward Theoclymenus or Menelaus, but toward herself. Instead of presenting herself as a passive object, victimized by her beauty, she has taken control of her appearance. She no longer merely voices the wish for an uglier appearance but has put that wish into action, demonstrating visibly that she does not take a dangerous pride in her beauty or view it as a source of power.

This symbolic renunciation of her beauty goes hand in hand with a willing suppression of her independence. Here in Egypt Helen succeeds in controlling her situation, against all the odds, through her own courage and initiative. But the "happy ending" that returns her to Greece also restores her to the marital status quo. She willingly and indeed joyfully sails back to Sparta—the place where she was denied the choice that traditionally defines her and from which she was simply removed, as a passive object, by the gods. Her *parthenos*-like

---

1. In one intriguing passage she rejects suicide by hanging because it would be unbecoming (299–302), possibly suggesting an improper vanity. But most editors reject the lines as inauthentic.

state, conveyed most strikingly at Proteus's tomb, furnished proof not only of her beauty but of the mobility that makes such beauty dangerous. When she reemerges from the palace in her new guise as a widow in mourning, her movements are presumably very different from the charming flightiness that she displayed earlier. She has become a wife, subdued and visually self-effacing, ready for the final journey to her husband's home.

This is the last Helen that we see on stage—the Helen who departs for Greece to live happily ever after with her first and only husband. Allusions to the *Odyssey*, particularly Hermione's future wedding (1476–78), lay the groundwork for a sunnier Odyssean outcome, not overshadowed by embarrassing Trojan tales. The reaffirmation of her marriage evokes, however, not just the *Odyssey* but the norms of Euripides' Greece at their most severe. Helen's haircutting may allude to specifically Spartan wedding customs, but the language used for her remarriage is equally applicable to Athens. A servant informs Theoclymenus that Helen ought by rights to be in the hands of the male guardian (*kurios*) to whom her father gave her (1634–35), and Castor, as deus ex machina, affirms the propriety of this "yoking" (1654–55). Helen herself speaks of her husband as a "master" (*despotēs*) (572), using the standard word for a master of slaves (cf., e.g., 1627). Cropped hair can also be a sign of slavery (e.g., Eur. *El.* 107–11), a way of marking a person as an object under another's control. A wife is not a slave, of course, even at Athens, but the use of the word "master" for a husband underlines the extent of his power over his wife (cf., e.g., Eur. *Med.* 233). Helen herself uses it for her feigned submission to the tyrannical Theoclymenus (1193). Yet she embraces Menelaus's authority with alacrity.

This attainment of rewedded bliss is contingent on Helen's symbolic rejection of her immortal beauty and the power that it implies. That beauty will, however, suffer no long-term impairment. As is the nature of mourning rituals, her transformation is strictly temporary. When they return to Sparta Menelaus will possess the most beautiful woman in the world, while remaining secure in the knowledge that she is willing to deface herself for his sake. Despite his initial entrance as an Odysseus figure, he is spared the dilemmas confronted by the hero of the *Odyssey*. Unlike Odysseus, who had to choose between his beloved human wife and marriage to an immortal goddess, Menelaus will be remarried to a future goddess (1667) endowed with eternally youthful beauty, and go on to live forever in the Isles of the Blessed (1676–77). Though recognizably similar to her own remorseful and ingenious self, the reformed Helen incorporates aspects of a whole series of Odyssean females, to become at once Penelope (virtuous faithful wife), Calypso (radiant ageless goddess), and Nausicaa (hospitable nubile maiden). Indeed she outdoes all of them. Unlike Calypso, she has no need to coerce her love object into remaining with her; unlike Nausicaa, she is available for (re)marriage without compromising Menelaus's fidelity to his "real" wife; unlike Penelope she is divinely beautiful (not to mention immortal), does not test or distrust her husband, and suffers no ambiguous dreams about geese (cf. above, p. 93). This Helen is, indeed, most beautiful and best.

In Euripides' Egypt, then, fantasy has full rein. It is not only a place where an assertive, intelligent woman may be a good woman and a beautiful woman may be faithful, but a place where a good, beautiful, intelligent, assertive, faithful woman ends up willingly and indeed eagerly resubmitting herself to a notoriously second-rate husband. For the fantasy to be complete, however, that second-rate husband must also be transformed into the hero of his own imagination.

Menelaus's imagination is, in this respect, a vivid one. He is obsessed with lineage and glory, specifically the glory of the Trojan War, on which he stakes his claim to fame and manliness (386–96, 453, 501–4, 808, 845–54, 947–53). He presents himself not as the supporting player with whom we are familiar, but as the war's principal or even exclusive hero. Though he and Agamemnon were, he says, a "glorious pair" of brothers (392), he talks as if he had been sole leader of the massive army (393–96) and personally conquered Troy (402, 806). He encroaches on other heroes too, recalling Achilles' death only to mention how he himself "deprived Thetis" of her son (847), and speaking of all the slaughtered men sent down to Hades "by my sword" (969–71).

Euripides deflates this self-image, however, with a healthy dose of theatrical mockery. There is an obvious comic dissonance between Menelaus's oversized heroic attitude and his degraded appearance. When he first enters, his usual magnificent garb, lost in the shipwreck, has been replaced with an outfit made from scraps of sail whose ugliness is remarked upon repeatedly (420–24, 554, 1204, 1284). Stripped of fine clothing, he is also stripped of his dignity. He is unrecognizable to his wife and unknown in Egypt, mocked as a nobody by a mere female doorkeeper who actually reduces him to tears at his own loss of status (455–58). This pitiful behavior undermines his scorn for tears and feminine weakness in favor of manly action (947–53, 991–92). The Odyssean overtones of his entrance also underline the fact that he is no Odysseus in the planning department. His contribution to the plotting process is laughable (1039–46). Helen is the driving force in crafting the plan, and as such, clearly his intellectual superior, evoking the Odyssean tension between the dull-witted Menelaus and the clever, manipulative Helen.

Menelaus thus makes a less-than-promising impression. But Helen's scheme allows him, too, to be reborn with a new, improved identity made visible in theatrical terms by a change of mask and costume. For their grand finale she mars her own appearance but bathes, dresses, and beautifies her husband. Menelaus reenters after this makeover wearing fine clothes and suitably martial accessories supplied by the grateful Theoclymenus (1281–84, 1375–84). He has probably also acquired a different mask, with elegantly coiffed hair, to go with his new outfit. His appearance is thus transformed along with Helen's, but in the opposite direction, from degradation to empowerment, in keeping with his self-proclaimed identity as the hero who conquered Troy.

This prepares him to reenact that identity in the play's denouement, which is not just a reformed elopement but also a rewriting of the Trojan War. Helen is not the only epic character to whom this drama gives a second chance. Once again there is to be a life-or-death struggle between Greeks and "barbarians" over Helen's marriage bed. Menelaus makes the parallel explicit when he invokes his men, prior to the final battle, as "you who sacked Troy" (1560). In the thick of the fighting Helen herself exhorts them, "Where is the glory of Troy? / Show these barbarians!" (1603–4). Relieved of his old identity as the archetypal cuckold, Menelaus can become *the* great hero of this struggle, re-deeming the sufferings at Troy that were rendered futile by the *eidōlon*. Despite his refurbished appearance, however, Euripides continues to undermine that heroism through the tone of the messenger's narrative. The Menelaus who reprises his "heroic" role, leading his men in a ruthless slaughter of unarmed Egyptian sailors until the ship runs with blood, is a disturbing caricature of the manliness by which he sets such store.

This characterization of Menelaus reveals the notion of an unproblemati-cally glorious war waged for a flawless Helen by her heroic husband as an absurdity. Euripides' Egypt is the kind of impossible fantasyland that belongs in comedy, like Cloudcuckooland, the avian republic of Aristophanes' *Birds*. The idea that this quintessentially second-rate male can be reimagined as a fit mate for the most beautiful woman in the world is, more specifically, a Spartan fantasy—that is to say, an Athenian fantasy about Spartans. Like *Trojan Women*, this drama was produced in the midst of the Peloponnesian War. Superficially, it seems to reverse the political sympathies of the earlier play, by making the Spartan Menelaus the hero of a just war against a nefarious barbarian. His manly heroism is, however, eviscerated by a mockery that exposes the fantasy for what it is.

The beautiful, virtuous Helen, by contrast, remains a fantasy for all Greece. Once again, Euripides exploits the resonance of her name. When Menelaus first sees her, he asks:

MENELAUS: Are you a Greek woman (*Hellēnis*) or a woman of this country?
HELEN: A Greek woman (*Hellēnis*); but I want to know your situation too.
MENELAUS: I have never seen anyone, woman, who looks so much
    like Helen (*Helenēi*).

(561–63)

In the Greek the wordplay is highlighted, as in *Trojan Women*, by placing the relevant noun first, at the beginning of each line, in a way that insists, rhetorically, on Helen's Hellenic identity (cf. above, p. 200). She must therefore be restored not merely to Sparta but to Greece. The Athenians, in particular, would be loath to let the Spartans claim this newly virtuous Helen exclusively for themselves. Sparta is, of course, the home to which she is sailing at the end of the play. But Euripides highlights the importance of Athena, his own city's divine patron, in Helen's Sparta (227–29, 244–46).

He also ends the drama by linking Helen to Attica itself. As deus ex machina, Castor informs her:

> The place where Hermes first brought you
> when he took you from Sparta, racing through the sky,
> stealing your body so that Paris would not marry you—
> I mean the island stretched along the Attic coast as a guard—
> from now on mortals shall give it the name "Helen,"
> since it received you when you were stolen from your home.
>
> (1670–75)

This gesture comes at the cost of some geographical awkwardness, since the island in question is far off the route of a direct flight from Sparta to Egypt. But it serves to recuperate a name that had become synonymous with destruction both through the tradition of negative punning and through the *eidōlon*, which is identified repeatedly with Helen's name (e.g., 42–43, 199). Renaming the island associates that name with an innocent, captured Helen instead of an active, capturing one, and implies that she belongs not only to Sparta but to Athens, whose coastline is protected by her island.

In contrast to the hostile dramatic treatment of her husband, neither the beauty nor the virtue of this reimagined Helen is undercut by mockery. This allows her to remain an ideal for all Greece, including Euripides' Athens. Yet the unattainability of that ideal is conveyed in other ways. Helen is, as she puts it, a *teras*, a "monster," "marvel," or divine portent, having been born from Zeus himself via an egg (256–61). Euripides humanizes her, like many of his characters, by making her question such improbabilities about herself (cf. 17–21). At the end of the play, however, she is fully remythologized. Castor informs us that Helen will be worshipped as a goddess after she "reaches the end of her life" (1666–69)—a careful locution, which avoids suggesting that she ever actually grows old or dies. Nor will this Helen be limited to the conventional gender role seemingly embraced by her human persona. There is no indication that she will accompany her husband to the Isles of the Blessed or be linked with him in cult. On the contrary, Castor specifies that she will be honored with ritual feasts at her brothers' side (1668). The divine Helen will, it seems, be active independently of her husband, transcending the geographical and ideological constraints of her human marriage. The woman who is most beautiful and best defies such limitations to become a goddess exempt from the rules restricting ordinary women's lives.

The illusory character of the romantic outcome—and of the glory of a bloody war fought for a virtuous Helen—is conveyed in a different way through Euripides' portrayal of the very double that is supposed to exculpate her. Despite the *eidōlon's* stipulated ontological independence it is in fact quite hard to keep it distinct from Helen. It is not only physically indistinguishable from her but embodies vital and intertwined aspects of her identity: her name, her reputation, and her beauty. As we saw earlier, she identifies with it personally to a remarkable degree (above, p. 207). Even the double's "character," as described by Menelaus's servant, resembles Helen's, to the point of echoing her language (compare 608–10 with 52–53).

Helen's double is, of course, not a natural woman but a fabricated object, made by Hera out of "air" (34) or "cloud" (705, 1219). Ex hypothesi, then, it lacks human subjectivity. But if it is an object, it is a very elaborate one. Like the Helen we see on stage, it can breathe (34), see (583), speak (608–15), and "be gone" (605), "leaving" others behind (607). It presumably had sex with Paris, with whom it presumably "eloped," and if you cut it, it presumably bleeds. It thus shows all the usual signs not only of life but of responsible agency, and is, in consequence, blamed by others for its actions (cf. 425–26, 620–21). The line between living females and their images is, moreover, an uncertain one in Greek mythology. Lifelike powers are attributed to statues—especially *agalmata*—and *eidōla* made of cloud are "physiologically functional" (above, pp. 12, 118). The ambiguous ontological status of such doubles is underlined by the fact that Cloud herself sometimes appears as a divinity. Thus, Pindar's description of the *eidōlon* of Hera, with which Ixion had sex, allows us to interpret it as "a cloud," or alternatively as Cloud. Nor is this kind of uncertainty confined to goddesses. Pandora, the first human woman, was fabricated by the gods to bring men harm. How, then, can we be sure Helen's *eidōlon* is not, like her, a living agent? If so, however, it is clearly the "real" Helen, since it has the salient characteristics of the bad old Helen and does the job that Zeus created her to do.

The dramatic plot stipulates, of course, that this is not the case. Like the heroine of the *Stepford Wives*, who unmasks the robot women by stabbing one of them with a knife, Euripides reveals the double as a fabrication when the messenger reports that it has vanished back into the sky (605–6, 612–13). But he complicates this stipulation metatheatrically by suggesting that the "real" Helen may be equally illusory. Throughout the play he points to his heroine's fabricated nature, equating her with the *eidōlon* in ways that constantly oblige us to confront her fictitiousness. Helen, as we saw, speaks of herself as a "statue" (*agalma*) (262), and the same word is used for her double (705, 1219). Similarly, when Theonoe calls the double a *mimēma*, or artistic "imitation" (875), she is echoing language used earlier by Teucer when he first lays eyes on

Helen. Believing her to be a stranger, he calls her "the murderous image of a woman"—which correctly describes the *eidōlon*—and perceives her as an "imitation" (*mimēma*) of the Helen who was fought over at Troy (72–75). He sees her, that is, as the double's double.

The Helen on stage is, in fact, as unreal as the *eidōlon*, even though she too moves, speaks, and acts (in more senses than one). Whereas her double is a divinely sculpted figure, Helen's fictitiousness is that of a masked and costumed actor "sculpted" by the playwright. As a literary construct, she is a "double" of her poetic antecedents, her virtuous persona parasitic on the adventures of her evil twin. As a dramatic character, her only "real" ontological difference from the double is that "she" is physically present on stage, visible to the audience. But the drama warns us repeatedly not to trust our eyes, especially where Helen is concerned. When Teucer tells Helen about the recovery of "Helen" at the sack of Troy, for instance, he declares, "I saw her with my own eyes, just as well as I see you" (118). In reply Helen warns him that it could have been an illusion—but so, of course, could she. The double, to be sure, disappears into thin air, but Helen, too, will vanish when the actor removes his mask and costume. To complicate matters still further, doubles like Helen's did sometimes appear as characters on the fifth-century stage. How, then, can we be certain that Helen in *Helen* is not, in fact, the *eidōlon*, as the messenger takes her to be (616–18)? Which is the "real" Helen, which the "imitation"? Euripides provokes such questions but does not answer them—not, at least, in any simple way.

This gives a new layer of meaning to Helen's rejection of her old identity, and specifically to her embrace of virtuous wifely submission through the symbolic act of changing her own mask and costume. She transforms her beautiful self using the kind of feminine agency that any woman might employ to manipulate her own appearance. But because she is a dramatic figure, not a real woman, this self-construction has another, metatheatrical dimension. As created by the author, and the actor who performs her, Euripides' Helen is quite literally an object made by men, an illusion crafted, like her double, to satisfy the desires of male viewers. Her purposeful self-effacement reveals the active construction of a virtuous female self to be itself a male fabrication. The reformed human Helen is thus, like Semonides' bee woman, a fantasy of female perfection that turns out to be, in essence, an illusion.

II

Helen MacGuffin: Isocrates

> The theft of secret documents was the original MacGuffin. So the "MacGuffin" is the term we use to cover all that sort of thing: to steal plans or documents, or discover a secret, it doesn't matter what it is. And the logicians are wrong in trying to figure out the truth of a MacGuffin, since it's beside the point. The only thing that really matters is that in the picture the plans, documents, or secrets must seem to be of vital importance to the characters. To me, the narrator, they're of no importance whatsoever.
>
> —Alfred Hitchcock

The last classical Greek author to make Helen the focus of a major work was the prolific Athenian rhetorician Isocrates. Isocrates was an aristocratic intellectual and student of the sophist Gorgias, who, some time in the early fourth century BCE, composed his own encomium of Helen. By this time the challenge to say something new and different was considerable, but Isocrates does not disappoint. His treatment of Helen is in many ways the strangest yet.

Isocrates viewed rhetorical skill as the foundation for educating elite Athenians in political leadership, and composed many "speeches"—though they were not intended for oral delivery—in which he expounded his thoughts on education and politics. But he does not classify his work as rhetoric. He calls it "philosophy," and insists that it is both serious and *useful*, as opposed to the sophists' frivolous disputations on the one hand and the impractical theoretical speculations of Plato's Academy on the other. He was, in particular, a tireless promoter of Panhellenism, the ideology aspiring to a culturally united Greek world based on shared Greek values in opposition to the "barbarians" to the east. Yet he was also stalwartly Athenian, and his Panhellenic vision calls for the leadership of Athens as the fullest embodiment of "Greek" ideals. His *Encomium of Helen* makes Helen into a symbol of this vision by using her to link the Athenian hero Theseus with the Panhellenic enterprise of the Trojan War.

The speech opens with a preface in which Isocrates differentiates his own seriousness of purpose from the alleged hairsplitting and intellectual triviality of his contemporaries. Gorgias is named as a founding father of such frivolity (3), and many of the traits Isocrates complains of were already evident in the sophist's own *Helen*, including paradox; a striving for novelty; a desire to dazzle; the promulgation of falsehood; the defense of things that are contemptible, trivial, or worthless; and joking and playfulness. If Isocrates is to be believed, recourse to these once-innovative rhetorical tricks had by his time reached epidemic proportions. He himself, by contrast, focuses on what is important and useful (5). One should praise only "things that are agreed to be either beautiful, or good, or exceptional for their excellence" (12). Such seriousness is, however, more difficult than merely "playing" (11), since anything worth talking about has already been treated by previous writers, making it hard to say anything original (13). Because Helen belongs, so Isocrates claims, in this category, he approves Gorgias's choice of her as a topic (14), ignoring the avowed playfulness of the sophist's treatment. He complains, however, with some justification, that his predecessor's speech is not really an encomium but a defense. A defense implies the existence of some accusation or blame, but an encomium should focus only on what is good (15). He declares that he, by contrast, will praise Helen genuinely, in a way that dismisses "everything" already said by others (15).

This lengthy preamble raises the stakes for Isocrates' encomium not only by promising originality but by declaring Helen a proper vehicle for important and useful ideas. It was not unusual for Greek writers to use mythic figures for serious purposes, typically by presenting them as ethical role models. Since most legendary heroes had at best rather checkered careers, this usually required a certain amount of rehabilitation. The most fundamental basic "facts" typically remain unchanged (Troy always falls), but embarrassing specifics are either omitted or reframed by reinterpreting the character or motive of the hero in question. Elsewhere Isocrates justifies this kind of approach by pointing out that legendary figures, though presumed to be historical, are shrouded in the mists of time, forcing us to rely upon conjecture (11.34–35).

Such conjecture should, in his view, be guided by a general principle that had been gaining ground in intellectual circles for more than a century. Despite the misbehavior attributed to gods and demigods in myth, they are, in fact, faultless; they have natural virtue and no share in evil; they are endowed with all the virtues and are guides for the "most beautiful" behavior (11.41). The poets, who ascribe to gods and heroes such wrongdoings as adultery, are often simply lying (11.38–40). One is therefore entitled to imagine creditable motives for legendary figures even if such motives cannot be proven (11.30–35). We can see Isocrates performing this kind of cosmetic surgery in his last speech, *Panathenaicus*, where he declares that Agamemnon had all the virtues to an exceptional degree (12.72), and glorifies him at length without mentioning, for example, the sacrifice of Iphigenia or Agamemnon's own shameful death (12.83).

Most male heroes have a variety of exploits that allow the moralist to pick and choose and reinvent at his own discretion. Helen, however, poses more of a challenge. She forces transgression—both male and female—into the legendary picture, because without it she has no story. Isocrates' claim that she is hard to praise because she is so well-known is a bit disingenuous, since she was not, in fact, well-known as an object of praise. What makes her hard to praise is, rather, the things that she is well-known *for*. Isocrates is therefore obliged to deviate from his usual strategy. He does edit the story of the Trojan War substantially, passing over in silence such unfortunate matters as human sacrifice. But he cannot entirely eliminate Helen's own transgression. He is careful, however, not to draw attention to it. He simply takes it for granted, neither defending nor accusing her but exempting her from moral judgment by ignoring her behavior almost entirely. The speech presupposes her complicity in her elopement but does not address the matter of her desire, not even, as in Herodotus book 2, in order to minimize it.

Isocrates focuses, instead, on Helen's beauty, which he presents as a divine, transcendent force endowing her with value regardless of her own intentionality or actions. He treats her not like a person (whose worth might be damaged by her complicity), but like a work of art whose value is increased by its circulation, regardless of the means. As an extraordinarily precious symbolic object she stands not for betrayal, emasculation, and strife but for heroic achievement and Panhellenic unity. The beauty that underwrites this totemic value renders the Trojan War an unequivocally glorious adventure, unshadowed by ambivalence. In order to allow Helen to fulfill this purpose, Isocrates, more than any other author, makes the war turn on the Greek men's collective desire to possess her. That desire is, however, de-eroticized, so that it can unite the Achaean army and even the Trojans without giving rise to emasculation or resentment. Since Helen's power to bring men together is no longer tainted by erotic passion, male or female, it is free to serve as a mythic expression of the noble Panhellenic cause.

This is not the only speech in which Isocrates uses the Trojan War as an antecedent for Panhellenism. In *Panathenaicus*, for example, Agamemnon is praised extensively for uniting the Greeks against the "barbarians." But this approach exalts Spartan leadership at the expense of Athens (which played essentially no role in the Trojan War). In *Helen*, Isocrates solves this problem by introducing Theseus, Helen's first abductor, as a predecessor to the collective desire that caused the war. Though insignificant in epic, Theseus was the Athenian hero par excellence, glorified both as the founding hero who unified the settlements of Attica politically and as a force for civilization to rival or surpass Heracles (who was associated with Sparta). Having brought together disparate Greek communities, and manifested the superior political

wisdom and virtue of Athens, Theseus supplied a ready-made mythic prece-
dent for Isocrates' particular brand of Panhellenism. His salience for contemporary Athenians, as the mythical founder of their distinctive political
institutions, also brings the heroic world into contact with Isocrates' own
time and place.

In *Panathenaicus* Isocrates explicitly avoids making Helen a symbol of
Panhellenism, asserting that the war was only nominally about her and really
about Greece (12.80). By ascribing to Agamemnon a concern for Hellas rather
than Helen he circumvents the problems surrounding her role as casus belli
and elevates the moral purpose of the war. But in order to introduce Theseus,
whose rather tenuous link to the Trojan War is the value he, too, placed on
Helen, Isocrates was obliged to reinstate her as a worthwhile object of struggle
and recuperate her luster as an emblem of Greek masculine identity. By his
time, however, that luster had become quite tarnished. In Euripides' *Trojan
Women*, for example, the sophistic Helen presents herself as the protector of
Greek freedom, declaring that she deserves a crown of honor for saving Hellas
from barbarian rule (932–37). Hecuba responds that *killing* Helen would be a
crown for Hellas (1030).

The idea that Helen was not worth fighting for, with the corollary that the
Greek men were fools or emasculated weaklings to pursue her, is therefore
the unspoken target of many of Isocrates' arguments. Helen's enemies had
belittled her as "just a woman" and used the devastation of the war as evidence
against her, but Isocrates reverses their logic. If the Trojan War took place,
Helen must have been worth it; if her beauty did, in fact, launch all those
ships, it must have been extraordinary enough to do so. The war itself is
circular proof of her supreme value (cf. 45–50). By presenting that value
as symbolic and transcendent—detached from the sexual allure of a "real"
woman—Isocrates can declare Helen unequivocally worth fighting for, something no previous author had accomplished.

Isocrates conveys the exceptional quality of Helen's beauty by insisting on its
uniqueness, power, and close ties to divinity. These interwoven themes are
introduced, after the preface, through an account of her divine parentage. As
Zeus's only female child with a human mother, Helen is unique; her divine
father gave her a beauty mightier than physical strength, which makes her
even more powerful than her half brother Heracles (Zeus's greatest mortal
son); this shows that Zeus honored her the most of all his children; since he
wanted both her and Heracles to be immortal, not only literally (as future divinities) but also through their reputations, he inclined his son to heroic labors
and risk taking and gave his daughter a "nature" that was "conspicuous" and
"fought over," since brilliant distinction comes from wars and struggles, not
from "quietness" (16–17).

This neat pairing of Helen and Heracles is in some ways predictable. Heracles is actively heroic, while Helen acquires glory solely as a passive object of male struggle. Her praiseworthiness depends on her value to the men who pursued her, which is itself a reflex of their need (or desire) to gain glory through fighting. This allows Isocrates to evade the fact that in Greek gender ideology a woman should certainly *not* be "conspicuous" and *should* stay hidden "quietly" at home. His interpretation of Zeus's paternal agenda is likewise a novel one. Traditionally, Zeus's goal in causing war through Helen's beauty was not to elevate his daughter but to punish mortals for impiety or reduce the human population.

Isocrates goes on to establish Helen's special value through the superior character of her many admirers. This argument is based implicitly on the pervasive Greek notion that like is attracted to like. The greatest proof of her praiseworthiness, he says, is the "wondrous" quality of those who "esteemed" her and thought she, too, was "wondrous" (22). Their excellence consists partly in their good judgment, which in turn reinforces the credibility of their estimation of Helen. Isocrates thus neatly reverses the traditional view that it is inferior men who value female beauty most highly, claiming instead that Helen's own superiority is demonstrated by the value accorded her by superior men. These men's admiration is, however, discreetly de-eroticized. We hear not of their desire but of their "esteem" (*agapē*) and "wonder" (*thauma*). The former is a distinctly nonsexual emotion, and the latter, though often a reaction to awe-inspiring beauty, is not intrinsically erotic (we have seen it applied by Aeschylus to the monstrous Furies and by Herodotus to "wondrous" exploits and other marvels). The good judgment of Helen's admirers seems to remain unimpaired by any erotic response to her beauty.

Isocrates' first example of such an exceptional man is Theseus, to whom I shall return. Next to show their "esteem" were Helen's official suitors. Isocrates presents their courtship as establishing a Panhellenic alliance like-minded in its values and attitudes. To begin with, he insists (unlike the tradition enshrined in the *Catalogue of Women*) that the suitors comprised not just most of the Greek rulers of the time but all of them (39, 40). Nor is any of them named; the emphasis is on the comprehensiveness and unanimity of the group. These men scorned the women of their own cities in comparison with Helen (39), suggesting the relative insignificance of local interests as compared with her importance for all Greece. Their unanimity is expressed, again, in terms more rational than erotic. The suitors all had "the same judgment" and a "shared opinion" about Helen (39–41).

In a unique variation on this part of the story, Isocrates has the suitors devise the oath of their own accord, as a group. Since it was obvious to all that she was going to be fought over—in other words, that she would be a source of glory (cf. 17)—they came together and pledged each other loyalty and mutual support (40). This ensured that the inevitable war would not pit Greek against

Greek. As we find out later, Helen's beauty induces even the gods to quarrel with each other (53), but it brings all the Greek kings together, thanks to their oath. To be sure, each man agreed to it thinking of the potential benefit to himself (40), but that is precisely the nature of political and military alliances. And in the end, as we shall see, they did indeed all benefit—albeit in a slightly different way—by participating in the glory that Helen represents and retrieving her as a blessing for all Greece.

Isocrates skims past the always slightly awkward choice of Menelaus, who, like the other suitors, goes unnamed. He does imply, however, that the selection was based on merit, not just property (40). He then moves directly to the Judgment of Paris (to which I shall return), which is followed by his explanation of the Trojan War. Here he insists strongly on Helen's exceptionality—as against those, like Herodotus's Persians, who would belittle her as merely "a Spartan woman." Helen *was* different from other mythical abductees. She was different, however, in Isocrates' telling, not because she was already married but because of the special value inherent in her supreme beauty. Like those Persian storytellers, Isocrates tells us that the Greeks had stayed "quiet" about earlier disagreements between Greeks and "barbarians" (49). But "quietness," he has already informed us, does not bring glorious distinction. For that the loss of Helen was required. The resulting war was, in proportion to her beauty, the greatest ever in all respects: martial passion, duration, and scale (49). In other words, it was the ultimate exemplar of the "wars and contests" that bring conspicuous distinction (17).

Isocrates has nothing to say about the moral reasons typically adduced to justify the war, such as justice or guest-friendship. This might seem surprising, given that he insists so strongly on the Greeks' shared outlook, which offers a convenient opportunity for dwelling on such values vis-à-vis the Trojan "barbarians." But the guest-friendship theme would run the risk of drawing unwelcome attention to Helen's complicity. More important, this kind of argument might suggest that the retrieval of her person was not enough to justify the war—and for Isocrates it is. He grants that person a symbolic importance transcending not only the erotic desire to regain a beautiful wife but the ethical and even religious demands of guest-friendship and justice. The sole motive he ascribes to the Greeks is therefore their desire to regain something of extraordinary value, which the "barbarians," for their part, want to keep for themselves (50).

As a uniquely precious object moving all Greek men into united action, Helen is an emblem of Greece itself. Isocrates conveys this by employing a familiar kind of wordplay. The names of Helen and the Hellenes are scattered liberally through the speech, but at this point the equivalence is hammered home. The Greeks (*Hellēnes*), he says, reacted to the abduction of Helen (*Helenēs*) as if all of Greece (*Hellados*) had been pillaged; the "barbarians," for their part, were as proud as if they had conquered all the Greeks—or all of "us," as Isocrates puts it, emphasizing the implications for his own time (49). The equivalence between Helen and Hellas is reinforced linguistically in the Greek through matching passive participles, which echo each other formally (Helen : abducted :: Hellas : pillaged).

The Greeks are, accordingly, united in their commitment to the war. After reaching Troy they preferred to stay put than return to their diverse home-lands without Helen (50). This unity of purpose is contingent on the de-eroticizing of their desire for her. The fact that only one suitor could win her as his wife is less important than their shared judgment of her value (41). As a result, neither they nor even the Trojans felt trapped or resentful as the war proceeded. Either side could have stopped the war if they had wanted (50), says Isocrates, but they chose not to. Nor is there any hint of bitterness toward Paris from either side. Isocrates emphasizes the hardships faced by both Greeks and Trojans for continuing to fight, but treats such suffering merely as further evidence of Helen's greatness (50). The attitude that Herodotus dismissed as evidence of derangement is, for Isocrates, proof of her transcendent value.

This value gives Helen a totemic significance that is inherent in her beauty. The armies were fighting, says Isocrates, not for Menelaus and Paris but for Europe and Asia, in the belief that Helen's physical presence—her "body" (sōma)—would make the whole land where she resided "more blessed" (51). As we have seen, the word sōma sometimes appears as a synonym for physical beauty, including Helen's (above, p. 196). Isocrates himself uses it like this, in reference to the radiant "bodies" of the three goddesses at the Judgment (42). Helen, too, was destined to be a goddess, as he has already reminded us (17). The choice of this same word to denote her protective power suggests that her beauty is somehow the source of the well-being bestowed on those who possess her.

Strange as this idea may sound, it is more plausible when viewed in its cultural context. As we saw earlier, beautiful women were often likened to agalmata, that is, to specially significant statues. Images of goddesses, in particular, may be invested with the power of the divinity herself and exercise a protective function. The most famous such numinous object was the Palladion, a statue of Athena in Troy with extraordinary properties (it could move, for example). The safety of the city depended on the Palladion, and only after Odysseus sneaked into Troy and stole it did the Greeks prevail. The uncertainty of the lines between the goddess, her statue, and a living woman is shown by a mythic variant in which the Palladion is not taken until the sack of Troy. In this account the statue is closely tied to Cassandra, whose abduction from Athena's sanctuary, while clinging to it, is symbolically equated with the Palladion's loss. (In some illustrations of the scene, like figure 1.3 above, p. 113, the statue of Athena seems to protect her actively, like a living goddess.) Regardless of how the Greeks obtained the Palladion, however, it became an object of dispute because of its protective value, and ended up in various places (notably Athens) in different versions of the story. From this kind of mythical and religious perspective, the suggestion that possessing Helen's beautiful "body" could guarantee prosperity seems less far-fetched.

Isocrates' odd claim draws further resonance from the institution of hero cult. Cult heroes live on beyond the grave to protect the land in which their bodies lie. An apparition (*phasma*) of Theseus, for example, was supposed to have appeared at the battle of Marathon fighting to save Greece from the Persian invaders (Plut. *Thes.* 35.5; cf. Paus.1.15.3). Greek cities therefore went to considerable trouble to acquire the physical remains of important legendary figures. In the case of Theseus, the Athenians conquered an island in order to repatriate their local hero's bones (Plut. *Thes.* 36.1–3). This kind of military role belongs primarily to male heroes, but Helen was an exceptionally active heroine, and her anecdotes include at least one defense in battle (above, p. 46). The Athenians' interest in Helen's cult was, moreover, related in part to the patriotic claim—promoted in many texts—that it was they who led the Greeks to victory over the barbarians in the Persian Wars (above, p. 43). Helen may therefore perhaps be imagined here serving, like the Athenian Theseus, as the protector of Greece as a whole.

Toward the end of his speech Isocrates will mention the growth and military dominance of the Greek people in his own time. As a result of the war, he says, the Greek race has flourished and expanded (68). This is presumably because Greece regained Helen, the emblem of beauty, heroism, and Hellenism, and has held on to her ever since. That she should have the same significance for "Asia," as Isocrates alleges (51), is far less plausible. Contrary to the hope that Isocrates attributes to the Trojans, her presence in Troy was very far from rendering the city "more blessed." But this is hardly surprising if she is, in her essence, a sacred emblem of *Greek* prosperity. Cult heroes, in general, tend to be local in their loyalties. The Trojans' mistake was their failure to understand Helen's Hellenism.

Only now, after Isocrates has asserted Helen's totemic value for both sides, does the word *erōs* make an appearance. The *erōs* in question is, however, aroused not by Helen but by the heroic "labors" of the struggle to possess her (52). This was the passion that filled the warriors in both armies and even the gods, thereby supplying the ultimate proof of Helen's value. *Erōs* is thus dissociated from Helen and displaced onto the war itself. Yet she and her beauty still underwrite the nobility of the heroic cause. Isocrates goes on to explain that *because* she was so beautiful the combatants fought over her "reasonably" (54). If the magnitude of the war shows Helen's excellence, the intrinsic value of her beauty—safely de-eroticized—justifies the war in its turn. The gods supposedly encouraged their mortal offspring, such as Zeus's son Sarpedon, to fight and die with the rest because they thought dying for Helen was "more beautiful" than life itself (52–53). Her physical beauty stimulates in men not a disgraceful, feminizing *erōs* but a praiseworthy passion for the "beauty" of masculine achievement.

If the threat of eroticism is expunged from Isocrates' Trojan War, so is the tragedy of death. Isocrates' portrait of divine enthusiasm for the war is at best an oversimplification of the heroic tradition. Homer portrays Zeus, for example, as grief-stricken at the prospect of Sarpedon's death. The heroes' own willingness to die is likewise stripped of its tragic dimension. Isocrates alludes to the heroic choice, faced most famously by Achilles in the *Iliad*, between a full life and a glorious but youthful death. But he erases the complexities of that choice and rewrites it, for all the warriors on both sides, in a way that makes Helen its entirely unproblematic focus. It was "more beautiful" for the sons of gods not just to win renown through death but to do so fighting for "the daughter of Zeus" (53). Helen, identified by means of her divine origin, is equated with heroic glory as such.

All this works reasonably well, on its own peculiar terms, as a justification for the Greek expedition against Troy. It is much harder to explain in any such lofty fashion the behavior of some of Helen's other admirers, starting with her childhood abductor, Theseus. The Athenian hero's abduction of Helen remained an embarrassment to those who wished to promote his newly idealized persona. But Isocrates could not avoid the episode, since it is this, as we saw, that connects Theseus with the Atreidae (unnamed in this speech) who actually led the united Greeks against Troy. The importance Isocrates attached to this link forged by Helen is shown by the lengths he is willing to go to in order to excuse the Athenian hero's shameful abduction of an underage girl.

Theseus is introduced as Isocrates' first and principal example of the claim that Helen's superiority is shown by the quality of her admirers. This justifies an extended excursus on his excellence, which occupies nearly a third of the entire speech. Theseus's heroic exploits, says Isocrates, made him equivalent to Heracles, but better, since his labors were more useful and more important both to Athens and to the Greeks in general (23–25). Besides these mighty deeds, the hero displayed his many excellences, including self-control, in his mode of government (31). He was a model leader, who ruled "lawfully and beautifully" (37), and his political virtues, shown especially in the unification of Attica, made Athens the greatest city in Greece (31–37).

This paean omits a number of less savory episodes in Theseus's myth. Isocrates' account of the slaying of the Minotaur, for example, omits the hero's well-known abandonment of Ariadne, the Cretan princess who assisted him (27). He cannot excise the abduction of Helen in this fashion, but he does take certain steps to palliate the deed. He ignores Theseus's other amours, making Helen his sole object of desire, and claims, uniquely among our sources, that the Athenian hero resorted to forcible abduction only after being refused her hand in marriage (19). He also emphasizes the courage required to steal her from her noble kinsmen, without mentioning the resulting war between Sparta and Athens (which made Helen a force pitting Greek against Greek). He even defends Theseus's supporting role in a still more heinous crime, traditionally linked with his abduction of Helen, namely the attempted abduction of the goddess Persephone by his friend Pirithous. Isocrates justifies this notorious act of impiety as a gesture of gratitude by Theseus in return for Pirithous's help with Helen; Theseus tried first to dissuade him, but when he failed, male loyalty won the day (20).

Despite making Helen the exclusive focus of Theseus's legendary interest in women, Isocrates de-eroticizes the hero's attitude toward her. Even though he describes Theseus as "conquered by her beauty" (18; cf. 16), he avoids cashing out that "conquest" in erotic terms. Nor does he resort to a Gorgianic denial of responsibility. He makes the abduction sound less like a crime of passion than a cool decision, a rational choice made in the interests of the best possible life. Theseus already had the greatest fatherland and most securely based kingship, we are told, but even so, he abducted Helen because he "believed" that life was not worth living unless he could have "familiarity" with her (18). The connotations of the verb "believe" (*hēgeomai*) are more cognitive than erotic, an implication that will be confirmed when Isocrates informs us that Theseus's "intellect" is the most trustworthy possible "witness" and "judge" of Helen's "good qualities" (38). What the hero seeks with her is, moreover, just "familarity" (*oikeiotēs*), a nonsexual word of broad application. The lack of any indication that the relationship is consummated, combined with a rather odd emphasis on Helen's underage status (18), reinforces the impression that her beauty's impact on the hero is not, in the first instance, erotic.

Isocrates' extended eulogy of Theseus foreshadows in several ways the account of the Trojan War that follows, inviting the reader to associate the war, and Helen, with the values embodied in the Athenian hero. In other sources, as we have seen, Helen's heroic male counterpart is Achilles, but Isocrates assigns this role to Theseus. Helen has "the greatest share of beauty" (54), and Theseus the greatest manly excellence (*aretē*), which, we hear later, is the most beautiful thing there is (55). By equivocating on different kinds of beauty—Helen is the most beautiful physically, but Theseus morally—Isocrates suggests that they share a fundamental likeness. Both, moreover, have the power to bring Greeks together. Just as Helen united the Panhellenic alliance against Troy through the suitors' "shared opinion" of her (41), Theseus brought the people of Attica together into a "shared fatherland" (35).

It is only natural, given this kinship between them, that Theseus should be the first to perceive Helen's value. His pursuit of her, since it precedes the Trojan War chronologically (as well as in Isocrates' narrative), suggests that he surpassed the other Greeks in insight. Isocrates describes it, moreover, in terms foreshadowing the Panhellenic values exemplified both in her courtship and in the Trojan War. Theseus's desire for Helen's beauty, like her suitors', is de-eroticized, and his judgment that life was not worth living without her anticipates both the warriors' heroic choice to risk their lives and their belief that reclaiming her will make Greece prosper. Since we are also told that Theseus thought it better to die than to rule a city under the sway of tribute to another (27), the value he places on Helen equates her, additionally, with political freedom, foreshadowing her role in the Trojan War as an emblem of Greek independence from "barbarians" (67–68). Even the attack on Persephone anticipates the Greek unity enshrined in the suitors' oath, by illustrating the kind of male camaraderie that was to result from the quest for Helen.

At the end of the day, however, Isocrates cannot deny the violence and lawlessness of Theseus's deed. The forcible abduction of an underage girl in defiance of her male guardians was a serious charge, which, he explicitly admits, would be grounds for legal action in contemporary Athens (21). It is, moreover, an archetypally "barbarian" and tyrannical way to behave. One of Theseus's own civilizing labors, applauded by Isocrates, was to punish the lustful centaurs (26), whose best-known crime was the abduction of a group of women in defiance of their male relatives. Stealing from the gods is another crime of tyrants, as Isocrates mentions (33), and the attempted abduction of Persephone was one of the most scandalous such incidents in myth. These behaviors stand in severe tension with Theseus's vaunted opposition to lawlessness (28, 29), rule by force (32), stealing from the gods (33), and tyrannical rule (34), and also with his alleged respect for the autonomy of others (36; contrast 31). The awkwardness becomes acute when Isocrates draws his conclusions from the Theseus episode. Helen should be praised and honored as the most exceptional woman who ever lived, he says, because she "overpowered" such great excellence and self-control (38). It is, of course, the ability to overpower men's virtue and self-control that makes Helen's beauty so problematic.

As this sophistic conclusion clearly shows, the decision to use Helen to connect Theseus with the Panhellenic glory of the Trojan War placed Isocrates in a difficult position. He needs Helen, and he needs Theseus, but the incident that links them is violent abduction, a fact that no amount of manipulation can, in the end, disguise. He therefore resorts to a most peculiar line of argument. As we have seen, he presents Theseus's admiration for Helen as proof of her value because of Theseus's excellence. But he also asserts that the abduction is not blameworthy *because* Theseus, uniquely among all heroes, lacks no part of virtue (such as courage or wisdom): he alone has "complete excellence" (21). Isocrates is arguing not merely that the abduction fades into insignificance compared to Theseus's great deeds, but that *anything* he does is beyond the scope of criticism, *because* he is a uniquely perfect example of male excellence. The logic is perfectly circular. This is a dubious type of argument in any circumstances, but especially for someone who regards demigods as models of virtue for our imitation. Isocrates himself worries elsewhere that palliating the crimes of a heroic figure when praising him may provide a cheap refuge for the defense of scoundrels (11.45). This is presumably why he insists so strenuously on Theseus's uniqueness, which not only assimilates him to the unique Helen but makes him an exception to the usual rules of moral judgment. The desperation of this reasoning is palpable.

The idea that Helen's praiseworthiness may be seen from the sterling quality of the men who desired her meets an even more serious stumbling block in the person of Paris. Since Isocrates cannot, for obvious reasons, excise Paris altogether, he is obliged by the logic of his own approach to defend him. The result is perhaps the strangest part of this very strange speech. Isocrates persists in his strategy of de-eroticizing Helen's beauty and emphasizing the rational, prudent judgment of the men who wanted her. In consequence, this is the first (and possibly the only) account of the Trojan War to expunge male erotic desire entirely from the story. Instead, Paris, like Theseus, and like the Greeks and Trojans collectively, sees the "possession" of Helen as a way of improving his life in quite practical ways.

Since Paris was defined as a legendary figure by the erotic susceptibility encoded in his famous Judgment, Isocrates was obliged to rewrite this incident in order to demonstrate his Paris's newfound prudence. At first it seems as though we will get the conventional narrative. Hera and Athena offer Paris the manly, political gifts of kingship over "the whole of Asia" and military dominance respectively, while Aphrodite as usual offers marriage to Helen (41–42). Confronted by the goddesses, Paris is *overcome* by the *sight* of their *bodies* (42), diction strongly suggesting submission to the power of *erōs*. But here Isocrates takes an unexpected tack. The supernatural vision does, to be sure, interfere with Paris's mental functioning, but not by making him succumb to Aphrodite's erotic beauty; rather, it impairs his ability to discriminate among the three goddesses at all. He is overcome by divine beauty as such, a sight that is, typically, overwhelming to mortals, but not intrinsically erotic. In the *Homeric Hymn to Demeter*, for example, a woman faced with the dazzling appearance of the goddess collapses, becomes speechless, and neglects her crying baby (*HH* 2.275–83). When the sight of Aphrodite, revealed as a goddess, overwhelms Anchises, this is distinct from the erotic impact of her earlier disguise as a "modest *parthenos*," and he reacts very differently (*HH* 5.181–90; cf. above, p. 6). By giving all three goddesses the same effect on Paris, Isocrates de-eroticizes the Judgment. He denies the specific character of Aphrodite's appearance, subsuming her and her power under a broader conception of awe-inspiring divine beauty.

This frees Paris to make a prudential judgment based on his assessment of the goddesses' various bribes. On due consideration he chooses "familiarity" (*oikeiotēs*) with Helen (42)—the same anodyne term used earlier in connection with Theseus. Isocrates insists, a touch defensively, that even though pleasure is not to be sneezed at in itself, this was *not* the reason for Paris's choice (42). Nor, in what follows, is there any mention of Helen's own desire. She is no longer Aphrodite's mortal proxy, with everything that this implies, but a *mere* gift, with no apparent say in the matter. Yet Isocrates does not use this fact to excuse her. He gives us no reason to doubt the traditional narrative of seduction on Paris's part and acquiescence on Helen's. Her participation is neither defended nor denied. Instead, she simply disappears as an agent. The ingenious Isocrates could certainly have devised a way to defend her had he so chosen. Any reference to her desire or agency would, however, have undermined the de-eroticizing of Paris, tainting his newly prudent persona by drawing attention to his seductive role.

If Paris did not choose Helen out of "pleasure," what *was* his reason? Not her personal assets, as it turns out, but her connections: "He desired to become the son-in-law of Zeus" (43). This was both more "beautiful" (*kalos*) to him than ruling over Asia and the most "beautiful" (*kalos*) thing that he could leave his children, since it endowed them with a noble lineage that would benefit the whole family (43–44). Family ties thus displace Helen both as the object of Paris's "desire" and as the most "beautiful" of the bribes that were offered him. Through repeated use of the multivalent word *kalos*, Isocrates reverses the traditional message of Paris's choice. What is most "beautiful" turns out to be family, good reputation, posterity, indifference to pleasure—in short, the polar opposite of what his choice normally implies. This interpretation of the Judgment ingeniously reintegrates Helen's abduction into the marital economy while reinventing heroic concern with reputation as a prudent attention to marriage alliance. Isocrates' defense of Paris is essentially that he made a sensible choice for a social climber.

This is not quite enough, however, to justify his abduction of Helen—even if we ignore, as Isocrates does, the fact that she was already married to someone else. The theft of such an extraordinarily precious object, even for the benefit of one's children, is an offense that must somehow be excused if Paris is to retain his claim to superior character. This Paris may be a sensible fellow, but he is no Theseus, whose crime can be justified by his uniquely perfect excellence—a position that is, in any case, already occupied. Isocrates therefore falls back on Helen's own uniqueness. Blithely ignoring the fact that Menelaus was "thought worthy" to marry Helen (40), his Paris reasons that obtaining her will make him unique in human history, since no one else will be "thought worthy" of such a woman (43). This both marks Paris as exceptional in his own right and implicitly excuses him for a deed made equally exceptional—and thus justified—by the uniqueness of the circumstances.

This is all mind-bogglingly implausible. In the event, Paris and Helen had no significant posterity, his reputation did not turn out quite the way he planned, and his choice did not exactly benefit the other members of his family (something he might have considered before rejecting military power and kingship at the Judgment). Isocrates is understandably defensive on this point, pointing out that hindsight is 20/20 (his sole admission that the war was less than beneficial, if only to the Trojans); but, he argues, one should not judge a decision by its consequences; it is Paris's critics who are the stupid ones (45).

He goes on to defend at length the claim that Paris was indeed a man of superior insight and prudence. This is proven, in the first place, by the alleged fact (not paralleled in other versions) that the goddesses themselves chose Paris, with great care, to decide the beauty contest; they selected him specifically for his intelligence and good judgment, as the best possible judge for their important dispute (46–47). This praise for Paris's intellect and judicial credentials echoes both Isocrates' earlier praise of Theseus, whose intellect made him the best possible judge of Helen's excellence (38), and the discriminating judgment of Helen's suitors (39). Such rational superiority is presumably what enabled Paris to judge the goddesses in a way that went beyond their uniformly dazzling appearance to comprehend a loftier conception of beauty.

If the goddesses' selection of Paris is prima facie proof of his judiciousness, his own choice of Helen confirms it. It is absurd, Isocrates maintains, to accuse Paris of "deliberating badly" (48). Helen has a transcendent value, as proven once again by the quality and the quantity of those who desired her. Not only Greeks and barbarians but even demigods were willing to die for her (48). Paris would have been stupid *not* to choose her, considering the weight placed on beauty by the gods themselves (or at least the goddesses), as evidenced by the very fact of the contest (46). Isocrates thus defiantly reverses the usual relationship between beauty and reason, eliding, once again, the erotic power of beauty by making reason its judge instead of its victim.

The importance attached to beauty by the goddesses made it clear, in addition, that "beauty" (i.e., Helen) was the greatest of the three gifts they offered, and thus the intelligent choice (48). Isocrates words this point in a way that conflates the value placed on their own beauty by the goddesses with the very different kind of value that a man like Paris places on the beauty of a woman like Helen. The effect is to equate Helen with beauty itself. This qualifies Isocrates' earlier claim that Paris chose Helen not for her erotic appeal but for the "beauty" of her family connections. It seems that he did choose her for her personal beauty after all. But since she has now become an emblem of beauty as such, his judgment remains untainted by mere "pleasure." The value of her beauty is, moreover, cashed out in patriotic as opposed to erotic terms. Who, Isocrates asks, would scorn marriage to a woman whom Greeks and "barbarians" alike valued as if she were identical with Greece itself (49)?

This prudent Paris not only reverses his own traditional persona but challenges the dichotomy between admirable Greeks and inferior non-Greeks that typically underpins the rhetoric of Panhellenism. Elsewhere Isocrates, like other Hellenic apologists, treats the Trojans as legendary ancestors of the "barbarian" Persians (4.159), for whom he expresses unmitigated contempt. Paris, in particular, with his scorn for Greek values and his unmanly erotic weakness, was a ready-made whipping boy. In his *Panathenaicus*, for example, Isocrates lauds Agamemnon for putting a stop to Paris and his "barbarian" arrogance (12.83). Why, then, turn Paris into a model of prudent judgment in his *Helen*? Why not, instead, make Helen a precious object belonging to the Greeks by right but nefariously stolen by a despicable barbarian—an approach that would seem to fit in neatly with the speech's identification of Helen with Hellas?

To begin with, in this particular speech Isocrates has no compelling need to malign Paris, since he does not make the Trojan War hinge on revenge. This points, however, toward deeper (though related) reasons for defending Paris, which have less to do with Panhellenism as such than with the use of Helen's story to support it. The rehabilitation of the barbarian Paris is required by Isocrates' larger project. In order to make her an emblem of Greek heroic excellence, and introduce Theseus as an antecedent for Athenian superiority, Isocrates relies heavily on his fundamental claim that Helen's value is shown by the quality of those she attracts. He could, theoretically, have confined this line of argument to Greeks, but that would weaken it considerably. Insofar as the point rests on the attraction of like to like, any admission that inferior men also desired Helen would automatically devalue her. It would also make the dubious argument from Theseus's exceptionalism appear even more glaringly as the special pleading that it is. If Isocrates was to maintain his basic approach consistently, he had to present all those who desired Helen, Greek and barbarian alike, as men of superior judgment.

Still more important, he works hard throughout the speech to render Helen's beauty "safe" by detaching it from the dangers of eroticism. If a single man—even Paris—is presented as motivated by strictly erotic desire for Helen, then we are obliged to confront the potentially negative effects of her beauty. And if she attracts not only heroic, virtuous men but weak, licentious barbarians, this opens the door to suspicion of the Greeks as well. To keep Helen pure of erotic contamination, as a glorious symbol of Hellenism instead of an emasculating threat, Isocrates needs to make *all* who desire her both admirable and prudent. Casting doubt on any man would cast doubt on them all, making Theseus's behavior even harder to paper over and opening the door to suspicion that the assault on Troy was, after all, prompted not by a worthy admiration for beauty in the service of great deeds, but by an unworthy subjection to erotic passion. Helen's extraordinary value as an emblem of Greek heroic manhood is grounded not just in the uniqueness of Theseus, or the number and quality of her other Greek admirers, but the uniqueness of Helen herself, who moves all and only exceptional men to seek to possess her, not out of erotic

weakness but out of a noble desire for her transcendent beauty and the blessed
life it bestows on those who possess it.

Having glorified Helen, more or less successfully, through the character and
exploits of Theseus, Paris, and the warriors of the Trojan War, Isocrates crowns
his argument with a celebration of beauty as such that adds several new in-
gredients to the brew. Though Helen remains his avowed subject he leaves
myth behind and turns, instead, to the power and value of beauty for his own
contemporaries.

He starts by explaining that the extremity both of men's reactions to Helen
(war!) and of his own discourse in her praise (over the top!) is justified by the
fact that "she had the greatest share of beauty, which is the most revered, precious, and divine thing that there is" (54). As such, beauty has extraordinary
power over human feelings and behavior. That power is not, however, in the
first instance erotic. Rather, beauty grounds any judgment of positive value. We
sometimes attach value to things deficient in moral virtue, Isocrates says, but
nothing is "esteemed" without beauty (54). The argument, once again, is circular. Beauty gives positive value to anything, and its own value is proved by the
fact that it is universally desired.

Isocrates goes on to declare "excellence" or "virtue" (*aretē*) the most beautiful activity there is (54), thereby dissociating supreme beauty from moral
transgression. Once this has been established, however, the word *erōs* reappears, for the second and final time. Beauty's superiority over all other things is
shown, he says, by the fact that "we" have an innate *erōs* for beautiful things or
people (the Greek is ambiguous); this is the most powerful kind of desire there
is, insofar as beauty, its object, is more powerful than anything else (55). The
erotic implications soon become inescapable: "As soon as we see beautiful
people, we feel goodwill toward them; them alone do we serve without fail as if
they were gods, enslaving ourselves to them with more pleasure than we rule
over others" (56–57). The beloved's godlike beauty and its divine power are
familiar erotic tropes. The slavery metaphor is particularly loaded, raising the
specter of a shameful subjection to mind-destroying *erōs*. Even here, however,
Isocrates' diction skirts the irrational power of such passion. "Goodwill" (*eunoia*)
is a rather mild term for the impact of erotically compelling sights. And although
Isocrates admits that "we" despise other forms of servitude, he claims that "we"
call beauty's slaves "beauty-loving" (*philokalos*) and "loving labors" (*philoponos*)
(57). These two adjectives, both of them nonerotic and strongly positive, evoke
the noble beauty of labors like those of the Trojan War, which, as we saw, inspire
a nonsexual *erōs* (52). Once again the potentially emasculating effect of physical
beauty is neutralized by making it an occasion for manly heroism.

Throughout this section (55–58), Isocrates extends the alleged connection
between beauty and praiseworthy action beyond legendary times into the

present by grounding the argument insistently in how "we" feel. The mythical reactions to Helen discussed earlier are shown, retrospectively, to exemplify a basic human emotional experience that "we" all share. Isocrates' initial claim that Helen's beauty is best judged by the opinions of those in her own time (22) is thus tacitly revised to embrace "us" as well, through "our" reactions to beauty as such, of which Helen is, by stipulation, the supreme example. Conversely, he implies that "we" too may be inspired by beauty to heroic, virtuous action like the exploits of the Trojan War. The power of beauty to influence male behavior is presented as both a transhistorical principle and an unalloyed good.

It is, of course, precisely the power of female beauty over men that makes it—and Helen—problematic. But Isocrates evades this issue by avoiding any reference at all to women. He begins his paean to beauty by speaking not of Helen, but of beauty as such, as an abstract entity (54). He then moves, as we saw, to *erōs* for beautiful things and/or people in the most general terms (55). When he does turn explicitly to beautiful people, the context reveals the people in question—as well as their admirers—to be male, since they are contrasted with others who are obviously men (since "we" resent them for their intelligence) (56). This admiration for masculine beauty resonates with the tropes of enslavement and the divinity of the beloved, both of which have strong homoerotic associations. "Our" *erōs* for beauty thus embraces a spectrum of enthusiastic reactions to various things and people, but remarkably—under the circumstances—makes no mention at all of female beauty.

This shift of focus, once sexual *erōs* is in play, from the power of Helen's beauty to the impact of male beauty on men, allows Isocrates to exploit a less problematic paradigm for the relationship between erotic beauty and heroism. In contrast to the ambivalence typically attending the exploits caused by female beauty, male desire for beautiful youths was often celebrated unequivocally as a stimulus to heroic deeds. According to Phaedrus in Plato's *Symposium*, the greatest of all armies would be composed exclusively of men and the male objects of their passion, who would spur each other on to noble deeds (178e–179b). Xenophon's Critobulus—the youth who was so proud of his looks (above, p. 2)—values his beauty in part because it "leads" men to "excellence," making them more "beauty-loving" and "loving labors" (the same two words employed by Isocrates); as a result, beauty like his benefits the whole human race (Xen. *Symp.* 4.15–16). This association of homoerotic beauty with noble action allowed Plato to build an entire metaphysics and ethics on *erōs* for beauty, redeeming the "enslavement" to beauty that is viewed, in other circumstances, as humiliating, by employing it in the service of wisdom and moral excellence (*Euthyd.* 282b, *Symp.* 184bc; cf. Xen. *Symp.* 4.14).

The most famous models of homoerotically inspired heroism at Athens were the tyrannicides Harmodius and Aristogeiton. As Thucydides tells it, Aristogeiton was the lover of the beautiful young Harmodius; a dispute with a rival, who happened to be the brother of the Athenian tyrant, induced the lovers to attack the royal family, a deed that led eventually to the monarchy's demise (6.54–59). The tyrannicides became semilegendary figures, celebrated in song and story. In the words of Plato's Pausanias, they are evidence that "heavenly" erōs between men generates lofty thoughts and powerful bonds of friendship and community; for this reason tyrants do not encourage it (Symp. 182c). In their case erotic passion for a beautiful object of desire generates not a destructive and morally doubtful war, for which that object is herself to blame, but a noble deed of male solidarity leading to political freedom. Removing men's desire for Helen from its heterosexual context, and reconfiguring it as a reaction to beauty as such, allows Isocrates to draw on such associations, thereby redeeming that desire for the cause of heroic Greek masculinity.

Only now does sex, at last, enter the picture. It is no surprise, at this point, to find it doing so in a way that disparages sexual behavior as a response to beauty. Because "we" have "reverence" and "regard" for the very idea of beauty, says Isocrates, we severely "dishonor" beautiful people who prostitute themselves; by contrast, "those who guard their youthful beauty as a shrine, keeping it untrampled by scoundrels, we honor for the rest of time like those who have done something good for the city as a whole" (58). He is referring here to the prohibition against sexual violation of the male body, which was considered so degrading that only a prostitute would submit to such treatment. The prostitutes in question are, by implication, Athenian citizens, since the implied penalty is loss of citizen rights (alluded to by the word "dishonor"), and slaves and foreigners (like women) had no such rights to lose. The strange assertion that those who refrain from prostituting themselves are honored like civic benefactors refers merely—one can only assume—to the retention of these rights or "honors." But self-control on the part of the lover and avoidance of sexual submission by his object of desire were essential to the idealized view of homoerotic relationships exemplified by Harmodius and Aristogeiton (cf. Aeschin. 1.132–33, 137–59). Isocrates' hyperbole therefore serves to link a desexualized respect for bodily beauty with this kind of heroic excellence.

The notion that reverence for beauty as such underpins Athenian opposition to male citizen prostitution is, of course, nonsense. But its very absurdity indicates that it serves some purpose for Isocrates. The primary effect is to draw a strict boundary between beauty and sex—between those who sully their beauty and those who "guard it as a shrine." Needless to say, Athenian law and custom also placed strict controls on the proper use of women's bodies, but under the right circumstances (i.e., marriage) even the most "revered" woman's body could—and indeed should—be used for sex. This makes it impossible to draw a bright line between beauty and sex where women are concerned. Any attempt to do so would, moreover, raise awkward questions about Helen's behavior, by defining the very line that she crossed when she so notoriously failed to "guard" her beauty from being "trampled by scoundrels." The beautiful, chaste male body, by contrast, is rendered by Isocrates a sacred object, whose very presence benefits the land in which it resides. It thus assumes, for the contemporary world, the function assigned by Isocrates to Helen's body in legendary times (51).

Now that he has brought the praise of beauty into his own world, and finally faced up to the indissoluble link between beauty and sex, Isocrates seems to have acquired a new attitude toward beauty and morality. Instead of excusing the men who pursued Helen's beautiful body and turning a blind eye to the way she acted in response, he has found a way to praise beauty that cleanses it from association both with her behavior and with her female body. This shift of focus, and newly moralizing tone, creates a disjunction between legendary times and Isocrates' own day. Despite his ingenious defense of Theseus and even Paris, and disregard for Helen's transgression, he cannot urge his audience to emulate their more reprehensible deeds. Nor can he eliminate those deeds, since he needs them for his larger argument. He therefore draws a tacit distinction between "our" world, where the value of physical beauty is shown by protecting it from immoral sexual "trampling," and the world of myth, where its value is demonstrated by a pervasive desire to trample the beauty of morality itself.

This distinction is maintained, in a buffoonish fashion, even when he returns once more to the world of myth. As further proof of the gods' esteem for beauty, Isocrates reminds us that Zeus, the most powerful of all, "thought fit to humble himself to approach it" in the persons of Alcmene, Danae, Nemesis, and Leda, among others (59). To be sure, these well-known amours contradict Isocrates' usual insistence on the virtue of the gods, but in this particular speech he has nothing to lose, since he has already linked Helen's beauty to her divine paternity and mentioned Zeus's many other mortal children (16, 52). He persists, however, in decoupling female beauty from the humiliation of powerful males. Erotic passion as such goes unmentioned, and it is beauty in the abstract, not embodied women, that supposedly draws the god's attention. Nor is that beauty presented as actively overpowering him. He freely debases himself to approach mortal women, manifesting not subjugation or helplessness but the high value he places on beauty in itself. Like the men who desire Helen, Zeus is not rendered helpless by *erōs*. The intrinsic value of beauty simply informs his choices.

At this point, female desire enters the story for the first time. As further evidence that the gods value beauty even more than "we" do, Isocrates claims that they forgive their "wives" when the latter are "overcome" by beauty (60). In contrast to the stern morality applied to those male, mortal scoundrels who trample on beauty by engaging in sex, married female divinities are apparently excused for sexual transgression—even by their husbands—because of the overwhelming power of (male) beauty. Female adultery, the most reprehensible of faults, is thus excused on the grounds that it is caused by the thing that always causes it. Isocrates makes light here of female desire and its consequences in a way that differs in kind, but not in essential import, from his trivialization of Helen's role in her elopement. But then he goes still further. Not only do the gods "forgive" such behavior, but the goddesses are proud of it! They do not try to keep their liaisons with mortal men secret, as something shameful, but want them sung about as "beautiful" deeds (60). The line between moral and aesthetic beauty is no longer merely blurred; physical beauty has the power, it seems, to make even female adultery morally *kalos* in the eyes of the gods.

As an assertion about traditional mythology, all this is preposterous. Unsurprisingly, Isocrates gives no examples at all (despite claiming that he could provide many). It is true that the best-known divine adulteress, Aphrodite, shows no sign of shame at her affair with Ares in the *Odyssey*, but she does not actively celebrate it; her husband is, moreover, extremely angry, and scarcely "forgives" her (8.266–367). In the *Homeric Hymn*, furthermore, she is acutely embarrassed by her liaison with the mortal Anchises and tries her best, pace Isocrates, to keep it a secret (5.247–90). Male gods, on the other hand, are not unknown to glory in their sexual exploits (though their spouses are not exactly forgiving when they do so). Isocrates thus erases the divine double standard, not, as philosophers typically do, by raising moral standards for divinities in general, but by giving goddesses the latitude of males and releasing all of them from any concern with sexual morality. This license presumably derives from their divine station, but Isocrates does not say so directly, distinguishing gods from mortals only by insisting that they value beauty even more highly (60).

The purpose of this bizarre reinvention can only be to justify divine female adultery in order to exculpate Helen through her future role as a goddess. Helen's erotic desire and agency are thus finally acknowledged, albeit extremely obliquely, and defended, if only through a specious assimilation of the mortal heroine to the goddess that she had yet to become. If one applies the argument about divinity retroactively to Helen's adultery with Paris, then that adultery becomes, in her own eyes, not only excusable but glorious and worthy of celebration in song. Helen is, in fact, the only mythic female who could plausibly be said to be exalted in song because of her adultery. As Homer's Helen knew well, however, that is scarcely the same thing as being celebrated *for* it. Nevertheless, as a goddess she will apparently come around to the divine view. This is implied in the encomium's final section, where the intimate relationship between beauty and the gods, which has threaded its way through the speech's various twists and turns, culminates in a celebration of Helen's own divinity.

Isocrates' last and "greatest" proof of the value the gods place on beauty is the number of humans who have been apotheosized for their beauty—more, he alleges, than for all other excellences (61). A number of mythic mortals (mostly male) were indeed immortalized for their beauty, as objects of divine desire. Helen, however, was not among them. Her beauty and her claim to immortality both derive, rather, from her divine paternity. Yet Isocrates suggests a causal relationship in her case, too, by declaring that the degree to which she surpassed other immortalized beauties was proportionate to the superiority of her beauty (61).

Helen's special status among such cult figures is shown by the alleged fact that she obtained not merely immortality but "power equal to the gods" (61). Isocrates is not referring here to the power of beauty, which plays no role in her divine activities as he recounts them, but to supernatural powers that seem to flow from her father's patriarchal authority. Unlike the goddess Helen in Herodotus, she does not focus on women's beauty or meddle destructively in the human world. Instead, she benefits mortals by making her brothers divine in their turn and assigning them special honors as the protectors of sailors (61). She also compensates Menelaus for the "labors and dangers that he endured because of her," by saving him from the disasters that dogged the rest of his family and making him, too, into a god (62). Uniquely among our sources, Isocrates gives their posthumous ménage an air of immortal domesticity: Menelaus is envisaged "dwelling with her and seated at her side for all time" (62). In contrast to her human self, Isocrates' divine Helen exercises powerful agency; like the most praiseworthy human heroines, however, she does so on behalf of her male relatives, both natal and marital.

Isocrates is also unique in giving Helen the stature of a major goddess comparable to the Olympians, and especially to the mightiest of them all, her father Zeus. Zeus is normally the one to deify the Dioscuri, but in this version it is Helen. Her dispensation of honors also evokes the authority enabling the king of the gods to reward his supporters with special privileges. Her relationship to Menelaus has likewise been adjusted. In the *Odyssey* he is to be immortal, presumably by the will of Zeus, because he "has" Helen, Zeus's daughter, as his wife (4.569). In Euripides' *Orestes*, the Olympian Apollo compensates him for his labors on her account (1662). But here Helen herself takes on both these roles, actively immortalizing her husband in compensation for his "labors." He is, moreover, to be "seated at her side," an expression sometimes used for lesser divinities who attend the most powerful gods (especially Zeus). This enhancement of Helen's stature is quite self-conscious. Isocrates declares that in their cult at Therapne she and Menelaus are worshipped not merely as cult heroes but as gods (63). He concludes that she should be celebrated and propitiated with sacrifices, petitions, and processions (66)—honors proper to a major goddess.

Despite the mention of Therapne, Isocrates' divine Helen is not tied narrowly to Sparta. His insistence that she is not a *mere* cult heroine (and as such a local divinity) may be a way of claiming her for larger Hellenic interests. In any case, her Panhellenic credentials are suggested by two further anecdotes adduced as evidence of her power. The first is the famous Stesichorus incident, which shows that she has the power to punish mortals as well as reward them

(66). When the poet "cast some kind of slur" upon Helen, says Isocrates, he became blind; but after he composed the Palinode she restored his sight (64). In Plato's version of this story (above, p. 117), Helen is not the subject of any verbs, and her power is merely implied; here she is actively in control. Plato goes on to quote the Palinode's denial that Helen went to Troy, but Isocrates has no interest in rejecting her canonical story. For him, this excellent anecdote is simply a way of demonstrating her supernatural power. He is therefore studiously vague about Stesichorus's transgression and says nothing at all about the contents of the Palinode. Instead he moves on quickly to a different story, one that demonstrates Helen's power in an entirely different way.

This next anecdote is attributed to the Homerids, a group dedicated to the performance of Homer's poems, on which they claimed to speak with special authority. Some of them, says Isocrates, assert that Helen appeared to Homer in a dream and "ordered" him to make poetry about the Trojan War; she did this because she wanted to glorify the Greek warriors' deaths at Troy by making them "more enviable than the lives of others" (65). Homer and his poetic skill were, naturally, essential to the finished product, but it is "mostly" because of Helen that the *Iliad* has "the charm of Aphrodite" and has become so famous (65). This story equates Helen with a Muse, even more overtly than the Palinode anecdote. Unlike the Muses of epic, however, she is herself a character in the story she inspires. This gives her a personal stake in Homer's narrative. Since epic poetry provides men with the conspicuous distinction and immortal glory that are rightly earned by fighting over Helen (cf. 17), it is in her interest to make sure the results are both "charming" and renowned.

This final anecdote is an implicit rejection of Stesichorus's Palinode, validating the canonical story of the *Iliad* by making Helen, in essence, dictate it. In so doing, it links Isocrates' celebration of the goddess Helen back to the glory of the Trojan War. The human Helen who brought men glory, in the earlier part of the speech, as a beautiful but passive object for which they fought and died, now uses her divine power to reward those deaths with the renown that is their due. The anecdote also gives Isocrates a new way of desexualizing Helen's beauty and its link to male heroic action, by transferring the "charm of Aphrodite" to the poetry that serves to immortalize them. Helen's role as cause of the war through her physical beauty is transposed into literary causation, in which she guarantees the war's commemoration by means of the charm that she bestows on epic. Both she and her beauty have become unproblematic producers of heroic glory.

This story conflicts not only with the Palinode anecdote but with Isocrates' own account of the Trojan War, since it endorses Homer's epic, which does not, for example, feature a rational, prudent Paris. By "correcting" certain aspects of tradition, however, Isocrates himself takes the divine Helen's project to its logical conclusion, transforming a notoriously ambiguous war into a source of unalloyed glory for the warriors and Helen alike. If Theseus, the suitors, and even Paris deserve praise for recognizing Helen's worth, then so does Isocrates himself. This was implied in the preface, where Isocrates spoke of Helen's excellence, unappreciated by others, and of his own intention to praise her properly. He concludes, similarly, by exhorting other thinkers to follow his example and honor Helen with more encomiums like this one (66). There is plenty more to be said, he adds encouragingly (if a bit disingenuously). One might, for instance, applaud the skills, ideas, and other benefits that are attributable to Helen and the Trojan War, including Greek freedom from "enslavement" to "barbarians," Hellenic unanimity and military alliance against "barbarians," and the military dominance of Europe over Asia (67).

Arriving at the end of this farrago of logical fallacies and mythological absurdities, we may well wonder how seriously to take it, despite Isocrates' initial protestations. Is there any coherence in this strange offering, or is it a mistake to seek such a thing? Is it merely an irresponsible romp through mythology, an intentionally incoherent joke? Many moments must surely be taken with a grain or more of salt. Isocrates was not, however, prone to frivolity, and has stern words in the preface for those who are. Moreover, Greek intellectual culture had always been hospitable to the use of playfulness in the service of serious ideas. Isocrates, I would argue, is very serious in this speech. He is just not serious about Helen.

He is extremely serious about establishing a mythic foundation for glorious Hellenic manhood, defined by the pursuit of a transcendent, divine embodiment of beauty. Helen is useful to him for this purpose—and usefulness is Isocrates' watchword. He is therefore willing to say anything at all to make her and her beauty seem admirable, and ignore anything that might undermine her emblematic value. He resurrects the epic Helen as a symbol of masculine glory, but uses all and any available devices to strip her and the war she caused of the ambivalence that traditionally shadows both of them. The guardedness of Homer's Trojan elders is to be transformed into unambiguous enthusiasm for the fight to possess such extraordinary beauty. In order to achieve this, the men who pursued Helen must be defended for their highly questionable behavior by any means possible. It is also essential to downplay the erotic threat to masculinity that such beauty typically poses. Helen's power *over* men must be transformed into a force that exalts them *as* men. Her beauty is therefore de-eroticized to become, instead, an emblem of moral "beauty."

In order to serve as a suitably glorious emblem of Greece, Helen herself must also be unsullied by blame, or the men will look like fools or worse for valuing her so highly. Isocrates achieves this not by excusing Helen's action, but by treating the moral threat posed by female desire as inconsequential. He does not pay Helen the respect of either blaming or defending her for the transgression that traditionally defines her. Rather, he treats her intentionality and guilt, and with them her erotic subjectivity, as irrelevant. Such matters are addressed only very obliquely—not to mention flippantly—through the alleged erotic misbehavior of the gods' "wives." The mortal Helen, however, who was actually guilty of such misbehavior, is neither excused (even by objectification) nor held accountable. Her agency and desire—along with female desire generally—are not denied, decried, or defended, but trivialized. Isocrates takes male behavior (among mortals) far more seriously, applying the norms of moral judgment both to legendary heroes and to men of his own time.

Ignoring the significance of Helen's action and exalting the men who abducted her both require Isocrates to depart, in this speech, from his usual practice of presenting gods and heroes as models for contemporary behavior. He therefore has to construct a firewall between legendary times and the present day. That firewall is a flimsy one, as we have seen. Where female behavior is concerned, it consists simply of refusing to take female eroticism seriously in the world of myth. The mortal Helen's desire is not a threat because she is not treated as a "real" woman: not a real subject or object of erotic desire but the symbolic object of a different kind of male aspiration. As a goddess, her power transcends the legendary past and persists into "our" world, in which she intervenes to control her own story and with it the production of heroic glory. This goddess is, on the one hand, remarkably loyal to patriarchal family values, and on the other retroactively exempt from judgment for her adultery, since such judgment is supposedly alien to the divine world.

Where men are concerned, the firewall is constructed primarily from the alleged uniqueness of legendary characters and their circumstances, whether Theseus's uniquely perfect virtue or Paris's unique opportunity to ally himself with Zeus. Since none of Isocrates' readers is presumably perfect, or will ever get the chance to abduct Helen or become the son-in-law of Zeus, the question of imitating such behavior is moot. The gulf between them and "us" is reinforced by reminding the latter both of the strong contemporary moral norms surrounding beauty and sex and of the license enjoyed by the gods of traditional myth, which distinguishes them even from the heroic mortals of the past. This leaves us free to use those heroic mortals as models for any behavior that is not excused by their uniqueness. As long as they abstain from abducting any women, Isocrates' audience of male Athenians can safely model themselves on their hero Theseus, and use him as a figurehead for the values that Helen represents: Greek unity, freedom, and prosperity, martial glory, and poetic renown.

The seed of Isocrates' Helen—like most other Helens—may be found in Homer, where she is both "real" and symbolic, a complex and compelling human figure who yet stands for the combined glory and horror of heroic warfare. Many subsequent versions of her character deprive her of symbolic significance, treating her as a beautiful but worthless "Spartan woman" who is doubly devalued as a mere woman and an adulteress. In face of such hostile treatments, Isocrates remystifies her. He does so, however, by stripping away her humanity and refusing to take her seriously as a moral agent. She regains her epic status as a symbol of heroic glory at the cost of trivialization, albeit in the guise of praise.

Epilogue

First you're another
Sloe-eyed vamp,
Then someone's mother,
Then you're camp.
Then you career from career
To career.
I'm almost through my memoirs.
And I'm here.
                    —Stephen Sondheim

When Isocrates ended his *Helen* by declaring that there was more to be said, little did he know how truly he spoke. Since emerging from the egg Helen has been praised, blamed, championed, and condemned in thousands of wildly disparate works of literature, art, and music, in every genre and from every conceivable point of view.

Even the ancient world knew more Helens than could be encompassed in this book. She appeared in Athenian comedy as a courtesan, in a caricature of Pericles' mistress Aspasia. Philosophers had a tendency to allegorize her. She is especially associated with the moon, because her name resembles the Greek word for it (*selēnē*). According to an obscure Pythagorean source, she came to earth from the moon, which was home to a colony of superhumans larger, more beautiful, and fifteen times stronger than ordinary mortals. Dio Chrysostom, a Greek writing under the Roman Empire, may be the only author to solve the problem of Helen's culpability by making Paris her first, legitimate husband. (The Greek men started the Trojan War out of resentment.) Virgil appropriated Menelaus's failure to kill Helen for his Roman hero Aeneas, transforming it into an act of virtuous self-restraint; meanwhile Helen herself reached a new low, betraying her current husband Deiphobus to Menelaus as a peace offering. Lucian, a century later, made comic hay out of the idea of an old, dead Helen withering away in Hades.

Helen thrived in late antiquity and on into the Middle Ages, a period of enormous popularity for the Troy legend. It is hardly surprising to find her equated, under Christianity, with Eve; much more so to find her encroaching on the role of the Virgin Mary. In the Renaissance Pierre de Ronsard composed no fewer than 142 sonnets to a woman named Hélène de Surgères, in which the "true" and virtuous French Helen, unlike the "lie" of the Greeks, becomes a path to redemption. Helen symbolized the antithesis to Christian faith, however, for Ronsard's younger contemporary, Christopher Marlowe, who gave us, in his *Doctor Faustus*, "the face that launched a thousand ships." This line—the most famous ever written about Helen—has long floated free of its original context, infiltrating popular culture and giving rise among contemporary philosophers to a unit for the measurement of beauty known as the millihelen (the amount of beauty sufficient to launch one ship).

Like Ronsard, Oscar Wilde gave a Christian inflection to Helen's ambiguity. His poem "The New Helen," published in 1881, celebrated his friend Lillie Langtry, known as "the most beautiful woman in the world," as Helen's reincarnation. This Helen is the antithesis of the Virgin Mary ("Her, before whose mouldering shrine / To-day at Rome the silent nations kneel"), but is endowed, at the same time, with aspects of Christ himself ("at thy coming some immortal star/Bearded with flame, blazed in the Eastern skies, / And waked the shepherds on thine island-home"). Helen was highly popular in this period among painters as well as poets, including Evelyn de Morgan, whose 1898 painting is reproduced on the cover of this book. It shows a more sexually assertive Helen than most, and is unusual in that it is the work of a woman. Among the many male painters who have taken up the challenge of portraying Helen's ineffable beauty special mention must be made of Salvador Dalí, who was fascinated with Helen from childhood onward and identified Gala, his wife and muse (whose birth name was Helena) with Helen of Troy, along with the surrealist muse Gradiva. His autobiographical *Diary of a Genius* is dedicated to "my genius Gala Gradiva, Helen of Troy, Saint Helen, Gala Galatea Placida."

Helen entered the silver screen early and has remained there ever since. Alexander Korda's farcical film, *The Private Life of Helen of Troy* (1927), turned the sensible, bourgeois heroine of John Erskine's best-selling novel into a shopaholic fashion maven. In one of the great missed cinematic opportunities of all time, Robert Wise—director of *The Sound of Music*—cast the young Brigitte Bardot as Helen's maidservant in his epic *Helen of Troy* (1956). The sixties saw Elizabeth Taylor, another "most beautiful woman in the world," fresh from reliving Helen's scandalous life, starring with her husband Richard Burton in a famously dreadful movie of Marlowe's *Doctor Faustus* (1968). On the small screen, that same year, *Star Trek* aired an episode entitled "Elaan of Troyius" in which, as the Internet Movie Database puts it, "Capt. Kirk must cope with her biochemical ability to force him to love her." Thirty years later, in a predictable yet original spin on the old tale, Xena the Warrior Princess liberated Helen for feminism. The *Xena* episode "Beware Greeks Bearing Gifts" challenged the romantic boilerplate typically applied to Helen in popular culture, by allowing Paris and Helen to fall out of love before sending her forth without a mate to find herself.

Nor has the stream abated in the twenty-first century. The turn of the millennium saw the debut of Eric Shanower's *Age of Bronze*, a massive graphic novel of the Trojan War that is still unfinished. The year 2004 produced both a major Hollywood movie (*Troy*) and a TV miniseries (*Helen of Troy*). There followed in quick succession a popular uncovering of the "real" Helen in 2005, with accompanying documentary, by Bettany Hughes (dubbed "Helen of Troy in jeans" by the British press), plus four novels by four women presenting four very different Helens: Margaret Atwood's *Penelopiad* (2005), Amanda Elyot's *The Memoirs of Helen of Troy* (2005), Margaret George's *Helen of Troy* (2007), and Tess Collins's *Helen of Troy: A Novel* (2012). Atwood's Helen, the cousin of her rather peevish heroine Penelope, is not only vain and manipulative but malicious and cruel; for Elyot (whose book is dedicated to her mother, Leda), Helen inherits from Zeus "the unabashed cravings for the blazing consummation that only two bodies can know," and, frustrated by the sexually inept Menelaus, cannot help "obeying her nature"; George's Helen really was begotten by Zeus in the form of a giant swan and is consequently endowed with second sight, which gives her, among other things, premonitions of Marlowe's *Faustus*. The most recent addition to the pack, Collins's *Helen of Troy*, is marketed as "a quirky and lively retelling of the classic Greek legend in small-town America."

This is only a tiny, biased, and necessarily arbitrary sample of the many later Helens that have crossed my path since I began working on this book. They suffice, however, to convey her persistence as a powerful yet elusive force, a MacGuffin whose absence offers an ever-refreshing screen for the projection of ideas and ideals about beauty, women, sex, and power. Demonized, idolized, allegorized, or humanized, Helen is still here.

Bibliographical Notes

The suggestions that follow are of four kinds. Useful or interesting or provocative discussions of the issues in question (many offering views different from those expressed in this book); fundamental works of scholarship; studies to which I am particularly indebted; recommended translations and commentaries (including information on some of the texts I have employed). The result is ruthlessly selective and to some degree arbitrary, and I apologize to the many scholars whose work would have been mentioned here had space permitted. Where appropriate, I have used the texts of the Loeb Classical Library, since they are widely available and accompanied by literal translations. The translations in this book are, however, my own unless otherwise indicated. Where the meaning of the text is problematic I have simply presented my preferred interpretation without discussion of alternatives. For scholarly articles I refer where possible to reprinted collections (even though this may give a misleading chronological impression), since these are usually more accessible than the original journals. I have limited what follows to English, except for a few items of special interest or importance.

CHAPTER I : FEMALE BEAUTY

For general background I suggest Skinner 2005 and Ormand 2009 on ancient sexuality; Just 1989 and Reeder 1995 on Greek women; Cartledge 2002 on Greek cultural identity; Dover 1974 on popular thought; Burkert 1985 on religion.

On *erōs*, female sexuality, and its relationship to women's biology, see Carson 1986, 1990; Hanson 1990; Dean-Jones 1992, 1994: chap. 1; Faraone 1999. On women and sexuality in art, see Kampen 1996; Ferrari 2002. Connections between the erotic, the verbal, and the magical are surveyed in Parry 1992. On the equivalence of *erōs* and death (esp. in battle), see Vermeule 1979: chap. 5; Vernant 1991: chap. 5. On feminine decorations as equivalent to male arms, see Vernant 1991: chap. 1. Cyrino 2010 provides an accessible general treatment of Aphrodite; on her association with gold, and its dangers, see A. S. Brown 1997; on her *kestos himas*, see Faraone 1999:97–102. Levaniouk 2011: chap. 5 elucidates the word *oaristus*.

Kirwan 1999 provides a concise history of conceptions of beauty. Beauty and beauty contests in Greece are discussed by Crowther 1985; Hawley 1998; Calame 1997. On the dazzling beauty of the gods, see Vernant 1991: chap. 1. For Greek artistic and philosophical theories of beauty, see Pollitt 1974, 1990. On the distaste for idiosyncrasy, see Blondell 2002:58–62. On the phrase *kalos kagathos*, see Donlan 1973 and Dover 1974:41–45; on *kakos*, Sluiter and Rosen 2008; on *aischros*, Cairns 1993:54–60.

The classic treatments of moral responsibility despite divine influence are Dodds 1951: chap. 1 and Lesky 2001 (first published in German in 1961). See also Dover 1974:133–60; Williams 1993: chap. 6; Holmes 2010: chap. 1. For the conception of objects with agency, see in general Kopytoff 1986. Women's position between object and agent and their likeness to dogs are both well treated by Franco 2003.

On Greek marriage, see Vernant 1990: chap. 3. Oakley and Sinos 1993 is a nicely illustrated description of the wedding. Consent, rape, and abduction are examined by Cole 1984; D. Cohen 1993; A. Cohen 1996; Deacy and Pierce 2002; Sommerstein 2006. For Persephone as a paradigmatic bride, see Foley 1994. On women's subjectivity and desire in marriage, see Ormand 1999: chap. 1; Kaimio 2002. On women as *agalmata*, see Scodel 1996; Lyons 1997:162–68.

Important discussions of Pandora include Vernant 1990: chap. 8; Loraux 1993: chap. 2; Saintillan 1996; Zeitlin 1996: chap. 2; H. King 1998:203–7. For the symbolism of wool working, see Jenkins 1985; Sebesta 2002; Ferrari 2002: chap. 6. Detienne and Vernant 1978 provides a thorough treatment of *mētis* (crafty intelligence). On the relationship of statues to living beings, see Spivey 1995; Steiner 2001; and cf. Stieber 2011: chap. 2. On the *Alcestis* passage, see Stieber 2011:163–68. For trust as constitutive of humanity, see Meyers 2005 (to whom I owe the Stepford wife example).

For physical controls on Greek women, see Llewellyn-Jones 2003; for social controls, D. Cohen 1991; for speech and silence, McClure 1999; Heath 2005. On praise and blame in Greek culture, see Vodoklys 1992; Nagy 1999: part 3; Gentili 1988:107–14. For self-control (*sōphrosunē*) as the virtue of women, see North 1977. Semonides' misogynistic poem is discussed by Lloyd-Jones 1975; Loraux 1993: chap. 2; Osborne 2001.

CHAPTER 2 : HELEN, DAUGHTER OF ZEUS

Gantz 1993 is an indispensable resource for all aspects of classical Greek myth, with its many sources and variants. My citations of the *Cypria* refer to vol. 5 of Allen's *Oxford Classical Text*. Davies 1989 gives a basic introduction to this and other early non-Homeric epic; see also Scaife 1995; M. J. Anderson 1997. On *Cypria* fr. 1, see Mayer 1996. Hesiod's poems, including the *Catalogue of Women*, are cited from the *Oxford Classical Text* of Hesiod, edited by Merkelbach and West, but are also conveniently consulted in Most's Loeb edition. My remarks on the *Catalogue* are indebted to conversation with Kirk Ormand; see further R. Hunter 2005, Doherty 2006, Ormand forthcoming. On Theocritus 18, see R. Hunter 1996: chap. 5; Sistakou 2008.

Among general works on the Greek Helen, Loraux 1995: chap. 11; Cassin 2000; and Meagher 2002 approach her as a symbol of the feminine; Lindsay 1974 combines a detailed survey of ancient sources with a focus on religion; Austin 1994 focuses on the *eidōlon*; Hughes 2005 offers a quixotic search for the historical reality of Helen's life; Calame 2009 addresses the problem of identifying a "myth of Helen" amid the diverse treatments she receives; Fulkerson 2011 is a recent examination of Helen's agency; Blondell, forthcoming, discusses the divine defense for her actions in the context of performance. Pallantza 2005 provides a weighty German treatment of the Trojan War tradition, including most of the works discussed in this book. For a comprehensive survey of Helen in art, see Kahil 1988. On images of Helen's birth and abduction by Theseus, see A. Shapiro 1992; A. Cohen 2007. On images of the elopement and Recovery, see Ghali-Kahil 1955; Clement 1958; Hedreen 1996.

On Spartan women, including their beauty and unusual wedding practices, see Millender 1999, 2012; Pomeroy 2002. For the importance of guest-friendship, see Herman 1987. On revenge in Greek culture, see esp. Lendon 2000. Women's symbolic relationship to household possessions is well discussed by Lyons 2003, and beautiful Trojan men by Clay 1989:185–91. On the attraction of like to like, see Blondell 2002:265. Sommerstein 2010:139 explains Agamemnon's various homes.

For an accessible introduction to the origins and nature of hero cult, with special attention to Helen, see Albersmeier 2009; see also Antonaccio 1995; Parker 2011: chap. 4. On heroines, see J. Larson 1995; Lyons 1997; Kearns 1998. On the evidence for Helen's cult, see esp. Edmunds 2007; he challenges the prehistoric goddess theory argued for by Clader 1976, West 1975. On her cult at Sparta see also Calame 1997:191–202, and for her appropriation by Athens, H. Shapiro 2009. Sutton 1997/1998 discusses Helen as paradigm of the bride in art, and Austin 1994:25 n. 2 mentions shrines honoring her sandals. For the links between Helen and Achilles, see Schmidt 1996; and for the latter's beauty, K. King 1987:3–4.

For Helen's equivalence to Aphrodite, see Meagher 2002: chap. 2, and for their iconographic similarity, Bron 1996. Ancient explanations of Helen's low fertility are cited by Kakridis 1971:50. Vernant 1991: chap. 2 explores the idea of the beautiful dead. For resistance to pleasure as definitive of masculinity, see, most influentially, Foucault 1985 (esp. 63–77). Maguire 2009: chap. 2 has an interesting discussion of the indescribability of Helen's beauty. On Zeuxis's Helen, see Sutton 2009. For her old age and death in later authors, see Maguire 2009:9, 17–18, 69–73.

CHAPTER 3 : THE *ILIAD*

Fowler 2004 is an invaluable resource for both Homeric epics. Schein 1984 is an excellent introduction to the *Iliad*, and Cairns 2001 assembles many influential articles.

Detailed documentation for much of this chapter may be found in Blondell 2010a. Of greatest interest are the general discussions by Clader 1976; Reckford 1964; Suzuki 1989: chap. 1; Austin 1994: chap. 1; Graver 1995 and Ebbott 1999 on Helen's self-blame; Jamison 1994 on the duel as a courtship scene; Bergren 2008: chap. 2 (cited in my article as Bergren 1979) and Kennedy 1986 on Helen's weaving; Worman 2001 on Helen's voice; Collins 1988 on ethical characterization; Arthur 1981 on the male and female worlds within Troy. A list of Helen's epic epithets may be found in Clader 1976: chap. 3.

Useful items not referred to in my article include Scodel 2008 on face and face-saving; Houston 1992 and Hieronymi 2007 on the conceptual relationships between blame, responsibility, and agency.

CHAPTER 4 : THE *ODYSSEY*

As with the *Iliad*, Fowler 2004 is invaluable. Schein 1996 is a useful collection of essays covering many aspects of the *Odyssey*. The following items from the previous note discuss Helen in both epics: Clader 1976, Suzuki 1989, Austin 1994, Worman 2001.

There are numerous studies of gender in the *Odyssey*, many of them focusing on Penelope's agency and her knowledge at the denouement of the epic. See esp. Murnaghan 1986, 1987; Katz 1991; Wohl 1993; Felson-Rubin 1994; B. Cohen 1995; Doherty 1995; Holmberg 1995a; E. Gregory 1996; Foley 2001: section 3, chap. 1; Clayton 2004; Buchan 2004; Levaniouk 2011. Many of these also discuss Helen's drug, the paired stories in book 4, and/or Penelope's reference to Helen (on which see also Kathleen Morgan 1991). What follows is additional.

On Helen's outspokenness, see Heath 2005:69–77. On female hospitality, including bathing and gifts, see Pedrick 1988; Helen's gift to Telemachus is well discussed by Mueller 2010; cf. also Lyons 2003 and, for the sinister connotations of starlight, Prier 1989:46–54. On "dread goddesses" and Odysseus's often sexually threatening female opponents and helpers, see Taylor 1963; Rose 1992:122–34; Nagler 1996.

Perceptive treatments of Helen's drug include Goldhill 1988:19–24; Bergren 2008: chap. 5. For the alleged travels of Greek sages and intellectuals to Egypt, see Lloyd 1975:49–60. On the paired speeches in book 4, see Dupont-Roc and Le Boulluec 1976, Andersen 1977, Olson 1989, Boyd 1998. For Helen's similarity to Odysseus, see Worman 2002 passim. On the song of Demodocus, see Newton 1987; Zeitlin 1996:32–42; Halliwell 2008:77–85.

For the household at Sparta as a negative paradigm, see W. S. Anderson 1958; Schmiel 1972. On the compatibility of Penelope and Odysseus, see Foley 1984; J. Winkler 1990: chap. 5; and on the test of the bed, Zeitlin 1996: chap. 1. For the importance of remembering, self-restraint, and caution, see Cook 1995:57–65. *Kleos* in the *Odyssey* is discussed by Katz 1991:20–29, 63–72; Segal 1996; Nagy 1999:36–41. For the overlaps among Clytemnestra, Helen, and Penelope, see Collins 1988:59–67; Katz 1991 passim.

CHAPTER 5 : ARCHAIC LYRIC

Detailed bibliography for my treatments of Alcaeus, Ibycus, and Sappho may be found in Blondell 2010b. On Semonides, see my notes for chap. 1.

I have followed the texts and numeration in Campbell's Loeb editions of the lyric poets, with the exception of Ibycus S151, for which I use Hutchinson's 2001 text and recommend his commentary. (This number refers to the supplement to Page's standard edition, but the poem may also be found in Campbell, as Ibycus 282.) Useful commentary on the Lesbians may also be found in Page 1955 (though his attitude toward Sappho is famously boneheaded). Translations are my own, but in some cases adapted from Campbell. Most 1982 and MacLachlan 1997 are helpful general introductions to lyric, and Stehle 1997 a thorough, valuable treatment from the perspective of gender. Boedeker 2011 looks at the ways in which various lyric poets use Helen to mediate their relationship to the past. Mythic background on such figures as Thetis and Troilus may be found in Gantz 1993.

On Alcaeus's life, poetry, dedication to brotherhood, and relationship to the heroic past, see Burnett 1983: part 2. Rösler 1980 gives a thorough treatment in German. On fr. 42, see also Davies 1986.

On Ibycus and the Polycrates fragment, see Barron 1969, Robertson 1970, Woodbury 1985. Readers should be warned that most scholarship on this poem is highly technical. The Ibycus fragment on the death of Troilus (S224) appears in Campbell on p. 241 as part of his 282B.

The bibliography on Sappho's poetry is enormous, and many aspects are highly controversial (notably issues surrounding sexuality and performance context). For a range of views, including some valuable articles on fr. 16, see Greene 1996. On fr. 16, see also Wills 1967; Koniaris 1967; Most 1981; Burnett 1983:277–90; Austin 1994: chap. 2; Segal 1998: chap. 4; Fredricksmeyer 2001; Bierl 2003. On its reception of Homer, in particular, see Rissman 1983; J. Winkler 1990: chap. 6; and Rosenmeyer 1997 (which goes well beyond Sappho in application).

For Stesichorus's life and works, see West 1971. Many questions about the Palinode are contested, including even the number of poems (was it one or two?). For detailed discussion, see Woodbury 1967; Bassi 1993; Austin 1994: chap. 4; Beecroft 2010: chap. 4. On Helen's doubleness, see esp. Bergren 2008: chap. 1; and on the doubling or splitting of women in myth more generally, Doniger 1999. For the creation of cloud-doubles to save goddesses from rape, see Kannicht 1969: 1.35–38, from whom I take the phrase "physiologically functional."

CHAPTER 6 : AESCHYLUS

Easterling 1997 is a superb general resource for the study of tragedy. See also Goldhill 1990 on the Athenian political context; Zeitlin 1994 and Goldhill 2000 on visuality; Halliwell 1993, Marshall 1999, Wyles 2010, Meineck 2011 on masks and acting style; Henderson 1991 on the composition of the audience; Mossman 2005 on women's voices and subjectivity. Sommerstein 2010 is an indispensable introduction both to Aeschylus generally and to many of the issues in this chapter.

The text of the *Oresteia* is monstrously problematic, and those familiar with it will see that I have ignored many alternative readings and interpretations; I beg their indulgence. My references are to Sommerstein's Loeb edition, but translations are my own. Also recommended is the translation with introduction and commentary in Lloyd-Jones 1979 (reprinted several times by the University of California Press). The Fraenkel quotation is from Fraenkel 1950: 2.346.

Because of space limitations Clytemnestra receives rather short shrift in this chapter, considering the importance of her role. She has, however, been discussed extensively in the scholarly literature, esp. as the focus of much that has been written about gender in the *Oresteia* (very little of which is about Helen). Two feminist classics, very different but both worth reading, are Winnington-Ingram 1983 (first published, well before its time, in 1949) and Zeitlin 1996: chap. 3 (first published in 1978). Among more recent work, the following are of particular interest: Neuberg 1991; McClure 1999: chap. 3; Fletcher 1999; Foley 2001: section 3, chap. 4; Lee 2004; Lyons 2003. Wohl 1998: part 2 includes an interesting analysis of Helen's significance. See also, on imagery, Lebeck 1971; Knox 1979: chap. 2 (which focuses on the lion cub); Ferrari 1997; on name play and magic, Peradotto 1969; on the Furies, A. L. Brown 1983, Frontisi-Ducroux 2007, Prag 1985 (for the visual evidence). On the resemblance of their red garments to the tunics worn by resident aliens, see Thomson 1966:231–33.

CHAPTER 7 : HERODOTUS

For an accessible introduction to all aspects of Herodotus, including his sources, methods, and relationship to epic, see Dewald and Marincola 2006. For deeper scholarly analysis, see Bakker et al. 2002. See also Thomas 2000: chap. 1 on Herodotus's rationalism and intellectual contexts; Nagy 1990: chap. 8 on his relationship to epic; Dewald 1981 and Gray 1995 on women, esp. "barbarian queens." For a survey of Herodotus's references to the Trojan War, see Neville 1977; for his treatment of legendary heroes generally, Vandiver 1991. On the overarching values of the *Histories*, including limit and transgression, revenge, reciprocity, and divine retribution, see Lateiner 1989: chap. 6; Gould 1989; Braund 1998; Harrison 2000: chap. 4; Fisher 2002; and cf. Lendon 2000.

On the abductions in the preface, see Harrison 2002. For the preface's pedestrian, commercial tone, see Flory 1987:24–29, and cf. Konstan 1987. The tale of Candaules' wife is discussed by Long 1987: chap. 1; Flory 1987:29–38; Hazewindus 2004: chap. 2; S. Larson 2006.

For the Greeks' "schizophrenic" view of non-Greeks, see E. Hall 1989:143–54. A. Lloyd 1975–1988 provides a wealth of learned information on Herodotus and Egypt, including archaeological details. For the historian's complex attitude toward Egyptians, see Vasunia 2001: chaps. 2–3; Haziza 2009 (esp. chap. 5 on women). On the Helen narrative, see esp. V. Hunter 1980: chap. 2; Austin 1994: chap. 5.

For the cult of Helen at Therapne, see my notes on chap. 2. The story of Demaratus's mother is treated by Vandiver 1991:102–7; Austin 1994:32–36; Burkert 2001: chap. 5. On Spartan kings, barbarism, and gender reversal in Herodotus, see Munson 1993; Millender 2009. On Protesilaus and Artayktes, see Boedeker 1988; Nagy 1990: chap. 9 (which also points out the Athenian potential for tyranny). Gould 2001:145–47 discusses the story of the raped Athenian women.

CHAPTER 8 : GORGIAS

Guthrie 1971 is an accessible introduction to the sophists. Fuller examination of their ideas and significance for Athens may be found in de Romilly 1992; Kerferd 1981. On their use of myth, see also Kathryn Morgan 2000: chap. 4. Ober 1989: part 4 discusses the Athenians' combined love of debate and fear of sophistic oratory. For the active scrutiny expected of Athenian audiences, see Goldhill 2000. On women in court, see Just 1989:33–39.

For the text of Gorgias's *Helen* I follow MacDowell 1982, which includes a useful translation, short introduction, and commentary. Other ancient sources for the sophists are cited from the standard edition by Diels and Kranz (DK), but may be more conveniently consulted in Graham 2010. Consigny 2001 surveys many aspects of Gorgias, including his persona as an epideictic performer. Kathryn Morgan 1994 gives the evidence for his golden statue. For his rivalry with poetry and interest in tragedy, see Duncan 1938.

On the genre of encomium, see Nightingale 1995:93–106. Pease 1926 supplies an entertaining survey of "paradoxical" encomia. On the nonpersuasiveness of *Helen*, see Porter 1993 and esp. Gagarin 2001, who emphasizes the professional and intellectual value of such "amusements." Cf. also Schiappa 1995 on Gorgias's rationalism and

Helen's intellectual contributions. Helen is treated as a figure for discourse, esp. rhetoric, by J. Poulakos 1983; Biesecker 1992; Zeitlin 1996:409–11; Gumpert 2001: chap. 5; Worman 2002; Bergren 2008: chap. 1.

For widely varied interpretations of Gorgianic *logos*, plus related issues concerning knowledge, truth, and "deception," see Segal 1962; Kerferd 1981: chap. 8; Verdenius 1981; Walsh 1984: chap. 5; Kathryn Morgan 2000:122–28; Consigny 2001: part 1. On determinism, voluntariness, and moral responsibility in *Helen*, see Calogero 1957; Donzelli 1985; Adkins 1983; Saunders 1986; Hankinson 1998:74–76; Holmes 2010:211–16. See also Ford 2002: chap. 7, on Gorgias's relationship to materialist thought. For the fundamental cultural distinction between persuasion and force, see Buxton 1982:58–62.

Horky 2006 argues that Gorgias influenced Platonic and Aristotelian ideas about the soul (though he is not concerned with gender). The *Republic's* view of the female *psuchē* has been much discussed; see esp. Pomeroy 1978, Smith 1983, Levin 1996. On the "feminist" implications of Medea's speech, cf. Blondell 1999:156–58. I hope soon to publish a more detailed version of this chapter's argument about gender, with full bibliography.

CHAPTER 9 : EURIPIDES' *TROJAN WOMEN*

On tragedy in general, see my notes for chap. 6. Conacher 1967 is an accessible general introduction to Euripides. Michelini 1987 provides a deeper analysis of many important aspects of his dramas, including the prominence of female sexuality and the deflating of epic heroism. Scodel 1999/2000 is a fine treatment of the characters' rhetorical performativity. Conacher 1998 supplies a short overview of sophistic themes.

I follow the text of Kovacs's Loeb edition of *Tro.* except in line 1114 (where with other editors I retain *helōn*). Goff 2009 provides a brief introduction to the play; Croally 1994 goes into more depth; Marshall 2011 examines its relationship to Homer. For a reconstruction of the whole trilogy, see Scodel 1980.

Marshall, forthcoming, discusses the dramatic representation of beauty, and argues that *Tro.* was probably Helen's first appearance as a substantial character, and perhaps her first appearance on the tragic stage (though she had already appeared in comedy). Thévenet 2009 analyzes the effect of translating a mythic character to the stage. On the pervasiveness of the cityscape of Troy in *Tro.*, see Stieber 2011: chap. 1; and for the imaginary staging of Athens as Troy, Hourmouziades 1965:109–10, 122–23. Dué 2006: chap. 3 discusses Athenian sympathy for the Trojans. Michelini 1987:161 notes the rarity of *kalos* for a woman's face or body in tragedy. For Hecuba as an iconic image of suffering, cf. Michelini 1987: chap. 6 (on her eponymous play).

On the debate in *Tro.* and the relationship of Helen's speech to Gorgias, see Donzelli 1985; M. Lloyd 1992:99–112. Worman 2002:124–35 emphasizes the importance of Helen's body; for the polishing metaphor in 1022–23, see Stieber 2011: 338–39. Goldhill 1990 discusses the announcement of crowns and parade of war orphans in the theater. On Socrates' physical ugliness and inner beauty, see Blondell 2002:70–74. For speech, esp. lamentation, as a mode of power for women in this play, see J. Gregory 1991: chap. 5; McClure 1999:40–47; Foley 2001: part 1; Dué 2006. Two outstanding analyses of women's agency in *Tro.* are Calabrese's as yet unpublished paper and Scodel 1998, which shows how all the women, not just Helen, use sex to make the best of a bad situation.

CHAPTER 10 : EURIPIDES' *HELEN*

On tragedy in general, see my notes to chap. 6; on Euripides generally, see the notes to chap. 9. For *Helen* I again use the text of Kovacs's Loeb, but readers should be warned that he brackets a number of lines that I (and other editors) accept.

Wright 2005 addresses many aspects of the play, as do Wolff 1973; Burnett 1971: chap. 4. Foley 2001: part 4 analyzes the play from the perspective of cult; her discussion of the ending is particularly valuable. On the importance of cult and ritual, see also Zweig 1999, which includes a useful survey of previous interpretations.

Helen is often considered a pioneer of "romance," both as a story of reunited lovers (see Trenkner 1958: chap. 4) and as a dream-like fantasy (see Segal 1986: chap. 4). For Egypt as a land of romantic fantasy, see also Nimis 2004. For the challenge Euripides presents to the Greek-barbarian polarity, see Saïd 2001; Wright 2005: chap. 3.3. The importance of Proteus is emphasized by Marshall 1995. Theonoe is discussed by Zuntz 1960; Sansone 1985. On the play's relation to the *Odyssey*, see Eisner 1980 and cf. Holmberg 1995b (on Helen as Penelope); Karsaï 2003 (on her retreat to the tomb and its evocation of Nausicaa).

For Helen's equivalence to Persephone and other mythic rape victims, see Robinson 1979; Juffras 1993. Voelke 1996 analyzes the significance of her beauty. On the statue passage, see esp. Stieber 2011:172–78. For the symbolism of hair and haircutting generally, see Levine 1995; and for haircutting at Spartan weddings, see the works on Spartan women cited in my notes to chap. 2. The chorus's rebuke of Helen in the Demeter Ode is discussed by Wolff 1973:70–74; Austin 1994:177–83; Voelke 1996:289–95.

On the mocking of Menelaus, see Papi 1987. Helen's equivalence to her double, and related questions about appearance and reality, fictionality and metatheater are examined by Solmsen 1934; Downing 1990; Austin 1994: chap. 6; Wright 2005: chap. 4.4; Meltzer 2006: chap. 5; Davis 2009; Stieber 2011: 169–72. For Cloud as a goddess, see Kannicht 1969: 1.36–37; and for doubles on stage, Bardel 2000.

CHAPTER 11 : ISOCRATES

The indispensable Zajonz 2002 includes a helpful general introduction to Isocrates. For the difference between his idea of "philosophy" and Plato's, see Nightingale 1995: chap. 1. On Panhellenism and Hellenic identity, see Flower 2000; J. Hall 2002; Mitchell 2007. Isocrates' attitude toward legend is discussed by Hamilton 1979; Papillon 1996a.

I cite Isocrates' *Helen* from Van Hook's Loeb edition. Mirhady and Too 2000 includes a short introduction and a good translation. Much of the scholarship on this speech is concerned with its structure (esp. the function of the prologue), its relationship to Gorgias's *Helen*, and its seriousness or lack thereof. Zajonz 2002 provides a survey; see further Braun 1982; J. Poulakos 1986a, 1986b. Kennedy 1958 discusses *Helen* as a Panhellenic speech, T. Poulakos 1989 its aristocratic values, Papillon 1996b its use of myth. For Theseus's evolving reputation, see Walker 1995; Mills 1997. On Isocrates' assertions about Helen as a goddess, see Edmunds 2007:20–24. Sourvinou-Inwood 2011: chap. 4 examines the complicated stories surrounding the Palladion; for its identification with Cassandra, cf. also Lyons 1997:165–66. On Greek homoeroticism, see Dover 1989; Halperin 1990 (esp. chap. 5 on prostitution and the integrity of the male citizen body).

EPILOGUE

On Aspasia as Helen, see Henry 1995: chap. 2. For the Pythagorean stories, see Detienne 1957. Dio Chrysostom's oration is the subject of Kim 2010: chap. 4. Lindsay 1974: chap. 7 covers ancient Helens from Hellenistic times to late antiquity. Backès 1984 and Homeyer 1977 survey works from antiquity to the twentieth century.

On Helen in the Middle Ages, see Baswell and Taylor 1988; Platte 2007 (who also discusses Ronsard); and for art, Scherer 1967. Suzuki 1989 has chapters on Virgil, Spenser, and Shakespeare. Gumpert 2001: part 2 concerns the reception of Helen in France. Maguire 2009 is scattershot but stimulating; it is best on the Renaissance. On Oscar Wilde and Lillie Langtry, see Ellmann 1988:110–19. Spentzou 1996 covers nine-teenth- and twentieth-century poetry. On Dalí, see further Chadwick 1980. Solomon 2001 lists most twentieth-century films involving Helen, and some screen Helens are featured in M. Winkler 2009. On the 2004 movie *Troy*, see Blondell 2009. "The most beautiful woman in the world" is the title of Amburn's 2000 biography of Elizabeth Taylor.

Bibliography

Adkins, A. W. H. 1983. "Form and Content in Gorgias' *Helen* and *Palamedes*: Rhetoric, Philosophy, Inconsistency and Invalid Argument in Some Greek Thinkers." In *Essays in Ancient Greek Philosophy*, vol. 2, edited by J. Anton, and A. Preus, 107–28. Albany: State University of New York Press.

Albersmeier, Sabine, ed. 2009. *Heroes: Mortals and Myths in Ancient Greece*. Baltimore: Walters Art Museum.

Amburn, Ellis. 2000. *The Most Beautiful Woman in the World: The Obsessions, Passions, and Courage of Elizabeth Taylor*. New York: Cliff Street Books.

Andersen, Øivind. 1977. "Odysseus and the Wooden Horse." *Symbolae Osloenses* 52:5–18.

Anderson, Michael J. 1997. *The Fall of Troy in Early Greek Poetry and Art*. Oxford: Clarendon Press.

Anderson, William S. 1958. "Calypso and Elysium." *Classical Journal* 54:2–11.

Antonaccio, Carla M. 1995. *An Archaeology of Ancestors: Tomb Cult and Hero Cult in Early Greece*. Lanham, MD: Rowman & Littlefield.

Arthur, Marylin B. 1981. "The Divided World of *Iliad* VI." In *Reflections of Women in Antiquity*, edited by Helene P. Foley, 19–44. New York: Gordon & Breach.

Austin, Norman. 1994. *Helen of Troy and Her Shameless Phantom*. Ithaca, NY: Cornell University Press.

Backès, Jean-Louis. 1984. *Le mythe d'Hélène*. Clermont-Ferrand: Adosa.

Bakker, Egbert J., Irene J. F. De Jong, and Hans Van Wees, eds. 2002. *Brill's Companion to Herodotus*. Leiden: Brill.

Bardel, Ruth. 2000. "*Eidôla* in Epic, Tragedy and Vase Painting." In Rutter and Sparkes 2000, 140–60.

Barron, John P. 1969. "Ibycus: To Polycrates." *Bulletin of the Institute of Classical Studies* 16:119–49.

Bassi, Karen. 1993. "Helen and the Discourse of Denial in Stesichorus' Palinode." *Arethusa* 26:51–75.

Baswell, Christopher C., and Paul Beekman Taylor. 1988. "The Faire Queene Eleyne in Chaucer's Troilus." *Speculum* 63:293–311.

Beecroft, Alexander. 2010. *Authorship and Cultural Identity in Early Greece and China: Patterns of Literary Circulation.* Cambridge: Cambridge University Press.

Bergren, Ann. 2008. *Weaving Truth: Essays on Language and the Female in Greek Thought.* Washington, DC: Center for Hellenic Studies.

Bierl, Anton. 2003. "'Ich aber (Sage), das Schönste ist, was einer liebt!' Eine pragmatische Deutung von Sappho Fr. 16 LP/V." *Quaderni Urbinati Di Cultura Classica* 74:91–124.

Biesecker, Susan. 1992. "Rhetoric, Possibility, and Women's Status in Ancient Athens: Gorgias' and Isocrates' Encomiums of Helen." *Rhetoric Society Quarterly* 22:99–108.

Blondell, Ruby. 1999. Introduction to *Medea.* In *Women on the Edge: Four Plays by Euripides,* by Ruby Blondell, Bella Zweig, Nancy Sorkin Rabinowitz, and Mary-Kay Gamel, 147–69. New York: Routledge.

———. 2002. *The Play of Character in Plato's Dialogues.* Cambridge: Cambridge University Press.

———. 2009. "'Third Cheerleader from the Left': From Homer's Helen to Helen of Troy." *Classical Receptions Journal* 1:4–22.

———. 2010a. "'Bitch That I Am': Self-Blame and Self-Assertion in the *Iliad.*" *Transactions of the American Philological Association* 140:1–32.

———. 2010b. "Refractions of Homer's Helen in Archaic Lyric." *American Journal of Philology* 131:349–91.

———. forthcoming. "Helen and the Divine Defense: Homer, Gorgias, Euripides." In *Logoi and Muthoi: Further Philosophical Essays in Greek Literature,* edited by William Wians. Albany: State University of New York Press.

Boedeker, Deborah. 1988. "Protesilaos and the End of Herodotus' *Histories.*" *Classical Antiquity* 7:30–48.

———. 2011. "Helen and 'I' in Early Greek Lyric." In *Greek Notions of the Past in the Archaic and Classical Eras,* edited by John Marincola, Lloyd Llewellyn-Jones, and Calum Maciver, 65–82. Edinburgh: Edinburgh University Press.

Bowersock, Glen W., Walter Burkert, and Michael C. J. Putman, eds. 1979. *Arktouros: Hellenic Studies Presented to Bernard M. W. Knox on the Occasion of His 65th Birthday.* Berlin: W. de Gruyter.

Boyd, Timothy W. 1998. "Recognizing Helen." *Illinois Classical Studies* 23:1–18.

Braun, Ludwig. 1982. "Die schöne Helena, wie Gorgias und Isokrates sie sehen." *Hermes* 110:158–74.

Braund, David. 1998. "Herodotus on the Problematics of Reciprocity." In *Reciprocity in Ancient Greece,* edited by Christopher Gill, Norman Postlethwaite, and Richard Seaford, 159–80. Oxford: Clarendon Press.

Bron, Christiane. 1996. "Hélène sur les vases attiques: Esclave ou double d'Aphrodite." *Kernos* 9:297–310.

Brown, A. L. 1983. "The Erinyes in the *Oresteia*: Real Life, the Supernatural, and the Stage." *Journal of Hellenic Studies* 103:13–34.

Brown, A. S. 1997. "Aphrodite and the Pandora Complex." *Classical Quarterly* 47:26–47.

Buchan, Mark. 2004. *The Limits of Heroism: Homer and the Ethics of Reading.* Ann Arbor: University of Michigan Press.

Burkert, Walter. 1985. *Greek Religion*. Cambridge, MA: Harvard University Press.

———. 2001. *Savage Energies: Lessons of Myth and Ritual in Ancient Greece*. Chicago: University of Chicago Press.

Burnett, Anne Pippin. 1971. *Catastrophe Survived: Euripides' Plays of Mixed Reversal*. Oxford: Clarendon Press.

———. 1983. *Three Archaic Poets: Archilochus, Alcaeus, Sappho*. Cambridge, MA: Harvard University Press.

Buxton, Richard. 1982. *Persuasion in Greek Tragedy: A Study of Peitho*. Cambridge: Cambridge University Press.

Cairns, Douglas L. 1993. *Aidōs: The Psychology and Ethics of Honour and Shame in Ancient Greek Literature*. Oxford: Clarendon Press.

———, ed. 2001. *Oxford Readings in Homer's Iliad*. Oxford: Oxford University Press.

Calabrese, Carin. unpublished. "Domination and Resistance in the *Trojan Women*."

Calame, Claude. 1997. *Choruses of Young Women in Ancient Greece: Their Morphology, Religious Role, and Social Functions*. Translated by Derek Collins and Janice Orion. Lanham, MD: Rowman & Littlefield.

———. 2009. "The Abduction of Helen and the Greek Poetic Tradition: Politics, Reinterpretations and Controversies." In *Antike Mythen: Medien, Transformationen und Konstruktionen*, edited by Ueli Dill and Christine Walde, 645–61. Berlin: de Gruyter.

Callender, Gae. 2012. "Female Horus: The Life and Reign of Tausret." In *Tausret: Forgotten Queen and Pharaoh of Egypt*, edited by Richard H. Wilkinson, 25–47. Oxford: Oxford University Press.

Calogero, Guido. 1957. "Gorgias and the Socratic Principle *Nemo Sua Sponte Peccat*." *Journal of Hellenic Studies* 77:12–17.

Carson, Anne. 1986. *Eros the Bittersweet: An Essay*. Princeton: Princeton University Press.

———. 1990. "Putting Her in Her Place: Woman, Dirt and Desire." In Halperin, Winkler, and Zeitlin 1990, 135–69.

Cartledge, Paul. 2002. *The Greeks: A Portrait of Self and Others*. Oxford: Oxford University Press.

Cassin, Barbara. 2000. *Voir Hélène en toute femme: D'Homère à Lacan*. Paris: Sanofi-Synthélabo.

Chadwick, Whitney. 1980. *Myth in Surrealist Paintings, 1929–1939*. Ann Arbor: UMI Research Press.

Clader, Linda Lee. 1976. *Helen: The Evolution from Divine to Heroic in Greek Epic Tradition*. Leiden: Brill.

Clay, Jenny Strauss. 1989. *The Politics of Olympus: Form and Meaning in the Major Homeric Hymns*. Princeton: Princeton University Press.

Clayton, Barbara. 2004. *A Penelopean Poetics: Reweaving the Feminine in Homer's Odyssey*. Lanham, MD: Lexington Books.

Clement, Paul A. 1958. "The Recovery of Helen." *Hesperia* 27:47–73.

Cohen, Ada. 1996. "Portrayals of Abduction in Greek Art: Rape or Metaphor?" In *Sexuality in Ancient Art*, edited by Natalie Boymel Kampen, 117–35. Cambridge: Cambridge University Press.

———. 2007. "Gendering the Age Gap: Boys, Girls and Abduction in Ancient Greek Art." In *Constructions of Childhood in Ancient Greece and Italy*, edited by Ada Cohen and Jeremy B. Rutter, 257–78. Princeton: ASCSA Publications.

Cohen, Beth, ed. 1995. *The Distaff Side: Representing the Female in Homer's Odyssey*. New York: Oxford University Press.

Cohen, David. 1991. *Law, Sexuality, and Society: The Enforcement of Morals in Classical Athens*. Cambridge: Cambridge University Press.

———. 1993. "Consent and Sexual Relations in Classical Athens." In *Consent and Coercion to Sex and Marriage in Ancient and Medieval Societies*, edited by Angeliki E. Laiou, 5–16. Washington, DC: Dumbarton Oaks.

Cole, Susan Guettel. 1984. "Greek Sanctions against Sexual Assault." *Classical Philology* 79:97–113.

Collins, Leslie. 1988. *Studies in Characterization in the Iliad*. Frankfurt am Main: Athenäum.

Conacher, D. J. 1967. *Euripidean Drama: Myth, Theme and Structure*. Toronto: University of Toronto Press.

———. 1998. *Euripides and the Sophists: Some Dramatic Treatments of Philosophical Ideas*. London: Duckworth.

Consigny, Scott. 2001. *Gorgias: Sophist and Artist*. Columbia: University of South Carolina Press.

Cook, Erwin F. 1995. *The Odyssey in Athens: Myths of Cultural Origins*. Ithaca, NY: Cornell University Press.

Croally, N. T. 1994. *Euripidean Polemic: The Trojan Women and the Function of Tragedy*. Cambridge: Cambridge University Press.

Crowther, N. B. 1985. "Male 'Beauty' Contests in Greece: The Euandria and Euexia." *L'antiquité classique* 54:285–91.

Cyrino, Monica S. 2010. *Aphrodite*. New York: Routledge.

Davies, Malcolm. 1986. "Alcaeus, Thetis and Helen." *Hermes* 114:257–62.

———. 1989. *The Epic Cycle*. Bristol: Bristol Classical Press.

Davis, Michael. 2009. "The Fake That Launched a Thousand Ships: The Question of Identity in Euripides' *Helen*." In *Logos and Muthos: Philosophical Essays in Greek Literature*, edited by William Wians, 255–71. Albany: State University of New York Press.

Deacy, Susan, and Karen F. Pierce, eds. 2002. *Rape in Antiquity*. 2nd ed. London: Duckworth.

Dean-Jones, Lesley. 1992. "The Politics of Pleasure: Female Sexual Appetite in the Hippocratic Corpus." *Helios* 19:72–91.

———. 1994. *Women's Bodies in Classical Greek Science*. Oxford: Clarendon Press.

de Romilly, Jacqueline. 1992. *The Great Sophists in Periclean Athens*. Oxford: Clarendon Press.

Detienne, Marcel. 1957. "La légende pythagoricienne d'Hélène." *Revue de l'histoire des religions* 152:129–52.

Detienne, Marcel, and Jean-Pierre Vernant. 1978. *Cunning Intelligence in Greek Culture and Society*. Translated by Janet Lloyd. Atlantic Highlands, NJ: Humanities Press.

Dewald, Carolyn. 1981. "Women and Culture in Herodotus' *Histories*." In *Reflections of Women in Antiquity*, edited by Helene P. Foley, 91–126. New York: Gordon & Breach.

Dewald, Carolyn, and John Marincola. 2006. *The Cambridge Companion to Herodotus*. Cambridge: Cambridge University Press.

Dodds, E. R. 1951. *The Greeks and the Irrational.* Berkeley: University of California Press.

Doherty, Lillian Eileen. 1995. *Siren Songs: Gender, Audiences and Narrators in the Odyssey.* Ann Arbor: University of Michigan Press.

———. 2006. "Putting the Women Back into the Hesiodic *Catalogue of Women.*" In *Laughing with Medusa: Classical Myth and Feminist Thought,* edited by Vanda Zajko and Miriam Leonard, 297–325. Oxford: Oxford University Press.

Doniger, Wendy. 1999. *Splitting the Difference: Gender and Myth in Ancient Greece and India.* Chicago: University of Chicago Press.

Donlan, Walter. 1973. "The Origin of Καλὸς κἀγαθός." *American Journal of Philology* 94:365–74.

Donzelli, G. Basta. 1985. "La colpa di Elena: Gorgia ed Euripide a confronto." *Siculorum Gymnasium* 38:389–409.

Dover, K. J. 1974. *Greek Popular Morality in the Time of Plato and Aristotle.* Berkeley: University of California Press.

———. 1989. *Greek Homosexuality.* 2nd ed. Cambridge, MA: Harvard University Press.

Downing, Eric. 1990. "*Apatē, Agōn,* and Literary Self-Reflexivity in Euripides' *Helen.*" In *Cabinet of the Muses: Essays on Classical and Comparative Literature in Honor of Thomas G. Rosenmeyer,* edited by Mark Griffith and Donald Mastronarde, 1–16. Atlanta: Scholars Press.

Dué, Casey. 2006. *The Captive Woman's Lament in Greek Tragedy.* Austin: University of Texas Press.

Duncan, Thomas Shearer. 1938. "Gorgias' Theories of Art." *Classical Journal* 33:402–15.

Dupont-Roc, Roselyne, and Alain Le Boulluec. 1976. "Le charme du recit (*Odyssee,* IV, 219–289)." In *Écriture et theorie poétiques: Lectures d'Homère, Eschyle, Platon, Aristote,* edited by Jean Lallot, et al., 30–39. Paris: École Normale Supérieure.

Easterling, P. E., ed. 1997. *The Cambridge Companion to Greek Tragedy.* Cambridge: Cambridge University Press.

Ebbott, Mary. 1999. "The Wrath of Helen: Self-Blame and Nemesis in the *Iliad.*" In *Nine Essays on Homer,* edited by Miriam Carlisle and Olga Levaniouk, 3–20. Lanham, MD: Rowman & Littlefield.

Edmunds, Lowell. 2007. "Helen's Divine Origins." *Electronic Antiquity* 10 (2): 1–45.

Eisner, Robert. 1980. "Echoes of the *Odyssey* in Euripides' *Helen.*" *Maia* 32:31–37.

Ellmann, Richard. 1988. *Oscar Wilde.* New York: Knopf.

Faraone, Christopher A. 1999. *Ancient Greek Love Magic.* Cambridge, MA: Harvard University Press.

Felson-Rubin, Nancy. 1994. *Regarding Penelope: From Character to Poetics.* Princeton: Princeton University Press.

Ferrari, Gloria. 1997. "Figures in the Text: Metaphors and Riddles in the *Agamemnon.*" *Classical Philology* 92:1–45.

———. 2002. *Figures of Speech: Men and Maidens in Ancient Greece.* Chicago: University of Chicago Press.

Fisher, Nick. 2002. "Popular Morality in Herodotus." In Bakker et al. 2002, 199–224.

Fletcher, Judith. 1999. "Exchanging Glances: Vision and Representation in Aeschylus' *Agamemnon.*" *Helios* 26:11–34.

Flory, Stewart. 1987. *The Archaic Smile of Herodotus.* Detroit: Wayne State University Press.

Flower, Michael A. 2000. "From Simonides to Isocrates: The Fifth-Century Origins of Fourth-Century Panhellenism." *Classical Antiquity* 19:65–101.

Foley, Helene P. 1984. "Reverse Similes and Sex Roles in the *Odyssey*." In *Women in the Ancient World: The Arethusa Papers*, edited by John Peradotto and J. P. Sullivan, 59–78. Albany: State University of New York Press.

———. 1994. *The Homeric Hymn to Demeter: Translation, Commentary, and Interpretive Essays*. Princeton: Princeton University Press.

———. 2001. *Female Acts in Greek Tragedy*. Princeton: Princeton University Press.

Ford, Andrew. 2002. *The Origins of Criticism: Literary Culture and Poetic Theory in Classical Greece*. Princeton: Princeton University Press.

Foucault, Michel. 1985. *The History of Sexuality*. Vol. 2, *The Use of Pleasure*. New York: Random House.

Fowler, Robert, ed. 2004. *The Cambridge Companion to Homer*. Cambridge: Cambridge University Press.

Fraenkel, Eduard, ed. 1950. *Aeschylus: Agamemnon*. 3 vols. Oxford: Clarendon Press.

Franco, Cristiana. 2003. *Senza ritegno: Il cane e la donna nell' immaginario della Grecia antica*. Bologna: Il Mulino.

Fredricksmeyer, Hardy C. 2001. "A Diachronic Reading of Sappho Fr. 16 LP." *Transactions of the American Philological Association* 131:75–86.

Frontisi-Ducroux, Françoise. 2007. "The Invention of the Erinyes." In *Visualizing the Tragic: Drama, Myth, and Ritual in Greek Art and Literature*, edited by Christina Kraus, et al., 165–76. Oxford: Oxford University Press.

Fulkerson, Laurel. 2011. "Helen as Vixen, Helen as Victim: Remorse and the Opacity of Female Desire." In *Emotion, Genre and Gender in Classical Antiquity*, edited by Dana Munteanu, 113–33. London: Bristol Classical Press.

Gagarin, Michael. 2001. "Did the Sophists Aim to Persuade?" *Rhetorica* 19:275–91.

Gantz, Timothy. 1993. *Early Greek Myth: A Guide to Literary and Artistic Sources*. Baltimore: Johns Hopkins University Press.

Gentili, Bruno. 1988. *Poetry and Its Public in Ancient Greece: From Homer to the Fifth Century*. Translated by A. Thomas Cole. Baltimore: Johns Hopkins University Press.

Ghali-Kahil, Lilly B. 1955. *Les enlèvements et le retour d'Hélène dans les textes et les documents figurés*. 2 vols. Paris: E. de Boccard.

Goff, Barbara. 2009. *Euripides: Trojan Women*. London: Duckworth.

Goldhill, Simon. 1988. "Reading Differences: The *Odyssey* and Juxtaposition." *Ramus* 17:1–31.

———. 1990. "The Great Dionysia and Civic Ideology." In *Nothing to Do with Dionysos? Athenian Drama in Its Social Context*, edited by John J. Winkler and Froma I. Zeitlin. Princeton: Princeton University Press.

———. 2000. "Placing Theatre in the History of Vision." In Rutter and Sparkes 2000, 161–79.

Gould, John. 1989. *Herodotus*. New York: St. Martin's Press.

———. 2001. *Myth, Ritual, Memory, and Exchange: Essays in Greek Literature and Culture*. Oxford: Oxford University Press.

Graham, Daniel W., ed. 2010. *The Texts of Early Greek Philosophy: The Complete Fragments and Selected Testimonies of the Major Presocratics*. Part 2, *Sophists*. Cambridge: Cambridge University Press.

Graver, Margaret. 1995. "Dog-Helen and Homeric Insult." *Classical Antiquity* 14:41–61.

Gray, Vivienne. 1995. "Herodotus and the Rhetoric of Otherness." *American Journal of Philology* 116:185–211.

Greene, Ellen, ed. 1996. *Reading Sappho: Contemporary Approaches*. Berkeley: University of California Press.

Gregory, Elizabeth. 1996. "Unravelling Penelope: The Construction of the Faithful Wife in Homer's Heroines." *Helios* 23:3–20.

Gregory, Justina. 1991. *Euripides and the Instruction of the Athenians*. Ann Arbor: University of Michigan Press.

Gumpert, Matthew. 2001. *Grafting Helen: The Abduction of the Classical Past*. Madison: University of Wisconsin Press.

Guthrie, W. K. C. 1971. *The Sophists*. London: Cambridge University Press.

Hall, Edith. 1989. *Inventing the Barbarian: Greek Self-Definition through Tragedy*. Oxford: Clarendon Press.

Hall, Jonathan M. 2002. *Hellenicity: Between Ethnicity and Culture*. Chicago: University of Chicago Press.

Halliwell, Stephen. 1993. "The Function and Aesthetics of the Greek Tragic Mask." *Drama* 2:195–211.

———. 2008. *Greek Laughter: A Study of Cultural Psychology from Homer to Early Christianity*. Cambridge: Cambridge University Press.

Halperin, David M. 1990. *One Hundred Years of Homosexuality and Other Essays on Greek Love*. New York: Routledge.

Halperin, David M., John J. Winkler, and Froma I. Zeitlin, eds. 1990. *Before Sexuality: The Construction of Erotic Experience in the Ancient Greek World*. Princeton: Princeton University Press.

Hamilton, Charles D. 1979. "Greek Rhetoric and History: The Case of Isocrates." In Bowersock, Burkert, and Putnam 1979, 290–98.

Hankinson, R. J. 1998. *Cause and Explanation in Ancient Greek Thought*. Oxford: Clarendon Press.

Hanson, Ann Ellis. 1990. "The Medical Writers' Woman." In Halperin, Winkler, and Zeitlin 1990, 309–38.

Harrison, Thomas. 2000. *Divinity and History: The Religion of Herodotus*. Oxford: Clarendon Press.

———. 2002. "Herodotus and the Ancient Greek Idea of Rape." In Deacy and Pierce 2002, 185–208.

Hawley, Richard. 1998. "The Dynamics of Beauty in Classical Greece." In *Changing Bodies, Changing Meanings: Studies in the Human Body in Antiquity*, edited by Dominic Montserrat, 37–54. London: Routledge.

Hazewindus, Minke W. 2004. *When Women Interfere: Studies in the Role of Women in Herodotus' Histories*. Amsterdam: Gieben.

Haziza, Typhaine. 2009. *Le kaléidoscope hérodotéen: Images, imaginaire et représentations de l'Egypte à travers le livre II d'Hérodote*. Paris: Les Belles Lettres.

Heath, John. 2005. *The Talking Greeks: Speech, Animals, and the Other in Homer, Aeschylus, and Plato*. Cambridge: Cambridge University Press.

Hedreen, Guy. 1996. "Image, Text, and Story in the Recovery of Helen." *Classical Antiquity* 15:152–92.

Henderson, Jeffrey. 1991. "Women and the Athenian Dramatic Festivals." *Transactions of the American Philological Association* 121:133–47.

Henry, Madeleine M. 1995. *Prisoner of History: Aspasia of Miletus and Her Biographical Tradition.* New York: Oxford University Press.

Herman, Gabriel. 1987. *Ritualised Friendship and the Greek City.* Cambridge: Cambridge University Press.

Hieronymi, Pamela. 2007. "Rational Capacity as a Condition on Blame." *Philosophical Books* 48:109–23.

Holmberg, Ingrid E. 1995a. "The *Odyssey* and Female Subjectivity." *Helios* 22:103–22.

———. 1995b. "Euripides' *Helen*: Most Noble and Most Chaste." *American Journal of Philology* 116:19–42.

Holmes, Brooke. 2010. *The Symptom and the Subject: The Emergence of the Physical Body in Ancient Greece.* Princeton: Princeton University Press.

Homeyer, Helene. 1977. *Die spartanische Helene und der trojanische Krieg: Wandlungen und Wanderungen eines Sagen-Kreises vom Altertum bis zur Gegenwart.* Wiesbaden: Steiner.

Horky, Phillip Sidney. 2006. "The Imprint of the Soul: Psychosomatic Affection in Plato, Gorgias, and the 'Orphic' Gold Tablets." *Mouseion* 6:371–86.

Hourmouziades, Nicolaos C. 1965. *Production and Imagination in Euripides: Form and Function of the Scenic Space.* Athens: Greek Society for Humanistic Studies.

Houston, Barbara. 1992. "In Praise of Blame." *Hypatia* 7:128–47.

Hughes, Bettany. 2005. *Helen of Troy: Goddess, Princess, Whore.* New York: Knopf.

Hunter, Richard. 1996. *Theocritus and the Archaeology of Greek Poetry.* Cambridge: Cambridge University Press.

———, ed. 2005. *The Hesiodic Catalogue of Women: Constructions and Reconstructions.* Cambridge: Cambridge University Press.

Hunter, Virginia J. 1982. *Past and Process in Herodotus and Thucydides.* Princeton: Princeton University Press.

Hutchinson, G. O., ed. 2001. *Greek Lyric Poetry: A Commentary on Selected Larger Pieces.* Oxford: Oxford University Press.

Jamison, Stephanie W. 1994. "Draupadí on the Walls of Troy: *Iliad* 3 from an Indic Perspective." *Classical Antiquity* 13:5–16.

Jenkins, Ian. 1985. "The Ambiguity of Greek Textiles." *Arethusa* 18:109–32.

Juffras, Diane M. 1993. "Helen and Other Victims in Euripides' *Helen*." *Hermes* 121: 45–57.

Just, Roger. 1989. *Women in Athenian Law and Life.* London: Routledge.

Kahil, Lilly. 1988. "Hélène." *Lexicon Iconographicum Mythologiae Classicae*, vol. 4, part 1, 538–50.

Kaimio, Maarit. 2002. "Erotic Experience in the Conjugal Bed: Good Wives in Greek Tragedy." In *The Sleep of Reason: Erotic Experience and Sexual Ethics in Ancient Greece and Rome*, edited by Martha Craven Nussbaum and Juha Sihvola, 95–119. Chicago: University of Chicago Press.

Kakridis, Johannes Th. 1971. *Homer Revisited.* Lund: Gleerup.

Kampen, Natalie Boymel, ed. 1996. *Sexuality in Ancient Art.* Cambridge: Cambridge University Press.

Kannicht, Richard. 1969. *Euripides Helena.* 2 vols. Heidelberg: C. Winter.

Karsaï, György. 2003. "Le corps d'Helene: La scène de reconnaissance dans l'Helene d'Euripide." *Kentron* 19:115–35.

Katz, Marilyn A. 1991. *Penelope's Renown: Meaning and Indeterminacy in the Odyssey*. Princeton: Princeton University Press.

Kearns, Emily. 1998. "The Nature of Heroines." In *The Sacred and the Feminine in Ancient Greece*, edited by Sue Blundell and Margaret Williamson, 96–110. London: Routledge.

Kennedy, George A. 1958. "Isocrates' *Encomium of Helen*: A Panhellenic Document." *Transactions of the American Philological Association* 89:77–83.

———. 1986. "Helen's Web Unraveled." *Arethusa* 19:5–14.

Kerferd, G. B. 1981. *The Sophistic Movement*. Cambridge: Cambridge University Press.

Kim, Lawrence. 2010. *Homer between History and Fiction in Imperial Greek Literature*. Leiden: Cambridge University Press.

King, Katherine Callen. 1987. *Achilles: Paradigms of the War Hero from Homer to the Middle Ages*. Berkeley: University of California Press.

King, Helen. 1998. *Hippocrates' Woman: Reading the Female Body in Ancient Greece*. Routledge: London.

Kirwan, James. 1999. *Beauty*. Manchester: Manchester University Press.

Knox, Bernard. 1979. *Word and Action: Essays on the Ancient Theater*. Baltimore: Johns Hopkins University Press.

Koniaris, George L. 1967. "On Sappho, Fr. 16 (L.P.)." *Hermes* 95:257–69.

Konstan, David. 1987. "Persians, Greeks, and Empire." *Arethusa* 20:59–73.

Kopytoff, Igor. 1986. "The Cultural Biography of Things: Commoditization as Process." In *The Social Life of Things: Commodities in Cultural Perspective*, edited by Arjun Appadurai, 64–91. Cambridge: Cambridge University Press.

Larson, Jennifer. 1995. *Greek Heroine Cults*. Madison: University of Wisconsin Press.

Larson, Stephanie. 2006. "Kandaules' Wife, Masistes' Wife: Herodotus' Narrative Strategy in Suppressing Names of Women (Hdt. 1.8–12 and 9.108–13)." *Classical Journal* 101:225–44.

Lateiner, Donald. 1989. *The Historical Method of Herodotus*. Toronto: University of Toronto Press.

Lebeck, Anne. 1971. *The Oresteia: A Study in Language and Structure*. Washington, DC: Center for Hellenic Studies.

Lee, Mireille M. 2004. "'Evil Wealth of Raiment': Deadly Πέπλοι in Greek Tragedy." *Classical Journal* 99:253–79.

Lendon, J. E. 2000. "Homeric Vengeance and the Outbreak of Greek Wars." In *War and Violence in Ancient Greece*, edited by Hans van Wees and Paul Beston, 1–30. London: Duckworth.

Lesky, Albin. 2001. "Divine and Human Causation in Homeric Epic." In Cairns 2001, 170–202.

Levaniouk, Olga. 2011. *Eve of the Festival: Making Myth in Odyssey 19*. Washington, DC: Center for Hellenic Studies.

Levin, Susan B. 1996. "Women's Nature and Role in the Ideal *Polis*: *Republic* V Revisited." In *Feminism and Ancient Philosophy*, edited by Julie K. Ward, 13–30. New York: Routledge.

Levine, Molly Myerowitz. 1995. "The Gendered Grammar of Ancient Mediterranean Hair." In *Off With Her Head! The Denial of Women's Identity in Myth, Religion, and Culture*, edited by Howard Eilberg-Schwartz, and Wendy Doniger, 76–130. Berkeley: University of California Press.

Lindsay, Jack. 1974. *Helen of Troy: Woman and Goddess*. London: Constable.

Llewellyn-Jones, Lloyd. 2003. *Aphrodite's Tortoise: The Veiled Women of Ancient Greece*. Swansea: Classical Press of Wales.

Lloyd, Alan B. 1975–1988. *Herodotus, Book II*. Vol. 1, *Introduction* (1975); vol. 2, *Commentary 1–98* (1976); vol. 3, *Commentary 99–182* (1988). Leiden: Brill.

Lloyd, Michael. 1992. *The Agon in Euripides*. Oxford: Clarendon Press.

Lloyd-Jones, Hugh., ed. 1975. *Females of the Species: Semonides on Women*. Park Ridge, NJ: Noyes Press.

———, trans. 1979. *Aeschylus: The Oresteia*. London: Duckworth.

Long, Timothy. 1987. *Repetition and Variation in the Short Stories of Herodotus*. Frankfurt am Main: Athenäum.

Loraux, Nicole. 1993. *The Children of Athena: Athenian Ideas about Citizenship and the Division between the Sexes*. Translated by Caroline Levine. Princeton: Princeton University Press.

———. 1995. *The Experiences of Teiresias: The Feminine and the Greek Man*. Translated by Paula Wissing. Princeton: Princeton University Press.

Lyons, Deborah. 1997. *Gender and Immortality: Heroines in Ancient Greek Myth and Cult*. Princeton: Princeton University Press.

———. 2003. "Dangerous Gifts: Ideologies of Marriage and Exchange in Ancient Greece." *Classical Antiquity* 22:93–134.

MacDowell, Douglas M., ed. 1982. *Gorgias: Encomium of Helen*. Bristol: Bristol Classics.

MacLachlan, Bonnie C. 1997. "Personal Poetry." In *A Companion to the Greek Lyric Poets*, edited by Douglas E. Gerber, 133–220. Leiden: Brill.

Maguire, Laurie. 2009. *Helen of Troy: From Homer to Hollywood*. Chichester: Wiley-Blackwell.

Marshall, C. W. 1995. "Idol Speculation: The Protean Stage of Euripides' *Helen*." *Text and Presentation* 16:74–79.

———. 1999. "Some Fifth-Century Masking Conventions." *Greece and Rome* 46: 188–202.

———. 2011. "Homer, Helen, and the Structure of Euripides' *Trojan Women*." In *Greek Drama IV: Texts, Contexts, Performance*, edited by David Rosenbloom and John Davidson, 31–46. Oxford: Aris & Phillips.

———. forthcoming. *Tragic Direction: Structure and Performance in Euripides' Helen*.

Mayer, Kenneth. 1996. "Helen and the Διὸς Βουλή." *American Journal of Philology* 117: 1–15.

McClure, Laura. 1999. *Spoken Like a Woman: Speech and Gender in Athenian Drama*. Princeton: Princeton University Press.

Meagher, Robert Emmet. 2002. *The Meaning of Helen: In Search of an Ancient Icon*. Wauconda: Bolchazy-Carducci.

Meineck, Peter. 2011. "The Neuroscience of the Tragic Mask." *Arion* 19:113–58.

Meltzer, Gary S. 2006. *Euripides and the Poetics of Nostalgia*. Cambridge: Cambridge University Press.

Meyers, Diana Tietjens. 2005. "Who's There? Selfhood, Self-Regard and Social Relations." *Hypatia* 20:200–215.

Michelini, Ann N. 1987. *Euripides and the Tragic Tradition.* Madison: University of
Wisconsin Press.

Millender, Ellen G. 1999. "Athenian Ideology and the Empowered Spartan Woman." In
Sparta: New Perspectives, edited by Stephen Hodkinson and Anton Powell, 355–91.
London: Duckworth.

———. 2009. "The Spartan Dyarchy." In *Sparta: Comparative Approaches,* edited by
Stephen Hodkinson, 1–67. Swansea: Classical Press of Wales.

———, ed. 2012. *Unveiling Spartan Women.* Swansea: Classical Press of Wales.

Mills, Sophie. 1997. *Theseus, Tragedy, and the Athenian Empire.* Oxford: Clarendon
Press.

Mirhady, David C., and Yun Lee Too, trans. 2000. *Isocrates I.* Austin: University of Texas
Press.

Mitchell, Lynette G. 2007. *Panhellenism and the Barbarian in Archaic and Classical
Greece.* Swansea: Classical Press of Wales.

Morgan, Kathleen. 1991. "Odyssey 23: 218–24: Adultery, Shame, and Marriage." *American Journal of Philology* 112:1–3.

Morgan, Kathryn. 1994. "Socrates and Gorgias at Delphi and Olympia: *Phaedrus*
235d6–236b4." *Classical Quarterly* 44:375–86.

———. 2000. *Myth and Philosophy from the Presocratics to Plato.* Cambridge: Cambridge University Press.

Mossman, Judith. 2005. "Women's Voices." In *A Companion to Greek Tragedy,* edited by
Justina Gregory, 352–65. Oxford: Blackwell.

Most, G. W. 1981. "Sappho Fr. 16.6-7 L-P." *Classical Quarterly* 31:11–17.

———. 1982. "Greek Lyric Poets." In *Ancient Writers,* vol. 1, edited by T. James Luce,
75–98. New York: Scribner.

Mueller, Melissa. 2010. "Helen's Hands: Weaving for *Kleos* in the *Odyssey.*" *Helios* 37:
1–21.

Munson, Rosaria Vignolo. 1993. "Three Aspects of Spartan Kingship in Herodotus." In
Nomodeiktes: Greek Studies in Honor of Martin Ostwald, edited by Ralph M. Rosen
and Joseph Farrell, 39–54. Ann Arbor: University of Michigan Press.

Murnaghan, Sheila. 1986. "Penelope's *Agnoia*: Knowledge, Power, and Gender in the
Odyssey." *Helios* 13:103–15.

———. 1987. *Disguise and Recognition in the Odyssey.* Princeton: Princeton University
Press.

Nagler, Michael N. 1996. "Dread Goddesses Revisited." In Schein 1996, 141–61.

Nagy, Gregory. 1990. *Pindar's Homer: The Lyric Possession of an Epic Past.* Baltimore:
Johns Hopkins University Press.

———. 1999. *The Best of the Achaeans: Concepts of the Hero in Archaic Greek Poetry.* 2nd
ed. Baltimore: Johns Hopkins University Press.

Neuberg, Matt. 1991. "Clytemnestra and the Alastor (Aeschylus, *Agamemnon* 1497ff)."
Quaderni Urbinati Di Cultura Classica 38:37–68.

Neville, James W. 1977. "Herodotus on the Trojan War." *Greece and Rome* 24:3–12.

Newton, Rick M. 1987. "Odysseus and Hephaestus in the *Odyssey.*" *Classical Journal*
83:12–20.

Nightingale, Andrea Wilson. 1995. *Genres in Dialogue: Plato and the Construct of Philosophy*. Cambridge: Cambridge University Press.

Nimis, Stephen. 2004. "Egypt in Greco-Roman History and Fiction." *Alif* 24:34–67.

North, Helen F. 1977. "The Mare, the Vixen, and the Bee: *Sophrosyne* as the Virtue of Women in Antiquity." *Illinois Classical Studies* 2:35–47.

Oakley, John H., and Rebecca H. Sinos. 1993. *The Wedding in Ancient Athens*. Madison: University of Wisconsin Press.

Ober, Josiah. 1989. *Mass and Elite in Democratic Athens: Rhetoric, Ideology, and the Power of the People*. Princeton: Princeton University Press.

Olson, S. Douglas. 1989. "The Stories of Helen and Menelaus (*Odyssey* 4.240–89) and the Return of Odysseus." *American Journal of Philology* 110:387–94.

Ormand, Kirk. 1999. *Exchange and the Maiden: Marriage in Sophoclean Tragedy*. Austin: University of Texas Press.

———. 2009. *Controlling Desires: Sexuality in Ancient Greece and Rome*. Westport, CT: Praeger.

———. forthcoming. *The Hesiodic Catalogue of Women and the Archaic World*. Cambridge: Cambridge University Press.

Osborne, Robin. 2001. "The Use of Abuse: Semonides 7." *Proceedings of the Cambridge Philological Society* 47:47–64.

Page, Denys., ed. 1955. *Sappho and Alcaeus: An Introduction to the Study of Ancient Lesbian Poetry*. Oxford: Clarendon Press.

Pallantza, Elena. 2005. *Der Troische Krieg in der nachhomerischen Literatur bis zum 5. Jahrhundert v. Chr.* Stuttgart: Steiner.

Papi, Donatella Galeotti. 1987. "Victors and Sufferers in Euripides' *Helen*." *American Journal of Philology* 108:27–40.

Papillon, Terry L. 1996a. "Isocrates and the Use of Myth." *Hermathena* 161:9–21.

———. 1996b. "Isocrates on Gorgias and Helen: The Unity of the *Helen*." *Classical Journal* 91:377–91.

Parker, Robert. 2011. *On Greek Religion*. Ithaca, NY: Cornell University Press.

Parry, Hugh. 1992. *Thelxis: Magic and Imagination in Greek Myth and Poetry*. Lanham, MD: University Press of America.

Pease, Arthur Stanley. 1926. "Things without Honor." *Classical Philology* 21:27–41.

Pedrick, Victoria. 1988. "The Hospitality of Noble Women in the *Odyssey*." *Helios* 15:85–101.

Peradotto, John. 1969. "Cledonomancy in the *Oresteia*." *American Journal of Philology* 90:1–21.

Platte, Ryan. 2007. "Hybrid Helen." *Genre* 27:30–47.

Pollitt, J. J. 1974. *The Ancient View of Greek Art*. New Haven: Yale University Press.

———. 1990. *The Art of Ancient Greece: Sources and Documents*. Cambridge: Cambridge University Press.

Pomeroy, Sarah B. 1978. "Plato and the Female Physician (*Republic* 454d2)." *American Journal of Philology* 99:496–500.

———. 2002. *Spartan Women*. Oxford: Oxford University Press.

Porter, James I. 1993. "The Seductions of Gorgias." *Classical Antiquity* 12:267–99.

Poulakos, John. 1983. "Gorgias' *Encomium to Helen* and the Defense of Rhetoric." *Rhetorica* 1:1–16.

————. 1986a. "Argument, Practicality, and Eloquence in Isocrates' *Helen.*" *Rhetorica* 4:1–19.

————. 1986b. "Gorgias' and Isocrates' Use of the Encomium." *Southern Speech Communication Journal* 51:300–307.

Poulakos, Takis. 1989. "Rhetorical Criticism. Epideictic Rhetoric as Social Hegemony: Isocrates' *Helen.*" In *Rhetoric and Ideology: Compositions and Criticisms of Power,* edited by Charles W. Kneupper, 156–66. Arlington, TX: Rhetoric Society of America.

Prag, A. J. N. W. 1985. *The Oresteia: Iconographic and Narrative Tradition.* Chicago: Aris & Phillips.

Prier, Raymond A. 1989. *Thauma Idesthai: The Phenomenology of Sight and Appearance in Archaic Greek Thought.* Tallahassee: Florida State University Press.

Reckford, Kenneth J. 1964. "Helen in the *Iliad.*" *Greek, Roman, and Byzantine Studies* 5:5–20.

Reeder, Ellen D., ed. 1995. *Pandora: Women in Classical Greece.* Baltimore: Walters Art Gallery, in association with Princeton University Press.

Rissman, Leah. 1983. *Love as War: Homeric Allusion in the Poetry of Sappho.* Königstein/Ts.: Hain.

Robertson, Martin. 1970. "Ibycus: Polycrates, Troilus, Polyxena." *Bulletin of the Institute of Classical Studies* 17:11–15.

Robinson, D. B. 1979. "Helen and Persephone, Sparta and Demeter: The 'Demeter Ode' in Euripides' *Helen.*" In Bowersock, Burkert, and Putnam 1979, 162–72.

Rose, Peter W. 1992. *Sons of the Gods, Children of Earth: Ideology and Literary Form in Ancient Greece.* Ithaca, NY: Cornell University Press.

Rosenmeyer, P. A. 1997. "Her Master's Voice: Sappho's Dialogue with Homer." *Materiali e discussioni per l'analisi dei testi classici* 39:123–49.

Rösler, Wolfgang. 1980. *Dichter und Gruppe: Eine Untersuchung zu den Bedingungen und zur historischen Funktion früher griechischer Lyrik am Beispiel Alkaios.* Munich: W. Fink.

Rutter, N. Keith, and Brian A. Sparkes, eds. 2000. *Word and Image in Ancient Greece.* Edinburgh: Edinburgh University Press.

Saïd, Suzanne. 2001. "Greeks and Barbarians in Euripides' Tragedies: The End of Differences?" In *Greeks and Barbarians,* edited by Thomas Harrison, 62–100. Edinburgh: Edinburgh University Press.

Saintillan, Daniel. 1996. "Du festin à l'échange: Les grâces de Pandore." In *Le métier du mythe: Lectures d'Hésiode,* edited by Fabienne Blaise, Pierre Judet de La Combe, and Philippe Rousseau, 315–48. Paris: Presses Universitaires du Septentrion.

Sansone, David. 1985. "Theonoe and Theoclymenus." *Symbolae Osloenses* 60:17–36.

Saunders, Trevor J. 1986. "Gorgias' Psychology in the History of the Free-Will Problem." *Siculorum Gymnasium* 38:209–24.

Scaife, Ross. 1995. "The *Kypria* and Its Early Reception." *Classical Antiquity* 14:164–91.

Schein, Seth L. 1984. *The Mortal Hero: An Introduction to Homer's Iliad.* Berkeley: University of California Press.

————, ed. 1996. *Reading the Odyssey: Selected Interpretive Essays.* Princeton: Princeton University Press.

Scherer, Margaret R. 1967. "Helen of Troy." *Bulletin of the Metropolitan Museum of Art* 25:367–83.

Schiappa, Edward. 1995. "Gorgias's *Helen* Revisited." *Quarterly Journal of Speech* 81:310–24.

Schmidt, Ernst Günter. 1996. "Achilleus und Helena—ein verhindertes antikes Traumpaar. Ps.-Hesiod, Frauenkatalog Frgm. 204, 87–92 M.-W." In *Worte, Bilder, Töne: Studien zur Antike und Antikerezeption*, edited by Richard Faber and Bernd Seidensticker, 23–38. Würzburg: Königshausen & Neumann.

Schmiel, Robert. 1972. "Telemachus in Sparta." *Transactions of the American Philological Association* 103:463–72.

Scodel, Ruth. 1980. *The Trojan Trilogy of Euripides*. Göttingen: Vanderhoeck & Reprecht.

———. 1996. "Δόμων ἄγαλμα: Virgin Sacrifice and Aesthetic Object." *Transactions of the American Philological Association* 126:111–28.

———. 1998. "The Captive's Dilemma: Sexual Acquiescence in Euripides' *Hecuba* and *Troades*." *Harvard Studies in Classical Philology* 98:137–54.

———. 1999/2000. "Verbal Performance and Euripidean Rhetoric." *Illinois Classical Studies* 24–25:129–44.

———. 2008. *Epic Facework: Self-Presentation and Social Interaction in Homer*. Swansea: Classical Press of Wales.

Sebesta, Judith Lynn. 2002. "Visions of Gleaming Textiles and a Clay Core: Textiles, Greek Women, and Pandora." In *Women's Dress in the Ancient Greek World*, edited by Lloyd Llewellyn-Jones and Sue Blundell, 125–42. London: Duckworth.

Segal, Charles P. 1962. "Gorgias and the Psychology of the Logos." *Harvard Studies in Classical Philology* 66:99–155.

———. 1986. *Interpreting Greek Tragedy: Myth, Poetry, Text*. Ithaca, NY: Cornell University Press.

———. 1996. "*Kleos* and Its Ironies in the *Odyssey*." In Schein 1996, 201–21.

———. 1998. *Aglaia: The Poetry of Alcman, Sappho, Pindar, Bacchylides, and Corinna*. Lanham, MD: Rowman & Littlefield.

Shapiro, Alan. 1992. "The Marriage of Theseus and Helen." In *Kotinos: Festschrift für Erika Simon*, edited by Heide Froning, Tonio Hölscher, and Harald Mielsch, 232–36. Mainz: P. von Zabern.

Shapiro, H. A. 2009. "Helen: Heroine of Cult, Heroine in Art." In Albersmeier 2009, 49–56.

Sistakou, Evina. 2008. *Reconstructing the Epic: Cross-Readings of the Trojan Myth in Hellenistic Poetry*. Leuven: Peeters.

Skinner, Marilyn B. 2005. *Sexuality in Greek and Roman Culture*. Oxford: Blackwell.

Skutsch, Otto. 1987. "Helen, Her Name and Nature." *Journal of Hellenic Studies* 107:188–93.

Sluiter, Ineke, and Ralph M. Rosen, eds. 2008. *Kakos: Badness and Anti-Value in Classical Antiquity*. Leiden: Brill.

Smith, Nicholas D. 1983. "Plato and Aristotle on the Nature of Women." *Journal of the History of Philosophy* 21:467–78.

Solmsen, F. 1934. "Ὄνομα and πρᾶγμα in Euripides' *Helen*." *Classical Review* 48:119–21.

Solomon, Jon. 2001. *The Ancient World in the Cinema*. 2nd ed. New Haven: Yale University Press.

Sommerstein, Alan H. 2006. "Rape and Consent in Athenian Tragedy." In *Dionysalexandros: Essays on Aeschylus and His Fellow Tragedians in Honor of Alexander F. Garvie*, edited by Douglas Cairns and Vayos Liapis, 233–51. Swansea: Classical Press of Wales.

———. 2010. *Aeschylean Tragedy*. 2nd ed. London: Duckworth.

Sourvinou-Inwood, Christiane. 2011. *Athenian Myths and Festivals: Aglauros, Erechtheus, Plynteria, Panathenaia, Dionysia*. Edited by Robert Parker. Oxford: Oxford University Press.

Spentzou, Effie. 1996. "Helen of Troy and the Poetics of Innocence: From Ancient Fiction to Modern Metafiction." *Classical and Modern Literature* 16:301–24.

Spivey, Nigel. 1995. "Bionic Statues." In *The Greek World*, edited by Anton Powell, 442–59. London: Routledge.

Stehle, Eva. 1997. *Performance and Gender in Ancient Greece*. Princeton: Princeton University Press.

Steiner, Deborah Tarn. 2001. *Images in Mind: Statues in Archaic and Classical Greek Literature and Thought*. Princeton: Princeton University Press.

Stieber, Mary C. 2011. *Euripides and the Language of Craft*. Leiden: Brill.

Sutton, Robert F., Jr. 1997/1998. "Nuptial Eros: The Visual Discourse of Marriage in Classical Athens." *Journal of the Walters Art Gallery* 55/56:27–48.

———. 2009. "The Invention of the Female Nude: Zeuxis, Vase Painting, and the Kneeling Bather." In *Athenian Potters and Painters*, vol. 2, edited by John H. Oakley and Olga Palagia, 270–79. Oxford: Oxbow Books.

Suzuki, Mihoko. 1989. *Metamorphoses of Helen: Authority, Difference, and the Epic*. Ithaca, NY: Cornell University Press.

Taplin, Oliver. 1992. *Homeric Soundings: The Shaping of the Iliad*. Oxford: Clarendon Press.

Taylor, Charles H. 1963. "The Obstacles to Odysseus' Return." In *Essays on the Odyssey*, edited by Charles H. Taylor, 87–99. Bloomington: Indiana University Press.

Thévenet, Lucie. 2009. *Le personnage: Du mythe au théâtre: La question de l'identité dans la tragédie grecque*. Paris: Les Belles Lettres.

Thomas, Rosalind. 2000. *Herodotus in Context: Ethnography, Science and the Art of Persuasion*. Cambridge: Cambridge University Press.

Thomson, George Derwent. 1966. *The Oresteia of Aeschylus*. Amsterdam: A. M. Hakkert.

Trenkner, Sophie. 1958. *The Greek Novella in the Classical Period*. Cambridge: Cambridge University Press.

Vandiver, Elizabeth. 1991. *Heroes in Herodotus: The Interaction of Myth and History*. Frankfurt am Main: P. Lang.

Vasunia, Phiroze. 2001. *The Gift of the Nile: Hellenizing Egypt from Aeschylus to Alexander*. Berkeley: University of California Press.

Verdenius, W. J. 1981. "Gorgias' Doctrine of Deception." *Hermes Einzelschriften* 44:116–28.

Vermeule, Emily. 1979. *Aspects of Death in Early Greek Art and Poetry*. Berkeley: University of California Press.

Vernant, Jean-Pierre. 1990. *Myth and Society in Ancient Greece*. Rev. ed. Translated by Janet Lloyd. New York: Zone Books.

———. 1991. *Mortals and Immortals: Collected Essays*. Edited by Froma I. Zeitlin. Princeton: Princeton University Press.

Vodoklys, Edward J. 1992. *Blame-Expression in the Epic Tradition*. New York: Garland.

Voelke, Pierre. 1996. "Beauté d'Hélène et rituels féminins dans l'Hélène d'Euripide." *Kernos* 9:281–96.

Walker, Henry J. 1995. *Theseus and Athens*. Oxford: Oxford University Press.

Walsh, George B. 1984. *The Varieties of Enchantment: Early Greek Views of the Nature and Function of Poetry*. Chapel Hill: University of North Carolina Press.

West, M. L. 1971. "Stesichorus." *Classical Quarterly* 21:302–14.

———. 1975. *Immortal Helen: An Inaugural Lecture*. London: Bedford College.

Williams, Bernard. 1993. *Shame and Necessity*. Berkeley: University of California Press.

Wills, Garry. 1967. "The Sapphic 'Umwertung aller Werte.'" *American Journal of Philology* 88:434–42.

Winkler, John J. 1990. *The Constraints of Desire*. New York: Routledge.

Winkler, Martin M. 2009. *Cinema and Classical Texts: Apollo's New Light*. Cambridge: Cambridge University Press.

Winnington-Ingram, R. P. 1983. *Studies in Aeschylus*. Cambridge: Cambridge University Press.

Wohl, Victoria Josselyn. 1993. "Standing by the Stathmos: The Creation of Sexual Ideology in the *Odyssey*." *Arethusa* 26:19–50.

———. 1998. *Intimate Commerce: Exchange, Gender, and Subjectivity in Greek Tragedy*. Austin: University of Texas Press.

Wolff, Christian. 1973. "On Euripides' *Helen*." *Harvard Studies in Classical Philology* 77:61–84.

Woodbury, Leonard. 1967. "Helen and the Palinode." *Phoenix* 21:157–76.

———. 1985. "Ibycus and Polycrates." *Phoenix* 39:193–220.

Worman, Nancy. 2001. "This Voice Which Is Not One: Helen's Verbal Guises in Homeric Epic." In *Making Silence Speak: Women's Voices in Greek Literature and Society*, edited by Andre Lardinois and Laura McClure, 19–37. Princeton: Princeton University Press.

———. 2002. *The Cast of Character: Style in Greek Literature*. Austin: University of Texas Press.

Wright, Matthew. 2005. *Euripides' Escape-Tragedies: A Study of Helen, Andromeda, and Iphigenia among the Taurians*. Oxford: Oxford University Press.

Wyles, Rosie. 2010. "Towards Theorising the Place of Costume in Performance Reception." In *Theorising Performance: Greek Drama, Cultural History, and Critical Practice*, edited by Edith Hall and Stephe Harrop, 171–78. London: Duckworth.

Zajonz, Sandra., ed. 2002. *Isokrates' Enkomion auf Helena: Ein Kommentar*. Göttingen: Vandenhoeck & Ruprecht.

Zeitlin, Froma. 1994. "The Artful Eye: Vision, Ecphrasis and Spectacle in Euripidean Theatre." In *Art and Text in Ancient Greek Culture*, edited by Simon Goldhill and Robin Osborne, 138–96. Cambridge: Cambridge University Press.

———. 1996. *Playing the Other: Gender and Society in Classical Greek Literature*. Chicago: University of Chicago Press.

Zuntz, Günther. 1960. "On Euripides' Helena: Theology and Irony." In *Euripide*, edited by J. C. Kamerbeek, 201–27. *Entretiens sur l'Antiquité Classique* 6. Geneva: Fondation Hardt.

Zweig, Bella. 1999. "Euripides' *Helen* and Female Rites of Passage." In *Rites of Passage in Ancient Greece: Literature, Religion, Society*, edited by Mark Padilla, 158–80. Lewisburg, PA: Bucknell University Press.

Index and Glossary

Plutarch, prolific 2nd-c. prose writer;
his works include biographies
of historical figures (including
legendary ones), and *Moralia*
("Moral Essays") on a wide variety
of topics, 42, 188, 214, 229
polis, "city-state," primary political unit
of classical Greece, consisting of
a central town and the rural land
surrounding it, *see* Argos, Athens,
Sparta
Pollux, *see* Dioscuri
Polycrates, 6th-c. ruler of the island of
Samos, patron of Ibycus, 104, 107,
110–11
Polyxena, daughter of Priam and Hecuba
sacrificed on Achilles' tomb, 40,
189
Poseidon, god of the sea, earthquakes, and
horses; angered by the sack of Troy,
he obstructs the Greeks' voyage
home, 183, 189
Polydamna, Egyptian queen who gives
Helen her drug in *Od.*, 80
Priam, king of Troy, husband of Hecuba,
father of Hector, Paris, Cassandra, Troilus (and many others),
murdered on an altar at the sack
of Troy, 53, 58, 60–61, 62, 64–65,
66, 152, 155
Prodicus, 5th-c. sophist from Ceos; his
fable on the Choice of Heracles
is cited from Xen. *Mem.* (the only
place it is recorded); *see Choice of
Heracles*
Prometheus ("forethought"), tries to
deceive Zeus then steals fire from
the gods for mortals, provoking Zeus to create Pandora in
revenge, 15, 16
prophecies and omens, 5, 78–79, 86–87,
90, 203, 204
prostitutes, 57, 239
Protesilaus, first Greek to set foot on
non-Greek land in the Trojan War,
156
Proteus, in *Od.* a shape-shifting sea god
living off the coast of Egypt, in
Hdt. and Eur. an Egyptian king,
86–87, 150–53, 156–57, 162, 202,
204
psuchē, "psyche," "soul," 168–71, 172,
175–76, 178–79, 180, 181
Pygmalion, sculptor who falls in love with
a statue of his own creation, 20

Pythagoreans, 247
Pythia, priestess of Apollo at Delphi, 137,
138
Pythian Games, Panhellenic festival
and athletic competition held at
Delphi, 165

rape (*see also* abduction of women; Cassandra, rape of), 7, 10, 13, 62–63,
118, 151, 161–62, 189, 206
Renaissance, Helen in, 248
reproduction, importance of, 1, 11–12, 14,
15, 32, 75, 86, 89, 92, 100, 102,
108, 139
responsibility, moral, 10–11, 22, 60,
66–67, 72, 169, 173–75, 178–79,
180–81, 194–195
and divine influence, 6–7, 37–38, 61,
64, 71, 93, 126, 157, 168, 170–71,
174–75, 189–90
Ronsard, Pierre de, 248

Saint Elmo's fire, luminescence on the
rigging of ships, associated with
Helen, 46
Sappho, lyric poet from Lesbos (active c.
600), 36, 111–16, 149
Sarpedon, mortal son of Zeus killed in
the Trojan War, 229–30
Seasons, goddesses of spring, youth, and
beauty associated with Aphrodite
and the Graces, 8, 16, 33
self-control (*see also sōphrosunē*)
Helen and, 36, 70–72, 79, 178, 189,
196, 204, 205, 215
men and, 6, 11, 17, 88–89, 95, 139,
145–46, 147, 149, 155, 157, 198–99,
212, 230, 232, 239, 247
women and, 10–11, 18, 23, 25, 79, 94,
95, 140, 149, 191, 199
Semonides, 7th-c. lyric poet from Amor-
gos, 23, 25–26, 96–97, 99, 101, 221
Shanower, Eric, 249
Sirens, female monsters, part bird and
part woman, who lure sailors onto
the rocks with their singing, 79
Socrates, 5th-c. Athenian philosopher
who wrote nothing but appears as
a character in many authors, notably Pl., Xen., and Ar.; tried and
executed in 399 for "corrupting
the youth and introducing new
gods," 10–11, 194
sōma, "body" (referring to physical beauty),
174, 196, 209, 228–29, 233

Troy, 2004 movie, 249

Trojan Horse, wooden horse filled with armed men enabling the Greeks to conquer Troy after the Trojans took it in as an offering to the gods, 40, 83–85, 89

Trojan War

as antecedent for Persian Wars, 38, 43, 124, 142, 145, 148, 153, 156, 160–61, 184, 232, 236, 244

justice of, 38–39, 60–61, 63, 101, 128, 144, 145, 151, 154, 155–57, 185, 227

length and scale of, 38, 39, 58, 116, 142, 227

Tyndareus, husband of Leda, biological father of Clytemnestra, adoptive father of Helen, 28–29, 31, 55, 117, 184–85

vanity, 7, 10, 50, 91, 96, 194, 196, 200, 215

veil, worn by Greek women, 9, 12, 14, 15, 22, 25, 40, 41, 51, 55, 58, 70, 94, 128

Virgil, 1st-c. Roman poet, 247

Virgin Mary, 248

voice, female (*see also* Helen, voice of), 5–6, 16, 21, 22, 23, 25, 79, 80, 84–85

Weaker Argument, character in Ar. *Clouds*; comic personification of sophistry who debates Stronger Argument and defeats him, 165, 168, 189

weaving, *see* wool working

weddings, *see* bride, figure of; Sparta, weddings at

White Island, site of a cult of Achilles in the Black Sea where Helen is said to cohabit with him, 46, 121

Wilde, Oscar, 248

Wise, Robert, 248

women

agency/objectification of (*see also* bride, figure of; Helen, agency/objectification of; statues and women), 7, 12–14, 16, 17, 19–22, 146, 148–49, 159–60, 161–62, 172, 190–92

Athenian, 9–11, 22–25, 140, 161–61, 172, 174, 181, 191, 216, 232, 239

weakness of (esp. sexual), 10–14, 17–22, 24, 63, 92–94, 146–47, 172, 173, 175–76, 181, 199, 240–41

virtuous (*see also* Helen as good woman), 1, 3, 10–11, 14, 22–25, 64, 90–92, 99–100, 102, 162, 191, 197, 206, 215

wool working/woven fabric (*see also* Helen as wool worker), 20, 21, 25, 76, 90, 125–26, 127, 128, 135, 138

xanthos, "tawny," hair color associated with aristocracy and divinity; name of one of Achilles' horses, 101, 102, 105, 208

Xena: Warrior Princess, 1990s TV series drawing in part on Greek mythology, 249

xenia, see guest-friendship

Xenophon, 4th-c. Athenian prose writer and associate of Socrates whose works include *Oeconomicus* ("Household Management"), *Memorabilia* ("Recollections of Socrates"), and *Symposium*, 2, 5, 10–11, 24, 25, 238

Xerxes, Persian king who invaded Greece in the Persian Wars, 149, 163

Zeus, king of the gods, ruler of the universe, father of Helen (and many others); governs many aspects of human life, notably justice, the weather, and guest-friendship

ambiguous gifts of, 15–17, 80

erotic susceptibility of, 5, 6, 143, 160, 168, 189, 195, 240

and Helen, 27–29, 55, 86, 87, 97–98, 129, 139, 184–85, 225–26, 242

Zeuxippus, little-known character praised by Ibycus for beauty, 107–108

Zeuxis, 5th-c. painter renowned for illusionistic realism, 49